Henry Fothergill Chorley

Henry Fothergill Chorley, 1841, by Count Alfred D'Orsay (1801-52)
By kind permission of the National Portrait Gallery, London

Henry Fothergill Chorley

Victorian Journalist

ROBERT TERRELL BLEDSOE

Ashgate

Aldershot • Brookfield USA • Singapore • Sydney

Published by
Ashgate Publishing Limited
Gower House
Croft Road
Aldershot
Hants GU11 3HR
England

Ashgate Publishing Company
Old Post Road
Brookfield
Vermont 05036-9704
USA

British Library Cataloguing in Publication Data

Bledsoe, Robert Terrell
    Henry Fothergill Chorley: Victorian Journalist.
    1. Chorley, Henry F. (Henry Fothergill), 1808-72.
    2. Journalists—England—Biography. 3. Authors, English—
    19th century—Biography.
    I. Title.
    070.9'2

Library of Congress Cataloging-in-Publication Data

Bledsoe, Robert Terrell.
    Henry Fothergill Chorley: Victorian Journalist/Robert Terrell
    Bledsoe.
    Includes bibliographical references and index.
    ISBN 1-84014-257-X (hb)
    1. Chorley, Henry Fothergill, 1808-72. 2. Music critics—
    England—Biography. I. Title.
    ML423.C55B54   1998
    780'.92—dc21   98-23743
    [B]   CIP
                                                          MN

ISBN 1 84014 257 X

Printed and bound in Great Britain by
MPG Books Ltd, Bodmin, Cornwall

Contents

For my father, mother, and brother
John, Helen, and John
'gone into the world of light'

Preface

Henry Fothergill Chorley was a major figure in mid-Victorian journalism. His book reviews, primarily in the *Athenæum*, appeared for more than thirty-five years, and he achieved recognition, too, as a playwright, novelist, and poet. His circle of friends and acquaintances included many of the major literary and musical figures in Victorian England. In his early years he was supported and influenced by Felicia Hemans, Maria Jewsbury, Mary Russell Mitford, and Elizabeth Barrett. Later he formed close and lasting personal attachments to Felix Mendelssohn and Charles Dickens. As a mentor, he worked arduously and successfully in the 1860s to help the beginning careers of Charles Santley, the singer, and Arthur Sullivan, the composer. In addition to reviewing books and musical performances each week from 1834 to his retirement in 1868, he wrote plays, poems, stories, and novels in Victorian abundance: all were almost as neglected then as they are now.

He achieved enduring significance, however, primarily as a musical journalist. As a chronicler of ephemeral musical life in London, especially operatic performances, his productivity was remarkable, his influence great, and his work permanently valuable. His book of musical travels, *Music and Manners in France and Germany* (1841), provided English readers with descriptions of romantic realms of Meyerbeer and Mendelssohn, and his widely-read book, *Thirty Years' Musical Recollections* (1862), not only brought to life more vividly than any other work of its time a golden age of singing, but also provided a cosmopolitan perspective on the formation of the nineteenth-century operatic repertory in London.

He was fervently engaged in the earnest struggle to define a canon of creative and re-creative musical greatness. He debated passionately the merits of singers such as Guilia Grisi, Mario, Jenny Lind, Pauline Viardot-Garcia, Adelina Patti, Sims Reeves, and Charles Santley. He took sides vehemently when the interests of the conductor Michael Costa appeared to conflict with the interests of managers such as Benjamin Lumley at Her Majesty's Theatre or Frederick Gye at Covent Garden. He held forth repeatedly on a question that endlessly fascinated the Victorians: was or was not England a musical nation? He responded favourably to Rossini, Meyerbeer, Gounod, Mendelssohn, Sullivan, and Schubert; he found Verdi's music noisy and vulgar; and he was concerned about the degenerate 'Music of the Future' and its creators, Schumann and Wagner.

In his literary reviews Chorley was a strong supporter of numerous women writers — Felicia Hemans, Lady Blessington, Elizabeth Barrett, Mary Russell Mitford — as well as of Nathaniel Hawthorne and Charles

Dickens. His literary journalism was generally competent but seldom inspired.

Susan Holland, indexer for the *Athenæum* project at the City University in London, has identified approximately 2500 book reviews written by Chorley.[1] That total, large though it is, understates his contributions to the *Athenæum*, since it counts neither his reviews during the several years for which the 'marked' office copies contain no attributions, nor his most important writing for the journal: the musical columns, 'Music and the Drama' and 'Musical and Dramatic Gossip', which appeared nearly every week for thirty-five years. These columns supported composers whose reputations were revised radically downward by the generation that succeeded them. In 1894, citing Chorley's views as representing 'what our fathers or our grandfathers admired' fifty years earlier, the *Musical Times* celebrated the great progress in musical taste made since then, while conceding that his 'trenchant and forcible style' still made for 'most entertaining reading' (1 June 1894: 383). Today the respect Chorley had for Rossini, Meyerbeer, and Mendelssohn no longer seems so quaint, and one need not share his contempt for Verdi, Wagner, and Schumann to find it worth examining.

Like many eminent Victorians, Henry Fothergill Chorley believed that well-bred people did not jeopardize reputations — their own or their acquaintances' — by leaving behind personal and delicate written records. Therefore, it is no surprise to learn from Henry G. Hewlett, who compiled and published parts of Chorley's journals and his unfinished autobiography, that 'some years before his death' Chorley destroyed 'many letters of too private a nature for preservation, and [returned] others to the friends of the deceased writers' (Hewlett, 1: vi). And only a few days before his death, according to his obituary in the *Athenæum*, 24 February 1872, he burned more than 5000 letters (250).

Chorley once wrote approvingly that his friend Sydney Smith was 'averse to the misuse which could be made, according to the flagrant fashion of our time, of every scrap of written paper, by the literary ghouls who fatten their purses in the guise of biographers' (Hewlett, 1: 199).

And yet, he wanted to be understood by posterity. On 22 March 1871, he wrote to Richard Bentley indicating that his autobiography was well underway:

> ... I conceive that the death of Mr. Blackett, released me
> from my contract with him — in regard to my own
> memoirs.[2] I am making daily progress with them, having
> materials so ample as to have made me determine thus,
> with respect to them — there will be two series — the first
> to close some twenty years ago. The second I shall com-
> plete while I can: — but it had better be deferred. I think

> the book will be as full of character & anecdote, as most
> that have appeared & I will take care that there shall not
> be a word that can give private pain, to any of those who
> have known & trusted me. It will make two groups of
> three volumes each. What are you disposed to offer? I do
> not wish to divide the work & should like to be paid on
> handing over the M.S. — I could not have believed I had
> so much to tell, as proves to be the case. ...[3]

Chorley's belief that his memoirs would be a matter of some value to publishers is emphasized by his confidence that they would be interested in publishing six volumes — a lengthy memoir even by the expansive standards of the 1870s. Bentley's response to Chorley's blunt query, 'What are you disposed to offer', must have been somewhat tentative, since Chorley again wrote to Bentley on 31 March 1871, offering the following more specific indication of the value he placed on his memoirs:

> As to the matter of business — Mr. Blackett promised
> verbally, to give me whatever I asked for the first portion
> of the memoirs. — I think he had confidence in the work
> &, more, in my not being exorbitant. I have thought
> much about the matter — The book, as it will be full of
> anecdote, is worth to me £250. I mean the first three
> volumes. I could at once send in the M.S. to be printed —
> as I am now occupied with nothing else. — I can
> undertake for its being finished by late Autumn.[4]

Bentley agreed with Chorley's estimate of the value of the first three volumes. In the Manuscript Room of the British Library is a contract signed by Bentley and Chorley on 9 May 1871, for two works. One is a biography of Mary Russell Mitford, for the copyright to which Bentley agrees to pay £100 'on delivery of the manuscript'. The other is his autobiography.[5] But when Chorley died suddenly, nine months later, on 16 February 1872, no autobiography had appeared.

Henry G. Hewlett wrote that Chorley had asked him to be his literary executor in 1870, perhaps because Hewlett was 'one of the few younger men who felt an interest in his writings' (Hewlett, 1: [v]). They had first met in the autumn of 1861, when Chorley had noted in the *Athenæum* the appearance of a book by Hewlett ('not otherwise worth recalling', the self-effacing Hewlett stated). That notice led to a letter from Hewlett to Chorley, which in turn led to 'a friendly invitation to dinner a few days afterwards ... and from that time until his death our intimacy was maintained with unbroken and increasing cordiality' (Hewlett, 2: 314).

On 18 December 1872, some months after Chorley's death, Bentley entered into another contract, not with Chorley's 'literary executor',

Hewlett, but with the person Chorley named in his will 'sole executor', Benson Rathbone of Liverpool, the nephew of Chorley's closest childhood friend. This contract called for a shorter, two-volume 'Life and Letters', at a price to vary depending on the book's sale:

> The said Benson Rathbone Esqre having written a work at present entitled "Memoirs and Correspondence of Henry F. Chorley" agrees to sell & the said Richard Bentley & Son agree to purchase the copyright of the said work upon the following terms: — viz One Hundred Pounds on the delivery of the M.S. Fifty Pounds on the sale reaching 750 copies Fifty Pounds on the sale reaching 1000 copies and a further sum of Fifty Pounds on the sale of every 250 copies over & above the thousand copies.[6]

Despite this contract, the two-volume work which Bentley and Son published in 1873, *Henry Fothergill Chorley: Autobiography, Memoir, and Letters* was explicitly 'compiled by' Henry G. Hewlett, not Benson Rathbone. The title is not inaccurate, but it is misleading, since Hewlett cut and re-arranged Chorley's manuscript freely. Hewlett included some sections of Chorley's manuscript autobiography, some excerpts from Chorley's journals, and some examples of such correspondence as had not been destroyed. He omitted the small amount of material that might have been too personal or too strongly worded, and, as Chorley had wanted, 'no passages have been printed likely to give needless pain to living persons' (1: vii). He added substantial passages of his own narrative and commentary, changing the nature of the work so that it is more accurately described as a book 'compiled by' Hewlett than one 'written by' Chorley.

The book's disjointed structure, lack of coherent organization, and chronological diffuseness make it awkward to read and difficult to use for reference. Moreover, Hewlett's knowledge of the world of Victorian music was superficial; unlike Chorley, he was an outsider, and not particularly interested in music. Therefore he was not well prepared to understand or evaluate Chorley's professional significance.

Nevertheless, his work is indispensable. He provided excerpts from Chorley's manuscript autobiography, plot summaries of Chorley's unsuccessful novels and plays, texts for some of Chorley's uncollected verses published in periodicals, and texts of some important letters to and from Chorley. Unlike many of Chorley's acquaintances, Hewlett had no musical axes to grind and no personal grudges to air.

Although I have not tried to replace him as Chorley's biographer, I have had access to works published after 1873 and to unpublished sources which were either not known by or unavailable to Hewlett (for example, manuscript material relating to Chorley's friendships with Felix Mendelssohn, Charlotte Cushman, Charles Santley, and Arthur Sullivan, among others).[7]

In keeping with my focus on Chorley's accomplishment as a writer, not on the story of his life, I have made much greater use of the weekly columns in the *Athenæum* than he did.

When quoting from Hewlett's compilation, I have indicated which passages are presented as Chorley's own words and which are Hewlett's commentary. In indented quotations, I have followed the original punctuation (authors and publishers generally used double quotation marks where current British usage calls for single). Chorley's handwriting is difficult for me to read; in quotations from unpublished sources, therefore, I have indicated in brackets places where I may have inadvertently mistranscribed words or punctuation.

Many people have helped and encouraged me with this project by answering questions, generously providing information, and in many cases offering hospitality during research trips to libraries in the United States and England. Among them are: David and Ann Allen, Miriam Allott, Micheline Beaulieu, Larry and Susan Bergstrom, Julian Budden, Wilsonia Cherry and Robert Williams, Martin Chusid, Robert and Vineta Colby, David Dickens, Richard and Carol Ekman, Wilfred and Thelma Grove, Susan Holland, Leanne Langley, Philip McCormick, the late William V. Nestrick, David Parker, Andrew Porter, Michael Slater, Kathleen Tillotson, Patrick Waddington, Janine Watrin, and Peter and Georgia Windhorst. Students and colleagues at the University of Texas at El Paso have directly or indirectly helped this project. I would like especially to thank Howard Daudistel, Mimi R. Gladstein, Carl Jackson, Lawrence J. Johnson, Carol Kelley, Joseph and Dorothy Ann Leach, Douglas Meyers, Diana S. Natalicio, and Stephen Riter. Support from the University, the University Interlibrary Loan Department, the College of Liberal Arts, and the Department of English has been sustained and indispensable. I am grateful to my editors at Ashgate, Rachel Lynch and Caroline Cornish, for their careful attention to the manuscript and their patience. For corrections and suggestions I am greatly indebted to Robert Colby, Vineta Colby, and Wilfred Grove, who read the work in typescript, and to Thelma Grove, who read it twice. The inaccuracies that remain are my responsibility.

Among the libraries and archives whose staff members have very kindly provided me with primary and secondary materials, either by mail or in person, are the following: American Institute for Verdi Studies, New York University; American University, Washington DC; Bobst Library, New York University; Armstrong Browning Library, Baylor University, Waco, Texas; Bodleian Library, Oxford University; Boston Public Library; Columbia University, New York City; Catholic University Library, Washington DC; City University Library, London; Fitzwilliam Museum, Cambridge; George Washington University Library, Washington DC; Houghton Library, Harvard University, Cambridge, Massachusetts;

Huntington Library, San Marino, California; Library of Congress, Washington, DC; Liverpool Record Office; London Library; New Mexico State University Library, Las Cruces, New Mexico; New York Public Library; Pierpont Morgan Library, New York City; Princeton University Library, Princeton, New Jersey; Senate House Library, University of London; Music Library, University of California at Berkeley; Harry Ransom Humanities Research Center, University of Texas at Austin; University of Texas at El Paso; and the Wigan Archives Service, Lancashire.

For permission to quote excerpts from unpublished material I would like to thank the Curators of the Bodleian Library, Oxford; the Trustees of the Boston Public Library; the Syndics of the Fitzwilliam Museum, Cambridge; Christopher Dickens; the Harry Ransom Humanities Research Center, University of Texas at Austin; the Houghton Library, Harvard University; the Huntington Library, San Marino, California; the Liverpool Record Office; the Pierpont Morgan Library, Gilbert and Sullivan Collection; and the Wigan Archives Service. For permission to reprint material originally published in journals, I would like to thank *The Dickensian*, *Victorian Studies*, *The Victorian Review*, and *Dickens Studies Annual*.

My greatest scholarly debt is to the British Library. I am very grateful for the generous help of its staff in the Main Reading Room, the Manuscript Room, the Music Reading Room, the North Gallery, and the Newspaper Library at Colindale.

Notes

1. For comparison it may be noted that the City University *Athenæum* project, using the marked office copies now in the library of the City University, London, identified just over 1700 reviews written by William Hepworth Dixon, and a similar number written by Geraldine Jewsbury and by John Cordy Jeaffreson.

2. Hurst and Blackett were the publishers of Chorley's *Thirty Years' Musical Recollections*.

3. MS, Wigan Record Office.

4. MS, Wigan Record Office.

5. British Library ADD MS 46 618 reads in part:

> The said Henry Chorley Esq. having also written a portion of his own Memoirs at present entitled "Half a Life" and which work is sufficient in extent to form a book of 3 vols post octavo hereby agrees to sell and the said Richard Bentley & Son hereby agree to purchase the copyright of the said Memoirs for Two hundred and fifty pounds, payable in cash one month after publication.

The last four words were crossed out; in their place was inserted 'on delivery of the entire manuscript'.

6. MS, British Library, ADD MS 46 618.
7. I have not discussed Chorley's *National Music of the World* (lectures which Hewlett edited and published in 1880) or his notices of art exhibitions, mainly written between 1836 and 1841 (Hewlett, 1: 138).

CHAPTER ONE

A Beginning:
Friends and Family

1

Henry Fothergill Chorley was born in Lancashire in 1808 and spent the first twenty-five years of his life in or near Liverpool. His childhood, his education, and his years working in Liverpool counting houses left him with few happy memories. For most of these years, he considered his life humdrum and his prospects for happiness slim. He was 'the third son and fourth child of John and Jane Chorley', he later wrote, 'and was born on the 15th of December, 1808, at Blackley Hurst, a house belonging to the Catholic family of the Gerards, near Billinge in Lancashire. My father and mother were nominally members of the Society of Friends, though neither the one nor the other ever wore the dress of that religious body, nor conformed to its ascetic discipline and testimonies. They were, both of them, superior and singular persons' (Hewlett, 1: 5).[1]

Earlier generations of Chorleys had been members of the gentry. In the early years of the eighteenth century, however, the family had come down in the world: the family property was confiscated and sold after Richard Chorley was hanged 'for complicity in the rebellion of 1715'.[2] Since that time the Chorley family had not been well-off, although, as if in compensation, several had manifested 'the artist temperament' (Hewlett, 1: 8).[3] None had the temperament like Chorley himself, however, and to it he attributed most of the joy and much of the pain he later experienced.

Henry Chorley's father, John, was the eldest of thirteen children — four sons and nine daughters; John Chorley's father was Alexander Chorley, an ironmaster at Stanley-Bank in Lancashire who married 'a rigid woman', born a Fothergill, 'another north-country family of some mark, which yielded a popular physician to London and a redoubtable preacher to the Society of Friends' (Hewlett, 1: 7).

All four sons died, said Chorley, 'in the very prime of life'. The oldest child, John — Chorley's father — died suddenly on 15 April 1816, when Chorley was just seven years old. Uncle Henry drowned on a voyage down the Rio del Plata. Uncle James Fothergill Chorley died 'of a wasted constitution'. Uncle Charles died in New Orleans of yellow fever. Of the nine daughters, Chorley mentioned only Aunt Rebecca, whose bright and entertaining personality he recalled affectionately (Hewlett, 1: 7, 9).

On his mother's side, Chorley's grandmother Wilkinson was strong-willed and domineering. A member of the Brownsword family of Cumberland, she had first married John Rutter, a merchant of Liverpool, by whom she had a son, also named John. After Mr Rutter died, she married Mr Wilkinson, whom she also outlived. Their daughter, Jane, Chorley's mother, was born after her father's death.

Chorley remembered his mother as loving, timid, and 'more alive to the pain of rebuke than any one I have known'. Like her son, she had 'fancies for poetry, romance, and art (as art was understood in those primitive, narrow days)'.

> I have before me the manuscript of a novel, the formal childish writing beautiful, and perfect as to spelling, by which it is evident that the small person had got hold of [Fanny Burney's] "Evelina." ... To the very last years of her life she could amuse herself and relieve her mind by writing verses; and in the rhymes of the old woman, as well as of the girl, there is a vein of true poetry, of real fancy, and of real feeling. She was very lovely on a small scale, with shy eyes, a fresh complexion, and a perfectly formed mouth, and hair of that sunny colour which womanhood ripens into auburn. (1: 14-15)

Chorley's mother was also 'weak', her character marked by 'want of courage, not want of affection' (1: 25). No one was 'less qualified to cope with the practical difficulties of life' than this sweet, timid woman (1: 41).

In 1800, when she was twenty one, Jane Wilkinson married John Chorley. During their sixteen years of marriage the couple 'maintained an unusual amount of affection for one another', Chorley recalled (Hewlett, 1: 5). Their honeymoon was in London. Some of the popular songs Jane Chorley heard there made a lasting impression on her, and Chorley remembered her picking out these melodies on the pianoforte when he was a child (1: 35). It was a pianoforte of the type, said Chorley later, 'which Dickens must have known, else he could never have described Miss Tox's instrument, with the wreath of sweet peas round its maker's name, in "Dombey"' (1: 51).[4]

After their honeymoon, John and Jane Chorley moved to Deane Cottage, near Warrington, where Chorley's only sister was born, the first of the four children. At Deane Cottage the family had a brush with the supernatural. Their landlord, a 'brutal, licentious man', was 'one of those wild provincial imitations of the town *Mohocks*' (1: 22). Perhaps something of a Heathcliff, too, since Chorley noted that '[f]rom among such people and such traditions did the Brontë sisters gather the materials for their novels — books which will have a value for the future historian of English society, if even they cease to be read for the rude power and romance put forth in them' (1: 22). After his death by apoplexy this wild Colonel's presence was felt by a family whose members 'noted omens; they dreamt dreams; they saw ghosts' (1: 11). John Chorley's family eagerly embraced the 'marvellous' and was convinced that the Colonel's ghost haunted their cottage.

At Deane Cottage, the appearances of the wicked Colonel's ghost were followed by more tangible troubles. Jane Chorley invested money she inherited from 'her north country ancestors' in the business of her young husband, an iron-worker at Ashton-in-Mackerfield (1: 26). The lock-making business did not flourish. Profits sank. John Chorley moved his young family from Deane Cottage to Penswick House. As the family's prosperity diminished, its size grew: the second child, Chorley's eldest brother, William Brownsword Chorley, was born while they lived at Penswick House.[5]

Then once again John Chorley moved his family, this time to Blackley Hurst, 'a dilapidated country-seat, near Billinge in Lancashire ... which was let to my father at a reduced rent' (1: 28-9). In that house the two youngest children were born: John Rutter,[6] and, ten days before Christmas, 1808, Henry Fothergill.[7]

Despite their very different temperaments, the emotional bond between Henry and his brother John was close:

> It is hardly possible for two children of the same parents, who lived to the verge of manhood together, and had been interested from childhood upwards in all that belongs to the world of imagination, to differ more widely in disposition, in many matters of opinion, practice, and the ordering of life, than did my brother and myself. But though there was little companionship between us, there was entire and unbroken confidence till the last. I felt that in any juncture of perplexity, or where essential and accurate service was required, I had a wall of strength to shelter under and to lean against, which nothing could shake; so deep were its foundations, so sound was its structure. (Hewlett, 2: 256)[8]

At Blackley Hurst matters continued to go ill with the lock-making business, and so, when Chorley was about four years old, John Chorley moved his family once again, this time to Smithy Brook, 'a square, ugly, new house by the side of the road betwixt Warrington and Wigan, near the latter town, with a square, ugly, new garden' (1: 31).

At Smithy Brook Chorley's education began. He remembered learning to write 'before I was three years and a half old' (1: 30), learning 'the rudiments of arithmetic' from a schoolmaster, 'an inefficient, civil old creature — who spoke broad Lancashire, at which we mocked' (1: 32), and learning that he had a 'fancy' for 'decoration' ('if I may not call it a love of art') (1: 32-3). He learned, too, his early political views from his dissenting elders — the child was a 'Liberal' who resented 'the powers that be' (1: 34). The adult Chorley, by contrast, was noted for his strongly expressed conservative views on art and politics.

Most importantly for his later life, at Smithy Brook he became aware of his mother's ability to 'pick out Scotch, or Irish, or Welsh melodies' (1: 35). It was thus through his mother 'that I recollect first hearing music, and hearing it with that passion which, if it had been understood and provided for, might possibly have conducted me to some eminence in the art' (1: 34). But his passion was not encouraged.

Chorley remembered a good deal of childhood sadness. He blamed his family's inability to understand and nurture his potential to be an artist. The mental worlds of John and Jane Chorley were too limited: 'I suspect that they loved each other dearly, and thought little of the future — nothing that the four children whom they brought into the world were to come after them, and however like them, MUST be "other, *though* the same"' (1: 26).

Contributing to family failings was the baneful influence of the Friends, whose bleak religion prevented his parents and his relatives on both sides of the family from enjoying life. Though Chorley believed that his parents and their relatives had managed to acquire a 'remarkable' amount of 'liberal culture' (1: 7-12), they were still drawn to — but did not achieve — a more complete spiritual 'escape':

> Over all these original, imperfectly-educated persons the ordinances and the usages of the Society of Friends hung like a pall of conformity, heavy enough to inspire them with certain characteristics, but so oppressive as to make escape and insincerity inevitable. It would be difficult to conceive a worse education for mind and heart. On the one side, a narrow, ascetic, mystical sectarianism, including the minute formalities of discipline, but not including the rallying-points of an established creed; on the other, worldly pursuits and pleasures, partaken of by snatches, without those safeguards which good breeding and good manners substitute for higher moral principle and precept among people of the world. (1: 18)

From an early age, Chorley saw himself as 'set apart', hoping that his differentness would bring him a future of exciting adventure, independence from relations and Friends, and soul-satisfying artistic creativity, but fearing that it might cause others to neglect him and to leave him unprotected, unguided, and unloved:

As boys from childhood, my two brothers "cronied" together, leaving the youngest, weakest, and ugliest as the odd one; and my sister early became my mother's companion. I have thus, from infancy, been alone as regards family confidence or comradeship; and the subsequent periods of life at which this condition of solitude has been partly counteracted have been few and far between. My father was fond of me, however, as of a sort of *Benjamin*, since he used to take me on his knee while he quoted that line from Chaucer —

   And spare my Gamelyn, because he's young[9]

I think, too, he must have discerned something of the adventurer in my composition; for I recollect his saying, when I was a small child, that "if I were turned loose in the streets of London, he should have no fear of my losing my way." (1: 28-9)

In 1816 John Chorley moved his family once again, for the fifth and last time in his too-short life — this time to Green End, 'about three miles from St. Helens, in Lancashire' (1: 35). From the front gate Henry Fothergill could see the house where he had been born. At last the Chorley family had a home with a lovely garden: cherry trees, lilacs, locust trees, laburnums, guelder-roses, syringas, a lime-tree — aspects of a smiling world where nature might nurture them.

Green End remained a soothing and restorative memory, an image of a site back to which Chorley could mentally travel during his adult years in London, transported there by something as seemingly inconsequential as the sight or the smell of shrubs in St James's Park. Many years after he had moved away from the country for good, he asserted that it was the city-dwellers 'who best relish and appreciate country sights, sounds, and things; and [I] know that with myself, at least — though I should not be believed on oath by any friend or acquaintance I have — it is a love that "fadeth not away"' (1: 37). The romantic memory of those bucolic childhood scenes was the cause of his love for landscape painting and for 'the wonderful new photographs of bare trees which I have lived to see brought to such perfection'. All in all, Chorley wrote, Green End was 'the happiest place of residence I ever inhabited' (1: 37).

Green End also provided another important memory, this one chilling. On 16 April 1816, a few weeks after the seven-year-old boy moved to the garden paradise, his father went off to work one morning as usual and never returned.

John Chorley had 'dropped down dead in his counting house' (Hewlett, 1: 7). 'Times had been growing worse with him for some years', Chorley later recalled,

> ... and this it may have been which had caused the hag-
> gard look and the loss of bulk, remarked after his death;
> or they may have been signs of the organic heart-disease
> which took him from us. The dismay, terror, and confu-
> sion of those days is like a thing of last week; and every
> minute detail comes back to me as I begin to think over
> the painful scene. My mother was like some timid crea-
> ture broken to pieces by the shock of an earthquake,
> unable to do much more than weep, and submit, and
> endure. (1: 38)

Chorley learned early the hard lesson that an Eden can quickly be transformed into 'dismay, terror, and confusion'.

2

In this crisis, help came to Chorley's mother from her half-brother, John
Rutter, the son of her mother's first marriage. Dr Rutter's assistance
allowed the family to remain in Green End from 1816 to 1819. Had he not
been so benevolent, Jane Chorley and her children would have lived in
poverty. Henry Chorley came to regard him almost in the light of a second
father.

An amiable bachelor who 'honourably practised physic' in Liverpool for
almost fifty years, he embraced 'wholly, nobly, devotedly' the responsibility of caring for Jane's children as if they were his own (Hewlett, 1:
15, 17). Though a life-long Friend, he played whist, read and dressed as he
pleased, and was altogether an admirable model in young Henry's eyes. Dr
Rutter, though 'courted' when young, did not feel 'justified in thinking of
marriage till he had reached the age at which romance (on either side)
ceases, and convenience begins.' And by the time he reached that age, his
self-imposed obligations to his half-sister and her fatherless children had
burgeoned, supplying all the 'duties' as well as the 'rewards' of family life
(1: 17). To the young Chorley children, Dr Rutter set an example of
generosity and familial loyalty in his willingness to assume responsibility
for them. He set another example, too: none of the four Chorley children
ever married.

During the three remaining years at Green End, the children's schooling
took two forms: first they had private tutors, one 'a man of humble origin',
another 'a crack-brained Irish Methodist' (1: 42). Then they attended day-
school at St Helens ('not bad'). But neither form of education nurtured
Chorley's 'artist temperament'.

> Had this [temperament] been understood, and had this
> been worked towards in forming character and in develop-
> ing such talents as God gave me, my life might have

> yielded special results, in place of the universal indica-
> tions which are all it ever will yield. ... Had I been
> apprenticed to a musician, or to a draftsman, or to an
> architect, I fancy I might have become distinguished. As
> it was, Latin and Greek did me small good. (1: 44)

There the mother and her four children stayed for about three years after
the death of John Chorley.

Then, in 1819, Dr Rutter caught typhus fever. His illness was severe: he
came close to dying. His cousins, the prominent Liverpool Rathbones,[10]
were alarmed. Hannah Mary Rathbone arranged for Jane Chorley to leave
Green End and come to stay with her in Green Bank, her house near Liverpool, along with the four children, in order to be able to care more easily
for her half-brother. When he recovered, Jane Chorley and her four children remained in Liverpool.

Going from the Chorley household, Green End, to the Rathbone
household, Green Bank, Henry entered a different, and considerably more
intellectual household. Though not ostentatious, life there was elegant and
prosperous, and Chorley began to get the kind of education that excited,
stimulated, and improved his mind — not by studying long hours in
solitude, but by mingling with and conversing with self-assured, distinguished people. From the impressive company around her, Mrs Rathbone
stood out as something of a wonder. Chorley paid her abundant tribute:

> Hannah Mary Rathbone was a noble and fascinating
> woman; the most faithful of wives, the most devoted of
> mothers, the most beneficent of friends. ... In 1819, when
> I stayed at Green Bank, she was in the last ripeness of her
> maturity, looking older than her years, but as beautiful as
> any picture which can be offered by freshest youth.
> Though she was nominally a member of the Society of
> Friends, she never conformed to its uniform. ... [Her]
> face was simply one of the most beautiful faces (without
> regularity) that I have ever seen; ... and the voice
> matched the face — so low it was, so kind, so cordial,
> and ... so irresistibly intimate, which means appreciating.
> The welcome of that elderly woman to the awkward,
> scared, nervous child who entered her house, is to me one
> of the recollections which mark a life, as having decided
> its aims, by encouraging its sympathies. (1: 48-9)

By contrast to Green Bank, the day to day world of schooling and studying proved much the same in Liverpool as it had been earlier. The three
boys began to attend the school of the Royal Institution, then headed by the
Revd John Monk. Chorley was admitted a year earlier than normal, and

endured teasing for his shabby clothes and lack of athletic ability (1: 56). He continued studying Latin and Greek, preferring the latter: Herodotus and Euripides' *Hecuba* were especially pleasing to his schoolboy frame of mind (1: 57). The training in classics, he realized, was intended not to make him a scholar, but to prepare him to be a clerk in some 'American merchant's counting house' in Liverpool (1: 58) — a situation he would soon term 'detestable' (1: 66), presenting him with 'intolerable drudgery' (1: 93).

For a few hours each morning, before going 'to the abominable school or the detestable counting-house', he painted still lifes, landscapes, and miniature portraits, finding pleasure in drawing (1: 66). But music was his early, great, and lasting passion, and he declared emphatically, 'A musician I should have been' (1: 65). It appeared in hindsight that an injury was done not only to him, but to England: 'It seems to me now, in putting together all these revelations, that had my elders understood the signs before them, and apprenticed me to a musical career, I might have done England an artist's service' (1: 67).

Many things in Liverpool nurtured Chorley's attraction to music. One of Mrs Rathbone's neighbours, for example, was a lady with five daughters, one of whom played Handel for Chorley, keyboard arrangements of the 'Overtures to "Acis", "Alcina", "Atalanta", — the royal "Occasional Overture"'. Although she did not play well, 'I derived a pleasure, an impression of power, and a feeling as if something magnificent and true had been shown me' (1: 53). At a music shop he heard Kalkbrenner's variations on the Hunting Chorus from Weber's *Freischütz* (1: 60). And at 'the Blind Asylum' he heard 'fragments of Haydn, Mozart, Handel, and Pergolesi' performed by the students' voices and organ (1: 59). To these occasions Chorley attributed the pleasure he took later not only in hearing an organ, but simply in seeing one: 'To this day I never see an organ-front without that sort of expectation with which one gets near a mountain-top from which the view is known to be wide, or opens a greenhouse door to get a feast of colour and odour' (1: 63). And one of Dr Rutter's patients, an Italian lady, was a fine pianist, who played for Chorley 'sonatas by Dussek and Clementi, an arrangement of Cherubini's Overture of "Lodoiska", and Beethoven's *Andante* in F for the pianoforte', pieces which, for the impressionable young Chorley, were 'so many introductions into Faëryland' (1: 62).

Glimpses of this Faëryland were tantalizing; becoming a musician, however, was unthinkable: 'In those days, and in that place, a musician was hardly a man' (1: 58). Indeed, 'I hardly know the middle-class family in the provinces forty years ago ... where such a disposition of a boy's life would not then have been considered as a degradation' (1: 65).[11] To this general feeling was added the specific objection of Dr Rutter, who 'despised music as a profession to such a point that I verily think he would rather have seen me a shop-boy than a second Mozart!' (1: 60). In a generally fatalistic way, Chorley sometimes blamed 'the stars' as well as his elders: fate was 'inexorably opposed' (1: 53).

Chorley's wistful belief that he 'might have been' a composer must have profoundly influenced his feelings later in life towards those who were.

3

There is a gulf between those who are thrilled by music and those who are knowledgeable about it. Henry Chorley's 'introductions into Faëryland' were followed by a period in which he began to combine passion with understanding. The transition period lasted over a decade, but it eventually took Chorley away from the hated world of Liverpool counting houses and into his life's work as a successful journalist in London. There, even if he did not write music, he at least wrote *about* it for more than thirty-five years.

Some time in the 1820s Chorley began his dreary job in the counting house, working with detested ledgers and invoices. This work, his family expected, was to be his life. His first position was as clerk with Messrs Cropper, Benson and Company, American merchants with offices in the inappropriately named Paradise Street. Much as he disliked his employment, he had kind things to say about the American merchants who employed him:

> I think of them as a fine, hearty, wholesome race of
> seafaring men; in general breeding and intelligence supe-
> rior to anything analogous of home-growth which Liver-
> pool could have produced. They brought an air, some-
> times a gale, of freshness into a society which, in those
> days, was restricted, and, therefore, given up to struggles
> and demarcations of petty class insolence, happily now
> over for ever. (Hewlett, 1: 78)

After a period with Cropper, Benson and Company, he worked at the offices of Messrs Woodhouse, Sicilian wine-growers. He loathed that job, too, finding in it another form of enslavement by the same Friends who vehemently opposed slavery.

> And the exactions of those Liverpool mercantile times ...
> were terrible — a slavery ill-compensated for by any
> indulgence or hope of advancement. The writing of
> "circulars," otherwise, the recopying of letters addressed
> at the last moment to the American cotton-ports, by the

> going packet, was not a light task. I have known it last as
> long as till two o'clock in the morning. The men who
> ordained such servitude for their gain's sake were the very
> same men who had protested against and broken down
> American slavery! (Hewlett, 2: 270)

Chorley's conflation of the abomination of slavery with the personal
inconvenience of being forced on occasion to work past midnight suggests a
self-centredness which helps explain why Chorley's life-long cries and
whispers of unhappiness sometimes seemed petulant. Sounding a little like
Charles Dickens recalling as a grown man the agony of his childhood experience as a common working boy in Warren's Blacking Warehouse, he continued:

> When I have a bad dream, now that I am old, the night-
> mare, as often as not, takes some form referable to an
> abhorred servitude. I see ledgers which will not be
> balanced, figures wrongly set down, and wake in the
> midst of such shame and self-disrespect as made up my
> normal state in those days. Had I not got up on summer
> mornings to draw, or rather paint, a little, ere the clock
> struck the abominable hour, I should not have been living
> to tell the tale of my failures in Cropper, Benson, and
> Co.'s office, in Paradise Street, Liverpool. (2: 271-2)

Although these jobs in the counting houses occupied most of his waking
hours, Chorley's mind and heart were not engaged with his work. Instead,
they were in the world where Liverpool's writers and musicians were to be
found. Among these new acqaintances he cut a striking figure in his
unusually colourful clothes. Criticized for being vain and a coxcomb, he
retorted: 'I was born with a love of gay and harmonious tints, and of rich
textures, and ... I have loved to wear them, for their sakes — not for mine'
(1: 63). He didn't dress to impress others (that was a 'ridiculous notion', he
wrote); rather, he simply chose to please himself with his clothes, since 'the
ruling passion for blue, and rose-colour, and yellow, worn about me and
upon me, broke out from the hour when I had a sixpence to call my own'
(1: 64). Throughout his life he stayed with those bright colours, despite the
mockery and criticism they provoked.

Among the people whose acquaintance the brilliantly-dressed though
semi-enslaved young man made while living in Liverpool, the most influential in the formation of his literary taste was the poet Felicia Hemans. She
had been widely known since the publication of *The Domestic Affections* in
1812; *Records of Women* in 1828 enhanced her literary reputation. Long
separated from her husband, in the autumn of 1828 she left Rhyllon, the
'last and most favourite of Mrs Hemans' residences in Wales' and moved to

Wavertree, a village near Liverpool, not far from where she had been born, thirty-four years earlier (Chorley, *Memorials of Mrs. Hemans*, 1: 130).[12] During the three years she lived there before moving to Dublin, Henry Chorley saw her often.

It appears that her acquaintance with the Chorley family was formed during a visit she made to Liverpool shortly before 18 June 1828, the date of the first letter printed from her to an unspecified member of the Chorley family (Chorley, *Memorials*, 1: 189-90). The link between her and the Chorley family (mainly the two brothers, Henry and John Rutter) was the 'annuals'. These, though much ridiculed by journalists like Thackeray, were important throughout Chorley's early career:[13]

> During the height of the 'Annual' fever, chance had thrown the editorship of one of those gay little ephemera into the hands of a member of our family;[14] — of course [Hemans] was among the persons first applied to for countenance and co-operation. How warmly and efficiently these were given, and continued and extended to other projects and pursuits, is a thing never to be forgotten. (1: 183-4)

Henry Chorley felt honoured knowing a famous artist, whom he described as 'almost the first distinguished literary person I had ever seen: one, too, whose writings I loved' (1: 184). She was also the first of several women interested in the connection between art and domestic affections about whom Chorley wrote and whose acquaintance Chorley cultivated. Under her influence he developed his understanding of the significance of 'womanliness' and its passive power. Her poems were, as William Michael Rossetti noted in 1873, 'gentle, sweet, pious and refined', and they appealed to similar 'souls'.[15] Chorley stressed her refinement:

> [I]ndeed, her shrinking from any thing like coarseness of thought, or feeling, or language ... may by some be thought to trench upon affectation, whereas it was only the necessary consequence of her exclusive and unchecked devotion to the Beautiful. If any passage in one of her most favourite writers offended her delicacy, the leaf was torn out without remorse. (*Memorials*, 2: 23)

Between Mrs Hemans and Chorley, 'the friendship was made in an hour, and only closed with her life'. Her poetry and her sensitivity to music elicited keen sympathy from him. At their first meeting 'one common taste disclosed itself — a fondness, I might say, a passion for music. ... There is no freemasonry so intimate and immediate, I believe, as that which exists among the lovers of music; and though, when we parted, I could not tell the colour of her eyes and hair, I felt that a confidence and a good understanding had arisen between us, which the discussion of no subject less fascinating could have excited' (*Memorials*, 1: 184-6). Their correspondence shows Mrs Hemans's interest not only in aspects of German literature — Körner, Grillparzer, Tieck (1: 275), Schiller (1: 277), Herder, A.W. Schlegel (1: 290) — but also in her own great contemporaries, Wordsworth and Shelley (2: 263). She visited Wordsworth at Rydal Mount in 1830 and shared with Chorley her assessment of the great man. Interestingly, considering her own sensitivity to indelicacy, she indicated that Wordsworth sometimes applied too rigidly a 'domestic' critical standard to literature, regretting that he 'is inclined to undervalue German literature from not knowing its best and purest master-pieces'. She discovered that Wordsworth undervalued Goethe:

> 'Goëthe's [*sic*] writings cannot live,' he one day said to me, 'because *they are not holy!*' I found that he had unfortunately adopted this opinion from an attempt to read Wilhelm Meister, which had inspired him with irrepressible disgust. (*Memorials*, 2: 145)

The virtues that comprised Hemans's womanliness were crucial influences on the literary taste that Chorley later supported and promulgated as a reviewer. Her long-suffering nature, and her acquiescence in, or celebration of, moral renunciation came to be central to the literary art Chorley reviewed. For her, '[r]enunciation, rejection and despair are thus gestures loaded with inherited, mythic meaning' (Leighton, 5; see also Clarke, 36). So too, for Chorley. Later, when Chorley began publishing criticism of the contemporary literary scene, these womanly virtues were frequently those he saw, or discovered, in the literature he extolled. He eagerly sought out other literary women (Elizabeth Barrett, for example), assuming (in Barrett's case, not entirely correctly) that domesticity and self-abnegation would be their moral anchors, and convinced that, as Ruskin taught, 'the best women are ... recognized chiefly in the happiness of their husbands and the nobleness of their children'.[16]

Mrs Hemans was supportive of the tentative efforts Chorley made as a composer during the late 1820s. 'I should have written sooner to thank you for the very sweet music to which you have set my "Rome, Rome"', she wrote to him (*Memorials*, 1: 197-8), and she inquired in a later letter, 'Have you composed any more music lately?'[17] In the early 1830s Chorley noted her self-described 'newly discovered power ... of composing melodies, by which I have been visited in the strangest manner. I have really succeeded in putting down a great many airs to lyric pieces of my own, which, though simple, as you may suppose, yet seem to me to express the character of the words' (2: 185).

She knew of, though she was not entirely sure she could share, Chorley's strong attraction to the conquering new composer of the 1820s, Gioacchino Rossini: 'my sister applauds to the skies your preference of Rossini to all others'. Hemans herself, however, continued to look to Mozart and Beethoven as providing something 'more spiritual and more profound' than Rossini (*Memorials*, 1: 199-200). Her musical taste is further illustrated in her strong reactions to music she heard at Dublin's musical festival in the autumn of 1831, after her move there from Liverpool to be near her brother: she praised highly Paganini's virtuosity and Neukomm's martial composition, 'Napoleon's Midnight Review' (2: 235).[18]

In a few years' time, Chorley had discovered that there was a musical world in Liverpool, and he had moved up from listening to his neighbours play the piano to hearing performances which conformed to prevailing European standards. In 1827, at the Liverpool Festival, he heard Mozart's 'Jupiter' Symphony performed and heard Pasta sing Zingarelli's 'Ombra Adorata' from *Romeo*. The response to Pasta in Chorley's journal was ecstatic: 'Her *reading* of that melody stands out distinct from anything I have ever heard. ... It has left an impression of majesty and first-rate talent which I cannot fancy any new pleasure will efface' (Hewlett, 1: 80-81). Then a visiting company performed Rossini's 'Turco in Italy'.[19] In 1832 Domenico Donzelli sang in Liverpool, and Chorley was struck by the beauty of his voice. He was becoming familiar with performances of the standard repertory. Hewlett tells us that around this time he heard:

> Beethoven's "Fidelio," Rossini's "Otello," Mozart's "Nozze," Handel's "Israel" and "Messiah," Haydn's "Creation" and "2nd Mass," Mozart's "Requiem" and "12th Credo," and Spohr's "Last Judgment." (1: 86)

He also heard the world famous sopranos, Wilhelmine Schroeder-Devrient and Maria Malibran, though it was not until later, in London, that he recorded reactions to them. These experiences slowly became, in effect, his credentials for his career reviewing music for the *Athenæum*, and they ensured that he was prepared to write about London music as one who had already heard the best that London, and the world, could offer.

Just as important for his musical education as performances by visiting artists was his familiarity with local Liverpool musicians. Between 1830 and 1833, he served as secretary for a local amateur musical society. Through it he was associated with James Z. Herrmann, later conductor of the Liverpool Philharmonic, who gave him the only systematic music training he ever received. Through it, too, he met several life-long friends: Harriett and Louisa Fletcher (daughters of a prominent banker), Samuel Kearsley, and Mrs Ambrose Lace (to whom in 1835 he would dedicate his first novel, *Conti the Discarded*). Gnosspelius, another friend from those days, told Hewlett that Mrs Lace in particular helped Chorley break away from office drudgery and from Quaker society (1: 84). He also knew Albert

Grisar, a young man from Belgium, and, like Chorley himself, a clerk in a counting house longing to get away.[20]

Chorley had become especially close to William and Hannah Rathbone's son, Benson. When Benson lived in Swansea, and later in Geldeston, Chorley visited him. Through his hospitality, Benson

> gave his young friend opportunities of hearing and practising music — [and the visits] were seasons of rare enchantment to him. It is probable, too, that his introduction to the Italian Opera in London was made under the same auspices. The cost of a journey thither from Liverpool was far too great for him to have undertaken it unassisted; and it seems likely that the visits which he speaks of having paid there before 1834, were in Mr. Rathbone's company. (Hewlett, 1: 74-5)

Chorley found other occasions for temporary escapes from Liverpool in the late 1820s and early 1830s, making, from time to time, 'hurried visits to London'. These get-aways renewed him enough to keep him going in the counting house until the next escape. Without them, he insisted, 'the hated drudgery of mercantile life among uncongenial spirits would have become intolerable' (1: 169). Brief and infrequent as the 'flying visits' were, they lasted long enough for him to attend some performances and to make some acquaintance with people he came to associate with more closely in later years.[21]

Increasing his knowledge and understanding of music provided Chorley with credentials. But credentials for what? Chorley seems to have reached his own answer to that question on reading some pieces by E.T.A. Hoffmann which Gnosspelius had translated at Chorley's request. Gnosspelius recalled that the works were, '[i]f I remember right, "An Evening with Kapellmeister Kreisler" and "A Critique on Don Juan"'.

Chorley's reaction to reading them was 'exultation' — 'That is what *I* can do, and what *I will* do', he exclaimed (Hewlett, 1: 87).

The possibility of writing about music professionally grew more likely: an important step toward the goal came through the agency of Mrs Hemans's friend from Manchester, Maria Jewsbury. She had already begun to write for the recently-established London weekly, the *Athenæum*. Some of her uncollected 'best compositions' were, according to Chorley, critical essays published there in 1831 and 1832 (*Memorials*, 1: 168-9). Hewlett believed that Maria Jewsbury recommended Chorley to the *Athenæum*'s new editor, Charles Wentworth Dilke (1: 88). Susanne Howe, too, stated that 'it was Maria Jane Jewsbury who, visiting their mutual friend Mrs Hemans in Liverpool in 1830, introduced him to Dilke, then editor of the *Athenæum*, and so had given him his start on a long career in journalism' (Howe, 136).

Dilke asked Chorley for a piece on the opening of the railway between Liverpool and Manchester in September 1830. Chorley's reply on 22 September 1830 revealed Chorley's well-developed sense of his own potential strengths as a journalist, and his keen awareness of the musical direction in which his interests and capabilities were taking him. Writing from 14 St Anne Street in Liverpool, Chorley informed Dilke that such 'scientific' assignments as railway openings were really not suitable for him, and he requested that Dilke keep him in mind for articles about music. It was these qualifications for writing *musical* papers that Chorley had been cultivating; he continued to improve them for the next three years. The son of John Francis, publisher of the *Athenæum*, recalled how Chorley formed his early association with the journal while he was still living in Liverpool, three years before he moved to London:

> It was towards the close of 1830 that Chorley first contributed to the *Athenæum* occasional musical criticism. Among these was a letter he wrote from Liverpool, which appeared on the 5th of May, 1832: "Music in the Provinces — The Chevalier Neukomm's Oratorio at Manchester." The opening paragraph shows the position he sought for music, and to promote this end it may be said that he devoted his life. (Francis, 2: 537)

Chorley's review of Neukomm's music, which he did not greatly respect, anticipated a theme of his later critical writing, the role of music for the middle classes, not only for the fashionable classes:

> The circumstances of a great musical work having been brought out with credit in a provincial town, and that too without the instrumental assistance usually derived from London, argues such an advance in the art amongst us, that it has seemed to me not altogether unworthy of a notice in your columns; and I furnish this, in the pleasant conviction, that that same delightful art has passed through one stage of its transformation from the state of a costly exotic, nourished and possessed as a luxury by the few, to that of a household delight and public recreation of the many who compose the middle class. (Francis, 2: 537 and *Athenæum*, 5 May 1832: 292, signed H.F.C.)

By this time, Chorley was involved in a variety of literary and musical projects. Bursting with energy, though with no clear prospect of leaving Liverpool, he began serious professional literary negotiations. A letter he wrote to F. Schoberl gives us an idea of his early activity in addition to the occasional pieces for the *Athenæum*. He was clearly unsure how much money his work was worth:

> My dear Sir ... I send by this opportunity the manuscripts
> of my Italian Tale of which you are kind enough to take
> charge. ... I should wish to dispose of the copyright for a
> sum & a certain number of copies, but feel so totally
> ignorant as to what the value of my MS. is, if it be wor-
> thy anything, that I must trust to your kindness, & supe-
> rior experience to assist me in making as favourable an
> arrangement as possible. My friends M[rs] Hemans & M[r]
> and M[rs] Howitt have been pleased to speak very
> encouragingly of my little book, and if you would trouble
> yourself to look it over, & could honestly add a
> favourable opinion of your own to theirs, it would be an
> obligation in addition to the other good offices on its
> behalf for which I have to thank you — I need not say
> anything about extending the book, as you are already in
> possession of my views on this point. ...
>
> I suppose the terms for contributions to the Forget-me-
> not remain the same — if you should wish another style of
> article I will endeavour to suit you. (7 March 1831)[22]

The 'little book' Chorley referred to was not identified: perhaps it was 'The
Adventures of a Merchant By Chance', a long novella which forms part of
Chorley's first published book, *Sketches of a Sea Port Town* (2: 202-323
and 3: 1-190). That work, together with other stories and essays, forms the
manuscript Chorley sent from Anne Street in Liverpool to Richard Bentley's office in New Burlington Street, London, on 30 November 1833 with
a cover letter requesting publication. Bentley was an established and important publisher; Chorley hoped to start at the top. His letter emphasized his
pride in being already a noted figure in Liverpool, suggesting that his position there would contribute to the sale of the *Sketches*:

> Sir, I believe my friend & correspondent M[r] Shoberl men-
> tioned to you the MS. which accompanies this — & I send
> it direct to you, as he desired me to do (I believe with
> your permission) in his letter of the thirtieth of October. I
> shall be glad to hear that it is approved — but, in common
> justice to myself, I must beg you to bear in mind that it
> has been for the most part transcribed in the midst of a
> noisy & interrupted family circle & there are of course,
> many errors & tautologies in style &c. &c. which must be
> corrected in the proofs. I may just further say that from
> the nature of its subject, as well as its Author's being
> tolerably well known here — I should expect that it would
> be likely to excite some interest in this place.

And he pressed Bentley for a response:

> I shall be glad to hear from you at your earliest con-
> venience how you like my sketches — & upon what terms
> should you like them, you would be disposed to undertake
> their publication. ... (30 November 1833)[23]

Bentley did respond promptly, accepting the work. Chorley wrote again, with attention to details of the financial side of their agreement that was to become characteristic of him. Clearly, Chorley had high hopes for his imminent success:

> Sir, I received your letter of the fourteenth last night: &
> take this opportunity of acknowledging the polite & early
> attention which you have paid to my MS. With respect to
> the arrangement which you propose, I should certainly
> have preferred disposing of the copy right of my sketches
> at once — but as this is my first work, & I am anxious to
> bring it before the public with as little delay as possible, I
> have decided upon closing with your offer — with the
> reservation of a further arrangement should the book go to
> a second edition — I must press the point of *early*
> appearance on every account — but as we shall meet early
> in the year (as I am coming up to town to join the
> Athenæum) we can talk the matter over more fully on a
> future occasion. ... (18 December 1833)[24]

By this time, December 1833, Chorley was preparing for his move from Liverpool to London. The contract (a fill-in-the-blank generic form used by Bentley's firm) was signed on 15 January 1834, just two weeks after Chorley arrived in London. It called for the profits to be split between author and publisher, 'after deducting from the Produce of the Sale thereof, the Charges for Printing, Paper, Embellishments, if any, and other Incidental Expenses, including the Allowance of ten per Cent. on the gross amount of the sale, for Commission and risk of Bad Debts'.[25]

Sketches of a Sea Port Town is a collection of long and short stories and sketches. Its general theme is that 'there is beauty every where, — ay — even in the bird's eye view of our Sea Port Town', that is, Liverpool (1: 2), and it was written for an audience whose romantic expectations of con-temporary story-telling were largely satisfied by the tales of Benjamin Dis-raeli, Frederick Marrayat, Edward Bulwer Lytton, Robert Surtees, Harrison Ainsworth, Catherine Gore, and the Countess of Blessington.[26] For the most part, their reputations were soon superseded, in large part, by Dickens and the sunshine of the *Pickwick Papers*. The essays, fanciful sketches, and romantic tales in Chorley's 'Liverpool Papers' revealed their family resem-blance to many other essays and stories of the 1830s. Their old-fashioned,

Annuals-related style remained characteristic of Chorley's fiction for the rest of his career, as did the topic of several pieces: the difficulties of becoming an artist.

Like a character in one of his own stories, Chorley had been complaining for years that in Liverpool his 'wings were perpetually breaking against the cage':

> No creature in prison was ever more resolute than I was
> to get out. But long and weary was the time ere extrica-
> tion came; and when it did come, it was only, as it were,
> along a byroad. (1: 68)

And now, at the end of 1833, he was about to be released from the prison of Liverpool. Bentley's acceptance of Chorley's *Sketches of a Sea Port Town* coincided closely with Charles Wentworth Dilke's offer of probationary employment with the *Athenæum*.

In December 1833, thanks to the 'byroad' of journalism, Chorley was given his opportunity to escape to London, faeryland of literature and music.

Notes

1. As discussed in the Preface, Henry Hewlett, an acquaintance of Chorley's in his last years, published long extracts from Chorley's manuscript diaries and manuscript autobiography, adding his own commentary, connecting material, and narration. These extracts were published in two volumes by Richard Bentley in 1873, the year after Chorley's death, under the title *Henry Fothergill Chorley: Autobiography, Memoir, and Letters*. When the context does not indicate clearly whether my quotations from 'Hewlett' were originally written by Hewlett or by Chorley, the author will be explicitly identified.
2. According to Hewlett, Richard Chorley's son, Charles, died in prison, although Chorley believed incorrectly that he too had been hanged (Hewlett, 1: 7).
3. Writing of his father's siblings, Chorley stated that 'they wrote verses far above the average of amateur verse; they read something of French and Italian. Two or three of them had aptitude for drawing; and almost all of them a love for out-of-the-way reading, and a raciness of expression and repartee to which I have since met nothing similiar' (Hewlett, 1: 8).
4. Dickens described Miss Tox's keyboard instrument as 'an obsolete harpsichord, illuminated round the maker's name with a painted gar-

land of sweet peas' (*Dombey and Son*, Chapter 7). In all his writings — starting long before the two men became close friends — Chorley frequently alluded to Dickens's novels.

5. Brownsword was the maiden name of Jane Chorley's mother.

6. Rutter was the surname of the first husband of Jane Chorley's mother.

7. Fothergill was the maiden name of John Chorley's mother.

8. For Chorley's elaborate tribute to his brother's talents see Hewlett, 2: 255-92. It pained him that his brother, whose literary efforts Henry respected and supported, did not seem to reciprocate that respect:

> Till within a very few years of his death, I was some-what misjudged by him, as one who had chosen my life for purposes of mere amusement. That my life had been turned aside from its natural current — that whereas he should have been a great and ruling power in the world of letters, I might have become a fair musical composer (my ideas, for better for worse, having always first occurred to me in that form,) never, during a long portion of our two lives, seemed to occur to him. I never had word or sign from him to testify that anything I have published gave him pleasure. (Hewlett, 2: 281)

9. Allusions to Genesis 35 (Benjamin, son of Jacob and Rachel, brother of Joseph) and to the *Tale of Gamelyn*, no longer generally attributed to Chaucer.

10. Hewlett noted that John Rutter was Mr Rathbone's first cousin, and that Mrs Rathbone was daughter of Richard Reynolds, 'the munificent Quaker philanthropist' from Bristol (1: 47). Members of the Liverpool Rathbone family had long been prominent both as abolitionists and successful merchants.

11. He noted as a possible exception a family 'so much before its age, as that of the Taylors of Norwich (1: 67). Richard Jenkyns observed that in Victorian England 'the classics tended to become an instrument of philistinism: the study and practice of art and music were regarded as womanish things' (Jenkyns, 64). On the low social status of the musician in England at this time see also Ehrlich, *Music Profession, passim*.

12. When she was 'little more than five years of age, domestic embarrassments, arising from the failure of the mercantile concern in which her father was engaged, led him to remove his family from Liverpool to North Wales' (*Memorials*, 1: 16).

13. In 1838, reviewing a large number of annuals for 1838 (i.e. published late in 1837), Thackeray, in *Fraser's Magazine*, sneered:

> such a collection of feeble verse, such a gathering of small wit, is hardly to be found in any other series. But the wicked critics have sufficiently abused them already. ... Miss Landon, Miss Mitford, or my Lady Blessington, writes a song ... about water-lily, chilly, stilly, shivering beside a streamlet, plighted, blighted, love-benighted, falsehood sharper than a gimlet, lost affection, recollection, cut connection, tears in torrents, true-love token, spoken, broken, sighing, dying, girl of Florence, and so on. The poetry is quite worthy of the picture, and a little sham sentiment is employed to illustrate a little sham art ('A Word on the Annuals' in *Fraser's*, December 1837, Thackeray's *Works*, 25: 73-5).

14. According to John Francis, John and Henry Chorley began the annual 'The Winter's Wreath' in 1827 (Francis, 2: 537).

15. Rossetti quoted in Leighton, 13. Mrs Hemans was further described in *The Three Histories* (1830) by her friend Maria Jewsbury as 'Egeria'. Chorley quoted approvingly Jewsbury's assertion that '[h]er strength and her weakness alike lay in her affections: these would sometimes make her weep at a word, — at others imbue her with courage. ... [S]he was a muse, a grace, a variable child, a dependent woman — the Italy of human beings' (quoted in Chorley, *Memorials*, 1: 188-9). As an example of the refining effect which the affections had on her daily behaviour, Chorley observed that, after she read extracts in some periodicals from Moore's memoirs of Byron showing the poet 'invested with a Mephistopheles-like character which pained and startled her', she stopped wearing her previously cherished relic of Byron, a lock of his hair (2: 22). Once she enclosed in a letter a copy of a critical study of herself — terming some parts of it 'beautifully written' (2: 173) — in which she was termed 'Speaker to the Feminine Literary House of Commons' (2: 174). When Fanny Kemble published a tragedy in 1832, Hemans censured the unwomanly aspects of Kemble's work: 'Have you not been disappointed in Miss Kemble's tragedy? — to me there seems a *coarseness* of idea and expression in many parts, which, from a woman, is absolutely startling' (2: 269).

16. *Sesame and Lilies*, preface, xxxiii.

17. I assume that this letter was written to Chorley because he prints it together with a group of extracts from letters 'addressed at this time to different members of our family circle' (Chorley, *Memorials*, 1: 189).

18. A fellow-writer for one of the annuals (*Forget-me-not*), Mrs Bowdich, had shown Chorley's verses to Chevalier Neukomm, with

whom Chorley then became acquainted (Hewlett, 1: 164-70). Chorley was not as impressed with Neukomm as Mrs Hemans was, remarking that 'for some five years, he held a first place in England, and was in honoured request at every great provincial music meeting', despite the fact that Neukomm had only a 'slender musical talent' (Hewlett, 1: 166).

19. Fanny Ayton, prima donna; Curioni, tenor; Giubilei, basso serio; and De Begnis, basso buffo (1: 81). Spagnoletti was 'leader'.

20. Grisar left Liverpool for Paris in 1830 and made a career writing for the Opéra Comique. See Chorley's obituary of Grisar in the *Athenæum*, 26 June 1869: 869 and Hewlett, 1: 85-6. Chorley's notices of Grisar's compositions during the 1860s were generally perfunctory.

21. Most importantly Ignace Moscheles, composer, teacher, and personal friend of Mendelssohn, Moscheles's family, Barry Cornwall and his family, and Mr and Mrs Basil Montagu (Hewlett, 1: 160).

22. MS, North Collection, Library of Congress, ML94.N67.

23. MS, Wigan Archives Service.

24. MS, Wigan Archives Service.

25. British Library, Bentley Papers LII, ADD MS 46 612.

26. As the following short summaries suggest, there were autobiographical elements in many of the stories. The three parts of 'The Furnivals' tell the story of Robert Douglas. By nature a painter, by nurture he seems doomed to become a merchant, but ends up, happily, a painter after all. In 'The Missionary and the Actress', a young woman who wants to be an artist is misunderstood by her relatives, enthusiastic dissenters. She attends some performances (*Macbeth* with Siddons, Kotzebue's *Stranger*, — 'that most lugubrious of all absurdities', [1: 259]) and she makes her debut as Juliet. In the end, however, she resolves to search for 'domestic happiness' (2: 57). In 'Parson Clare' Herbert marries for money, not love; his wife dies in an accident — or so it is thought. It turns out, eighteen years later, that she has been living secretly, a madwoman in the house. Then she really dies, this time at the feet of the sad, aged woman whom Herbert might have married eighteen years ago, had he married for love instead of money. Chorley recalled this story when he reviewed *Jane Eyre* in 1847, though he did not suggest that Brontë had been influenced by it. In 'The Adventures of a Merchant By Chance', Walter, thought drowned, works hard, and is a good merchant. His honest career shows that 'it is better to make a name than to inherit one' (3: 190). In 'The Story of Madame Fabbroni', the appearance of a glamorous opera singer in the provincial sea port town causes the narrator to uncover her history. Born Miss Robinson, married to Mr Smith, who was as proud of his beautiful wife 'as others have been of a picture or

a statue purchased at an immense price' (3: 226), she was one day deserted by him. When he eventually returned, Mrs Smith decided to leave: she studied hard, became a celebrated opera singer, and returned to the sea port town as Madame Fabbroni.

CHAPTER TWO

Beginning Again:
Journalism and Literature

On the recommendation of Maria Jewsbury, the editor of the *Athenæum*, Charles Wentworth Dilke, had accepted articles from Chorley while he still lived in Liverpool. In 1833 Chorley applied for a position, suggesting £80 as an acceptable yearly wage.[1]

After some correspondence, Chorley and Dilke agreed on the conditions of a trial position on the *Athenæum*: he settled in London, lived near Dilke, and did anything Dilke deemed needed for the journal — writing or rewriting — six days a week for six months. For this he was paid £50. Dilke warned Chorley candidly about what he could expect:

> It may, indeed, be presumed that I mean to shift from my shoulders to yours *as much of the drudgery as possible*, being heartily weary of it. I am, however, of opinion [*sic*] that at least one whole day a week would be at your disposal, and perhaps some hours of one or two other days. Nor would your occupation be *always* disagreeable; but as much of it would be to *rewrite* papers — a wearisome business, as I know — I think it better to declare at once that [your occupation] will be generally *drudgery*. (Hewlett, 1: 92-3)

Chorley, for whom there could be no drudgery worse than enslavement in a Liverpool merchant's office, accepted the offer 'with pleasure and without hesitation' (1: 93). He moved from Liverpool on New Year's Eve, 1833. The trip to London took twenty-six hours in miserable weather. Chorley rode outside the coach and remembered that

> [t]he weather was of the very worst winter kind; the horses could hardly make head against a storm of wind, which, as we passed through Derbyshire, blew over a worse-appointed stage-coach before us. It snowed heavily, and my hat was blown off. The bitter cold at dawn of that new year's day is a thing never to be forgotten; and when I arrived at my destination (Mr. Dilke having kindly invited me to his house till I could establish myself), I was numb, stupid, hardly able to speak, to think, or to move.

> ... But it was something to begin a man's life in London,
> and during the early months of my probation ... I never,
> for an instant, repented the step I had taken. (1: 94, 95)

He left with best wishes of friends from Liverpool days. A few weeks after entering the new world, Mrs Hemans wrote to encourage and to warn him of dangers ahead. She was uncertain

> whether or not to congratulate you on having at last so gallantly launched yourself upon the tumultuous yet dazzling sea, which has been so long the arena of your hopes. ... I only fear that you may sometimes want someone like your old friend to be near you, 'to babble of green fields'[2] and primroses, and win you back occasionally to childhood and nature, and all fresh and simple thoughts, — from those gorgeous images of many-coloured artificial life by which you will be surrounded, and which may possibly, at first, seize on your spirit with irresistible sway. But I am convinced that nothing really worthy and *permanent* in literature (such as I sincerely think you have the power with steadfast purpose to achieve) is ever built up except on the basis of simplicity. (26 January 1834, Chorley, *Memorials*, 2: 304-5)[3]

Chorley arrived in London on New Year's day, 1834. He moved into lodgings at 5 Stafford Row, Buckingham Gate, Pimlico. He soon established chains of acquaintances. One began with the 'very agreeable' American, N.P. Willis, whom Chorley met in Italy in 1834.[4] Willis had a letter of introduction to Chorley's brother John; somehow he mistook Henry, who was on one of his Continental visits, for John (1: 170). Despite the mistaken identity, the two men struck it off well together, and, back in London, Willis introduced Chorley to Lady Blessington, who took him up and invited him frequently to Gore House. Chorley reciprocated Lady Blessington's friendship wholeheartedly.[5]

He was eager to meet more literary people. He already knew the literary society of Liverpool, of course — Hemans, William and Mary Howitt, etc. And, on his 'flying' trips before he moved to London, Chorley had met other distinguished people, some of whom were naturally among his close early acquaintances in London: Barry Cornwall (B.W. Procter) and his family, for example, and Henry Roscoe (son of 'the Italian historian' (1: 162), about whom he spoke in 'unqualified terms of admiration' (Hewlett, 1: 164), and Ignaz Moscheles. It was thanks to Moscheles that Chorley was introduced in 1839 to one of the most influential people in his life, Felix Mendelssohn.

The integrity of Chorley's employer, Charles Wentworth Dilke, played a role in his friendships, partly because he was determined that reviewers for the *Athenæum* would not write puffs or favourable reviews as personal or professional favours to their personal friends or potential benefactors. Thus we learn that

> Mr. Dilke wrote to [Chorley], that he might go to Lady Blessington's, "because she is Lady Blessington," but nowhere else, and Chorley replied that he agreed that "of all tuft-hunters, literary tuft-hunters are the worst." (Dilke, *Papers of a Critic*, 1: 31)

Dilke's wife took a 'motherly interest' in Chorley's well-being, and he was grateful for her kindness (Hewlett 1: 218).

At Lady Blessington's Chorley became acquainted with Count D'Orsay, Prince Louis Napoleon, Theodore Hook, Teresa Guiccioli, Walter Savage Landor, Isaac Disraeli, and Edward Bulwer Lytton, a vain and 'thoroughly *satin* character' (Hewlett, 1: 194).

An important friendship began in 1836 when he met Mary Russell Mitford and formed an immediate attachment to her. It endured despite the occasionally unsympathetic or sharp comments she made about him to others, and one of Chorley's final projects before he died was to publish a collection of her letters. Through Mitford Chorley came to know Mr Justice Talfourd, who became much angered by thinking that Chorley reviewed his play *Ion* harshly, though in fact the reviewer of *Ion* had been George Darley. Once this was cleared up, Chorley and Talfourd came to be on good terms (1: 113-17, 211).[6] Through Mitford also he met John Kenyon, William Harness, Charles Kemble's family, and Robert Browning (1: 205).[7]

Still more significantly, it was Mitford who introduced him to Elizabeth Barrett, writing to her around 31 July 1836 that she should make an exception to her no-visitors policy and receive the admirable Mr Chorley:

> ... my friend, Mr. Chorley ... will be the bearer of my letter and of a few flowers, and if he have the good luck to be let in, as I hope he may, will tell you all about our doings. He is worthy of the pleasure of seeing you, not merely in right of admiration of your poems, but because he is one of the most perfectly right-minded and high-minded persons that I have ever known. (*Brownings' Correspondence*, 3: 184)

This friendship remained epistolary for many years. Strongly encouraged by Mitford, Barrett from time to time seemed on the verge of agreeing to meet Chorley face to face at Wimpole Street, but in fact she never did. Although Chorley was a trustee of the Brownings' marriage settlement in 1846,[8] she met him personally only in 1851, on one of the Brownings' visits to London from Italy. (The significance of their epistolary friendship is examined more fully in Chapter 4.)

In Paris (between 1836 and 1839) he became acquainted with the Duc de Grâmont (brother-in-law of Count D'Orsay) and his family, Paul de Kock (259), and Alfred de Vigny, in whose company he saw Rachel in Voltaire's 'Tancrède' (Hewlett, 1: 265).[9] In Paris, too, he saw the early success at the *Théâtre de la Renaissance* of Albert Grisar, the composer whose path had briefly crossed Chorley's among the counting houses of Liverpool in 1830:

> The music of the opera aforesaid, ('*Lady Melvil*' being its name,) is by Grisar — a young Belgian, not many years since learning commerce in a Liverpool counting-house. After a very few months of forced application, he took flight thence, for pursuits more congenial, and here he is figuring by the side of Victor Hugo, and Meyerbeer — for the latter has promised a new work to the *ci-devant* Ventadour! (*Athenæum*, 24 November 1838: 841)

In 1838, at a party given by the author Harriet Martineau, he met the great actor William Charles Macready and also the Berry sisters, elderly and gracious holdovers from late eighteenth-century society (1: 276; *Macready's Reminiscences* 2: 104). By 1839 Chorley also came to know George Grote, the historian (Hewlett, 1: 212), Fanny Kemble, the actress, her sister Adelaide Kemble, the singer (Mrs Sartoris), Letitia Landon (L.E.L.), the poet (1: 249), as well as Mrs Somerville (1: 255), and Lady Morgan.[10]

The growing circle of well placed social connections during the 1830s was impressive: Prince Louis Napoleon Bonaparte (1: 269), and eminent literary figures like Robert Southey, Thomas Hood, Thomas Haynes Bayley, and the American author, George Ticknor. And then there was Miss Sedgwick (1: 276-9). She, after being kindly received in England despite her American 'twang' and backwoods 'dowdiness', published some letters which were not 'of good taste' (1: 280). 'I fear the next cage of Transatlantic birds will not run much chance of being very liberally din-nered and soiréed here', Chorley sighed (1: 281).

He found a comrade in the highly eligible bachelor, Henry Reeve, with whom he shared living arrangements for about four years. Reeve recalled that early in 1838 'Henry Chorley and I agreed to take lodgings in com-mon, and established ourselves at No. 9, Chapel Street, Grosvenor Place. We set to work to make our house agreeable. He supplied the music and I part of the company. Through Chorley I became intimate with the Procters, Browning, Moscheles, and especially at Gore House' (Laughton, 1: 86; also Hewlett, 1: 268). Reeve was himself socially very well connected and the two men gave many entertainments. Chorley recalled that their servant Jonathan was much impressed by the importance of the guests whom Chorley and Reeve entertained (Hewlett, 1: 271).

On 4 March 1841, the two men moved from the house in Chapel Street, Grosvenor Place, to new quarters at No. 2 Wilton Street, Grosvenor Place. (Several months later, in December 1841, Reeve married Hope Richardson. After that their personal intercourse seems to have become intermittent. The living arrangements between Chorley and Reeve had worked well for them, and their friendly relations lasted until Chorley's death. He entered into no other house-sharing arrangements.)

In Chorley's later days, strained relationships with other people were so common that it is pleasant to note how during these early energetic years he seemed to enjoy swimming in an almost endlessly extending stream of amicable social relations and friendships which were, at least superficially, cordial. Of course, not everyone who knew him in the 1830s liked him. For example, at the Grotes' (and at the Kembles' and the Procters') Chorley ran into the distinguished elderly man of letters, Samuel Rogers. Whether because of Chorley's 'coxcombical' dress or his 'affected' manner (Hewlett, 1: 220), or because he didn't like Chorley's friend Reeve, Rogers was implacably hostile (1: 221). At dinner parties, he made his distaste for Chorley known by asking

> loud enough to be heard, "Who is that young man with red hair?" (meaning me). The answer would be, "Mr. Chorley" … "Never heard of him before," was the rejoinder: after which Rogers would return to his dinner, like one who, having disposed of a nuisance, might unfold his napkin, and eat his soup in peace. (1: 221)

Chorley in turn deplored Rogers's smug, self-satisfied musical taste: 'How one, who had been hearing music for so many years, and who would never keep away from any place where it was going on, could have made so little progress in taste and knowledge as Rogers, used to excite my wonderment' (1: 224).

Thus Chorley entered quickly and easily into an active social life in London, and his personal acquaintances were legion. He moved with the successful and the rich. He took his own Chesterfieldian advice — 'live with your superiors' — and associated with people whom he could happily look up to.

2

Professionally during the 1830s Chorley became known as an important member of the staff of the *Athenæum*. He was increasingly valued not only as a reviewer of novels but also, within a year, as the journal's authority on all musical matters. His contributions first supplemented and then replaced those of John Ella.

Leslie Marchand, in *The Athenæum, A Mirror of Victorian Culture* (1941), related how Charles Wentworth Dilke, assuming editorship in 1830 turned a floundering new periodical started by James Silk Buckingham into an extremely influential general-interest journal, providing a large public with opinions on new literature, art, drama, musical compositions and performances. Some other members of Dilke's 'inner circle' in addition to Chorley were John Hamilton Reynolds, Allan Cunningham, W. Cooke Taylor, Lady Morgan, and George Darley (Marchand, 172-211).

Dilke's grandson recorded that in 1830 he 'obtained the sole control of the *Athenæum* with which he continued to be more or less associated until his death in 1864' (Dilke, *Papers of a Critic*, 1: 24), although in a drastically reduced capacity after his move to the *Daily News* in 1846. In 1831 Dilke lowered the price from eightpence to fourpence (Marchand, 34); the journal flourished, achieving the very large circulation of about 18 000 per copy. Under Dilke's editorship, Chorley's career prospered.

Dilke's *Athenæum* was widely regarded as a journal of integrity. Not everyone, however, appreciated his efforts. In retaliation for perceived slights, Bulwer, for example, termed the journal *The Asinaeum* in his novel *Paul Clifford* (1830) (Marchand, 23). On the other hand, in Dilke's eyes, Bulwer himself was part of the author-editor problem, and Dilke was determined to render periodical criticism more disinterested:

> In one of [Bulwer Lytton's] letters, he admits that he had
> on one occasion presented a silver inkstand to Mr. Jerdan,
> the editor of the *Literary Gazette*, a curious instance of the
> state of journalism forty years ago, and one which shows
> how necessary it was for Mr. Dilke to avoid all society
> himself, and to lay down rules, which at first sight might
> seem harsh and pedantic, to guide the conduct of the con-
> tributors to the *Athenæum*. (Dilke, 1: 45)

Dilke's grandson further remarked that he 'pushed his principles to the extreme only because of the bad system which had grown up in other quarters' (48). Dilke let his staff know when they used poor judgment:

> In 1835 we find Chorley receiving a "wigging" from Mr.
> Dilke for naming to his friend, Miss Mitford, George
> Darley as the author of an article in the *Athenæum*. Chor-
> ley humbly acknowledges his transgression. (Dilke, 1: 33)

Chorley's strong sense of professionalism and integrity generally blended comfortably with Dilke's. When, for example, the publisher Richard Bentley sent Chorley some material in care of the *Athenæum* office, Chorley responded that such material should be sent to his Stafford Row residence, not to the office.[11]

During the 1830s English journals did not generally identify their authors or reviewers: the practice of anonymous reviewing lasted for most journals well into the 1860s and for some journals considerably later.[12] Chorley's name, however, was much talked-about in connection with *Athenæum* business. Marchand writes that Chorley expected eventually to become editor himself on Dilke's departure (77-9). Indeed, by the end of the 1830s some people assumed he already *was* the editor: Elizabeth Barrett, for example, reported to Hugh Stuart Boyd in 1838 that 'I have seen an extract from a private letter of Mr Chorley editor of the Athenæum, which speaks *huge* praises of my poems' (*Brownings' Correspondence*, 4: 50).[13]

When Dilke began sending Chorley to the Continent as a correspondent, Chorley reported frankly and vividly to Dilke about the literary figures he met. In 1836 he wrote from Paris that Eugène Sue was 'a fierce, black hearted fellow, who looked ready and willing to eat me up' (Dilke, *Papers of a Critic*, 1: 43). The next year

> Chorley, who had been again sent to Paris on *Athenæum* business wrote: "I saw Janin yesterday. He is wilder and dirtier than ever. His dressing-gown full of holes, and his braces very immodestly absent. He piques himself on the mildness and sobriety of his article, written, he says, *à l'Anglaise*, and on the extreme moderation of his criticisms. Said I, '*Par exemple, sur Paul de Kock!*'" (Dilke, 1: 44)

The mutual respect between Chorley and Dilke never altered, and Dilke was an encouraging mentor to Chorley until he left in 1846 to succeed Charles Dickens as editor of the *Daily News*. Chorley reviewed literature and music for the journal until 1866, and wrote weekly about music until his retirement in 1868. Even after his retirement he contributed occasional pieces to the *Athenæum* and other journals until his death in 1872.

In Marchand's view, Chorley 'perhaps ... mirrored more truly the average opinions of the majority of the readers of the journal during the first three or four decades than did almost any other critic associated with the periodical in the same period' (193).

3

Bentley seems to have delayed publication of *Sketches of a Sea Port Town*. But at last it appeared, and on 21 February 1835, Chorley saw a review of his first book in the *Athenæum*. The magazine prided itself on disinterestedness; being on the staff didn't guarantee a favourable review. This first review was indulgent. The *Athenæum* allotted to the *Sketches* a column of quotation from 'Night in the Streets: Snow', which revealed a 'gentle and genial spirit'. The introductory commentary was modestly favourable:

> We have been much pleased with these volumes, for the good feeling which pervades them, and for the obvious sincerity of spirit in which they are written. The best part, however, is not, in our opinion, that which is peculiar to the Sea Port Town, but the pretty romantic stories which are grafted upon the sketches. These stories, indeed, are connected with the town, and touch upon its peculiarities; but they awaken interest from the almost irresistible impression that they are not altogether fictions: the reader feels that he is looking through a glass slightly tinged with the colours of imagination, on real romances; and, though the author frequently uses the first personal pronoun, he never gets inconveniently between the spectacle and the spectator, and rarely imposes his discussions wearisomely or prosingly on the reader, but lets his characters speak and act for themselves. The two longest and best stories are 'The Missionary and the Actress,' and 'The Merchant by Chance.' (*Athenæum*, 21 February 1835: 142)

The London Literary Gazette, a rival review, was still more encouraging. It allotted Chorley's book five columns of extensive quotation, terming him a talented provincial author with a modest, but already well-established reputation:

> Mr. Chorley is, however, known to the public in his own name as one of those who take a graceful and active part in the literature of the day, so as not to allow the metropolis to monopolise it. Conjointly with friends of similar tastes and talents, he has raised the standard of the *Belles Lettres* in Liverpool. (7 March 1835: 150)

In placing Chorley's 'class of writing', the reviewer seems to allude to Chorley's reputation as one who has established a position in 'womanly' literature:

> Of the present single-handed attempt we can also speak favourably, though it does not reach the high elevation at which this class of writing has arrived in Master, and we may add, in Miss and Mistress hands. (150)

Thus, Chorley's career as an author of books was off to a good start in 1835. Only a few weeks later appeared his first first novel, *Conti the Discarded; With Other Tales and Fancies*. Saunders and Otley paid £100 for it.

It was dedicated to Mrs Ambrose Lace, his friend from Liverpool who had introduced him to people more interesting than the Friends, 'for the sake, and in remembrance of many days gone by'. In the Preface, he wrote that he was attempting 'something in the style of the German *Kunstromanen* (Art Novels) [*sic*] with such modifications as might seem called for by the peculiar spirit of our national tastes and literature' (1: vi) — presumably the very kind of work that Chorley had encouraged Mrs Hemans to write, examining the relations between society and the artist (*Athenæum*, 23 May 1835: 392). He was concerned that the 'unreckoned-up account of misunderstanding and suspicion which exist between the World and the Artist' degraded art into a 'plaything'. And artists sometimes saw their 'calling' as 'a mere engine of money-getting' (vii).

Beginning with its epigraph from Barry Cornwall ('Come! — Sweet music hath a smart / And a balm for every heart!'), the novel emphasized music, relating an involved story of a celebrated singer from Naples, Giulia Zerlini, who at eighteen falls in love with a thirty-year-old Englishman, Colonel Hardwycke, and comes to live with him at Maldham Court, bearing his son Giulio. When the Colonel decides to marry an eligible English girl, Georgina Featherstone, Giulia dies of a broken heart.

The story moves to the Continent, where their son, Giulio, is moulded into a musician by the kind-hearted Master Silbermann. The complications are melodramatic: Giulio and the great singer La Celestina are revealed to be brother-sister (same father) just before their marriage (1: 265).[14] The narrative of *Conti* ends on page 214 of volume 2. The rest of that volume is taken up with essays labelled *Fancies of Music*, and a novella, *Margaret Sterne; or, the Organist's Journey*.[15] The essays deal with four subjects that reappear frequently throughout the next thirty-five years of Chorley's writing on music: Rossini, Mendelssohn, Handel's 'Messiah', and 'National Music'. His perspective may be summarized as follows:

1. Rossini is a great operatic composer and *Otello* is his masterpiece. 'Nor can I, for an instant, join those who abuse it as a desecration of our own Shakspeare's stupendous tragedy' (2: 241).
2. Mendelssohn is a great instrumental composer (Midsummer Night's Dream, Melusine overture — 'how charming and full of poetry', and the Symphony 'I believe in A natural' which inspires Chorley to write a three-part poem, 'The Village Beauty's Wedding') (2: 265-76).
3. Handel's 'Messiah' is 'an immortal work' (2: 299).
4. National Music 'is essentially the music of nature, inasmuch as it existed in a ruder form than it now

> wears, before science began to systematise and correct'
> (2: 303).

The *Athenæum*'s notice of *Conti the Discarded* on 17 October 1835 — six columns of quotations interspersed with commentary — was largely positive. As a story-teller, it stated, Chorley was improving:

> We have been greatly pleased with these volumes, and we say so at once, because we were somewhat chary of kind and encouraging words on a former occasion to this same writer ... [*Conti*] shows manifest progression: the writer has advanced with a bold manly stride — he evidently sees his way more clearly, writes more directly to his purpose; indeed, there are scenes in 'Conti' (we would instance the interview between the father and son,) of sustained interest and power that, to us, are an earnest of better things to come. (*Athenæum*, 17 October 1835: 776)

But the reviewer singled out the jumbled, confusing narrative style for notice:

> the very slovenly manner in which he has gathered up, or rather crushed together, incidents which ought to have been carefully unravelled. This is a fault of haste or inexperience; he raises a giant power, and is then perplexed to know what to do with his giant. (778)

These problems — seeming haste and carelessness — were cited more than once in reviews of Chorley's later attempts at fiction as reasons for his failure to reach many readers.

The next major literary task Chorley assumed concerned Mrs Hemans. In the Spring of 1835, Chorley published an essay on Mrs Hemans under the title 'Original Papers' in the *Athenæum* on 23 May 1835 (391-2). This initial article was followed by a series of three articles, 'Personal Recollections of the late Mrs. Hemans', published in the *Athenæum* on 2 June 1835 (452-4), 27 June 1835 (493-5), and 11 July 1835 (525-30). All were signed 'HFC'. Although '[w]e have laboured but a few years in our present vocation' (391), Chorley was already struck by the number of his acquaintances who had died. In Mrs Hemans's case, death came before 'she had reached the full strength of her powers' (392).[16]

The articles were followed the next year by the publication of Chorley's book about Mrs Hemans made up of commentary, anecdote, and substantial quotations from her correspondence. Much of his material came from correspondence to the Chorley family which Chorley himself possessed. For other material, he wrote to her friends. He solicited manuscript material from Professor Norton of Cambridge, for example, writing to him on 19

January 1836:

> I think by extracting merely from these precious letters &
> linking them together with some notice of her works, &
> remembrances of happy days passed by our & her
> firesides — I shall be able to produce a delightful & valu-
> able work.

He was interested in knowing

> whether you are disposed to allow me the benefit of any
> letters, or *passages of letters* you may have by you. They
> would enrich my collection as throwing a light on M^rs
> Hemans' American fame — which would be most inter-
> esting — & any remarks or criticism from the journals of
> your country (or still better from your own pen) would be
> most valuable. ... If I might hope for such aid, & your
> interest with your excellent & distinguished townsman
> Doctor Channing in my behalf — I should be highly
> gratified — .[17]

Chorley's inquiry apparently was rebuffed or ignored, since the book
contains only brief reference to Hemans's 'lasting and cordial' friendship
with Professor Norton (1: 132), and Chorley regretted that 'I have not
permission' to quote from letters by Dr Channing (*Memorials*, 1: 134). Perhaps for this reason, Chorley's discussion of Mrs Hemans's American
reputation is sketchier than might be expected:

> ... it may be well to allude to the fame which she had
> already gained in America by her writings. The circula-
> tion of these was almost unprecedented; and its influence,
> as has been already remarked, might be presently traced
> in the host of imitators that sprung up there. (*Memorials*,
> 1: 132)

This inquiry, and others like it which had more success, led to the pub-
lication of *Memorials of Mrs. Hemans With Illustrations of Her Literary
Character From Her Private Correspondence* (2 vols, London: Saunders
and Otley, Conduit Street, 1836). The two volumes were published in
Philadelphia the same year in a single volume by the firm of Carey, Lea
and Blanchard, which noted across from the title page that 'this edition of
Mrs Hemans's Memorials is published for the pecuniary benefit of her
Family'.[18] The English edition was reprinted in 1837 with some additions
and minor pagination changes.

Chorley undertook the task as a delicate one, tactfully and 'purposely
refraining from touching upon any such details of the delicate circumstances

of her domestic life, as were not necessary to the illustration of her literary career' (1: vi). He claimed for his work a special social significance not only because it treated the 'annals of English Poetry', but also because it focused on an important aspect of the 'spirit of the age', namely 'the popularity and prevalence of female authorship' (1: 2). Chorley quoted Maria Jewsbury's opinion that 'we still secretly dread and dislike female talent ... because it interferes with our implanted and imbibed ideas of domestic life and womanly duty' (1: 8). He was convinced that female authorship could maintain and reinforce 'womanly duty'.

The *Memorials* included copious quotations from Mrs Hemans's letters; Chorley explored and discussed her inquisitive mind regarding contemporary literature and music in England and the continent. He marvelled at her talent for establishing deep friendships (citing as examples her friendly relationships with Wordsworth and with the Chorley family, among others). He stressed, too, her gift for 'female friendships' and her correspondence with Joanna Baillie, M.R. Mitford, Mary Howitt, and Maria Jane Jewsbury.[19]

In 1836, three years after the publication Chorley's *Memorials*, controversy arose. After the publication of another memoir of Hemans by her sister, Chorley felt a need to defend his own integrity against statements in various journals (among them, he named *The Spectator* and *The Examiner*) that members of Hemans's family were not pleased with his biography. In an extended *apologia* (a signed letter to the *Athenæum*), Chorley quoted correspondence with Major Browne (Hemans's brother and executor) who suggested that some 'worthy people' were offended by some of the letters. Brown himself was sure that Chorley 'would not have published the letters in question had you supposed they would have given pain'. Chorley also confirmed (as he had mentioned when asking Professor Norton for help) that after 'having remunerated myself for the task of writing and compiling', he gave the proceeds from the work to Hemans's children, and he quoted approving correspondence with Mrs Hemans's sister and nephews (*Athenæum*, 17 August 1839: 620-21).[20]

Chorley's next work was another novel. He had high hopes for the success of *The Lion: A Tale of the Coteries* (3 volumes, London: Colburn, 1836) — 'To the Right Honourable the Countess of Blessington, this Tale of Modern Life and Literature is Respectfully Inscribed by The Author'). Chorley received £100 for this novel, as he had for *Conti*. It too was a *Kunstroman*, about a genius and 'his relations with society — a subject that haunted Chorley's imagination almost to the close of his life, and of which he has attempted three or four distinct illustrations' (Hewlett, 1: 146). The hero — this time a poet, not a musician — is spoiled, taken up by society, and dropped; he behaves badly, he repents. Hewlett described the opening chapters as 'pervaded by the sham-romantic, sentimental tone that widely infected English literature at the period when Chorley was writing, and for which his mind had a natural bias' (1: 150).

But Chorley was again disappointed. The work had no success. It was, however, well received by *Tait's Magazine*, though a review in *Tait's* was 'little likely to influence the sale or reputation of a book'. Chorley was, nevertheless, grateful for the review — its sympathetic tone was an 'unexpected blessing', he noted in his private journal:

> I do believe my "Lion" to be true, and I do think that it ought to find an acceptance among the middle classes, as a true picture of one section of English life. ... I feel sorely withered this time by the want of sympathy under my own roof and in my own parish; and I have been surly, irritable, and distrustful. May it be forgiven me! I am humbled by this unexpected comfort and blessing. (Hewlett, 1: 152-3)

Chorley's anguish that the novel had no success with the *Athenæum* ('under my own roof and in my own parish') was somewhat overstated. In fact, the *Athenæum* reviewer (T.K. Hervey) judiciously found things to praise and to blame in its one-column notice:

> We are somewhat puzzled in what terms to express our opinion of these volumes. ... It is seen, at once, that the author is a writer of more than ordinary powers, and the result of the expectations thereby raised is a consequent sense of disappointment. [The author exhibits a] fine talent of observation, skill in the use of the weapon of satire, which implies a practised hand, and a command of pathos, [but also reveals] what the reader feels all the time to be rather carelessness than inexperience. ... The work leaves throughout an impression that the author can not only do better hereafter, but could have done better this time, if he had chosen to take the pains. ... The satire against the coteries is well deserved and well meant, but too broad. It will raise a laugh, notwithstanding, and probably work its effects none the worse for being delivered in caricature. (*Athenæum*, 29 June 1839: 482)

Chorley's last large-scale work to appear during this highly productive phase was another volume of literary appreciation: *The Authors of England: A Series of Medallion Portraits of Modern Literary Characters, Engraved from the Works of British Artists by Achille Collas with Illustrative Notices by Henry F. Chorley* (1838). This book contains portraits and analyses of: Felicia Hemans, Sir Walter Scott, Lord Byron, Dr Southey, the Countess of

Blessington, Samuel Taylor Coleridge, Edward Bulwer Lytton, Lady Morgan, Percy Bysshe Shelley, Thomas Moore, Charles Lamb, Mary Russell Mitford, Thomas Campbell, and William Wordsworth. The publisher, Charles Tilt, paid Chorley £150 for it, and a second edition was issued in 1861. According to Mitford, Chorley had at one point intended to include Maria Edgeworth instead of Sydney Morgan.[21]

The Preface asserted that the main interest of the work lay in the medallic engraving process of M. Collas, and that other modern authors would soon be included. Chorley was sensitive to his own relatively humble position, when compared to that of his distinguished subjects:

> To avoid the language of flattery, on the one hand and of presumption on the other, is not easy; and the difficulty is increased, when a writer, comparatively young and untried, has his contemporaries and not his predecessors for his subjects. In the following slight notices I lay no claim to any merit, save such as belongs to a genial and respectful sympathy with all — whatever be their political creed or poetical school — who have laboured well and honestly in the cause of literature. (Chorley, *Authors of England*, vi)

Each author's portrait was followed by a short biography and a few paragraphs of tribute.

Several of those tributes were related to themes of his later career. For example, Chorley's chapter on Hemans (his third published work on her) stated that her separation from her husband 'contributed largely ... to increase her disposition to dwell upon the sacrifices and regrets of life in preference to its more cheerful scenes' (3).[22]

The chapter on the Countess of Blessington praised the constantly improving 'construction' in her fiction:

> Her last work, the "Victims of Society," combines a fearless and searching picture of the manners of certain higher circles, (manners, be it remarked, so false and corrupt, as hardly to be worth the painting,) with a story of adventure and retribution of great interest and originality: ... Her style is always graceful in its total absence of affectation — she excels, too, in the constructiveness, which we have sometimes fancied was peculiar to her sex, — in the power of weaving a plot. (36)

Interestingly, it was the lack of that 'constructiveness' in Chorley's work — 'the power of weaving a plot' — which the *Athenæum* reviewer of *The Lion* had recently reproved.

Edward Bulwer Lytton's works were profusely praised, with *Eugene*

Aram and *Rienzi* singled out for commendation. Bulwer's play, 'The Duchess de La Vallière' at Covent Garden (1837) was too harshly attacked, Chorley asserted,[23] and in general Bulwer 'has hardly received fair treatment from the hands of his critics' (49). The reason for this unfair treatment was partly Bulwer's own responsibility, partly the fault of corruption, which too often succeeded where critical integrity, objectivity, and disinterestedness did not.

> [T]here have been few epochs of English literature wherein criticism has been more largely a system of puppet-work, more deeply steeped in personality, than during late years. Mr. Bulwer may regard the fame he has already won with the proud satisfaction that he owes it not to the crowd of interpreters who stand between the man of genius and the public, and like the *claqueurs* of the French stage, sell themselves to him who bids the highest. (50)

In another chapter Chorley discussed Mary Russell Mitford. He considered that her prose, like Barrett's poetry, was central to contemporary female literature. He noted that we are 'too apt' to think of her name as 'connected with all that is lovely in the rural scenery, and characteristic in the rural society of Southern England, and to forget that it also appertains to a dramatist of no common power' (77). He reviewed her successes as a playwright — *The Two Foscari, Julian, Rienzi, Charles the First* — and her plays as yet unperformed: *Inez de Castro* and *Otto of Wittelsbach* ('Miss Mitford's last, finest work').

> In all these plays there is strong vigorous writing, — masculine in the free unshackled use of language, but wholly womanly in its purity from coarseness or licence. ... As also in Joanna Baillie's fine tragedies, the poetry of these plays is singularly fresh and unconventional; equally clear of Elizabethan quaintness and of the modern Della-cruscanisms. ... (78)

Despite the importance of her plays, the rural writing, especially *Our Village*, achieved greater permanent significance:

> But the claims of Miss Mitford to swell the list of *inventors* ... rest upon yet firmer ground, they rest upon those exquisite sketches, by which — their scenery all, and their characters half real — she has created a school of writing, homely but not vulgar, familiar but not breeding contempt (in this point alone *not* resembling the highly-finished pictures of the Dutch school) wherein the

> small events and the simple characters of rural life, are
> made interesting by the truth and sprightliness with which
> they are represented. (79)

Thus *Our Village* differed from the rural writings of Crabbe, who 'lingers like a lover in the workhouse and the hovel, and dwells rather upon decay, and meanness, and misery, than the prosperity, and charity, and comfort with which their gloom is so largely chequered. He may be called the Caravaggio — Miss Mitford the Claude of village life in England; and the truth lies between them' (80).

Finally, the case of Wordsworth showed how party spirit caused reputations to rise and fall. Scorned when he first wrote, later he was considered 'the regenerator of our literature' (87). With Wordsworth, Chorley seemed somewhat unsure of his own critical perspective. Perhaps for that reason, he mentioned Wordsworth's works through the 1820s straightforwardly, then relied on quotations from Coleridge's *Biographia Literaria* to account for Wordsworth's poetical strengths (92-3). The *Authors of England* ended with its assertion that Wordsworth had 'a purifying, rather than a corrupting influence' (93).

Chorley was also expected by the *Athenæum* to write articles on subjects outside his area of expertise: between 1836 and 1841 he wrote numerous reviews of painting exhibitions, though he stated in a column of 1841 that '[t]o criticise painting and sculpture I have little pretension'.[24]

In October 1838, Dr Rutter, Chorley's benefactor, uncle, and 'second father' died. Chorley returned to Liverpool at that time and was present at the death. Chorley's mother inherited enough money to be described as 'affluent' (Hewlett, 1: 219), and Chorley himself inherited £1400. Only seven months later, another loss followed: Mrs Rathbone of Green Bank, benevolent and much-admired, died in May 1839.

These early losses initiated what seemed to Chorley an unending stream of bereavements throughout his life. Domestic happiness, rooted in security, remained the powerful ideal for Chorley's imagination throughout his life. One of the central attractions for him of Hemans's works, and her womanliness, lay in her ability to create an emotional expression of domestic felicity as a 'fictional state', as Anne Mellor termed it. As a fictional state, the ideal could be yearned for: it did not necessarily have to be experienced literally. It could be treasured romantically, as an expression of the desire to regain that which one had never possessed.[25]

In this sense, Hemans's womanliness, the kind that 'finally collapses upon itself, bringing nothing but suffering, and the void of nothingness, to both women and men' (Mellor, 142) had a powerful impact on Chorley, since his image of happiness focused on the ideal of perfected human sympathy, of loving domestic intercourse between a man, his wife, and their children. For him, this relationship was overwhelmingly important, difficult to achieve, and subject to disappointment, dissolution, and decay. Thus Chorley could experience the warmth of womanliness, in Hemans and other writers, as a fictional state providing an imagined validation of, alternative to, and consolation for his own constant loneliness and suffering.

Notes

1. Chorley's joining the London staff was facilitated 'by the intervention of a Quaker acquaintance, Mr. Pringle, the African traveller' (Hewlett, 1: 91).
2. *Henry V*: ii, 3, 17.
3. The recipient is unspecifed but the context suggests Chorley himself.
4. In Thackeray's *Vanity Fair* (1847-48) Willis was ridiculed as John Paul Jefferson Jones, 'titularly attached to the American Embassy, and correspondent of the *New York Demagogue*' (Chapter 48, 'In which we enjoy three courses and a desert'). According to the *Dictionary of American Biography*, Willis's writings about his experiences abroad began appearing in *The New York Mirror* in 1832; *Pencillings by the Way* appeared in 1844.
5. Unlike Greville, who dined at Lady Blessington's on 16 February 1839 and noted in his diary that after dinner appeared 'Foster [*sic*, John Forster], sub-Editor of the "Examiner"; Chorley, Editor of the "Athenaeum"; Macready, and Chas. Buller. ... [T]he woman herself ... is ignorant, vulgar, and commonplace' (Strachey and Fulford, 4: 128).
6. The *Athenæum*'s later review of the printed text of *Ion* covered seven columns: 'Ion may answer very well as an acting tragedy while we have nothing better' (28 May 1836: 373).
7. Philip Kelley and Ronald Hudson suggest that Chorley met Robert Browning either at Harriet Martineau's in 1838 or shortly before the first letter from Browning to Chorley in January 1844 (*Brownings' Correspondence*, 8: 326).
8. Along with John Kenyon and Joseph Arnould, see *Brownings' Correspondence*, 8: 327.
9. He also saw Rachel in Paris in 1840 and described her acting to Mendelssohn: 'She is indeed, a wonderful Genius & it is wonderful to see so young and childish a creature capable of such a concentrated scorn & hatred as she shows in her great scene in "*Les Horaces*"' (MS, Green Books, XII, 27 November 1840).
10. Lady Morgan's diary for 23 December 1838 notes that 'Count Alfred de Vigny was presented to me' at a 'soirée' given by Chorley and

Reeve (Owenson, *Lady Morgan's Memoirs*, 2: 445). According to Chorley, she was once introduced to 'the stately, grave, and accomplished Mrs. Sarah Austin, on which occasion she complimented her sister authoress on having written "Pride and Prejudice"' (1: 241).

11. 'Please to send any further notes &c to my address as above. I am never at the Athenæum office — & keep my private business as much separate from its concerns as possible' (21 March 1834, MS, Wigan Archives Service).

12. Christopher Kent in Alvin Sullivan, *British Literary Magazines*, 2: xiii. The *Athenæum* from time to time used initials: see, e.g., the 'Foreign Correspondence' from 'Leipsic' and Brunswick signed H.F.C., 26 October 1839 and 2 November 1839, 9 November 1839, 16 November 1839.

13. 21 June 1838. Chorley's favourable review of Barrett's *The Seraphim* appeared in the *Athenæum*, 7 July 1838: 466-8. R.W. King also termed Chorley 'the editor of the *Athenæum*' (King, 259).

14. Several narrative asides allude to current operatic practice, e.g.: 'The Italian Opera [in London then] was a much more aristocratic amusement than it is now' (*Conti*, 2: 41) and 'Our periodicals are grown something more liberal than to expend anathemas upon the King's Theatre in the Haymarket, as a temple of effeminate pleasure fatal to English manliness' (2: 42). In a footnote, Chorley commented on the quality of acting on the 'stage' compared to the opera:

> ... where are we to look for the really first rate actors
> of the years in which we are living? The English stage,
> I suspect, would find some difficulty in furnishing
> superiors, or even equals, to Pasta, Schroeder, Grisi,
> Malibran, Lablache, Tamburini and Donzelli, (in some
> of his parts). (2: 42)

15. Like the narrator of *Vanity Fair* ('A novel without a hero') twelve years later, the narrator of *Margaret Sterne* writes of 'the heroine of my story (it hardly boasts a hero)' (3: 377).

16. A friend of hers (presumably Chorley himself) had urged her 'to undertake a prose work, and a series of "Artistic Novels", something after the manner to Tieck, and Goethe's *Kunst-Romanen* [*sic*], as likely to be congenial to her own tastes and habits of mind, and to prove most acceptable to the public' (23 May 1835: 392). This would be something not unlike the task Chorley set for himself in *Conti*. But Hemans countered that 'I cannot help sometimes feeling as if it were my true task to enlarge the sphere of sacred poetry, and extend its influence' (392). These *Athenæum* articles emphasize the importance to her work of her feminine nature, that is, her refinement and her

patient suffering.

17. MS letter to Andrew Norton, Autograph File, Houghton Library, Harvard University.

18. Chorley wrote to Professor Norton that he intended the book to aid Mrs Hemans's sons, but, like many English authors, he might not have been satisfied with the 'pecuniary' arrangements of American publishers, as is suggested by his signature on a petition to the United States Senate in 1834 from more than sixty British authors requesting the establishment of copyright protection (MS Huntington Library).

19. The book also provided much information about the close relationship established between Chorley and Mrs Hemans during her time living at Wavertree, near Liverpool. For example, we learn that she, like Chorley, studied music with James Z. Herrmann, that he had put to music two of her poems (2: 165), and that she had begun to compose music for her own poems (2: 185). Chorley worried that her inspiration was bad for her health.

> The fervour with which these [lyrics] were poured forth, seriously endangered a frame already underminded by too ardent a spirit, whose consuming work had been aided by a personal self-neglect, childish to wilfulness. So perilously, indeed, was she excited by the composition of Mozart's Requiem, that she was prohibited by her physician from any further exercise of her art, for some weeks after it was written. (1: 128-9)

Chorley's belief that her sensibility caused her suffering is illustrated by his comment that in her own copy of Madame de Staël's *Corinne* she marked the passage beginning 'De toutes mes facultés la plus puissante est la faculté de souffrir' and added in the margin: 'C'est moi' (*Memorials*, 1: 304). Hemans's suffering was as inseparable from her womanliness, as her life was from her works, since 'the works of the *really* gifted ... *must*, in some sort, mirror their lives' (1: 2).

20. Barrett wrote to Mitford on 23 November 1842: 'Is it not true that Mrs Hemans's friends took offence at his work respecting her? I inferred so from the memoir written by her sister & could not make out *why* — for surely nothing could be more delicate, even hyperdelicate, than his manner of treating the subject' (*Brownings' Correspondence*, 6: 165).

21. In a postscript to her letter to Elizabeth Barrett on 22 February 1837 she wrote, 'Henry Chorley wishes me to go to town to sit for the "Portrait Annual;" Miss Edgeworth, Mrs. Hemans, Lady Blessington, and myself being the ladies chosen for this first volume'

(*Brownings' Correspondence*, 3: 226).

22. He called attention to her great popularity in the United States, where 'The Pilgrim Fathers' had made her famous (4), and noted her restlessness during her years in Wavertree, when her mind was 'more subject to painful alternations [*sic*] of mood than at any previous or subsequent period' (6).

23. This opinion, read in the light of a comment by Dilke's grandson about Bulwer and the *Athenæum*, suggests some mending of fences.

> [Bulwer] having on another occasion stated that the unfavourable criticism on "La Vallière" was "written by one who, having himself an interest in a play the production of which was (as to time) incidental on the success of 'La Vallière,' had every motive of personal interest to induce him to assist and procure its failure," was assured by Mr. Dilke that he was mistaken, and apologised. He meant Chorley, but the criticism was probably written by George Darley, though Chorley was in the house on the first night. Chorley certainly did not write it, but did write a private one equally unfavourable. (Dilke, 1: 46)

24. *Athenæum*, 'Foreign Correspondence' signed H.F.C., 9 October 1841: 779. In April, 1856 he published 'Ruskinism' in the *Edinburgh Review* and near the end of his life, he considered but abandoned the idea of writing a book on Holbein.

The range of Chorley's assignments and the direction of his creative and critical publications in London are seen in other works written around this time in addition to his regular journalism for the *Athenæum*: A drama, *Fortibel*, (1838, not produced), poems in the *Athenæum* and in Lady Blessington's annuals, reviews and articles in the *London and Westminster Review* (all attributions from *Wellesley Index to Victorian Periodicals*):

1. 'Concerts and Operas', July 1837: 53-77. (*The Crucifixion* by Louis Spohr, version arranged by Edward Taylor; *Malek Adel* by Costa, and *Catherine Grey*, text by George Linley, music by Balfe).
2. 'Works of Mrs. Trollope', October 1837: 112-31.
3. '[Thomas] Hood's Own [Style]', April 1838: 119-45.
4. 'England and Brittany', August 1838: 352-72. (review of E. Souvestre's *Les Derniers Bretons*, Paris 1836, and William Howitt's *Rural Life in England*, London, 1837).

    5. 'The pianoforte', April 1839: 306-56.

and reviews in the *British and Foreign Review*:

    1. a review of Anna Jameson's *Winter Studies, Summer Rambles*, January 1839: 134-53.
    2. a review of the works of George Sand, April 1839: 360-90.

25. See also Tucker (especially 533-42), who noted that 'home for Hemans is less imagined than *imaginary*, a fancy past fulfillment' (542).

CHAPTER THREE

Chorley and Music, 1834-41

1

Chorley's musical tastes were formed early and for the most part remained constant throughout his life. His writings group themselves into four chronological periods. The first lasted from his full-time employment in 1834 as a staff writer for the *Athenæum* to the publication in 1841 of his three-volume *Music and Manners in France and Germany: A Series of Travelling Sketches of Art and Society*. The second, the 1840s, culminated in his involvement with the theatre war which resulted in the formation of the Royal Italian Opera at Covent Garden as a rival to Her Majesty's Theatre in the Haymarket managed by Benjamin Lumley. The third period, the 1850s, was Chorley's journalistic prime, when he was an arbiter of London's musical scene, along with J.W. Davison at *The Times*. The final period, the 1860s, is characterized by Chorley's bitter conviction that his work had not been understood or appreciated. This final period began with the publication of *Thirty Years' Musical Recollections* in 1861, which, more than any other book of his, has survived, influencing readers and critics to the present day. Chorley's railing — especially at the 'music of the future' — increased as his effectiveness decreased. Even after his retirement from the *Athenæum* in 1868, Chorley blustered on in final jeremiads, signed articles in the *Athenæum* and the *Orchestra*.

In Chorley's weekly columns for the *Athenæum*, several issues during the 1830s assumed particular importance:

1. the English careers of Italian opera composers: Rossini, Bellini, and Donizetti.
2. the Grand Opéra at Paris and the Music Drama of the Future.
3. the establishment of the golden age group of singers; performance standards at the opera in London.
4. the promotion of British musicians and English operas.
5. the English careers of Mendelssohn, Liszt, and other foreign musicians.

Although Chorley began working for the *Athenæum* full time in January, 1836, he was not its music critic at first: John Ella was. The marked file in 1834 attributes numerous musical articles to him. Sometime between 1835 and 1840 Chorley assumed responsibility for these articles, but the marked files are frequently unmarked during these years.[1] Therefore, the authorship of some of the opinions in the late 1830s is presumed, rather than known, to be Chorley's. The first marked identification 'Chorley' is on 26 April 1834 (*Don Giovanni*); it is preceded and succeeded by many reviews attributed to Ella, and by many other reviews left unattributed.

It is certain that Chorley wrote most reviews from 1835 on. And it was because of Chorley's reviews that by the end of the 1830s the *Athenæum* earned a reputation as a musical authority unusual for a general-interest publication. By then, at least from Elizabeth Barrett's perspective, the *Athenæum*'s strength in music could at times be grounds for (private) complaint about its other departments, as she wrote Mary Russell Mitford: 'But I wish sometimes that it's [*sic*] poetical were like its *musical* criticisms, justified & beautified by the love of art' (18 July 1841, *Brownings' Correspondence*, 5: 83). And the next year, to the artist Benjamin Robert Haydon, Barrett stated: 'The truth is, that the Athenæum gives all the enthusiasm it has to spare for Art, away from Poetry & Painting to *music* ...' (20 October 1842, *Brownings' Correspondence*, 6: 113). Looking back in 1872, John Edmund Cox stated that best way to document London's musical life in the period since the 1830s was by referring first to Richard Mackenzie Bacon's *Quarterly Musical Magazine and Review*, then the *Harmonicon*, and 'from the year 1830 to 1867' to the criticism in the *Athenæum* 'from the pen of the late Mr. Henry F. Chorley' (Cox, *Musical Recollections*, 1: ix). Cox endorsed Chorley's opinions and quoted them extensively.

The production which defined the possibilities of music drama to London audiences in the early 1830s was *Fidelio*, as presented in Monck Mason's season of German Opera in 1832. Though financially the season was unsuccessful, artistically the production of *Fidelio*, conducted by Chelard, with Schroeder-Devrient as Leonora, 'amounted to a revelation' of opera as drama:

> Her eyes, quickened by the yearnings of her heart, were everywhere; her quivering lip, even when her countenance was the most guarded, told how intensely she was listening. It was impossible to hear the "Prisoner's Chorus" ... without tears. ...
>
> But the principal feature of the German performance of "Fidelio" which marked an epoch in London, was the spirit and reality of the stage chorus — ... a company of earnest folk, with stout voices (and those of the women fresh), who showed that they took pride in their work ... and that they understood the scene. ... (Chorley, *Thirty Years' Musical Recollections*, 1: 52, 57-9)[2]

Although the Italian opera season at the King's Theatre in the Haymarket began during the winter, the performances after Easter were more important: — 'There is a sort of traditional allowance extended to the performances at this theatre before Easter, which we have no wish to withhold', the *Athenæum* noted after a performance of Bellini's *Beatrice di Tenda* (labelled 'merely a rifacciamento of "Anna Bolena"', 26 March 1836: 227). The principal singers from the Théâtre des Italiens in Paris joined the London company after Easter and stayed through July. That year a performance of Rossini's *Gazza Ladra* with Grisi, Rubini, Tamburini, and Lablache ('so familiar that every tenth person among the audience could act as prompter' [276]) marked the 'real' beginning of the season.[3] The journal's overview of the 1836 season stated that the upcoming Paris season 'promises well' because a good French season was needed for a good London season 'as all the efficient rehearsal and preparation which is done at all is done there, and not in London' (6 August 1836: 555).

And, indeed, when the principal singers returned from Paris to London in April, 1837, the *Athenæum* rejoiced:

> Once more we have an opera! The arrival of *the* company from Paris — and there is not such another company collected, or *to be* collected, 'from China to Peru' — has changed the King's Theatre from a pillory — that is, a place where ears are *bored* — to a 'paradise of dainty devices'.[4] In plainer phrase, Grisi, Rubini, Lablache, and Tamburini, re-appeared in 'I Puritani' this day week, and were greeted by the heartiest of welcomes from a densely crowded audience. ... (15 April 1837: 268)

2 Relative Positions: Rossini, Bellini, and Donizetti

Rossini's music in the 1820s was fashionable. In England, the first version of Stendhal's adulatory life of Rossini had been translated and rushed into print early in 1824, even before it appeared in Paris.[5] Although some old-fashioned curmudgeons like Mount Edgcumbe deplored the noise and vulgarity, Rossini's popularity remained at a peak during the 1830s, and the newer Italian opera composers, judged by standards applied to his operas, were found wanting by many critics. In 1835 George Hogarth expressed in his *Musical History, Biography, and Criticism* a critical perspective which Chorley shared and frequently articulated:

> The present Italian composers are mere imitators of Rossini; and are much more successful in copying his defects than his beauties. They are, like him, full of mannerism; with this difference, that his manner was his own, while theirs is *his*. ... This general description applies to them

all. PACINI, MERCADANTE, BELLINI, and DONI-
ZETTI are all alike — *"fortem Gyan, fortemque Cloanthum,"*[6] — and have not a single distinctive feature.
(398)[7]

The *Athenæum*'s notices of operatic performances in the middle and late
1830s reflected precisely this assessment of the relative worth of Rossini
and the other Italian opera composers.

Bellini's inferiority to Rossini was asserted in comments such as this:

> Bellini's operetta, 'La Sonnambula,' was produced on
> Thursday week, for the benefit of Madame Caradori, but
> did not attract a full house; as, in spite of great occasional
> sweetness of melody, the effect of one of Bellini's com-
> positions cannot fail to be feeble and unsatisfactory to the
> ears that have been lately enjoying the brilliancy and pas-
> sion of Rossini. (24 May 1834: 396)

In reviewing the fourth edition of Mount Edgcumbe's *Musical Reminiscences*[8] the *Athenæum* stated that the book's weakness was its old-fashioned
lack of enthusiasm for Rossini:

> The latter part of the book is professedly chiefly written
> from hear-say, and to this we attribute no little of its
> author's severity upon Rossini. No one has mourned over
> this master's mannerism more than ourselves — but to
> speak of him, as a composer, slightingly or indifferently,
> or reproachfully, is, we think, "professing" something
> "too much." (22 November 1834: 852)

The issue of 16 May 1835 noted that Grisi's singing in Bellini's *Sonnambula* was greatly applauded, but the opera is 'insipid' (379). 'Marino
Faliero' by 'Donnizetti' was produced for Lablache 'with questionable success' (23 May 1835: 395). The *Athenæum* recognized the success of Bellini
and Donizetti as dependent on the quality of the singing, rather than — as
with Rossini — the innate quality of the music and the music drama. The
reception of Bellini's *Puritani* illustrated this point; its success was
attributed Grisi, Rubini, Tamburini, and Lablache, the golden-age quartet
of principal singers who were associated with it.

At the end of the 1835 season, the *Athenæum* complained that the
management of the Italian opera should produce more Rossini: 'why have
we not heard ... his "Mosè", his "Assedio di Corinto", above all his
"Guillaume Tell"?' (22 August 1835: 651).

The *Athenæum* noted Bellini's death in 1835 with regret — he was
'affectionate and refined' (3 October: 747); his music, however, was no
more worthy of succeeding Rossini's than that of his contemporaries: 'Italy

has the singers — but if we ask where are its composers, echo answers 'where?'' (3 October 1835: 747).

In the 'Musical and Dramatic Gossip' section for 27 February 1836, not long after Bellini's death, the journal announced a production of Bellini's 'Beatrice Tenda' [*sic*] and asked querulously, 'Why produce so much sickly and characterless music, when so many of Rossini's fresh and glorious works are left unperformed, or, at best, given imperfectly?' (160).

As for Donizetti, the following bluntly dismissive reaction was characteristic: 'Donnizetti's [*sic*] (*sixtieth*?) opera, "Belisario", was given this day week. ... The music is beneath criticism — the weakest work of a weak writer' (8 April 1837: 252). This may be compared to Chorley's hostile reaction to Donizetti's 'insipid' *Lucia di Lammermoor* with Persiani, Rubini, and Tamburini: 'a weaker musical composition it would be impossible to imagine' (7 April 1838: 259). And though a performance of Donizetti's *Parisina* (Grisi, Rubini, and Tamburini) was 'excellent', the opera itself 'must be pronounced wholly worthless' (9 June 1838: 413). Further complaint was made that in Italy such works 'are permitted to push the best operas of Rossini from the stage' ('Our Weekly Gossip', 4 August 1838: 555).

The relief was palpable when Her Majesty's Theatre performed Rossini again — *Mathilde di Shabran* (Persiani, Rubini, Lablache):

> It would be hard to express with what an intense sprightli-
> ness, and melody, and freshness, the music of 'Mathilde'
> came upon our ears, saturated as they have recently been
> by the thoroughly dull and dismal tragedy of Donnizetti
> [*sic*]. (16 June 1838: 430)

Balfe's *Falstaff* was presented at Her Majesty's with Grisi and Lablache (not as an English opera but part of the Italian opera season, its libretto from the extremely busy pen of Manfredo Maggioni). Chorley objected to Lablache's uncharacteristically vulgar 'introduced morsels of English'. Though he praised the stretto of a trio for its 'liveliness', he was more concerned to point out (as a flaw) a resemblance between the compositional styles of Balfe and Bellini, since Balfe 'has therein chosen to extend Bellini's illegitimate device in "Suoni la tromba" and, in repeating the theme, to make the three denounce the "ridicole vechiacchio" *in unison*!' (21 July 1838: 516).[9]

The music of 'Donnizetti's' *Lucrezia Borgia* was termed 'even less inviting' than that of *Parisina* (8 June 1839: 437). Mario was styled the new 'Romeo', with a 'delicious voice'. But he must 'work hard to make it [his success] lasting' (437).[10] It was interesting to Chorley that this performance (though it was Grisi's benefit) was 'but moderately well attended' (437); a few weeks later, this time after *L'Elisir d'Amore* with Persiani, Mario, Tamburini, and Lablache, he again noted that the performance was not well attended (29 June 1839: 490).

In 1840 Her Majesty's opened with 'Donnizetti's' *Torquato Tasso* (commendable singing only from Coletti). It resembles *Parisina* and *Lucrezia Borgia* in being 'so weak in structure, familiar in every phrase of melody, and harmonic combination, and instrumental effect, as to be beneath the reach of analysis' (7 March 1840: 195).

Longing for an improvement, Chorley inquired about the possibility of bringing to London a new Italian opera composer, Mazzucato. Another name merited a passing reference: 'The music of Verdi, too, whose "Oberto" introduced Mrs A. Shaw to the Italian stage, should be inquired after, were we in the management' (7 March 1840: 194). Chorley lived to rue the day when management did inquire after Verdi's music, since he soon became most hostile to it.

Meanwhile, there were more operas by Rossini's rivals to complain about. Bellini's *Beatrice di Tenda* 'remains the worst and weakest opera we ever endured. ... By this time, we hope it is dead and buried, past the power of even a Persiani to resuscitate' (4 April 1840: 278).

Not even the splendid voice of Persiani could rescue the music composed by her husband for *Inez di Castro*. Despite vocal fireworks (Rubini 'touching E flat *altissimo*' and Persiani singing 'a high soprano note, which we will not name, lest our ears have deceived us'), and despite characteristically splendid acting from Lablache, the opera was 'barren, poor, and common-place' and the libretto was 'weak and hackneyed' (6 June 1840: 461):

> A week ago, we should have thought it impossible that we could think wistfully of Donnizetti [*sic*]; yet we did, while suffering our first weariness under the infliction of 'Inez di Castro.' Are there no operas by Pacini ... which, if revived, would be more agreeable to the ear than this hackneyed and ungracious music? (6 June 1840: 461)

There was, at least, a visiting German company at the Prince's Theatre giving performances of operas more durable than Pacini's — *Don Giovanni*, *Fidelio*, and *Freischütz*. Although the company was deemed mediocre on 9 May 1840 (378), Chorley spoke encouragingly of the production of *Euryanthe*. It was not a popular draw, but it was an opera which, despite its poor libretto, 'stands by the side of the "Fidelio", on the highest pinnacle of excellence, as a specimen of the legitimate German lyric drama' (6 June 1840: 461). The notice directly followed the review of *Inez di Castro*, perhaps with some consciousness of irony at its placement there, since Chorley believed that 'none of the barrel-organ operas of the modern Italian school ... deserves to be mentioned in the same day with this German work, so rashly voted incomprehensible' (461). Later in the summer there was praise for Staudigl in Spohr's *Jessonda* (11 July 1840: 557) and the greatness of Gluck's *Iphigenia in Tauris* was discussed in that issue and the following (18 July 1840: 578). (Chorley's period for championing Gluck most energetically, however, was the early 1860s.)

Thus, as the 1840s began Chorley found himself an advocate for Rossini, somewhat surprised and displeased that any advocacy should be needed for works which in the 1820s had made their way in triumph. The same operas that had formerly delighted audiences were now being revived somewhat less often and to somewhat less enthusiastic audiences. *Tancredi* in 1841 was a case in point:

> To ourselves, the music had all the genial freshness of novelty, the opera not having been given, save once for Brambilla, and an act of it for Pasta, since the year 1834. But the audience seemed to find it flat and uninteresting, and were warmed with difficulty by Persiani's best singing in the part of *Amenaide*, and by the magnificent sallies of Madame Viardot-Garcia as the hero. (27 March 1841: 245)

The large-scale modification of audience taste, however, and its effect on the recently established canon lay ahead. Rossini's loosening grip on the English audience still seemed a passing aberration.

3 The Paris Grand Opéra: the Music Drama of the Future

During the 1830s a new repertory was being created in Paris and introduced at the Académie Royale de Musique (the Opéra), a repertory dominated by the last works of Rossini, several works by Auber, and the first operas of Meyerbeer. Although many of the operas of the new French repertory were brought from Paris to London, they did not achieve the popular success in London that they had in Paris.[11]

Chorley saw it as his mission to open the eyes and ears of the English to the repertory of the French Grand Opera — Rossini, Auber, and above all Meyerbeer and *Les Huguenots*. In the 1830s he was in the forefront of those recognizing that the direction which dramatic music had taken in Paris was to form the core of new repertory for decades. Not until the late 1840s — with the Meyerbeer craze at Covent Garden — did London catch up with Chorley's early enthusiasm. Reviewing Hogarth's 'very pleasant book', *Memoirs of the Musical Drama* (30 June 1838: 453-5) Chorley digressed: 'It is enough for us to say, that our highest hopes, for the future of the lyric drama, are from French composers' (455).

Meyerbeer's *Robert le Diable* (1831, libretto by Scribe) established the dramatic and musical norms of the grand opera.[12] The new manager of the Opéra, Louis Véron, made a commercial success of the genre by using the combined talents of several extraordinary men of the theatre: composers like Auber, Halévy, and (especially) Meyerbeer along with the librettist Eugene Scribe and stage designers Ciceri and Duponchel.[13] To some observers, the 'commercial' aspect was pronounced. William Crosten pointed out that, while the established audience, 'the older aristocracy', still 'took its patronage to the Théâtre-Italien, the bourgeoisie stormed the doors of the Académie Royale de Musique'.[14]

In London, there was an important difference: the King's Theatre (renamed Her Majesty's Theatre in 1837) functioned in terms of repertory and casts almost as an English version of the Théâtre-Italien. There was no rival to function as a kind of English analogue to the Académie in Paris. For the English, French opera would be translated into Italian.

Some of the differences between audience expectations in Paris and London were exemplified by the lukewarm reception obtained in London by the great Parisian box office hit of 1831, Meyerbeer's *Robert le Diable*. Soon after its Paris premiere came the first English production at the Adelphi Theatre in an arrangement which dropped most of the music (only two pieces remained). The scene of the ghostly nuns, the opera's most sensational part, was 'most admirably managed' (*Athenæum*, 28 January 1832: 69). The Adelphi version was produced quickly, but was overshadowed in a few weeks when the rival Patent houses came out with alternative versions: Covent Garden, under Elliston's management, produced it in a version arranged by Michael Rophino Lacy as *The Fiend Father*. The production at Drury Lane, under Bunn's management, was altered and adapted by Henry Bishop.

Alternations, substitutions, and adaptations were standard practice in the 1830s, but the alterations made in *Robert* and in some of the succeeding French grand operas were substantially more drastic than those made in the new and recent Italian operas performed at the King's Theatre. According to Chorley and the *Athenæum*,[15] they were formidable obstacles, preventing the English from forming an appropriate appreciation of the works' significance.

But the English audiences did have at least a brief opportunity to experience the work in its French form, since, as part of an extravagant and anomalous season at the King's Theatre under the short-lived direction of Monck Mason, much of the original company from the Opéra was imported at the end of the regular 1832 season to perform *Robert* in all its Parisian glory. Presenters of French Grand Opera believed in spending money in order to make it. The importance of this unprecedented event was heralded in the *Athenæum* by items designed to arouse its readers' attention and curiosity, and to lay the ground for a sympathetic hearing of the opera. On 9 June 1832, for example, the *Athenæum* announced that '[t]he cost in producing this opera for scenery, costume, and machinery alone, will, we are told, exceed three thousand pounds', and the total cost was to be approximately £7,000 (*Athenæum*, 9 June 1832: 373).

The reviewer for the *Harmonicon* conceded that 'the French have made vast strides in composition', and that the singers were good,[16] but cautioned: 'That the opera is too long for us, is admitted by all' (10 [1832]: 159, 160). The criticism of French grand opera on the grounds of excessive length seems odd since performances at English opera houses were notoriously long, lasting from as early as 7 p.m. until well past midnight. Perhaps the complaint was really levelled at what was to the English an unconventional use of time: the whole evening's being devoted to a single opera. English audiences expected a ballet after the opera.[17]

The reviewer for the *Athenæum* asserted that the success of *Robert le Diable* 'was complete' (16 June 1832: 388), singling out Grieve's scenery for special praise. *Pace* the *Athenæum*, the success of *Robert* was *not* 'complete'. Meyerbeer, reported to be displeased, left England after the first rehearsal, and Cinti, singing Isabelle, withdrew after the first performance. Subsequent performances were given without the second and fourth acts (*Athenæum*, 23 June 1832: 420).

Looking back on the production from the vantage point of 1861, Chorley analysed why *Robert* had failed in London despite its triumph in Paris:

> In England some ill fortune, as will be seen, has always attended this opera, which has never been accepted as a favourite by our public. It is impossible to account for inconsistencies like these, frequent as they are in the world of Music. — In 1832, however, 'Robert', with its piquant melodies, its daring stage effects, and magnificent instrumentation, had no chance of establishing itself in London; since it was only completely performed once — and then after insufficient rehearsal. The singers quarrelled with the management, and had to be replaced by inferior ones. The work was curtailed, and on it, given in this mutilated form, descended the curtain of the season 1832 — a season of disasters. ... (Chorley, *Thirty Years'*, 1: 48-9)

Though *Robert* failed to make a lasting impression in 1832, some versions of other French grand operas did enjoy temporary success in London, though in drastically altered form. J.R. Planché wrote that Alfred Bunn believed that his audiences did not want to have to hear much music in their operas (Planché, 1: 82). In the adaptation of Auber's *Gustavus* (in Planché's version with music by T. Cooke) for London audiences, Gustavus was *not* in love with Madame Ankarstrom, a change introduced in order to accord with conventions of English stage morality, more sensitive than French (see Planché, 1: 211-22). With these radical alterations, Bunn noted that the 'town became literally *Gustave-mad*' (Bunn, 1: 195). The reviewer in the *Athenæum* concurred, praising the 'exquisite scenery' and terming the adaptation 'the most splendid and most gratifying of its sort ever placed upon the English stage' (16 November 1833: 780).[18]

Two years later the Bunn-Planché-Cooke team produced an even more successful version of a grand opera: Halévy's *La Juive*. At Bunn's insistence, the ending was altered so that Rachel lived.[19] The *Athenæum* stated that 'Mr. Planché's is an admirable adaptation' of Scribe's 'admirable play' — a 'splendid and interesting drama' (876), with praiseworthy scenery by Messrs Grieve (21 November 1835: 876).

When the English opera at Drury Lane produced Rossini's *The Siege of Corinth* in November, 1836, the journal praised it. The adaptor, Planché, 'has substituted the leading personages of "the late" Lord Byron's poem', and the 'scenery was very splendid, and added to the already heaped-up fame of the Messrs. Grieve'. The best singing came from Giubelei ('one of the very best second-rate singers') and in general 'the opera met with a brilliant reception' (12 November 1836: 803).

Still, *Gustavus* and *La Juive*, and even Rossini's own *Siege of Corinth*, however admirably adapted, were considerably less important than Rossini's great *Guillaume Tell*. Produced at the Opéra in 1829, the opera reached London in an English version at Drury Lane in December, 1838. Chorley reported on the performances with enthusiasm, qualified by his reservations about the libretto for being 'at best, dull and harmless':

> But the music by Rossini! It may appear exaggerated to
> the rigid admirers of the German school, for us to rank
> this opera — whether as a whole, or in parts — by the
> side of 'Fidelio,' and 'Don Giovanni,' and 'Oberon;' and
> yet, according to our principles of criticism, this is what
> we must do. (*Athenæum*, 8 December 1838: 881)

Chorley was struck by the 'exquisite adaptation of sound to sentiment' when Tell interrupted the fisherman's song, and when he embraced his son at the height of the suspense:

> Then what an exquisite propriety of colour has Rossini
> diffused over all his scenes — throughout all his choruses!
> ... [N]ot even in his already-mentioned 'Otello,' has he
> risen to the height which he reached, when writing for
> Arnold the great duett [*sic*], the great *solo*, and the *trio*,
> the slow movement and *stretto* of which carry passion and
> melody united as far as they can legitimately go. ...
> ... [This production] is one of the best attempts ever
> made on the English stage to realize the intentions of a
> great composer; and if it be followed up, it will be

regarded as a era in the progress of the musical drama in England. (8 December 1838: 881)

The singers (Romer as Matilda, Allen as Arnold, Giubelei as Gesler, and Braham) were not fully in command of their roles; and yet this did not entirely explain why the English public resisted *Tell*. Chorley searched for reasons why the time for French grand opera had not yet come. Perhaps in order to establish a defence against a possibility that the time would *never* come, he suggested that it was necessary to direct 'attention to the disadvantages attending the performance of this opera, in order to account beforehand, should there be a failure in point of attraction, of an experiment in many respects highly commendable, and, on the whole, extremely interesting to the lovers of music' (*Athenæum*, 8 December 1838: 881). The 'disadvantages' Chorley specifically cited were the quality of the singers (Allen as Arnold, Romer as Matilde), who were unable to match the high quality of the singers at the Opéra (Nourrit and Cinti Damoreau). The best singer was Braham as Tell, who, 'though labouring under the disadvantage — the greater considering his age — of contending with music below the compass of his voice, at times blazed out with great success'.

When *Tell* was produced at Her Majesty's the following season (1839), where one might assume that the disadvantages of the English Drury Lane production could be overcome by the resources of London's main opera house, and by a cast including Persiani, Rubini, and Lablache, the results seemed inconclusive. As an explanation of some of Chorley's critical preoccupations during the late 1830s, this review of *Tell* at Her Majesty's Theatre is revealing:

> On Thursday, M. Laporte honourably kept *the* promise made at the outset of the season, by producing [in Italian translation] 'Guillaume Tell,' as efficiently as lay in his power. The fact that the success of this opera was less brilliant than we could have desired, is worth explaining. In the first place, the work was largely retrenched, so as to bring it within the customary limits of a London performance. [Chorley here enumerated various cuts made in the score.] ... Add to these drawbacks, the want of any predominant female interest throughout the opera (during the whole of the first act the principal *soprani* were scarcely audible), and the grandeur of scale upon which the music is written, which may, in the first instance, be felt as oppressive by uninitiated ears, — and we think that Rossini is vindicated, without any too severe reflection upon an English audience — still less, any ill-natured carping at a management, which has made the most of the imperfect materials it had to work with. [Rubini was mis-

cast, Persiani good, Lablache magnificent] ... The orchestra was, throughout, very good ... The chorus, too, was well-trained, and powerful; and we can but hope that the public will recognize the pains which have been taken, on the present occasion, to represent one of the noblest lyric dramas extant, in a fitting manner. (*Athenæum*, 13 July 1839: 525)

That *Tell* was not as successful as might have been hoped confirmed Chorley's intimation that the new French school of grand opera, for him the most interesting development in contemporary music drama, might be able to achieve public acceptance only under the special conditions of the Opéra in Paris.[20]

Sometimes French Grand Opera reached London in German rather than English or Italian translation. In 1841 a German company visiting London performed Auber's *Muette*, though not entirely satisfactorily:

We have rarely heard a translated opera without a feeling of dissatisfaction: each school has its own characteristics, which are weakened, if not lost, in the process of substituting one language and one body of executants for another. Most especially does our remark apply to French music.

Nevertheless, on grounds of significance, Chorley recommended that people see this production:

But we are inclined to believe that our Germans do all that any Germans can do for this French music; and while we pray those who are innocent of Paris not to accept theirs as a final version of any work originated in France, we cannot sufficiently commend the zeal, diligence, and resolution to be sprightly as well as correct, which every one, from the cymbaleer to the least important chorus singer, threw into his performance. (*Athenæum*, 27 March 1841: 245-6)

Despite the fact that Germans did not do justice to French music, when Drury Lane announced that in the coming season the Germans planned to present *Les Huguenots* 'under the direction of its composer', Chorley commented eagerly that the prospect of *Les Huguenots* '*is* indeed a promise, which, with all our musical hearts, we hope may be fulfilled' (6 March 1841: 191). Still, French grand opera in German translation was artistically acceptable only by comparison with the abysmally low quality of the earlier English versions by Planché, Cooke, Bishop, et al. Chorley never considered the German translations adequate substitutes for the originals.

The same reasoning did not hold for Italian translations. Through them, finally, with the production of *Gli Ugonotti* at Covent Garden in 1848, French Grand Opera achieved popularity in London.

4 The Golden Age: Performance Standards in London

The beginning of Chorley's career coincided with one of the greatest golden ages of operatic singing. In April 1834 Giulia Grisi's debut was rapturously received. She became almost overnight the single most important woman singer on the London stage until her retirement in 1861. Ella's comment on the debut in Rossini's *Gazza Ladra* of *la jolie* Grisi (so called by Parisians to distinguish her from her unsuccessful sister, Giuditta), was that '[i]t is long since we have seen so triumphant a first appearance upon these boards' (*Athenæum*, 12 April 1834: 275). She joined Rubini, Tamburini, and Lablache to anchor the post-Easter repertory of the Italian opera seasons.

In April 1835, the singing of Grisi, Tamburini, and Lablache in the trio, 'O nume benefico', from Rossini's *Gazza Ladra* was praised as 'the most perfect piece of dramatic concerted singing we ever heard' (18 April 1835: 324). Another kind of recognition of a golden age came with the notice given to Malibran and Grisi who — at different theatres — were both singing *Sonnambula*:

> ... we could almost fancy that the old days of Cuzzoni and Faustina are about to be acted over again; and that the high *soprano* of the Haymarket [Grisi at Her Majesty's Theatre] is to be set up in rivalry against the mellow contralto of Covent Garden [Malibran in Bunn's Company]. For our parts, we like both; and all the better for the entire difference of their voices (396).[21]

Grisi and Malibran sang together at Mr Benedict's Morning Concert, performing an electrifying 'Ebben ferisci' (from Rossini's *Semiramide*) and 'this magnificent performance awakened in us feelings, which we had almost thought, and *feared*, we were too hackneyed in pleasure ever to experience again' (18 July 1835: 552).

The reviews in the *Athenæum* evaluated not only the principal singers, but also, from time to time, the chorus, the scenery, and the band (orchestra). Chorley complained on 26 March 1836, after a pre-Easter *Beatrice di Tenda*, that 'we cannot overlook the deficiencies of the chorus' (227). On May 28, 1836, commenting on a performance of Rossini's *Otello*, it noted: 'The band is at its best this year: ... — the chorus is not quite at its worst' (386). The next season the journal noted not only new faces in the *corps de ballet* but also an 'opera chorus, which is now sufficiently strong' (4 March 1837: 163).

Grisi appeared as Norma in 1836, approaching Pasta in her mastery of the role, and the *Athenæum* asserted that the performance was a bright spot in an otherwise 'tedious and unsatisfactory' season: 'The most obstinate and fantastic *anti-Grisi* must have been startled out of his prejudice by the passion and brilliancy of her whole performance of this part' (6 August 1836: 555). Her excellence made the opera seem better than Chorley believed it was, but not even the combination of Grisi, Rubini, Tamburini, and Lablache could rescue the season's 'less than mediocre' new opera, *I Briganti* by Mercadante (based on Schiller's *Die Räuber*), in which there was 'nothing to remind us of the original "Robbers"' (2 July 1836: 473). Anticipating its reaction to Verdi's setting of the same source eleven years later, the *Athenæum* labelled it 'a total failure' (6 August 1836: 555).

The next season, after welcoming the return of 'the' company from Paris, the *Athenæum* stated that

> Grisi, at least, is assuredly improved; as superb in the fulness [*sic*] and flexibility of her voice as formerly, and far more impulsive and unconstrained in its management. Her performance of the part of *Norma* was beyond all praise.
> (15 April 1837: 268)

Malibran's death was lamented for two and one half columns: her best role in England was remembered as Leonore in *Fidelio*. '[I]n the lyric drama of Europe, she who has died has left no peer behind her!' (1 October 1836: 707). The *Athenæum* regretted that she was not well served by the *Memoirs* of the Countess of Merlin. 'Nothing, in short, can be more childish and unsatisfactory than the concoction of this book' (14 March 1840: 209).

When Clara Novello gave a benefit concert in April 1837, the *Athenæum* commented that she would be 'shortly proceeding to Italy to complete her studies. ... She *may be* our best English *soprano* if she pleases ...' (29 April 1837: 309). Her welcome home was not so warm: 'Her voice is improved ... but to make Miss Novello a singer of the first class, almost as much is wanting as was required before she left England' (15 February 1840: 138).

The conducting of Michael Costa was usually praised, but it came in for criticism after a *Don Giovanni* because of 'the constant disposition shown by Signor Costa, in the first finale, to accelerate: this, though it be of little consequence to the flimsily-contrived music of the modern Italian school, is most detrimental to the more substantial compositions of the Germans' (6 May 1837: 331). Costa almost immediately regained his place of honour with the *Athenæum*: his new opera, *Malek Adel*, was performed that season several times with Grisi, Lablache, Rubini, and Albertazzi; on May 27, 1837, the *Athenæum* noted that the 'first favourable impression ... has been confirmed by a second and third hearing' (388).

Pasta's return in Zingarelli's *Romeo* was noted: 'She was received most enthusiastically. ... And well does she deserve such honour. What matter if Time has made her voice at times tremulous, at times uncertain, and coarsened the outlines of her figure and the traits of her fine countenance? She is still ... the unapproached Queen of the Italian stage' (24 June 1837: 469). Though she did not sing well in Mayr's *Medea* — 'to say the sad truth, singing a quarter of a note too flat, from the *entrata* to the *finale*' — her acting was 'incomparable' (15 July 1837: 523).

Schroeder-Devrient around the same time was appearing at Drury Lane in Planché's English version of *Norma*: the *Athenæum* noted that Malibran's English was better than hers, and that 'her deportment [was] classically correct, though somewhat classically cold' (1 July 1837: 485).

The season of 1837, in complete contrast to that of 1836, was 'the most brilliant and most satisfactory season within our remembrance' (19 August 1837: 602). A tone of glowing satisfaction was evoked in reports of the 'real', after-Easter season of 1838, which began exactly as that of 1837:

> It is scarcely necessary to do more than announce the reappearance of Grisi, Rubini, Lablache, and Tamburini, in the well worn 'I Puritani.' ... The only change to be remarked, was a variation of exceeding brilliancy introduced by Grisi at the *da capo* of her polacca ["Son vergin vezzosa"]. The orchestra and chorus of the establishment are in a riper state of perfection than we remember them to have been. Sig. Mario (*alias* the Marquis de Candia) is announced to appear next month, to replace Sig. Tati. (13 April 1839: 283)

That season brought, too, the appearance of Persiani, who showed 'great merits' in *Sonnambula*, though her 'ornaments' are not 'such as made Sontag *par excellence*, and Pasta grand, and Malibran astonishing' (31 March 1838: 242). Persiani was Zerlina in a performance of *Don Giovanni* which provoked Chorley to remark on the 'exceeding perfectness' of the cast (26 May 1838: 379). Complaints about Persiani's ornaments did not continue; indeed, her 'cadences' [cadenzas] were soon held up as models to Madame Balfe (notice of Philharmonic Concert, 13 April 1839: 283).

Generally Chorley's reports on the King's Theatre seasons after Easter focused on the high quality of the singers and the need for the manager (Pierre François Laporte from 1833 to 1841) to present the highest quality music (more Rossini, less 'Donnizetti'); he objected to 'the dishonourable system of puffery now carried on with such activity, in particular as regards the Italian Opera, and certain benefit concerts' (12 May 1838: 348).

The debut of Pauline Viardot-Garcia as Desdemona in Rossini's *Otello* was perceived by Chorley as especially significant. Later he became close to her professionally and personally; her voice was not entirely beautiful, but artistically there was something unique about her:

> The first appearance of the sister of Malibran, so long talked of, so eagerly anticipated, — and yet, strange to say, so meagrely attended, — made Thursday evening the most remarkable one in this season's musical chronicle. A *début* so interesting to witness, yet so puzzling to describe, does not come within the scope of our recollections. ... On future occasions, we shall have much to say concerning the peculiarities of Mdlle. Garcia's singing. ... And now a word or two on her acting: her *physique* prepared us for eccentric, unstudied attitudes, at time happily conceived — at times almost uncouth. But ... we need only add, that the intenseness with which Mdlle. Garcia is obviously possessed of her part, must lead to her impressing her audiences and swaying them according to her own mood — in spite of great disqualifications of form and feature. Long and bright be the career thus remarkably begun! (11 May 1839: 357-8)

Two weeks later Chorley wrote after her singing at Benedict's benefit concert:

> Mdlle. Garcia justified, to the very highest point, all the praise we had bestowed upon her, as a thoroughly finished singer ... — and this at the early age of seventeen, in her first season of intercourse with the public! (25 May 1839: 398)

If she resists 'strange and startling' ornaments, 'she may become the greatest singer of her century' (25 May 1839: 398).

The glories of the singers at Her Majesty's Theatre were profusely acknowledged, as were some aspects of generally improving performance standards. For example, after praising Persiani's *Sonnambula*, Chorley wrote: 'We cannot close this paragraph of praise without one word laudatory of the Opera orchestra this year — and another of the chorus. ...' (21 March 1840: 237).

And yet the next year, 1840, brought tension. The troubles of the manager, Pierre Laporte, anticipated by a few years the vastly more protracted and bitter struggle between a group of journalists and Laporte's successor, Benjamin Lumley. The 'Tamburini riots' in April 1840, like the anti-Kemble O.P. ('Old Price') riots in 1809,[22] revealed fissures produced by sources deeper than the ostensible cause. In this case, when Coletti was substituted for Tamburini in *Puritani*, the audience rioted. Chorley sided with the rioters, and exhibited a long set of grievances (interestingly, the least of the grievances seems to be the substitution of Coletti for Tamburini).[23] 'We cannot regret that M. Laporte has at last been called to account', he wrote.

> The case between him and the public stands thus: — a progressive encroachment on the purses of the subscribers — witness the raised rents of the boxes, and the fifteen nights retrenched from the subscription, — and on the comfort of the casual public — witness the six rows of stalls subtracted from the pit, (another measure tending to enrich the treasury), has been accompanied by a constant disposition on M. Laporte's part to attempt such changes and economies as seriously impair the excellence of most operatic performances, — as entirely preclude the possibility of others. In proof: besides the vexed question under notice, since the time (two years ago) when Ivanoff was dismissed, the place of second tenor has been filled by persons such as Tati and Ricciardi, whose singing would disgrace a minor theatre. Again, last year Madame Albertazzi, the established contralto of the company, was dispensed with: — the engagement of Mdlle. Pauline Garcia, for *a few* nights, as *prima donna*, by no means filling the void; inasmuch as that lady naturally declined the secondary occupation falling to the share of the person missing. This year we have neither Albertazzi *nor* Pauline Garcia, and hence we can have no 'Tancredi,' no 'Semiramide,' no 'Donna del Lago,' — no opera, in short, with a prominent contralto part. (2 May 1840: 354)[24]

Having warmed to the subject, Chorley returned to it the next week. Chorley accused Laporte of trying to destroy 'the association of his principal performers in Paris, where (we speak advisedly), by constant private practice and frequent public rehearsal, most of the operas performed here, have been *got up*' (9 May 1840: 378). Chorley attributed the 'cold reception' given the previous Saturday to Rossini's *Otello* to 'Signor Ricciardi's incompetence' and added to his list of singers who should not be hired, 'Madame Bellini, a *mezzo soprano*' (378). He rounded off the diatribe with a sentence whose sentiment is still a favourite of critics attacking operatic management in London and elsewhere: 'Such things should not be permitted to pass at the most expensive place of public amusement in the world' (378).

When Laporte issued the 'programme' for the 1841 season, his last, Chorley found one section of it commendable: Laporte's insistence that the orchestra attend all rehearsals. Chorley's position is interesting because it conflicts with that taken a few years later during the battle between Lumley and Costa.[25]

The complaints about mismanagement returned, however, when Laporte added 'two or three rows of stalls' by way of encroaching on the pit,

> making that once favourite resort of idle rank and fashion about the best imaginable theatre for the exhibition of experiments in the compressibility of animal matter. We are so vexed at being thus eternally called on to take exceptions at M. Laporte's selfish policy, that we escape gladly from all matters of objection, to the music of Cimarosa's master-work [*Gli Orazi*] (13 March 1841: 213)

Chorley's favourite singer fell temporarily out of favour: 'Garcia-Viardot' singing Orazia, 'gave us painful pleasure. There is no disguising the truth, that her admirable musical skill, and her fine dramatic conception of the dignity, the tenderness, and the agonized despair, of the part, are not seconded by Nature. Her voice *will* be weak' (13 March 1841: 213).

Regaining her standing in Chorley's eyes with her 'magnificent sallies', Viardot displayed 'her fancy in its most fertile abundance' in Rossini's *Tancredi* (27 March 1841: 245). The 'genial freshness' of the music, however, made little impression on the audience, which 'seemed to find it flat and uninteresting' (245), a reaction which boded ill for Chorley's devotion to the continuation of Rossini's central place in London's operatic canon.

For Chorley, and for English audiences, it was not Viardot but Grisi who became and remained the queen of song during the golden age. Time and time again, Chorley wrote glowing notices of her exemplary performances: 'Madame Grisi never performed "Norma" with such deep passion, such grandeur of voice, and such brilliancy of execution, as on Tuesday evening' (22 May 1841: 411).

Grisi owned the role of Norma, as even Jenny Lind was to discover in a few years.

Great singers fascinated Chorley; occasionally so did other performers. When Liszt came to England in May 1840, Chorley was overwhelmed. Liszt's first public appearance was on 8 May, only two days after his arrival, at the Hanover Square Rooms; on 11 May he played at the Philharmonic Society concert. Although much of the press was indifferent or hostile, Chorley was thrilled. He called Liszt's playing 'the musical event of the week — of the year' (16 May 1840: 403). Chorley reminded his readers that Liszt had previously appeared in England fifteen years ago as a child prodigy. Now his performances of his own music (a 'Marche Hongroise', a Valse, and a 'Galop Chromatique'), of opera fantasies (from

Puritani and *Lucia*), and — with the Philharmonic — of Weber's 'Concert Stück' — confirmed his status as 'Poet of the Piano', and 'all anticipations of M. Liszt have been exceeded by the reality' (16 May 1840: 403). Before we knew of him by reputation as associated with the 'romantic school', that is with Victor Hugo and George Sand, those who worship 'Shakspeare [*sic*] and Goethe, and Byron and Hoffmann' (403). In his performances now, 'the peerless feature is, the bright, eager, elevated poetical genius to be heard in every tone and touch — the utterance of a high-soaring enthusiasm, if at times near to, never wholly coincident with extravagance' (403).

On 9 June and 19 June, Liszt performed his 'recitals', a new concept. Henry Reeve recorded in his diary that he 'took Mme. d'Agoult to his recital' at the Hanover Square Rooms on 9 June (Laughton, *Reeve*: 117); in July Liszt gave a recital with the violinist Ole Bull at Willis's Rooms, 55 St James's Street: Alan Walker quoted the review in *The Times*, by now favourably disposed (2 July 1840). According to Walker, it was Chorley's review in the *Athenæum* of 4 July which 'rightly gauged the historic importance of what was happening, and which seized on the essential point'. That point was that Liszt could, all by himself, hold the attention of an audience for two hours — 'The critics may not understand M. Liszt, but the musicians crowd to listen to him' (cited in Walker, *Liszt: The Virtuoso Years*: 357).

After the Philharmonic's fifth concert of 1840, 'led by Mr Loder and conducted by Mr Bishop' (with Liszt and Molique as guests), Chorley criticized Bishop severely because he 'set many of the movements going in times which their composers did not intend'.

> Strong nationality makes our ears tingle and our cheeks burn, whenever foreigners, armed with musical science to their fingers' ends, like M. Liszt and Herr Molique, should witness such incompetence — the shame of which must be divided equally among the directing committee, the conductor of the night, and the orchestra, vaunting itself to be one of the finest in Europe! (16 May 1840: 103)

Chorley liked to meet and socialize with his favourite musicians. Since Henry Reeve knew Liszt through Alfred de Vigny,[26] Liszt soon was introduced to Chorley. Within a month of his arrival in England, Liszt was appearing with Chorley at Lady Blessington's parties at Gore House (Allsobrook, 33). During Liszt's stay in London, the musical parties given by Chorley and Reeve 'were very brilliant. We had Liszt, the Battas, Ole Bull, Moscheles, Benedict. On June 1st, M. Guizot and the Richardsons came. Liszt and Batta played the great Beethoven Sonata, *en doublant les passages*' (Laughton, 116-17).

5 Is England a Musical Nation?

If you are told often enough that you are no good, you will eventually believe it. So claimed the *New Monthly Magazine* in 1835 — 'Our countrymen have been told until they believe it, that they are not musical; and they acquiesce in spite of the evidence of their own senses (February 1835: 146). *Is* England a musical nation? In the opinion of the author of 'Notes of A Musical Student: Progress of English Music in the Past Year', the answer, happily, was becoming obvious to all except, perhaps, snobs:

> That "the English are not a musical people," is a saying
> which by frequent repetition has become a proverb. It is
> surprising how long a fallacy keeps its ground. ... It has
> been a pet piece of cant among even musical professors,
> to say, that the Italian Opera was only supported by the
> world of fashion, as a splendid lounge; and when the
> German company came over, and drew crowded houses,
> not of fashionables merely, but of the middle and even
> humbler classes, "novelty" was the cause assigned for
> their success; and the failure of the last German company,
> on account of their inferiority, was, by the same persons,
> attributed to the lack of novelty. ... [I]n short, the
> English, not being a musical people, went to hear music
> for any other reason but because they liked it. (*The New
> Monthly Magazine*, February 1835: 146-7)

The author rejoiced in the formation of the 'Society of British Musicians', suggesting, however, that it needed to admit certain 'foreigners' who, like Moscheles, Crevelli, and Cramer, have 'lived for years in this country' (152).

Even more worthy of celebration was English Opera, a topic of critical concern from the beginning of Chorley's career till its end:

> The establishment of a *bonâ fide* English Opera House,
> contemporaneously with the formation of a Society of
> British Musicians, is a remarkable event in the past year.
> ... Up to 1834 it was said that there was no Englishman
> capable of composing a grand opera. ... Yet no sooner
> was it understood that Mr. Arnold intended to give the
> experiment of English opera a fair trial, than composers
> set to work, and the result was the production, in one
> short season, of three grand operas, with various degrees
> of success, the lowest being far removed from failure.
> (*New Monthly Magazine*: 153-4) [Loder's *Nourjahad*,
> Barnett's *Mountain Sylph*, Thomson's *Dark Diamond*]

Eric Walter White, in his *History of English Opera*, termed the year 1834 'something of a milestone' (262) — the *New Monthly Magazine* said rather 'an epoch' (146). It was the year when the rebuilt Lyceum opened as 'The New Theatre Royal Lyceum and English Opera House'.

And yet only a few years later, George Hogarth suggested that the milestone was more apparent than real: 'About the year 1834, there was a revival of English opera which lasted for a time, and gave a deceitful promise of being permanent' (*Memoirs of the Opera*, 1851: 373).[27]

Much of the history of British music, especially English opera, vacillated between two viewpoints much like these, one continually expressing hope, the other disappointment. Sometimes, as was the case with Chorley, both viewpoints were held by the same person.

The *Athenæum* had a reputation in some circles for not supporting English talent, or at least not doing so enthusiastically and consistently enough. Chorley was sensitive to this accusation. The *Athenæum*'s 'Weekly Gossip on Literature and Art' for 3 May 1834, stated:

> ... there is also a Committee of Professors, who are interested in the establishment of a National Opera. Until we accomplish this — and until our composers work therein for future good, as well as present gain, we shall not overtake our continental neighbours. (335)

On 26 July, 1834, the *Athenæum* saw fit to encourage English talent: E.J. Loder's 'Nourjahad' at the English Opera House was said to show 'considerable promise' (555).

The *Athenæum* returned to the subject in more detail. Under the title, 'Society of British Musicians', the journal took note of the burst of activity:[28]

> The year Eighteen hundred and thirty-four just gathered to its father, has been a remarkable one in the annals of English music. We regard the re-opening of the English Opera House, the Amateur Festival at Exeter Hall, and the establishment of the Society of British Musicians, as forming an era, from which we hope to date the commencement of a long a brilliant season of prosperity. (17 January 1835: 58)

This positive note was immediately checked by disapproval of the anti-foreign sentiment that motivated some pro-British developments:

> ... we cannot but regret that, in considering the state of native musical talent, many have fallen into the common error of mistaking partizanship for patriotism. ... They have ... raised a *cri de guerre* against foreign composers

and artists — as interlopers — locusts, who eat up the
fruits of the land upon which its own children should be
fed. We shall endeavour to place this question in its true
light. (58)

Its 'true light' was that British composers and performers had simply not
demonstrated themselves to be as good as foreign musicians. This cosmopolitan standard is one that Chorley returns to numerous times during his
career, often seeing the cry to 'buy British' as having a hidden personal
agenda for those making it. He ended the notice with a warning about
'patriotism':

Let us not, however, in our satisfaction at the coming
change, forget by whom it has been brought about or be
ashamed to own, that it is to the teaching of foreigners,
and the influence of their works — to the Philharmonic
Concerts, and the Italian and German Operas, that we are
indebted for the cultivation of our public taste — and
thence the arising of a new and better spirit among us.
There is room enough among us for the welcome and protection of all talent, foreign as well as native. (17 January
1835: 58)

He then turned to the concert sponsored by the Society, singling out W.S.
Bennett's Symphony; its movements 'fully justify our high expectations
from the future works of this young writer: — we are beginning to look for
his name in the concert bills' (58).[29]
   The next few seasons offered many performances of new English music.
At Drury Lane, Balfe's *Catherine Grey* (libretto by George Linley)
'experienced a very good reception' (2 June 1837: 404). The opera was
noted for being the first English opera to use sung recitative throughout,
instead of spoken dialogue. Chorley was not impressed, singling out the
words as 'not well fitted' for continuous recitative and the plot as 'not only
poor, but absurd'.[30] Although it was not so good as the *Siege of Rochelle*,
it was not so bad as *The Maid of Artois*, and was, at any rate, 'much
applauded' (404). Nevertheless, in his critical retrospective on the season of
1837 (*London and Westminster Review* July, 1837) he reiterated his negative judgement emphatically, asserting that *Catherine Grey*,

... though clever and lively and graceful, is a reflection,
and nothing more, of the modern French and Italian
music, and save as being the first specimen of an opera
conducted throughout in the Italian fashion (that is, with
sung recitatives) since the days of the over-praised
Artaxerxes, contains few salient features upon which to
predicate improvement, or to found hope. (75)

The season of 1837 demonstrated that performance standards and the audiences' musical tastes were improving, but the quality of English music remained derivative and imitative:

> So much for the past concert-season of London. We should point to it with unalloyed satisfaction had we detected in it any encouraging traces of English *music*, as well as of English musicians, but for this (with one solitary exception perhaps, Mr. Bennett's overture, "The Naiades," performed at the Philharmonic concert), the ear has longed and listened in vain. (72)

Chorley's reviews of new music by English composers sometimes took the form of bland statements about an English opera's success or popularity, with little comment on its quality. In August Barnett's *Blanche of Jersey* (at the 'English Opera House', libretto by Peake) was a 'complete success' with Romer and Seguin (*Athenæum*, 12 August 1837: 589).[31] Balfe's second opera of 1837, *Joan of Arc* (Drury Lane, libretto by Fitzball), was 'carefully rehearsed' and, on the whole, 'decidedly successful'. And in May, 1838, at Drury Lane, *The Gipsy's Warning* by the 'clever composer' Benedict had a 'justly awarded share of popularity' (5 May 1838: 331), though later in 1838, again at Drury Lane, Loder's *Francis the First* (libretto by Mckinlan) was deemed a disappointment after the promising *Nourjahad* (10 November 1838: 812). In February 1839, *Farinelli* (Drury Lane, libretto by C.Z. Barnett) was termed Barnett's 'very best opera' (16 February 1839: 140).[32]

At other times, Chorley's reviews of English operas were more bluntly controversial. The case of *Fridolin* provides an example. John Barnett and Morris Barnett (not related) sponsored an English Opera season at the Prince's Theatre in 1840 and their first production was *Fridolin* (music by Frank Romer, libretto by Mark Lemon).[33] It closed in December 1840, after eight performances, and the English season ended. Angry at what he saw as the provincial and the second rate nature of English musical life, Chorley lashed out. Far from being sympathetic with English artists, he was exasperated with them:

> The ballad of the man "who married his wife on Sunday, and quarrelled with her on Monday," sets forth, in small compass, the history of all recent undertakings having the establishment of an English Opera for their object. ... The case, we think, needs but be stated, to substantiate as a melancholy truth, the fact that, with all the cry for nationality in music, there are none who are willing to sacrifice so small an amount of pretensions and profits to the well-being of English Art, as English artists; and that they are

wanting in will as much — the truth *must* out — as in
power! ... [Under such conditions] the lyrical drama of
England can never be raised from its prostrate condition:
... [and] we shall, again and again, be humiliated in the
eyes of Europe, by exhibiting a National Opera House,
which but opens its doors to close them again in eight
days. (12 December 1840: 990)

Throughout Chorley's career, managers and singers presented new
English Opera seasons, but neither during his lifetime nor for many decades
after it did a 'National Opera' enterprise achieve the prestige or the critical
acceptance of foreign opera in London. English literature and art were
known and respected through Europe. English music was not, and Chorley
suggested that perhaps English musicians themselves were to blame.[34]

Notes

1. Consistent attributions in the marked file begin in 1844.
2. Schroeder-Devrient's 'death', reported in the issue of 20 February
    1836 (145), occasioned quick back-pedalling: 'Within the last eight-
    een months, they [newspapers] have had the pleasure of killing and
    bringing to life again, Zingarelli and Paganini, and a day or two
    since, Madame Schroeder, for whom we were all grieving, walked
    quietly into their columns ...' (192). In 1833 there were three German
    performances at the King's Theatre (Pirshcher as Fidelio, Binder as
    Florestan, Johann Nepomuk Hummell conducting; Schröder-Devrient
    [sic] returned for six performances at Drury Lane in May 1833 and
    five at Covent Garden; in June 1835 Malibran sang an English ver-
    sion (John Templeton sang Florestan) eight times at Covent Garden
    and five times at Drury Lane. Malibran sang seven performances
    again beginning in May 1836 at Drury Lane; Schröder-Devrient
    returned for thirteen performances beginning in May, 1837 at Drury
    Lane. There were other performances in London by visiting com-
    panies, with less notable casts, in 1840 at the St James's, 'then called
    the Prince's' (12), 1841, and 1849 (Northcott, *Fidelio*, 10-12).
3. In the 1850s Chorley saw some chance that the new social conditions
    caused by the railway might change the fashion. He reminded readers
    that in Handel's time fashionable opera began in the autumn:

> Thanks to the railroads, — which make intercourse
> easy, and have thus suggested a new class of enterprise
> to speculators, while they have assisted largely in keep-
> ing London full of a play-going public, — the spell of
> autumn silence seems to have been broken here. We

> may live to see our musical year again arranged as it
> was at the period when Handel directed his own operas
> at the harpsichord, — when Gray wrote words to an air
> by Geminiani for Miss Speed to sing, — when Horace
> Walpole stuck sweet peas in his hair, and was to be
> found sitting singing to his "sorcières" over the card
> table.

4.   'Let observation with extensive view, / Survey mankind from China to Peru' is from Samuel Johnson's 'Vanity of Human Wishes'. 'Paradise of Dainty Devices' is the title of a collection of poems compiled by Richard Edwards (1576).

5.   See Richard Coe's discussion (Stendhal, xvii).

6.   Gyas and Cloanthus were brave companions of Aeneus ('fortemque Gyan fortemque Cloanthum', *Aeneid*, 1: 222 and 612).

7.   These volumes were reviewed in nos 429, 430, and 431 of the *Athenæum*. Hogarth's revised work, published in 1838 as *Memoirs of the Musical Drama*, received two generally positive reviews (23 June 1838: 435-6 and 30 June 1838: 453-5). Though the author is not identified in the marked copies of the *Athenæum*, the reviews are typical of Chorley's style and interests: for example, one reprimanded Hogarth for devoting disproportionate space to English opera (23 June 1838: 435), and another insisted that the future of the lyric drama lay with French composers (30 June 1838: 455).

8.   Spellings of his name were inconsistent: the *Athenæum* reviewer wrote 'Lord Mount Edgecumbe'; on the title page of the fourth edition of the *Musical Reminiscences* he was 'The Earl of Mount Edgcumbe' (Da Capo Reprint, 1973).

9.   Michael Hurd has also noted (though, unlike Chorley, approvingly) that the soprano-bass duet which opens Act II ('Nell'orror de notte oscura') is 'worthy, surely, of Bellini (or John Field)' (in Temperley, 320).

10.   John Edmund Cox, recollecting the debut of this most long-lived of tenors, commented in 1872:

> [B]y relying upon his magnificent sympathetic voice
> and handsome personal appearance alone, he managed
> on the instant to win the affection of the public — a
> privilege that even now in his terrible decay he can by
> no means be said to have in the slightest degree lost.
> (Cox, *Musical Recollections*, 2: 84).

11.   For discussions of opera in Paris at this time see, i.a. Barbier, Bloom, Crosten, Ellis, Fulcher, Gerhard, and Johnson.

12.   Because of its emphasis on local colour and its use of the full resources of nineteenth-century stage design, Auber's *La Muette de*

Portici (1828, libretto by Scribe) is often cited as the first of the French grand operas, see Crosten, 60.

13. The importance of the stage designers to a romantic fusion of the arts was often stressed. 'C'est de Ciceri que date la rénovation ou la révolution littéraire et dramatique, dont les Victor Hugo, les Dumas, les Alfred de Vigny fuent les principaux instigateurs' (Séchan, 7).

14. Crosten, 130. For a political perspective, see Fulcher.

15. The musical notices in the *Athenæum* in the early 1830s were generally by John Ella; during the middle of the decade it is sometimes unclear whether Ella or Chorley is the author, since the journal's copies are incompletely marked at this time.

16. Nourrit, Levasseur, Cinti-Damoreau, and De Meric.

17. See Chorley's comment in *Music and Manners*, 1: 254-5: 'Talk of the English as lukewarm in the matter of public amusements! Where else shall we find audiences willing to be shut up in the strait seats of a theatre, or the cramping benches of an opera pit, from seven o'clock in the evening till an hour past midnight'. The German traveller Frederick von Raumer insisted that English theatre managers should 'reduce the performance from five or six hours to three (as with us)' (*England in 1835*, 2: 221).

18. Chorley stated that in *Gustave* Auber had 'spread himself over too wide a canvas. The passion is cold'. He qualified his censure by conceding that '"Gustave" is full of delicious music finely wrought, beginning with the first notes of the overture, which has a fascination approaching those which open Signor Rossini's opera-preludes' (*Thirty Years'*, 2: 107, 134).

19. Planché appended a note of self-exculpation to the printed libretto:

> I feel it due to Mons. Scribe, and to myself, not to suffer these pages to go to press without recording in them, my deep regret that it was considered vitally important to the success of the Drama, on the English Stage, that the catastrophe should be altered; — that truth, power, and poetical justice should be all sacrificed, as in the recent case of 'The Red Mask', to a prejudice; — an amiable one I acknowledge — but still a prejudice — I might almost say a caprice, looking at the permitted catastrophes of many of our finest Tragedies, and most popular living Dramas. (Planché, *The Jewess*, 47-8).

20. Chorley made a distinction between the Grand Opéra composers and the operas of Hector Berlioz. When the Académie Royale performed *Benvenuto Cellini*, the *Athenæum* reported that 'it does not appear as if its reception justifies the high hopes entertained of M. Berlioz by

some of his friends' (15 September 1838: 683).

21. Malibran is termed a contralto here. She transposed parts of some of her roles down. Her high notes also aroused astonished comment. Henry Phillips wrote of her in Balfe's *Maid of Artois* (libretto, Bunn, 1836):

> She had the lower range of the contralto, with the highest compass of the soprano, and a conception of her subject truly wonderful. ... In the finale of this opera, her shake on the upper C was one of the most extraordinary vocal efforts I ever heard. She seemed to me, resolved to outstrip all competitors, and did it so vigorously that I fear it accelerated her death. ... (Phillips, 1: 219)

22. The Old Price riots are described in numerous theatrical histories and memoirs; see, i.a., Wyndham, 1: 339-48.

23. A year later, Chorley demonstrated decreasing patience with Tamburini's position: 'Apropos of this artist, he appears to be coquetting with his London patrons, in a manner which, to say the least of it, is in bad taste. The Opera, we suppose, means to do without him, if possible: and he, we suppose, means to be rioted for again. The subscribers, if they mean to interfere at all, should look to these things, we repeat it, early in the season' (27 March 1841: 245).

24. Chorley continued, complaining about the ballet: '... it was customary, formerly, that the *corps de ballet* should contain a fair proportion of fixed stars, besides the Elssler or Taglioni of the night: this year, however, we have had, till now, *ballets* without one single male dancer. It is time, then, that the audience should speak out ...' (354). The true 'palmy days' of the ballet came in 1844 and 1845, according to Lumley (83), but by then Chorley complained that it was receiving *too much* attention from the management. Of this time, John Ella later remembered: 'In my younger days the ballet was not only the most costly part of the entertainment, but frequently the chief attraction, at Her Majesty's Theatre. *On a changé tout cela*' (Ella, 50).

25. 'Another point of M. Laporte's management, much found fault with among the musicians, seems to us defensible: we mean his insisting upon the attendance of his orchestra at all rehearsals, come what will to tempt them thence. The collision to be apprehended was between the Philharmonic Concert and the Opera; we presume, too, the Ancient Concerts. His motives in enforcing such a regulation have been questioned, but be they what they may, the regulation itself is good for Art. It is indispensable for the maintenance of a lyric theatre, that its orchestra should be under strict call and command' (27 February 1841: 171).

26. See Allsobrook, 23.

27. Hogarth quoted the prospectus of the Society of British Musicians in his chapter, 'Present State of Music in England' (*Musical History*, 418-32). His overview noted that the Concerts of Ancient Music were too monotonous (425), that the Philharmonic Society used vocal music to be 'attractive' to the public (425), and that the Royal Academy (founded in 1823) was 'successfully and beneficially conducted' (426). Thus, his main disappointment was with English Opera.

28. The article was by Chorley or possibly Ella. The marked office copy at the City University, London, attributes part of a musical notice for 26 April 1834 to Ella (notice of *Otello*), and part of the same notice to Chorley (notice of *Don Giovanni*). This is the first attribution to Chorley in the marked file. Ella's contributions dwindled, but did not immediately cease.

29. In one instance, British music drama was represented by the combined talents of Charles Dickens, librettist — suddenly famous as the dazzling creator of Mr Pickwick and Sam Weller — and John Hullah, composer. Their 'burletta' at the St James, 'The Village Coquettes', was not praised. Although the music 'gives fair promise of future excellence', Boz 'is likely rather to diminish than increase his reputation by his dramatic efforts' (17 December 1836: 891). The whole thing was a little tedious — 'weak and languid throughout' (891). The notice was probably not by Chorley, who did not usually cover theatres like the St James. The notice came out two weeks after the *Athenæum* reviewed the opening nine numbers of Dickens's *Pickwick*: 'The writer of this periodical (for such it is) which is now before us, has great cleverness' but is derivative: 'two pounds of Smollett, three ounces of Sterne, a handful of Hook, a dash of a grammatical Pierce Egan — incidents at pleasure, served with an original *sauce piquante*'. Still, 'we like him' (3 December 1836: 841). Although Hullah set no more of Dickens's works, he did set poems by Chorley. Published as 'Six Duets for Soprano Voices', these were reviewed in the *Athenæum* (4 January 1836: 841).

30. For this and other grievances, Linley struck back at Chorley twenty-five years later in a long satiric poem, *Musical Cynics of London* (1862), in which Chorley's own libretti and translations were belittled with gusto.

31. Not recorded in Biddlecombe's 'List of Operas' in *English Opera*.

32. Like a number of contemporary novelists (or at least their narrative *personae*) the *Athenæum* seemed nostalgically drawn to the good old days, the simple British tunes of yesterday. '"[T]he songs our fathers loved" for melody and sweetness, have far more claim on the musician's favour, than the would-be Italian insipidities, or would-be

German crudities of more ambitious modern native composers' (14 December 1839: 950). Compare this with the narrator of Thackeray's *Vanity Fair* (1847-48), for example, who deplored 'the milk-and-water *lagrime, sospiri*, and *felicità* of the eternal Donizettian music with which we are favoured now-a-days' (Chapter 4) and the narrator of Charlotte Bronte's *Villette* (1853), who marvelled at a singer who 'made her voice run up and down', but asserted that 'a simple Scotch melody ... has often moved me more deeply' (Chapter 20).

33. The prima donna, Emma Romer, was the sister of Frank Romer and the sister-in-law of Mark Lemon; she accepted the engagement on the 'express stipulation' that the first work was to be written by them. See White, 276. Chorley says she refused to take a temporary cut in her salary, and this refusal forced the cancellation of the season (12 December 1840: 990).

34. The review in the *Athenæum* (not attributed in the marked file, but probably by Chorley) stated that Hogarth's *Musical History* praised English music too highly: '[I]f our national musical compositions have not travelled so widely [as our other arts], may it not be that they are not of fibre strong enough to bear the journey?' (30 January 1836: 86).

CHAPTER FOUR

Elizabeth Barrett
and Felix Mendelssohn

1 'Miss Barrett's genius is of a high order'
Athenæum, 7 July 1838

In 1836, Chorley happened to read a poem in the *New Monthly Magazine*, 'The Romaunt of Margret'. He was overwhelmed by it: he copied it over and over until he had memorized it. In Elizabeth Barrett's work he recognized 'a strange, seizing, original genius' (Hewlett, 2: 33).

His acquaintance with Barrett's relative, John Kenyon and his cordial relations with Barrett's best friend, Mary Russell Mitford, opened the door in 1836 to correspondence with the reclusive poet. Barrett did not permit Chorley to meet her in person until she had become Mrs Browning and returned to London from Italy for a visit in 1851. Nevertheless, her personal interest in Chorley's life and career was genuine and it reveals much not only about her estimation of his talents and potential, but also about her own pleasure and interest in his reviews of her work in the *Athenæum*.

Barrett wrote to Mitford that she was out when Chorley first called. Mitford's letter to Barrett, however, suggests that he may never have called:

> Did Henry Chorley call himself? He told me that his
> heart had failed him ... I was myself in all the grief of
> parting from this same Henry Chorley, one of the most
> affable companions I have ever known. (16 August 1836,
> *Brownings' Correspondence*, 3: 184)

The next month Barrett read Chorley's newly published *Memorials of Mrs. Hemans*, and commented to Mitford that 'Mr Chorley seems to have done his task in a spirit she w^d herself have chosen for such a task' (*Brownings' Correspondence*, 3: 193). Comments made in letters by Barrett over the next few years suggest that Chorley's view of Hemans intrigued her and was in her mind as she formulated her own ideas about 'female literature'. She liked it well enough to read it for a second time in July, 1844 (9: 62).

A few months later Chorley was working on *The Authors of England* essays, a volume of critical and biographical essays accompanying engravings by Achille Collas. On 22 February 1837 Mitford wrote to Barrett that 'Henry Chorley wishes me to go to town to sit for the "Portrait Annual";

Miss Edgeworth, Mrs Hemans, Lady Blessington, and myself being the ladies chosen for this first volume' (*Brownings' Correspondence*, 3: 226). Like Chorley's novels, *The Lion* and *Conti the Discarded*, his *Authors of England* did not sell well: Barrett commented to Lady Margaret Cocks:

> Have you seen Mr Chorley's annual of living authors [*The Authors of England*]? which did not sell, & to no surprise of hers Miss Mitford says, as she always feared for the fate "of 13 ugly profiles & a long volume of short lives". Her own profile is among the "ugly" ones! & notwithstanding this liveliness & fear *I am* very much surprised that a book of a character so lastingly interesting, could not sell for one Christmas day. (?29 January 1838, *Brownings' Correspondence*, 4: 9)[1]

Barrett was flattered by Chorley's continuing support for her poetry, and on 21 June 1838 she wrote to Hugh Stuart Boyd that 'I have seen an extract from a private letter of Mr Chorley editor of the Athenaeum, which speaks *huge* praises of my poems. If he were to say a tithe of them in print it w^d be nine times above my expectation!' (4: 50). A few days later, Chorley's review of Barrett's *The Seraphim* did print those huge praises, with reservations: 'This is an extraordinary volume — especially welcome as an evidence of female genius and accomplishment — but it is hardly less disappointing than extraordinary. Miss Barrett's genius is of a high order; active, vigorous, and versatile, but unaccompanied by discriminating taste' (*Athenæum*, 7 July 1838, reprinted in *Brownings' Correspondence*, 4: 375-8). Although Chorley regretted that the text of the 'Romaunt of Margret' had been altered somewhat since its first publication in the *New Monthly Magazine*, he nevertheless quoted from the book extensively to support his claim that it was extraordinary. By way of explaining why the works were at the same time somewhat disappointing he concluded by advising Barrett that her poetry could be improved: 'her language' was wanting 'in the simplicity of unaffected earnestness' (7 July 1838: 466). All Barrett's poems needed to gain wide acceptance was 'a simpler and less mannered clothing than they at present wear' (468).

Mary Russell Mitford was concerned: would Chorley's negative remarks hurt Barrett's feelings? Barrett disabused her of the notion emphatically:

> And I wish besides to impress it upon you my very dear & generous friend, that so far from being annoyed or even disappointed by the review in the Athenæum I was abundantly satisfied & gratified by it. There are more who will complain of its praising me too much than of its blaming me at all — and I have good reason to be obliged to the critic, to Mr Chorley both for the actual praise he

gives my poetry & for the willingness to praise, manifest I
think in all parts of his criticism. As to the blame — ...
But you know if things appear so to critics, it is quite
right & *honest* for corresponding statements to be made.
(14 July 1838, *Brownings' Correspondence*, 4: 60)

Barrett began to take an interest in Chorley's writings: her comments to
Mitford demonstrated her interest in his career and belief in his potential:

I have read Mr Chorley's Lion — and if we of the multi-
tude, we of the literary laity, dared to remark upon persons set in authority over us, I sh^d wish the election of a
hundred books off, & more unity, — or rather more of
that composure which arises from the *sense of unity*, —
throughout the work. But it is a work highly indicative of
ability — of an ability to come, as well as present — brilliant with allusion, yet not too dazzling to think by. A
great part of the first volume & the greater part of the
third struck & interested me — only the Robin of the
opening is too good for the Robin of the close — surely he
is. (11 August 1839, *Brownings' Correspondence*, 4: 184-
5).

She read Chorley's *Sketches of a Sea Port Town*, too: '[I] was much struck
by the power it indicated, & the constructiveness of the stories — a rare
characteristic, even in these story telling days' (4: 185).

Shortly after *The Seraphim* was published the edition of the annual
Findens' Tableaux for 1839 appeared, edited by Mitford (published in the
autumn of 1838). It included Barrett's 'Romaunt of the Page', which
attracted favourable comment from several reviewers, including the
reviewer in the *Athenæum*, who stated that it 'seems to us one of the most
beautiful things from a woman's hand which has appeared for many a day'
(*Athenæum*, 20 October 1838: 758). On 30 October Barrett mentioned how
pleased she was with the *Athenæum* for the review: 'I am indeed grateful to
the Athenæum. Will you say to Mr Chorley how it pleased me with its
honor *undue*' (*Brownings' Correspondence*, 4: 102).[2]

Although Barrett's work was generally well received in the *Athenæum*,
on occasion she expressed sharp disagreement with some of their editorial
positions. Writing to Richard Hengist Horne (8? February 1841), she
expressed her exasperation:

Talking of critics . . oh . . the Athenæum! — Have you
seen it? — & seen in it how tender-hearted people keep
themselves warm this cold weather by tomahawking their
neighbour? — Everybody belonging to Chaucer is
executed, — & *you* hacked at, with the degree of malice

> extraordinar[i]ly done to you as editor! ...
>
> Now I am quite sure, or next to quite sure that Mr George Darley, is the perpetrator of 'the article.' I have no reason for it, except the *crossness* — which however is to myself unanswerable. This "Cynical poet" as some of his fellow citizens in the Rep. Lit. call him, achieves I rather believe most of the Athenæum bitterness. ...
>
> Yet I have an interest in the Athenæum, for all its sins. They have been as kind to me, I do believe, on different occasions, as their consciences would let them. ... (*Brownings' Correspondence*, 5: 17)

In the early 1840s Horne was preparing his *New Spirit of the Age*, with Barrett's support; this caused a certain amount of awkwardness with Chorley, who did not like Horne. Horne's *New Spirit* — a series of essays on important contemporary authors — was to be somewhat comparable in design to Chorley's *Authors of England* (published in late 1837). Barrett wrote to Mitford on 18 July 1841 that

> I shall *therefore* be correspondingly open with you & confess that I have not for a moment since the ringing of Mr Chorley's alarm-bell, felt frightened or embarrassed or distrustful of my invisible friend with his visible kindnesses . . Mr Horne. Certainly the dreadful black book[3] is his own perpetration. It is his acknowledged work. There is no mystery about it. I never read it: & I remember hearing of it ... [before she knew Horne] — as a clever & eccentric work — eccentric — no more — Mr Chorley's "silent gravity" being 'the full sum' of evil imputation in relation to it that ever reached *me*. (18 July 1841, *Brownings' Correspondence*, 5: 80)

She suggested that Chorley might be on firmer ground as a music critic than as a critic of new literature:

> The Athenæum has not done the most limited justice to Mr Horne the poet. I like the Athenæum! — I am interested in it, & Mr Dilke is kind enough, do you know, to send it to me regularly. But I wish sometimes that it's [*sic*] poetical were like its *musical* criticisms, justified & beautified by the love of art. When however the critic passes to the poets, he grows blue with cold, & his finger-ends insensate! (18 July 1841, 5: 83)

There was a moment of light banter about Chorley's personal life. Mitford suggested that Miss Pardoe was hoping to inspire Chorley to take some romantic interest in her. Barrett thought the idea was droll:

> You cannot think how your letter has amused me. ONE of
> the portraits of Miss Pardoe, engraved & attached to her
> work upon Hungary, suggests certainly *twice eighteen*.
> And so she w^d take Mr Henry Chorley in lieu of the
> Sultan! You know how *he* turned a longing lingering look
> upon her in the streets of Constantinople . . with a view
> probably to the seraglio. And she w^d catch Mr Chorley's
> handkerchief after *that* . . & settle down into the armchair
> of an English matron! — as if she had never touched a
> Turkish cushion — or seen a dervish spin!! Allah Kerim!
> It is astonishing indeed! — ... Not that I wish her ever to
> marry y^r friend unless you desire it! — (11 January 1842,
> 5: 207)

Then Mitford wrote to Barrett about her play, *Otto of Wittelsbach*. In her response, Barrett compared Mitford's work favourably with a play of Chorley's. She then commented on Chorley as a literary jack-of-all-trades:

> I think we may venture to count on the excellence of your
> Otto above the three unnamed Acts of the Uncom-
> panioned! I think we may! At the same time I do quite
> appreciate his pleasant & lively, & sometimes elegant
> writings — yes, & do it so heartily as to feel more sorry
> than the strangership justifies perhaps, that he sh^d be
> entangled *with the theatres*. Well! I am ignorant enough
> of it all . . but from my own impressions, & from what
> you have said of your experience, it seems of all literary
> positions in the world the one least calculated for a young
> author whose object & ambition it is to pass out of the
> periodical low atmosphere of literature into the high
> serene of a success which will not in its turn, pass. It
> sounds impertinently — but is'nt [*sic*] it true that M^r
> Chorley tries all sorts of literature — as if he were bent
> rather on trying his faculties than using them? (14 May
> 1842, *Brownings' Correspondence*, 5: 345)

The reference to Chorley as 'the Uncompanioned' may refer to matchmak-ing, as in the lighthearted speculation about Miss Pardoe, or may be a term used more seriously to refer to his own complaints about loneliness.

Barrett returned to her sense that Chorley's strength, and therefore the *Athenæum*'s strength, was musical journalism in her letter to Benjamin Robert Haydon: 'You made me smile with your *theory* about the Athenæum. The truth is, that the Athenæum gives all the enthusiasm it has to spare for Art, away from Poetry & Painting to *music*' (20 October 1842,

6: 113).

Mitford believed that Barrett should get to know Chorley personally, and Barrett tentatively agreed: 'I will hope some day to know your Mr Chorley, — because I like so much the most of what you tell me of him' (21 November 1842, 6: 163).

Two days later she repeated this, with comments on his *Memorials of Mrs. Hemans*:

> I hope to know him some day both for your sake & his own — and *my* own, as the person benefitted [*sic*]— for I like what you say of him & what his books say of him too. Is it not true that Mrs Hemans's friends took offence at his work respecting her? I inferred so from the memoir written by her sister & could not make out *why* — for surely nothing could be more delicate, even hyper-delicate, than his manner of treating the subject. ... I admire her genius — love her memory — respect her piety & high moral tone. But she always does seem to me a lady rather than a woman, & so, much rather than a poetess — her refinement, like the prisoner's iron . . enters into her soul. She is polished all over to one smoothness & one level, & is monotonous in her best qualities. We say "how sweet & noble" & then we are silent & can say no more — perhaps, presently, we go to sleep, with angels in our dreams. (6: 165-6)

She consulted Chorley among others, indirectly through Mitford, about the possibility of publishing some work in early 1842, but decided not to (*Brownings' Correspondence*, 6: 259 and 336). She was interested to learn from John Kenyon about Chorley's social life:

> Mr Kenyon met four & twenty ... not fiddlers . . but harmonious spirits in different degrees, at your friend Mr Chorley's the other evening. The new German wonder Mr D. ... [Dreyschock] (I really am afraid to write him down, so little sure of him am I) raised thunderclouds & lightenings out of the piano forte . . and Moscelles [Moscheles], who is only a demi-god followed the miraculous with his heroic — and Adelaide Sartoris sang like a spirit — and Mrs Butler read Shakespeare. And your Mr Chorley lives in an enchanted house in Victoria Square . . (a new square with tiny houses) — in a sort of gold . . not "vinegar-bottle" . . but *vinaigrette* . . with ceilings & chains of gold, & hangings of silken crimson — "It is like a jewel-case," says Mr Kenyon — and Mr Chorley lives

like a ruby in the glory of it. (To Mary Russell Mitford, 4
May [1843], *Brownings' Correspondence*, 7: 109-10)[4]

Later in 1843, as Horne's plans for *The New Spirit of the Age* advanced,
there was more awkwardness involving both Chorley and Mitford.[5] Barrett
gently reminded Horne of the existence of Chorley's book, noting the
wounded feelings that might result from the publication of a volume by
Horne resembling Chorley's *Authors of England* in scope.

> Are you aware that M[r] Chorley published a work called
> 'The authors & authoresses of England' some time ago,
> with profiles & short notices? When I say 'some time ago'
> I mean some years. And your book will probably assume
> a higher character, & go deeper. (5 October 1845,
> *Brownings' Correspondence*, 7: 356)

And she gently defended Horne to Mitford:

> I am very much surprised that your head will not smile
> out of his book — if it will not — but of course you will
> be there. He could not intend a bare corollary to M[r] Chor-
> ley's work, & give it the name of Hazlitt's, — although
> he may think it wise and necessary to restrict his notices
> to such men & women as are actually living. (13 October
> 1843, 7: 369)

Horne then protested to Barrett on 20 October 1843 that he had little or
no control over the illustrations, and suggested that she write some critical
material for the book:

> How you *do* go on in the dark about this new dark work
> of mine as to who sh'[d] be in it, portrait-wise or not, when
> *I* have no deputed power over the illustrations — *my* part
> is the literature. Be sure I will not forget to make mention
> of Miss Mitford — [...] No — others were in Chorley's
> picture-book. Miss Mitford was *there*. *Now*, dear E.B.B.,
> you begin to see? ... I did suddenly arrive at a very high
> opinion of your critical powers where the subject suited
> you, in reading your remarks on Shakespeare, and on
> Beaumont and Fletcher, in the Athenæum. Therefore, oh
> Friend in need, will you write me four or five pages ...
> on "William Wordsworth *and* Leigh Hunt."[6] (*Brownings'*
> *Correspondence*, 7: 379)

So Horne was not going to exclude *all* authors treated in Chorley's *Authors
of England*, since Wordsworth was extensively eulogized there. After this,
Barrett provided a little back-tracking and further explanation when she

wrote to Mitford on 4 March 1844:

> He [Horne] told me that you would *be in it*, — altho' his
> publishers, . . going upon the circumstance of Mr Chorley
> having introduced you bodily, . . would permit no repeti-
> tion, in the form of an independent article. On the same
> ground, there is no paper on Rogers, nor on Joanna Bail-
> lie &c. And the apparent contradiction of giving one to
> Wordsworth & Leigh Hunt, he explains by treating them,
> he says, in reference to their influence on the age. (8:
> 240-41)

The warmth of Barrett's friendship with Mitford was reflected in her
invitations to Mitford. To other would-be guests (so far including Chorley)
she was inaccessible.

Interestingly, one of the ways she undertook to make Mitford feel welcome to visit her was to write repeatedly that Mitford could invite Chorley
to call at Wimpole Street (to see Mitford that is, not to see Barrett). On 30
October 1843 she wrote Mitford:

> Will you come? WILL you come? And Mr Kenyon is
> away, . . at least talked of being away when I last saw
> him. Still you may bring alms to *me* & to Mr Chorley —
> for of course you will desire him to meet you here, & any
> other person you may wish to see. (*Brownings' Cor-
> respondence*, 8: 17)

A few days later, on 2 November 1843, she exclaimed, 'Oh — do let M^r
Chorley meet you here. You shall have a room to yourself to meet
anybody' (8: 28). Her enthusiasm continued:

> My dearest friend I do hope that you have made a contract
> with Mr Chorley to be ready to meet you here on
> whatever day you please to come — and in the case of
> uncertainties, that you are prepared with a word for us to
> send down to him immediately on your arrival in
> Wimpole Street. Do not scruple to see *any* OTHER
> *friend*, I beseech you moreover. (14 November 8: 45)

When the *Spirit* appeared in early 1844, Barrett continued friendly relations
with Mitford and Chorley as well as Horne, with whom she sympathized on
account of the mixed press reaction. Horne was angry with critics:

> Your kind and good advice is not lost upon me, as to
> replying to critics. I shall not do so hastily, nor by
> *wholesale*; nor perhaps at all in the Second Edition. But
> either in 2nd or 3rd (for I think a third very probable) I

shall 'make an example' (except I find that scorn can do better) of two or three of these pests of Literature. The "Morning Chronicle" is only worth a laugh (turned back, though, upon the writer of that silly article) — and perhaps I shall not address *Mr Thackeray* by name, but rather as an Irish Moon-raker. As for the Athenæum, which led the way, and gave the *tone* to the press, it was certainly Mr Chorley. I am told this on all sides. I wonder if he is the Pen that has been screeching on paper after every work I have published for some years — and in the Athenæum. I shall find him out, if so, and then stop him, unpleasantly (23 April 1844, *Brownings' Correspondence*, 8: 305-6)

In fact, Chorley's reviews of Horne's *New Spirit of the Age* — assuming, as is likely, that the reviews were his[7] — were not so much hostile as patronizing. The first appeared in the *Athenæum* on 23 March 1844. Many of its observations about Horne's study were positive, and Chorley agreed with Horne's assessment of Dickens's standing: 'seldom, if ever, has any man been more beloved by contemporary authors, and by the public of his time' (quoted in *The Brownings' Correspondence*, 8: 371).[8] Chorley mentioned the other authors discussed by Horne and, as was customary, quoted from them extensively.[9]

In the *Athenæum*'s second review of *A New Spirit of the Age*, volume two (*Athenæum*, 30 March 1844: 291-2), Chorley complained that the analysis of Tennyson is 'vague and feeble' (quoted in *Brownings' Correspondence*, 8: 378), adding that '[t]his remark applies, also, to the chapters on Mr. Marston and Mr. Browning, and the one strangely uniting Mrs. Norton and Miss Barrett!' (8: 378). The chapter following Macaulay 'on Messrs Hook and Hood, is one of the flimsiest in the volume' (8: 379).

> Next come Miss Martineau and Mrs. Jameson, yoked together in right of their energetic sympathies for the anomalous position of woman in society. Here, in truth, was a fine text for a chapter essential to our contemporary history, ... But such a chapter would have claimed a wider range of illustrations. (8: 379)

Chorley mentioned 'a feeble flagellation of Mr. Ainsworth' (8: 381) and concluded that, if Horne's work were rewritten, it 'might become a library book. As it is, its day must end with the circulating libraries, as not the least pleasant *ephemeron* of the season' (8: 379).

When Chorley and Horne encountered one another, Barrett suggested that it would be 'a meeting of thunderclouds' (13 June 1844, 9: 14). Horne, however, in a pacific reply to her, suggested that perhaps Chorley had been taken in by someone else's malice:

> One thing I sh'd tell you in extenuation [... several words
> missing] You know he set all the press "a-going" with the
> cry of *clique* and *coterie*. He was misled. Hoaxed and led
> astray by the dancing vanity of a gentleman who lent
> some portraits — knew some booksellers — had authors to
> dine with him &c[.] ... As to *clique* or *c[o]terie* it was all
> a mistake — natural for Mr Chorley to fall into at the
> vision and hearing of Mr Powell's rodomontade and
> romancing — but he (Mr Powell) did *not write one line in
> the book*, and I refused to tell him the name of a single
> contributor! (*Brownings' Correspondence*, 9: 18)

2

Barrett's interest in Chorley's critical opinions was complemented by an
interest in Chorley's personal life. On a number of occasions, Barrett wrote
Mitford that she was worried about Chorley's low spirits:

> Mr Chorley speaks very kindly! Thinking over what you
> said, I wonder to myself whether he may not have some
> mournful reason for *particularly wanting* change of scene
> this year! Did it strike you that it might perhaps be so? I
> hope not — but his note seems to have a grave keynote in
> it — & then your words recurred to me. (?29 June 1844,
> 9: 39)

Perhaps with this view of him in the back of her mind, she wrote to Chorley in August words of support and kindness:

> Dear Mr. Chorley, —
>
> Kindnesses are more frequent things with me than glad-
> nesses; but I thank you earnestly for both, in the letter I
> have this moment received. You have given me a quick
> sudden pleasure which goes deeper (I am very sure) than
> selflove; for it must be something better than vanity that
> brings the tears so near the eyes. I thank you, dear Mr.
> Chorley.
>
> After all we are not quite strangers. I have had some
> early encouragement and direction from you; and much
> still earlier (and later) literary pleasures from such of your
> writings as did not refer to me. I have studied 'Music and
> Manners' under you, and found an excuse for my love of
> romance-reading from your grateful fancy. Then, as dear

Miss Mitford's friend, you c^d not help being (however against your will!) a little my acquaintance; and this she daringly promised to make you so in reality some day, till I took the fervour for prophesy.

Altogether I am justified, while I thank you as a stranger, to say one more word as a friend — and *that* shall be the best word, . . *'May God bless you!'* The trials with which He tries us are all different, but our faces may be turned towards the end in cheerfulness, for *'to* the end he has loved us.' (26 August 1844, *Brownings' Correspondence*, 9: 115-16)[10]

Meanwhile, Barrett took to heart Chorley's comment in the *Athenæum* about the need for 'simpler and less mannered clothing'. On 1 September 1844 she wrote to Mitford:

That I have made progress, and particularly improved in clearness appear general admission — & made not only by the Athenæum. By the way I do not at all doubt that Mr Chorley is the author of that criticism; & I am sincerely grateful to him for it. It is a review of the minor poems, — with a reference to a purpose of taking the long poems into consideration on a future occasion. (9: 122)

She was pleased to inform Mitford on 5 December 1844, that

Mr Kenyon tells me that Mr Chorley is writing another review of my poems, to add to my obligation on account of the first Athenæum notice. He is very kind & good indeed. (9: 263)

and

Indeed my dearest Miss Mitford, I cant [*sic*] answer your question about the names of my critics. I know the name of not one of them, except of Mr Chorley, in the instance of the notice in the Athenæum . . (*Brownings' Correspondence*, 11 December 1844, 9: 272)

Chorley's own writings continued to interest and intrigue Barrett. For her, Chorley's *Memorials of Mrs. Hemans* was an important and interesting work. Reading it occasioned a meditation on women authors. She wrote to Mitford on 22 July 1844:

I have been reading for the second time, that interesting memoir of Mrs Hemans by Mr Chorley — full of interest certainly. Still I stand by my position, that she was too conventionally a *lady*, to be a great poetess — she was

> bound fast in satin riband. Her delicacy restrained her sense of Beauty — and she had no reverence for Humanity, through the morbid narrowness of her sympathies. I took up Blanchard's memoir of LEL just after M[r] Chorley's book, & was struck by an undefinable vulgarity spreading all through it, in obvious contrast to the refinement of the other work. Do you remember enough of the two, to think with me? (*Brownings' Correspondence*, 9: 62)

For his part, Chorley continued to call attention publicly and prominently to Barrett's poetry during the 1840s. His review essay on her *Poems* in two volumes, published by Moxon, was printed as the lead review in the *Athenæum* for Saturday, 24 August 1844. In it he raised to a still higher level his previously published praise of her genius, asserting that there was a great gap between the quality of her poems and 'the slighter lyrics of most of the sisterhood', that is, England's poetesses (763).

> ... there appears to us a decided effort on Miss Barrett's part, since she last met her critics (vide *Ath.* No. 558), to clear her verse of the entanglements which formerly obscured some of its finest passages. 'The Romaunt of the Page,' for instance, is much simplified since we quoted it from 'Finden's [*sic*] Tableaux,' and now stands foremost among 'Records of Woman,' to be added to the beautiful lyrics in which Joanna Baillie, and Mrs. Hemans, and many another earnest songstress, has honoured herself in her sex. ... But the new poems strike us as yet more emphatically betokening advance, though still the execution is not always equal to the conception.[11]

The review was taken up largely by quotations, the most substantial from 'The Rhyme of the Duchess May', and 'The Romance of the Swan's Nest'. One of her 'bolder flights', he noted, was 'The Dead Pan', where she worked in a mood opposite to Schiller's in 'Götter Griechenlands' and similar to Mrs Hemans's in her 'Antique Greek Lament'. In short, Chorley concluded, these two volumes were 'remarkable manifestations of female power' (764).

Chorley sensed that Barrett now brought 'power' to her womanliness. As Barrett became more involved in realizing her poetic power, Chorley's positive reaction to her work was modified somewhat and by the time of her *Poems Before Congress* (1860), Chorley grew less tolerant of Barrett's engagement with a poetry of empowerment than he had been in the mid-1840s. Moreover, their increasing differences about the politics of the Italian revolt came to a head in 1859 with the publication of Chorley's novel *Roccabella*. Given the book's intense hostility to Italian revolutionary politics, his decision to dedicate it to her seemed odd.

These tensions lay ahead; in the 1840s, their disagreements related to more specific issues. For example, Harriet Martineau was a occasion for disagreement: had the *Athenæum* treated her badly because of her views on mesmerism and clairvoyance, or was she just naive, gullible, and deserving of public reproach? Martineau's writings on the subject in the *Athenæum* were answered and sharply rebuked by Dilke, its editor. Martineau's anger at the journal's scepticism was referred to frequently in Barrett's correspondence in December 1844 and thereafter. Barrett believed that Dilke had treated Martineau badly. As she explained to Mitford,

> I understand that Mr Chorley used some entreaty to her, *not* to publish her papers in the Athenæum, — for that Mr Dilke w^dnt believe a word, though Moses & the prophets asked him, — & that she must therefore look to having her views opposed in the very journal which out of respect to herself personally, had accepted the office of conveying them to the public. (28 December 1844, 9: 295-6)

Harriet Martineau wrote a couple of days later to Barrett expressing her own anger:

> In *Dilke* I am wholly disappointed. I knew him only f^m Chorley's report. But he is sordid & dishonourable, to a degree impossible to be mistaken, or even exaggerated. I never was before concerned with a person so dishonest. … Truth is with us — clear & strong, — & we are happy. (30 December 1844, *Brownings' Correspondence*, 9: 306-7)[12]

In the January 1845 issue of *The New Quarterly Review* Chorley wrote a review article of works by three women authors: Mrs Butler (Fanny Kemble), Frances Browne, and Barrett herself. Barrett responded to his article with intensity:

> It has been long 'a fact,' to my view of the matter, that Joanna Baillie is the first female poet in all senses, in England; and I fell with the whole weight of fact and theory against the edge of your article. (3 January 1845, 10: 4)

She expanded on this subject in another letter to Chorley written on 7 January 1845:

> You are very good to deign to answer my impertinences, & not be disgusted by my defamations of "the grand-

> mothers". ...
>
> I look everywhere for Grandmothers & see none. It is
> not in the filial spirit I am deficient, I do assure you —
> witness my reverent love of the grandfathers! — ...
>
> It is very pleasant to me to have your approbation of
> the sonnets on George Sand ['To George Sand: A Desire'
> and 'To George Sand: A Recognition']. ... (10: 13-14)

Barrett's relation to the 'grandmothers' was still not completely worked out. Her evolving relation with them, with her father, and with male and female authority in general, can been seen at this time in connection with an invitation from the Anti-Corn Law League to write a poem in support of their cause. She wanted to say yes, but declined.

Barrett's self-reproaches and self-analysis, seen in her letters to Mitford, show her articulation of a side of 'female authorship' which would later lessen some of the bonds of sympathetic understanding between her and Chorley. Her father and her brothers told her not to write the poem. Accordingly, on 10 February 1845, she declined. The next day she wrote to Mitford that 'Papa was against it, which, if he stood his ground, was enough of course to decide the question'.

> And then, to close the scene & clench the whole series of
> arguments, Mr Kenyon came, & told me that he had seen
> Mr Chorley, & that Mr Chorley declared it w^d ruin me for
> ever if I attempted such a thing, . . that my poetical
> reputation was at a crisis, . . & that from the moment I
> trusted it into the air of that region, it w^d fall flat, . . that
> nobody w^d read or buy me any more, as a matter of prin-
> ciple, . . nobody! & that my utility, from that hour, w^d be
> circumscribed, shackled, undone, — that the act w^d be
> fatal to me as a writer! Well! (10: 65)

Far from objecting to Chorley's reported narrow-mindedness, however, she wrote of him warmly later in the same letter, suggesting that she was now willing to receive him and even meet him personally, for his own sake as well as for the sake of Mitford's friendship with him:

> For Mr Chorley, . . even if you did not command this
> house when you are in it, . . which you are liberty to do,
> . . the door of it would yet be open to *him* as a respected
> visitor. (10: 67)

Five days later she returned to the ideas which the Corn Law poem were causing her to consider, reporting to Mitford:

> Mr Chorley told Mr Kenyon he felt so strongly about it,
> that if he had heard accidentally of my having such an

intention in my head, he w^d have written to give his
opinion of it unconsulted. Oh — I did not consult him. I
consulted Mr Kenyon. But it was Papa in the first place —
or I sh^d have written at once to accept. Seeing Papa
adverse, I wanted a quick opinion on *my* side, & consulted dear kind Mr Kenyon. As to my brothers, . . they
just made me angry, chafed, & out of sorts, — & sh^d not
have minded (as I told them) the great storm of their
'most sweet voices'[13] ... if it had not been for Papa.

Papa's denial was central to Barrett's declining the request, and she
believed that his attitude was characteristically male:

> The secret of the bearing of men towards women, let it be
> ever so much "made up of adorations"[14] & the like, is
> just . . contempt: they make idols of them because they
> recognize their raw material to be wood or brass. I see
> this every day in a [...] (15 February 1845, *Brownings'*
> *Correspondence*, 10: 77)

Here Barrett broke off, adding that the person is emphatically *not* 'dearest
Mr Kenyon' (10: 77).

On 19 February 1845, Barrett wrote to Mitford that she had many
opportunities to observe this male contempt for women — masked as
respect for them. It was expressed every day by Mr Hunter, who considered women to be 'divine angels' (10: 83):

> I tell him, . . the feeling is all to be analyzed into con-
> tempt of the sex. It is just that, & no less. [...]
>
> Angry as all this makes me, I am *not*, as you are per-
> haps aware, a very strong partizan [*sic*] on the Rights-of-
> women-side of the argument — at least I have not been,
> since I was twelve years old. I believe that, considering
> men & women in the mass, there IS an *inequality* of
> intellect, and that it is proved by the very state of things
> of which gifted women complain, — & more than proved
> by the manner in which their complaint is received by
> their own sisterhood. (*Brownings' Correspondence*, 10:
> 84)

Her written dialogue with Chorley seemed to imply acceptance of a
certain inequality, at least of relative professional positions, if not necessarily of intellect. On 10 March 1845, she wrote to him:

> Never was a child, who cared more for 'a story,' than I
> do — never even did I myself, *as* a child, care more for it
> than I do. My love of fiction began with my breath, &

> will end with it. (10: 116)
>
> I have forgotten what I particularly wished to say . .
> viz — that I never thought of *expecting* to hear from you.
> I understand that when you write, it is pure grace, &
> never to be expected. You have too much to do — I
> understand perfectly. (10: 117)

But a few days later, she wrote to Robert Browning more confidently about her own knowledge of the art of writing.

> Mr Chorley made me quite laugh the other day by recom-
> mending Mary Howitt's 'Improvisatore,' with a sort of
> deprecating reference to the *descriptions* in the book —
> just as if I never read a novel, . . *I*! — I wrote a confes-
> sion back to him which made him shake his head per-
> haps — & now I confess to *you*, unprovoked. I am one
> who could have forgotten the plague, listening to Boccac-
> cio's stories, — & am not ashamed of it. I do not even
> "see the better part," I am so silly. (*Brownings' Cor-
> respondence*, 20 March 1845, 10: 135; allusion to I
> Henry IV, V, 4)

These, then, were the subjects around which the epistolary friendship developed and revolved: Mesmerism, the position of women authors in the world of literature, the position of women in society, Barrett's own genius, and whether she should see Mr Chorley in person or not. Barrett did not drop her interest in any of these subjects. But in 1845 she had added an interest: Robert Browning. That new circumstance altered the direction of the developing relationship between her and Chorley. As a wife, mother, and poet living in Italy she saw him as less imposing, perhaps somewhat less promising, than he appeared to her in the early years of their friend-ship.

At first she told herself, and Mitford, that she still intended to see Chorley in due course, writing on 18 March 1845:

> Ah — Mr Chorley. But you know, I cannot exchange him
> quite for Mr Browning. Mr Browning & I have grown to
> be devoted friends I assure you — and he writes me letters
> praying to be let in, quite heartmoving & irresistible. In
> the summer I must see him — & Mr Chorley too. I shall
> like to see *both*. And then for Hyéres & everybody! —
>
> You see what Mr Chorley says of Paracelsus! You see
> it is not merely a dream of mine! — he is full of genius.
> (10: 127)[15]

Then her tone combined a 'by-the-way' casualness with some sense of urgency:

> and oh! — did I tell you in my last letter that I had seen
> lately (*now I beseech you to keep my counsel & not tell M*^r
> *Horne — and not tell M*^r *Chorley!*) Mr Browning? [...]
> Younger looking than I had expected — looking younger
> than he *is*, of course — with natural & not ungraccful
> manners [...] & we shall be good friends I hope. You and
> I differ about his genius. ... (26 May 1845, 10: 242-3)

Despite her fast growing love for Browning, she maintained her interest in
Chorley's welfare, writing to Mitford in March of her concern for him:

> What does Mr Chorley mean by saying that he is 'all sur-
> face'? Of course it is a "voluntary humility" — but what
> does he mean by it? I do not like to hear people say such
> things even in deprecation & melancholy jest — nobody
> who thinks & feels is all surface, or can really think so of
> himself — now can he? In relation to Mr Chorley, you
> know how prepared I am to see a friend in him, in the
> best sense of being a friend, & to hold the pleasure of it
> for a privilege. In principle, in feeling, in ability, he
> seems to draw the esteem of all men & women, — & I am
> personally obliged to him, — besides having been long
> personally interested in him for your sake. Then I like the
> Music & Manners, & Mrs Hemans's Memoirs, & much
> besides. You know it all as well as I can, — now do you
> not? I do not speak meanings "on the surface," but deep
> & true. (25 March 1845, 10: 138)

And a month later, to Chorley himself:

> I congratulate you (amid all cares & anxieties), upon the
> view of Naples in the distance[16] — but chiefly on your
> own happy & just estimate of your selected position in
> life. It does appear to me wonderfully & mournfully
> wrong, when men of letters, as it is too much the fashion
> for them to do, take to dishonouring their profession by
> fruitless bewailings & gnashings of teeth, — when, all the
> time, it must be their own fault if it is not the noblest in
> the world. ... Men & women of letters are the first in the
> whole world to me, & I would rather be the least among
> them, than "dwell in the courts of princes." (28 April
> 1845, 10: 178-9)

Nevertheless, as Robert Browning's visits continued, she wanted to hear
no more of possible personal visits from Chorley (or from Horne, or

anybody else). Even a visit from Mitford herself produced some anxiety; in a long, rambling letter of 21 June 1845, Barrett repeatedly excused herself from Mitford's clear expectation that Chorley was finally to meet Elizabeth Barrett:

> But I appeal to your known goodness & indulgence my dear dear friend, & open my heart to you, & entreat you (taking courage from the imagination of your smile) to *forgive me if I do not see Mr Chorley* — though of course YOU shall see him, & he is as welcome as the air to this house. (10: 269-70) [...] & my dear friend, I must confide to you besides that a peculiar reason why, just now, I object to receiving Mr Chorley, (whom, for the rest, I honour for many reasons & to whose acquaintance I look forward with hope for another brighter day,) is, . . that if Mr Horne were ever to know of my having given a welcome to his critic before I had done so to *him*, he would think it (not unnaturally) a mark of extreme unkindness on my part. You know I am grateful with reason to Mr Horne — he is my friend . . & I owe him my regard — . Well! I *could not*, comfortably to my own consciousness, receive Mr Chorley without receiving him — and really & really I am not equal to receiving all those men [...] And for Mr Chorley, I will see him some time ... [EBB's ellipses] you will see. (10: 270-71)

Two days later to Robert Browning she wrote:

> Miss Mitford talked of spending wednesday [*sic*] with me — & I have put it off to thursday: — and if you sh^d hear from Mr Chorley that he is coming to see *her & me together on any day*, . . do understand that it was entirely her proposition & not mine, & that certainly it wont be acceeded [*sic*] to, as far as *I* am concerned, — as I have explained to her finally. I have been vexed about it — but she can see him down stairs as she has done before, — [...] (23 June 1845, 10: 277)

Meanwhile, Charles Hemans, son of Felicia Hemans, had written asking to see her. Chorley came in handy, as Barrett was able to write to Mitford sincerely on 2 July 1845: 'I wish I c^d have seen him! — But it was out of the question — particularly after the refusal to Mr Chorley' (*Brownings' Correspondence*, 10: 289).

Although she was still not prepared to meet Chorley, she retained her affection for him. When Mitford mentioned in 1846 that with his fine clothes and effeminate manners, Chorley could sometimes be exasperating,

Barrett conceded her point, granting that his intellectual limitations and personal weaknesses were real. Nevertheless, she defended him sincerely:

> ... I do quite understand that your Mr Chorley moreover is somewhat of a *trial* notwithstanding his excellences [...] That he is admirable essentially, I have no manner of doubt — Not only *you* say so, but other of my friends . . who have no tenderness for the finery . . & who shrink from the waistcoats & the effeminacy — but the truth is, that he is very highly esteemed on grounds of morals & intellect by men who exceed him in power & are without his weaknesses . . & so, altogether, that we should all admire him, is as clear to me as the sun [...] Also, I have received letters from him . . full of good sense & fine sense, & free from affectation to the last line of them — and I like him . . seen so in the letters . . & am prepared to hold him in high esteem & regard even, whenever the time comes for personal knowledge. Still . . I understand how those faults must strike — strike a manly man — I, who am a woman only, cannot endure that class of faults — so we will not talk of them any more. Tell Mr Buckingham, instead, of the goodness & earnestness — He is a man of letters, not a man of genius — He can write agreeable books, . . but of great conceptions he is not capable, I always think, & it seems to me an injustice to expect great things from him (10? February 1846, Raymond and Sullivan, *EBB/Mitford Letters*, 3: 158-9)

In Elizabeth Barrett's life as Mrs Browning, she made some room for Chorley; she corresponded with him, corresponded *about* him (especially with Mitford), and fussed over him. Why wasn't he appreciated? Why wasn't he happy? Why wasn't he married? 'I do count him in the forward rank of our friends', she wrote to Mitford (19 December 1846, *Brownings' Correspondence*, 14: 81).

In 1851, she met him face to face when she and Robert Browning returned to London from Italy for a visit. In 1852, the next year, on another visit to London, the Brownings visited Chorley at his elegant little house in Belgravia. She described her courteous reaction to that second meeting to Mitford: 'We went to dine with [Chorley] in his new house & liked host & house as they deserved' (*Brownings' Correspondence*, 8: 327). By the 1850s, however, the time of close intellectual companionship had passed. Memory of their correspondence remained, as did gratitude that he had recognized her genius early, but contact was intermittent.

3 'I believe I have known you all my life'
(Chorley to Mendelssohn, August 1840)

Mendelssohn was central to English musical life in the 1840s and to Chorley's understanding of the nature of musical genius. The *Athenæum* had celebrated Mendelssohn's compositions from the first. Its review of the first English performance of his oratorio, *St Paul* (Liverpool, 1836), enumerated the score's beauties one by one, commended John Braham, Henry Phillips, and the conductor, Sir George Smart, and concluded by noting that the work gave music lovers reason to hope for the future of music:

> The Liverpool Festival, though confessedly occupying a low rank among our provincial music meetings, deserves, on the present occasion, a separate notice, for the sake of the new work which it has introduced to the English public: the successful performance whereof it gives us sincere pleasure to record.
>
> ... We have long felt that, as regards the future, it was to M. Mendelssohn that we were to look for works, not merely of the subtlest intellectual refinement, but also of the brightest original genius. ... In his Oratorio of 'St. Paul,' M. Mendelssohn has taken a yet more exalted flight: while he has grasped his subject in its most picturesque and striking aspect, he has wrought out his conceptions with science indeed, but that science refined into a grand simplicity. ...
>
> The work may be said to be linked together, and its interest wonderfully heightened by the introduction of *Corales*, after the older German manner. ... [The narrative is summarized.] Paul replies, and a chorus and *corale* follow, prophetic of the glory to the Christian cause, about to be won by the new convertite, — which have a power and sublimity almost alone in modern music. This scene is, without doubt, the gem of the Oratorio. ...
>
> In giving the above hasty sketch of this excellent work, we cannot but congratulate our musical friends, upon another composition of the highest order added to their modern stores, — to the contradiction of those who have declared that the art is exhausted, and that its decline and fall must succeed the triumphs of Handel, Mozart, and Beethoven. ... (15 October 1836: 739)

Chorley met Mendelssohn in 1839, during one of the September journeys to the Continent which Chorley undertook for the *Athenæum*. They quickly became friends. Mendelssohn had none of Barrett's reservations about personal intercourse. Twice they considered becoming collaborators, once in 1840 on a biblical cantata, 'Dives and Lazarus', and later, in the last year of Mendelssohn's life, on an opera based on Shakespeare's *Winter's Tale*, and their friendship lasted until Mendelssohn's sudden death in 1847.[17]

The period of Chorley's first acquaintance with Mendelssohn contributed largely to the formation of his opinions about the general state of German musical culture, which in turn became an important general theme in his musical journalism for the next thirty years. As Werner Ruprecht noted: 'The entire musical development of Germany from 1830 to 1860 is in him paraded forth through English eyes; thus he revealed himself as one of the most significant mediators between the countries.'[18] Felicia Hemans had impressed on Chorley the significance of German culture; through Mendelssohn his understanding was broadened and deepened.

There were numerous hospitable individuals and families in London in the 1830s whose connections with Mendelssohn, and with each other, nurtured German-English connections. Among the most frequently mentioned were the families of William Horsley (organist at the Asylum for Female Orphans), Friedrich Rosen (Professor of Oriental Languages at University College from 1828 till his unexpected death in 1837), Karl Klingemann (attached to the Hanoverian Embassy since 1827), and Ignace Moscheles (musician and teacher in London since 1826). Through Moscheles, Chorley met Mendelssohn. Even when he lived in Liverpool he had known Ignace and Charlotte Moscheles, and he became a respected friend of the family shortly after he moved to London.[19] Not long after Chorley moved to London to begin working for the *Athenaeum* he became acquainted with their friends, the Klingemann family, with whom he was also on excellent terms.

On 17 August 1839, Moscheles wrote a letter of introduction to Mendelssohn[20] and gave it to Chorley in London to carry with him on his trip to the Continent in September. On 3 September Chorley left the house which he was sharing with Henry Reeve (No. 9 Chapel St, Grosvenor Place). He sailed to Hamburg through a gale fierce enough to cause his housemate Henry Reeve anxiety about Chorley's safety (Laughton, 1: 91). After the rough crossing, Chorley's ship docked in Hamburg the next day. From Chorley's published account of the journey in *Music and Manners in France and Germany* (1841) we can follow his travels in some detail. Finding the scenery around Hamburg bleak, and thinking of the long day and night ahead of him as he proceeded by wagon through 'the dreariest country conceivable', he exclaimed to himself, 'What a fool have I been ... ever to think of this Musical Festival at Brunswick' (Chorley, *Music and Manners*, 1: 210). Reaching Braunschweig (Brunswick) at 8:30 a.m. he took quarters in the 'Blue Angel' and went for a stroll, impressed with the city's 'cleanliness' and its 'quaintly picturesque architecture' (1: 218).

He then wrote the first of many letters to Mendelssohn which Mendelssohn preserved in his 'Green Books':

> Brunswick. Thursday morning Sept^m 4
>
> Dear Sir. — I should not have intruded the inclosed [*sic*] notes upon you at so busy a time, had not Klingemann told me that he had written to you to keep tickets for me for the Festival: & as I have made a rather long journey to enjoy a pleasure long expected, & do not know the ways of the place — I have not taken any steps to provide myself till I hear from you. If the affair, however, has been forgotten — I beg that I may not add to your occupations in any way — but will endeavour, if you will favour with me [*sic*] a line, to do the best I can, in securing places. I should be much the best pleased if I might be treated by you not as a stranger but as a lover of your art — that is, wholly without ceremony.
>
> Very respectfully yr^s
>
> Henry F. Chorley (Green Books, X: 39)

After lunch, as Chorley related in *Music and Manners in France and Germany*, 'the thread of my musings was cut short by the entrance of a clean civil little boy, with a message from Dr. Mendelssohn, who was then in the Egydien Kirche, superintending the rehearsal' (1: 220). Chorley immediately went to the rehearsal and, when it was over, finally met Mendelssohn, who 'till then personally a stranger, came down to me, and gave me a friendly welcome to Germany' (1: 226). He was struck by Mendelssohn's simplicity and considerateness, as well as his appearance, thinking that 'none of the portraits of Dr. Mendelssohn do his face justice' (1: 227).[21]

At the Festival Chorley was especially impressed by a performance of Mendelssohn's *St. Paul*, which he 'had heard two or three times before, but never so thoroughly enjoyed' till hearing it at Brunswick (*Music and Manners*, 1: 236). In the report of the Festival which he sent back at that time to be printed in the *Athenæum*, Chorley reported that the performance 'as a whole, went excellently well'. He praised the Germans for doing without the 'offensive' male counter-tenors found in English choirs and noted that '[i]t was another agreeable novelty to hear the whole oratorio executed without one solitary change, cadence, or ornament on the part of any singer'. Nevertheless, the German soloists, Madame Fischer Achten, Herr Schmetzer, and Herr Fischer (Paul) were inferior to Phillips, Mrs Shaw, and other singers in London (*Athenæum*, 9 November 1839: 846). Moreover, Chorley was surprised and a little 'disappointed with the audience', whose reaction was not so warm as he had expected (*Music and Manners*, 1: 245). A further disappointment occurred at the banquet following the oratorio, when he was seated 'too near one of my countrymen' — the loud, coarse type whose boorish behaviour made Chorley wonder '[h]ow the young travelling Englishman is endured in Germany' (1: 249).

On the second day at Brunswick, Mendelssohn 'kindly' paid Chorley a visit and the two inspected some Bach manuscripts, then visited the town's Cathedral where Mendelssohn wound up 'nearly an hour's magnificent playing, by one of Bach's grand fugues' (*Music and Manners*, 1: 255, 259).

These few hours in 1839 formed the basis for their friendship. A few weeks later, Chorley approached Mendelssohn again to arrange another meeting, this one in Mendelssohn's home, Leipzig, where they could spend more time together.

But before that second meeting, Chorley gathered further impressions of German musical life, taking the opportunity of staying in Braunschweig after the three day Festival was over to hear his first performance of an opera in Germany. He looked forward to the experience with 'great interest', though not expecting much of the voices. The opera was Halévy's setting of Scribe's melodramatic *Guido and Ginevra*, a libretto which, 'after its coarse kind', was 'exceedingly effective' (1: 288). The principal singers

> went through their parts moderately well, but no more. Indeed, the peculiar structure of the French language, piquant in its separate words, but lending itself so unwillingly to rhythmical purposes, that the elongated "patri-ē," and "voya-gē," become indispensable; [*sic*] stamps, too, so much individuality of form upon its music, that the latter, when mated with a translated text, becomes singularly ungracious to speakers and singers. Even Rossini's "Guillaume Tell," which is not wholly French, loses (so to say) its *bouquet*, when given with Italian words. How much more must the music of M. Halévy suffer, — every note of which tells of Paris and the Conservatoire, — by being fitted with the heavier and less tractable German rhymes and phrases! (*Music and Manners*, 1: 295)

Although Chorley criticized operas performed in translation, he himself later translated into English numerous libretti for performance in London.

Chorley then proceeded to Berlin by way of the Harz mountains, fancying himself something of a sentimental traveller in the manner of Sterne. And from Berlin, he reported to the *Athenæum* about the current fashion in Germany for French light music, for Marryat's novels, and for the 'uprisings and downfallings' of the family in Dickens's latest novel, the '*familie* Nickleby' (*Athenæum*, 5 October 1839: 762). From Berlin Chorley wrote a second time to Mendelssohn on 23 September 1839, thanking him for hospitality received from Mendelssohn's relatives in Berlin and expressing his hopes for meeting again soon (Green Books, X: 66). Mendelssohn's reply clearly was encouraging, for it prompted a short note from Chorley announcing that he intended to leave Berlin on the 27th by the *schnell post*, and that he was grateful for Mendelssohn's 'offered kindness, as to engaging a room for me' (Green Books, X: 71). During his visit to Leipzig in 1839, he saw more of Mendelssohn and his family than he had been able to at Braunschweig and also met Mendelssohn's friend, the violinist Ferdinand David.

From Leipzig Chorley went to Dresden. By far the most significant musical events there were performances of Weber's *Euryanthe* with Schröder Devrient and Tichatschek as Adolar (*Music and Manners*, 3: 140).[22] Characteristically, he reacted strongly to the libretto as well as the music: although the opera was 'the most remarkable expression of passion in Music which the lyric drama has hitherto possessed', it also had a weak libretto, one that should be improved by 'some well-skilled but not over-arrogant dramatist' (*Music and Manners*, 3: 145).[23]

Later in October, Chorley returned to England, happy in his new friendship and eager to nurture it by collaborating with Mendelssohn on a new work, and to share some of his anxieties about his own artistic career with a sympathetic spirit.

In his letters, we can trace the progress of this proposed collaboration: Chorley's initial warmth and Mendelssohn's coolness. Writing on Sunday, 3 November 1839, Chorley hoped for 'a partnership in some great lyrical work, on the back of which my name may ride behind yours — no one knows through how many biographical dictionaries!!!!' The very salutation of his letter moved the friendship to a more intimate level than before — 'My dear Mendelssohn (for I cannot follow the only one bad fashion I saw in Leipsic — namely, that of your calling me "*Sir*")'. Chorley mixed expressions of gratitude with small talk:[24] He hoped earnestly that 'a connexion so pleasantly commenced, will not be easily let drop'. The letter continued with the proposal for collaboration: a motet based on Chorley's treatment of the Biblical story of Dives and Lazarus.[25]

> What think you of making the story of Dives & Lazarus the frame work of such an *opus*? — Say, in the first part for *Earth* [double underlining] — a chorus or choruses descriptive of natural beauty — Spring for instance — or presenting the cheerful images of busy, domestic life — (one might vary the picture by airs, duets &c, if desired) — & then, the contrast afforded by the deep sadness & solitariness of the leper whom all the young & the active & the prosperous passed by — none pitying him!

Then, to proceed, — a harvest feast for the rich man's banquet — (with the poor beggar at the gate) & here (to link as it were, the *present* with the *future*) might be introduced that parable of the same import with the story of Lazarus — where the rich man rejoices in the houses he has built, & the barns he has filled, & bids his *soul take its ease, in the goods he has laid up in store for many years* — while, in the midst of his rejoicing the voice of God summons him with that awful summons. *"Thou fool! this night thy soul shall be required of thee!"* Do you not think that in the poem thus arranged — *Earth* might be shadowed forth, with sufficient variety & distinctness for musical purposes? [...] Then, the second part, would comprise the rich man, placed amid the flames & torments of Hell — agonized for one drop of water — & afterwards with the remembrances of his unconverted brethren — while the poor despised beggar, reposes in Abraham's bosom, & answers the petitions of Dives, with gentle but passionless reply. [...] If this idea were adopted, you would have two contrasted characters throughout — & both, offering scope for a wide range of expression and development — I think moreover, that the whole could be accomplished with scriptural words — & that whatever variety of voice, musical form &c. &c. was wanted, might be naturally & and easily introduced without spoiling or overencumbering the main great purpose. If my notion be at all such an one as you approve, let me hear soon from you — & I will then send you my ideas as to details &c. &c. &c. To me it seems that there is in it the *material* for a great work of universal application & interest. I need not say what pleasure it would give me to be associated with you, even in the humble capacity of compiler of *libretto*.

Having proposed himself for the 'humble capacity of compiler of *libretto*', he informed Mendelssohn about the progress of one of his own plays (perhaps *Fortibel*), the production of which seemed imminent. A successful production would strengthen his qualifications to serve as an opera librettist for Mendelssohn:

But I don't know whether any more aspiring notions as to opera may not come out sooner than I fancied, when we talked together — for the negociations concerning my play are assuming a very agreeable appearance — & I think I

> have more than a chance of its being produced. The pros-
> pect of coming to my trial so soon, has excited me not a
> little — I am trying hard to subdue my too sanguine
> nature, so as not only to be prepared for — but even to
> expect *failure* should my dramatic child make its
> appearance soon as now seems likely. — I mention this —
> believing I have your good wishes — (Green Books, X:
> 120)

Mendelssohn's reply to Chorley's letter was cordial. In one crucial respect, however, it was unsatisfactory: Mendelssohn refused to set *Dives and Lazarus* unless Chorley could convince him that the structure of the text (and its treatment of moral rewards and punishments) was dramatically motivated and justified. Mendelssohn wrote to Klingemann that he was not entirely comfortable with Chorley's proposal and had been putting off the unpleasant necessity of explaining that to Chorley.[26]

In writing to Mendelssohn, Chorley showed his continuing determination to make his name 'ride behind' Mendelssohn's in future biographical dictionaries. He exerted himself in his letter of 11 February 1840, to justify his original proposal. It is significant to our understanding of the determined, perhaps somewhat stubborn, way Chorley's creative mind worked.

> Sunday, February 11/40
>
> [T]his is almost the first moment I have had to thank you
> for remembering me so kindly — & for the careful atten-
> tion you have given to the idea I submitted to you
> immediately on my return from Germany. [...] I feel, to
> the fullest point, the weight of your objection to Dives &
> Lazarus, on the score of their insignificance — So should
> I, did I consider them as historical characters, or even
> individual *dramatis personae*, as anything, in short, but
> types of humanity or children of Earth. [...] I would have
> the first part of such a work as the one I contemplated be
> purely Earthly in its joy & sorrow — of the familiar
> incomings & outgoings of daily life — rising to the mysti-
> cal sublimities of blessedness & truth when the veil is
> raised which separates the finite from the infinite, the
> visible from the invisible. — And I thought that [...] in
> such a Poem (for the work with its Music makes a poem)
> might be nobly symbolized a picture of the lofty & fearful
> destinies which await Mankind — so as to touch all hearts
> & to belong to all times. [...] It seemed to me that the dif-
> ficulty is now very great, again to treat what I may call
> the historical events & passages of Scripture, particularly

those of the New Testament. There are a few noble &
mystical stories in the Old Testament still untouched —
among others, Elijah as the type of Prophecy[27] — The
fate of the Temple — (a grand subject!) comprising the
building — the sojourn of God among his people — the
Time of War — of ruin & Captivity & of restoration: —
but I wish I could put you into the point of view, whence
I regard the subject — & I think you would find it
afforded good scope for contrast — for passion — & those
sublime effects (clear of all tawdriness & exaggeration)
which no living composer knows better to give than yourself. At the same time do not, for an instant conceive me
capable of imagining that a subject can be crammed down
any man's throat — still less that I have energy & persuasion to do it. If when you have considered it again — you
find it still antipathetic, I will once more *think my best*, in
default of some one else. — But the rich man's feast — &
the voice through the chamber summoning him to
judgement — contrasted with Lazarus carried by Angels to
Abraham's bosom! — I would not beg you to give these a
second thought, were they inventions of my own! — but
do consider them!

After a long explanation of his determination to insist that Mendelssohn
reconsider, Chorley concluded with general news and information, including information about such topics as his bad health, his recent stay in Paris,
the production of his play, Clara Novello's voice, etc.

A substantial portion of Mendelssohn's reply to this letter was a detailed
critique of Chorley's manuscript, with a request for clarifications and further explanations. Mendelssohn seemed to be indicating a willingness to
reconsider his opposition to Dives and Lazarus.

Leipzig, 28th Feb., 1840

My Dear Friend. [...] Thanks for your ideas on the plan
of Dives and Lazarus — be sure that I am fully aware of
your kindness in thus discussing the matter with me,
instead of leaving it off at once, as I unfortunately experienced so often; and I thank you more for it than I can well
express. After what you say, I see that I have not been
able to form an exact idea of what you intend the whole to
be; the fact is, that I did not quite understand what part
both figures should act in hell or in heaven, because I do
not quite understand the part they act on earth — and
indeed the true sense of the story itself, as I find it in the

> Evangile [Luke] — or is there another source, which you
> took your notions from? I asked some of my theological
> friends here, but they knew none. — I only find Dives
> very rich and Lazarus very poor, and as it cannot be only
> for his riches that one is burning in hell, while the other
> must have greater claims to be carried to Abraham's
> bosom than his poverty alone, it seemed to me as if some
> very important part of the story was left in blank. Or
> should Lazarus be taken as an example of a virtuous poor
> man; the other of the contrary? But then we ought to
> know or to learn (by the poem) what he *does* or *has done*
> to deserve the greatest of all rewards; the mere reason (as
> given in St. Luke) that he suffered want, and that the
> other has had his share of happiness on earth already,
> does not seem sufficient to me to give interest to the prin-
> cipal figure of such a poem as that which you intend. Per-
> haps you have another view of the whole; pray let me
> know it and tell me what part you would give to both of
> them in earth, hell, and heaven. If once delivered of this
> scruple, I should quite agree with your opinion, and the
> great beauties you point out I certainly should feel and
> admire with all my heart. Do not lose patience with me; I
> am of a rather slow understanding, and can never move
> forwards until I have quite understood a thing. The best
> is, that in all such discussions one always draws nearer,
> not only to the subject, but also to each other. But what is
> this return of your illness, and the continual complaint of
> which you write me? You seemed so well and so high in
> your spirits when we met here. ... (Hewlett, 1: 309-11)[28]

Chorley's third letter on the proposed collaboration had two main pur-
poses: the first to urge the appropriateness of the subject Dives and
Lazarus; the second to ask whether Mendelssohn would be interested in
Chorley's accompanying him back to Leipzig from London at the end of
Mendelssohn's next visit in the autumn of 1840. Writing on 10 March
1840, he attempted the justification which Mendelssohn requested:

> My dear friend — [D]o, first, believe me, when I say,
> that I feel much obliged & flattered by your willingness to
> give me another hearing. — But no more speeches; for I
> have a good deal to say. —
>
> It seems to me that we are misunderstanding each
> other, in consequence of your fancying, that I meant
> *literally* to adhere to the story of Dives & Lazarus as told

in the Bible. I think I would follow its spirit (or rather, let me say, *not contradict it*) but, my plan would be to fill up the outline largely. I never believed Dives was punished *because* he was "rich" or Lazarus beatified *because* he was a leper! Why then? — because Dives was worldly, or cruel, or unjust, or vainglorious — the *"rich man" par excellence*, of the Parables. [...] [T]his, then, is the extreme figure of my group — the black shade of my picture. — For light, I would have my "poor man" — [...] Taking these two figures as *extremes* — I think, that a picture of the human lot of vicissitude — here plenty, there beggary — here discontent in the midst of splendour, there patience in despite of suffering & agony — might be combined of the materials they would furnish — with a slight intermixture of other shades of *the world* (Dives) against the *spirit* (Lazarus) displayed in subordinate figures. — And how strikingly might this lead on to the *second part* or the Future! After such a suite of movements as might display the various moral torments of the condemned [...] I would then show Dives, tormented by his own earthly appetites following him [... and] I would show Lazarus not among the palms & the seraphs of a visible Paradise, but reposing in the certainty that his agonies had been wisely ordained & in the deep thankfulness, that he had been taught & tried on Earth, so as to be qualified for Heaven! [...]

In looking into my Bible this moment, I find that superb passage — *Matthew Chap. 25.* beginning verse 31st *"When the son of Man shall come in his glory &c. &c."* to the end of the chapter — Why, that in itself is such an opening to the second Part on Heaven & Hell, as we could find no where else! — the whole scheme of reward & punishment — the finite & the infinite, set forth in language of surpassing grandeur, — ready for you to look upon as artist! — I was never more vexed at the want of clearness in explanation, which I know to be my fault, than in this instance: for it seems to me that this might be one of the newest & noblest works ever done in Christian art! I have talked over the subject with Klingemann, who took fire immediately — Had I only time & energy I would complete the book, in the hope, that when you had the whole before you, you might feel its coherence & significance as intensely as I do. — Do not turn away from it, I beg of you, without doing your best to understand my clumsy English!

Chorley then turned to his hope to see Mendelssohn again in England and to return with him to the Continent in October:

> ... [Y]ou are anxiously wished for, & will be affectionately welcomed — [...] I hardly think, I should go abroad, *at least till October*, if I knew that I should see you here — My own future is not an easy one to arrange: but a dream [?] *has* crossed me, more than once, of the pleasure it would give me, could I return with you — [...] &, could we come to any agreement, I might perhaps settle myself for a month or so at Leipsic or Dresden. [...] These are, perhaps, mere *chateaux d'Espagne* — but come, & help me make realities of them! [...] The "good spirits" you saw at Leipsic, have carried my weak body on these thirty years — but you did not see, how many headaches, & languid hours I had, when I was by myself, even in your pleasant and friendly town. If I was, perhaps, too critical about the *Conservatoire*, I am sure today, it is perfect, thanks to the coarse and noisy doings of our Philharmonic band last night. Bennett played Beethoven's C Major Concerto — very fairly — but I was not content with his cadence: & there was a new symphony of Spohr in C minor — very *laudanum*, very! — I believe Moscheles & Klingemann are both writing to you, as well as I — & the former will tell you of a psalm he is composing — Bennett brings out a new Pianoforte trio at the Quartett Concert on Thursday. — I will not believe that you will not come — [...] And pray when is a certain work with certain themes, something like those in the margin [three brief themes are sketched in the margin], to see the light? I have been inflaming the curiosity of every pianist here & in Paris, about it. — Good bye. God bless you & believe me Affectionately y^{rs} Henry F. Chorley (Green Books, X: 96)

Mendelssohn was genuinely pleased with the idea of Chorley's visit. The subject of the cantata, however, was dropped from further serious consideration.

4

Chorley wrote again on 11 May 1840, after he learned that Mendelssohn might indeed visit England in a few months:

> My dear Mendelssohn. — Though a good deal hurried by
> having my mother & sister here: & by the exigencies of
> the season, I must avail myself of a moment, to tell you
> how happy I was last night made by Klingemann's news
> that you have said "*yes*" to the Birmingham Committee &
> are coming to pay us, I hope, a long visit this Autumn. I
> have not heard a piece of news which has given me more
> pleasure for a very long time: though I know how little I
> can hope to do, so as in any way to testify my grateful
> remembrance of your kindness to me when I was in
> Germany. Still it is delightful to think we shall have you
> here — & you will find few among your friends old or
> new, more eager to welcome you. — You have not kept
> your word as regards bringing the P.[iano]F.[orte] trio —
> for it was played for the first time, yesterday, by Mos-
> cheles, Molique & Hausmann — each movement twice —
> that some familiarity with the work might be gained: & it
> went well, for a first performance. I think you would have
> been satisfied by the impression it produced. Did your
> ears burn about two o'clock in the day? You know that
> the English believe when their ears are hot that some one
> is talking of them. — Have you not made some slight
> changes at the end of the first movement from the M.S.
> copy? — I ask, in great humility.
>
> Liszt arrived on Wednesday — & showed himself *chez
> moi* in the evening: & I have heard him, about once a day
> since. I am excessively crazy about the *man*, as well as
> the pianist: he keeps my mind so wide awake! Besides
> making my ears (not burn) but *jump* with astonishment. —
> There is far less eccentricity too, about his appearance, &
> behaviour than I had expected. [...] (Green Books, XI:
> 150)

Not only was Mendelssohn contemplating another visit to England, he
was also about to accept another position at home and move from Leipzig
to Berlin. Chorley had heard this piece of news, too, and referred to it in a
letter written 20 June 1840:

> There are rumours of musical changes at Berlin, which
> affect us with close interest. We wait for their confirma-
> tion with great anxiety — I know (being a prophet) what
> the end *will* be — but I want the end to come soon — &
> your family to have the full joy of seeing you in your

right position *at home*!

When Mendelssohn wrote to Chorley with more details about his coming trip to England, he tactfully refered to Chorley's proposal for an oratorio (or motet or cantata) on Dives and Lazarus as something that might some-day lead to some *other* collaboration:

Leipzig, 21st July, 1840

My Dear Sir,

... I have thought very often of our Oratorio plan; and although I could not reconcile myself to the idea of intro-ducing Dives and Lazarus, your sketches have given me another idea for the introduction of my favourite plan, which I think is the right one, and which I long to com-municate to you, and to hear your opinion of it. But I must do it in person, not in writing, and we must talk it over, not only correspond about it; and, therefore, pray keep much leisure time open for me and for my plans. Perhaps I shall annoy you very much with them, but then you must only accuse your own kindness, which induces me to think you more of an old friend than a new one. As for your opening of the second part, with the verses 31, &c., from Matthew, chap. xxv., it is a glorious idea, and that of course must remain, but "mündlich, mündlich."

I was glad to hear that you like Liszt so much; he is such an extraordinary artist. [Ferdinand] David sends his best regards and wishes: he is in better humour for play-ing and composing than ever, and his new *concerto* at the Schwerin Festival was capital. I am now finishing the *concerto* for him, of which you recollected the last move-ment so perfectly. By-the-bye, what an extraordinary memory you must have, to write three subjects of a piece, which you only heard once, without missing a note! But I have not altered anything at the end of the first movement of my trio, and cannot make out what might have been the cause of your thinking so. Did they play it fast enough? I hope you will like my new 'Lobgesang,' or 'Song of Praise,' which we performed here at the Festival [25 June 1840], and which they will give at Birmingham on the second morning. ... It is rather long, but I think and hope you will like some parts of it better than my other things. I will also bring some other new compositions; and this leads me to a question which I will also put to Klingemann,[29] and to which I should like to know your answer and very sincere opinion, as I shall be guided by

> it. It is now so long since I have not been heard in public in London, that I should like to arrange a concert for some charitable institution during my stay in September next: it might either be in a church, and there I could only play the organ, or (which I would prefer) in a room, where I could perform my new pianoforte music, a new overture, &c. But the question is, first, whether such a thing is possible in the month of September, when everybody is out of town? ... (Hewlett, 1: 314-20)

As the time for Mendelssohn's visit to England came closer, Chorley became more and more excited, thinking not only of Mendelssohn's arrival but also of his own plans for a second trip to Leipzig to be at home with the Mendelssohn family, a prospect that was becoming increasingly likely. On 3 August 1840 he wrote:

> I really deserve to receive letters: so much pleasure do they give me. Yours (to speak like a man of business) of the 21st arrived here on Friday morning — & I should certainly have answered it by the same day's post, had I had a moment's leisure. *Now* I can thank you for it, in a little more peace & quietness, than I could have done, had I written *then*. There is no need, between us, for you to explain why you write to me so seldom, any more than for me, I trust, to apologize for writing to you so often — But to come to matters of more consequence than civil speeches, we are all delighted to think that you are coming we hope not alone, for it will give us more of your company — & to some of us the great pleasure of making the personal acquaintance of Madame Mendelssohn & of doing our poor best to make England agreeable to her: and you, too, will be more content & willing to stay as long as your engagements permit, if so pleasant an arrangement be possible. If I was not another man's servant, I should say *positively* that I will return with you at least as far as Frankfort — as it is, I can only declare such to be my best intention — ... I need not tell you what a pleasure & privilege I shall esteem it ... to be allowed to go so far on my way, under the shadow of your wing.

As it happened, Mendelssohn's wife, Cécile, did not accompany him to England, nor was Mendelssohn's visit to be protracted, as Chorley hoped. But Chorley did return to Germany, 'under the shadow' of Mendelssohn's 'wing', along with their mutual friend Moscheles.

In this same letter of 3 August 1840, Chorley returned briefly to the by now almost exhausted topic of the oratorio, thanking Mendelssohn for his 'patience', and noting his own determination to bring up the topic for renewed discussion when the opportunity should arise:

> I thank you very much for your patience with my oratorio [...] & sketches: because I mean to try it still further, when we meet face to face, & can talk of the matter, instead of trusting to the post.

Then Chorley turned his attention to practical comments on Mendelssohn's plans for his visit, speaking positively about the coming performances of the 'Lobgesang' at Birmingham, negatively about the possibility of giving successful concerts in London in September, when as many people as possible leave town.

> I long to hear the "Lobgesang" & (D.V.) shall.[30] But my dear friend, I am sorry not to be able to encourage your concert scheme for London: & having shown Moscheles what you say, I may add his infinitely more valuable opinion to mine. Neither orchestra nor audience is in London in September (London's emptiest month) & we will not have your new work given in a corner, & to a handful of people. It is neither fair to them, nor to the public — least of all to your own position.

Chorley's next comments are characteristic behind-the-scenes gossip.

> There is little news here. Every one is gone or going from London as fast as possible. Miss Novello (totally unsuccessful here) is I see trying Germany again — & we have been all set on fire, by a very mediocre German opera company, which, nevertheless has been almost a blessing, as giving us an opportunity of becoming acquainted with *the forms* of some of the great music Gluck's "Iphigenie," among the rest. — And you know, I hope, that at the Queen's private concert — "Our sovereign Lady Victoria" as the prayer-book calls her, & Prince Albert, with sundry amateurs among the nobility — *and* Rubini — *and* Lablache, sung a chorus from the "Paulus." — Good bye, & God bless you till we meet. Excuse my writing to you in this familiar manner: but I cannot help it. I believe I have known you all my life, & *not* that I saw you for the first time last year: & I am sure that I think of all y^r kindness with a warm gratitude that will not let me be formal. (Green Books, XII: 39)

Mendelssohn arrived in London on 18 September 1840 at four o'clock in the afternoon; by seven he was with Moscheles. That night Mendelssohn and the Moscheles family all shared their memories of happy times spent together.[31] The next night Chorley and Klingemann were invited to join the family circle. Moscheles's wife, Charlotte, wrote to her relatives that it had been seven years since Moscheles and Mendelssohn had played duets together. It was so beautiful it had been worth waiting for.[32] A few days later, during the stay in Birmingham for the performance of the 'Lobgesang', Moscheles decided to accompany Mendelssohn back to Germany. It was also agreed that Chorley would indeed be a third member of the travelling party (Moscheles, *Leben*, 1: 57).

On the night of their departure, Chorley, Mendelssohn, and Moscheles were in high spirits, and on parting they each made light-hearted entries in Mrs Moscheles's Album.[33] They gathered at the Dover Mail Coach, transferred to a ship for the eight hour crossing to Ostende, then set out in 'Mendelssohn's Wagen mit Postpferden' until eventually the axle broke and they sat down for a meal at Lüttich while it was being repaired. At noon the next day the coach was ready to go on, and the party made it to Aachen on the evening of 5 October. Supper at Aachen proved memorable because at their Gasthof they encountered Ole Bull, the violinist, and Anton Felix Schindler, whose biography of Beethoven Moscheles translated into English the next year.[34] Mendelssohn was happy to be back on the Rhine; he knew 'all the points of the river like a lover, and showed them to me with the eagerness of one who has sympathy in his heart' (Hewlett, 1: 321). Chorley enjoyed the company of both men:

> Moscheles of a humour quaint and curious and more genial than I had at all expected from one habitually so calm and reserved; Mendelssohn warm and petulant about small troubles and hindrances, but good-natured to an excess, and *spirituel* and cheerful passing common cheerfulness. (Hewlett, 1: 321)

The route took them on to Cologne, up the Rhine, through Frankfurt, where on Wednesday they stopped again. Next came Weimar, and finally, after two more days, Leipzig, where they finally arrived at 11 in the morning on Friday, 9 October 1840.

Chorley had been looking forward eagerly to his second stay with Mendelssohn. It began well, with dinners and visits. Chorley wrote some occasional verse in Mrs Mendelssohn's honour and Moscheles set it to music (Moscheles, *Leben*, 66). On Monday, Chorley visited Robert Schumann, who jotted in his Diary on October 12: 'Früh Bür[c]k, David, Landsberg, Moscheles, Chorley'.[35] Moscheles recorded that this visit was especially interesting because Frau Schumann played for them a Bach fugue.[36] Chorley too was impressed by Clara Schumann's playing.[37] His reaction to Robert Schumann's music was ambivalent, as he recorded in *Music and Manners*, where he termed Schumann 'the German Berlioz', an uncomplimentary phrase signifying that his works 'are in the very wildest strain of extravagant mysticism' (3: 126), and he cited 'Kreisleriana' as an example. In a note, Chorley explained that the title referred to 'one of Hoffmann's most fantastic creations', a figure 'of whom a sort of Shandean use is made by that strange humourist':

> [H]ence the fragments bearing his name (and bearing out his character) are as near regular and symmetrical musical compositions as Coleridge's "Kubla Khan" is to a complete epic. Herr Schumann has too much talent and learning to lose himself for ever in such mazes, which lead to nothing, when the broad highways of the art lie open before him. (3: 126)

In his private journal Chorley recorded still more of his reaction to hearing *Kreisleriana*:

> [They are] fantasy pieces with that affected and Hoffmannish title, and written studies, neither songs without words, nor *notturni*, nor recitatives in rhythm, but partaking of all these natures; exceedingly wild, exceedingly clever, with some passages of very sweet melody, and some middle work of very fine construction; but, after all, clouded, and dreamy, and heavy: a sort of answer to the spirit of Berlioz talking on the pianoforte. Surely music is neither to end nor to stay here, else will it become a house for no sane man to dwell in! (Hewlett, 1: 325)

This comment about Schumann in 1840 recurred in various forms as a basic justification for Chorley's increasing hostility to Schumann's music during the 1850s and 1860s.

Mendelssohn and David provided 'ceaseless musical entertainment' (Hewlett, 2: 323). From Moscheles's letter to his wife (2: 64) we learn that the next night, Tuesday, Mendelssohn gave a musical soirée. But Chorley's health was poor. At some point in the week he took to his hotel room to recuperate. Mendelssohn tried to cheer him up by sending over a piano for him, even coming himself to play music by Moscheles and Schubert on it.[38] Because Chorley was confined to his hotel room, Tuesday's soirée was probably the last social function in Leipzig he enjoyed with Mendelssohn. Mendelssohn good-naturedly transformed himself from host to nurse. This kindness made an impression which Chorley never forgot:

> I was lying down ... in all the fullness of wretchedness ...

when a little bustle at the door announced the arrival of a concert-flugel from Breitkopf and Härtel. I shall always think of this with emotion. Mendelssohn had sent it, and he and Moscheles were coming to make their evening's music by the side of my sofa! One hardly knows how to take these things without seeming extravagant; and I could not help running over, in thought, years of struggle, and obscurity, and longing, when such a visitation would have seemed to me a positive faery-dream. ... Then one's mind so strongly and sadly associates with its thoughts at such times all who are gone; and I could not but remember what a sympathy poor Benson [Rathbone] would have had in seeing my tastes thus ministered to, and without, I hope, any obtrusiveness or flattery on my part. (Hewlett, 1: 323-4)

Chorley's visit was disappointingly shorter than he had hoped it would be. From Frankfurt on 29 October Chorley wrote to Mendelssohn in order to

... do what I could not do on leaving Leipsig, — namely thank you, with all my heart. [...] Indeed, I have lived years in places in which I have felt less at home than in your dear, hospitable town. — & though my ambition cannot help wishing for you some metropolis as the sphere of your exertions, I do not think I shall ever visit you under pleasanter circumstances, or those more calculated to make me feel regret when my visit is over.[39]

Chorley visited not only Berlin and Frankfurt, but also Nuremberg ('I was never so excited by a place in my life ... the old streets & churches & works of art were seen to every possible advantage', Green Books, XII: 145). Finally he arrived in Paris, hoping to hear some of Berlioz's music (he mentioned to Mendelssohn that Berlioz's 'usual habit' made him expect 'several concerts at this time of year'). As it happened, no works by Berlioz were being performed. Rachel's acting, Duprez's singing (in Meyerbeer's *Robert le Diable*), and a great deal of church music thus constituted the main attractions of Paris (Green Books, XII: 145).

Chorley wrote to Mendelssohn next after he was re-established in London, on 27 November 1840. Full of the usual musical gossip, the letter was an elaborate thank-you. At the same time, its tone suggested that the visit had perhaps not quite lived up to Chorley's high expectations — or perhaps that Chorley feared that, on further acquaintance, he was becoming a disappointment to Mendelssohn.

My dear Mendelssohn. It was not my intention to have been even thus long without writing to you — as my hasty

> &, I fear, ill tempered note from Frankfort cannot count as a letter: but in Paris, I was not only much hurried, but suffering from extreme fatigue. ... I have been too long in thanking yourself — & Madame Mendelssohn for the friendly kindness, which made Leipzig so delightful to me — I was languid, & unwell, & (as we say here) *good for nothing* all the days I was there & I fear I may have thrown the burden of bad health and bad spirits upon other people. If it was so, I can only entreat the indulgence of my friends — I hope they are not visited by those feelings of constant fatigue of body, which alone, could make them thoroughly sympathise with my *triste* looks & grieved[?] speeches. It is only within the last two days that the cloud has begun to pass away — we have now a little frost: & that always gives me life and spirits.
> (Green Books, XII: 145)

This letter sounded a refrain that recurred in the letters to many correspondents in later years in which he apologized for poor spirits due to ill health.

When Chorley left Leipzig, he had absent-mindedly left behind a knife which was associated with his much-loved boyhood friend from Liverpool, Benson Rathbone, who had died in 1834. Fortunately, Mendelssohn found the knife and enclosed it in a letter to Chorley of 24 January 1841. He also mentioned that he hoped to see Chorley's sonnet to his son (Hewlett, 1: 327-35). Chorley responded on 13 February 1841:

> My dear Mendelssohn. . . many thanks for my knife —
> It is all I have to remind me of the best friend I ever had,
> and I grieved over its supposed loss, more than I could
> tell you: — though grown indifferent to relics, for the
> love is poor that will not last without them. ...

He enclosed his 'poor sonnet to your little boy':

> To C. Mendelssohn Bartholdy
> Now, while the Night with sad embrace hath kissed
> The earth to silence, save for winds that grieve,
> My heart is counting o'er the things I leave
> With tender watchfulness that none be missed:
> And 'mid the ties which Life will scarce untwist,
> O blooming, bright-haired Boy! thou, too, did'st weave
> A tiny thread — with looks that all believe,
> And gladsome voice. Oh, may it aye resist,
> Merry as now, the harsher tones of Time!
> Thou wilt forget me ere we meet;

And I am townward bound — to play the mime
'Mid worldly men — perchance myself to cheat:
Fit is it then that one atoning rhyme
So fair a gift of Heaven should simply greet.[40]

Although the friendship lasted without interruption until Mendelssohn's death in 1848, Chorley's second visit to Leipzig, in September 1840, marked an end to the initial warmth and intimacy. Though the relation between the two never withered into mere acquaintance, neither was it sustained by constant personal contact, as Chorley's late-blooming friendship with Charles Dickens was to be. Nevertheless, for the rest of Chorley's life Mendelssohn's work and his personal good will meant much to him. Privately he took pride and comfort in being Mendelssohn's friend, while he expressed his admiration for Mendelssohn as a great composer often and publicly. Indeed, it was the genius of Mendelssohn, even more than that of Rossini, which came to be the yardstick by which Chorley judged subsequent European musical culture.

Notes

1. Publication date given as 1838 (actually appeared in late 1837; reissued by Griffin, Bohn, and Company in 1861).

2. Other reviews of *Findens' Tableaux* are reprinted in *Brownings' Correspondence*, 4: 400-408. Kelley and Hudson refer to Chorley's review of the *Seraphim*, but the context suggests to me a review of *Findens' Tableaux*. Barrett's remark of 30 October indicated that she attributed the review to Chorley, but there are no attributions in the marked *Athenæum* volume for the year 1839.

3. *Exposition of the False Medium and Barriers Excluding Men of Genius from the Public* (1833).

4. A few days later she compared Kenyon's description of Chorley's 'enchanted house' in Victorian Square with Kenyon's description of his own new house in Regent's Park:

    > ... and the drawing rooms with walls of tender green according to the tint of a duck's egg, & gilded cornices, and crimson silk curtains, & tables of red granite, & carpetings with the chequered brightness of a cathedral-window, will be beautiful if I fancy them aright from his description; & I shall like them better (*I should*, I mean) than Mr Chorley's more gorgeous vanities. But the best furniture, after all, is books — books. (7: 112)

5. Barrett to Mitford 26 August 1843: 'I was not aware that Mr Chorley

had any personal acquaintance at all with him [Horne] — I thought the sin lay in the *book*!' (7: 292). This was a reference to *Exposition of the False Medium and Barriers Excluding Men of Genius from the Public*, which Horne had published in 1833. Two years before, EBB's letter to MRM of July 18, 1841 stated that Chorley's 'silent gravity' about Horne's *Exposition* was the only 'evil imputation in relation to it that ever reached *me*' (5: 80).

6.   Kelley and Hudson state that it is 'impossible to determine the exact extent of her share of authorship of *A New Spirit of the Age*' (*Browning's Correspondence*, 7: 374, note 2).

7.   Phillip Kelley and Ronald Hudson, editors of *The Brownings' Correspondence*, attribute the review to Chorley (8: 373). Although there are no attributions in the marked copies of the *Athenæum* for 1844, the attribution is plausible.

8.   Chorley once again revealed his own admiration for Dickens's novels:

> This 'New Spirit' opens with an elaborate analysis of the works of Mr. Dickens, accompanied by a portrait engraved after one of Miss Gillies's miniatures. As fitly might the professor of architecture attempt to revolve the *Adler Strasse* of Nuremburg into first principles of harmony and proportion, as the critic to reason philosophically on Tony and Sam Weller, Mrs. Nickleby, and Mrs. Jarley and Miggs, and last, but not least lovely, Mrs. Gamp, with her idea of friendship at her side — the enduring Mrs. Harris!

9.   Chorley commented on Horne's treatment of Dr Southwood Smith, Walter Savage Landor, the Howitts, Edward Pusey, Marrayat, Gore, Francis Trollope, Monckton Milnes, Hartley Coleridge, etc. Of the first performance of Thomas Noon [Serjeant] Talfourd's *Ion*, Chorley commented that it was 'a spectacle not to be forgotten by those who were present' (*Brownings' Correspondence*, 8: 373). The *Athenæum* had reviewed *Ion* coolly, and for a time Talfourd incorrectly assumed that Chorley had written the review.

10.   Allusion to John 13: 1, as noted by Kelley and Lewis.

11.   *Athenæum*, 24 August 1844: 763-64; rpt. in *Brownings' Correspondence*, 9: 320-24.

12.   Martineau was told that Chorley as well as Dilke had treated her unscrupulously, and she informed Barrett on 15 May 1845:

> Poor Mr Chorley! It must be his own consciousness w^h makes him suppose he has lost my friendship, for it so happens, I have not mentioned his name, more or less, since the Athen^m assault. Surely his case must be clear to him, as to every body else.

> He is supposed to be sub-editor of the Athen^m, & to
> have his portion of respons^y for the doings of the
> paper. He cannot, of course, have both that respons^y &
> my friendship, or that of any honourable person, —
> [...]
> [She was warned that Dilke was 'dishonest &
> malicious'] but took Chorley's engagement for him that
> it was not true, & he w^d be gentlemanly to me. And
> Mr Chorley has not yet expressed his remorse for
> having so misled me, though he knows the fact from
> myself. I am now assured on very high authority, that
> Chorley is no friend of mine in his present conduct &
> conversation; but I keep this to myself; & wait to hear
> what he has to say for himself. Thus stands the matter.
> (*Brownings' Correspondence*, 10: 220)

13. Allusion to *Coriolanus*, II, 3, 172, as noted by Kelley and Lewis.
14. Allusion to *As You Like It*, V, 2, 95-6, as noted by Kelley and Lewis.
15. Kelley and Lewis state: 'Since there is no evidence of a review of *Paracelsus* by Chorley, it seems reasonable to infer that his opinion of RB's poem must have been expressed in correspondence with EBB which she may be sharing with Miss Mitford' (10: 127, note 7).
16. Kelley and Lewis note that this is probably a reference to his going to Italy in the autumn of 1845.
17. The relationship between the two men between 1839 and Mendelssohn's death in 1847 is documented in several published and unpublished sources. Hewlett printed several letters from Mendelssohn, but Hewlett's book was published too early to take into account the published reminicences of Ignaz Moscheles and Karl Klingemann, and Hewlett was unaware that Chorley's letters to Mendelssohn were in fact not lost but preserved in Mendelssohn's 'Grüne Bücher', now at the Bodleian Library, Oxford. The following are the most relevant sources:
     1. Mendelssohn, Grüne Bücher ('Green Books'), Bodleian Library, Oxford University.
     2. [Moscheles, Charlotte], *Aus Moscheles' Leben* and *Life of Moscheles* (the English translation is not only 'adapted' but somewhat condensed, with fewer references to Chorley than the German edition).
     3. Chorley, *Music and Manners in France and Germany* and his re-issue of part of that book, along with much new material, as *Modern German Music*.
     4. Klingemann, *Mendelssohn-Bartholdys Briefwechsel mit Legationsrat Karl Klingemann in London*.
18. Ruprecht added that as mediator his efforts were not always positive:

'Die ganze musikalische Entwicklung Deutschlands von 1830 bis 1870 is durch ihn an englischen Augen vorübergezogen; so hat er sich als einer der bedeutendsten Mittler der Nationen bewiesen. Freilich hat er nicht immer eine glückliche Hand dabei gehabt'. (Ruprecht, 42).

19. Moscheles's widow is the source for information about the family friendship: 'Chorley wurde bald Hausfreund und blieb der vieljährige hochgeactete und stets dienstfertige, ja unentbehrliche Anhänger der Familie' (Moscheles, *Leben*, 1: 245).

20. English translation printed in Felix Moscheles, *Letters*, 191-2. For a reference to the letter of introduction, see letter of 4 September [1839] from Chorley to Mendelssohn (Green Books, X: 39). Hewlett stated that the introduction came through Moscheles (Hewlett, 1: 306).

21. Thackeray asserted that 'Mendelssohn's face is the most beautiful face I ever saw. I imagine our Saviour's to have been like it' (from R. Doyle's *A Sketch Book of Reminiscences* [1880], quoted in Jacob, 233). Henry Phillips was reminded of the beautiful 'Jew's eyes' of his own mother when he saw Mendelssohn's face (Phillips, 1: 3). When Chorley published *Modern German Music*, after Mendelssohn's death, he added to this passage: '[Our acquaintance] soon ripened into indulgent friendship on the one side, and faithful regard on the other. ... I thought then, as I do now, his face one of the most beautiful which has ever been seen. No portrait does it justice. ... Perhaps there was no contemporary at once strong, simple, and subtle enough, to paint such a man with such a countenance' (1: 14, 15).

22. '"Euryanthe" is too little known in England as yet. ... It is difficult to understand what freak of prudery drove the German adaptors of the exquisite "Cymbeline" of Shakspeare [*sic*] so utterly to transform and distort and weaken its incidents' (*Music and Manners*, 3: 143).

23. For a discussion of this section of *Music and Manners* in relation German romantic opera in general, see Aubrey S. Garlington, '*Mega*-Text, *Mega*-Music'.

24. Hewlett printed several letters from Mendelssohn to Chorley and stated that 'I have found no copies' of Chorley's replies. The replies are now in the Bodleian Library, Oxford ('Green Books'), my source for quotations from Chorley's letters to Mendelssohn, with exceptions as noted.

25. For a discussion of other Victorian literary treatments of this subject see Williams.

26. 'Aber auch Chorleys Idee vom Lazarus sagt mir nicht recht zu, obwohl es damit freilich ein ganz andres Ding ist. Ich schreibe ihm heut oder morgen darüber, und hab es bisher nicht getan, weil mich das Englischschreiben mehr geniert, als ich selbst gedacht hätte,

namentlich in solchen Dingen, wo die Muttersprache mir auch nicht bequem genug ist' (2 January 1840, Klingemann, 242).

27. Mendelssohn's *Elijah* with German text arranged by Julius Schubring from Biblical passages was first performed at the Birmingham Festival on August 26, 1846, in the English version by William Bartholomew.

28. Hewlett noted: 'All these letters [from Mendelssohn] are transcibed *literatim*' (1: 308).

29. Mendelssohn asked Klingemann in a letter from Leipzig on 21 July 1840 about the possibility of a benefit concert in London, noting that he was going to seek Chorley's opinion on the subject: 'Wär's nicht gut, wenn ich mich bei der Durchreise durch London wieder einmal mit meinen neuen Sachen öffentlich hören liesse, und könnte ich zu dem Zweck nicht ein Konzert für irgend eine wohltätige Anstalt geben? Oder ist die Zeit zu ungünstig, und die ganze Sache in England nicht angebracht? Wollten es die Birminghamer wieder nicht vor dem Fest leiden, so bliebe mir noch ein oder zwei Tage nachher Zeit, wenn Du überhaupt dazu rätst. Ich schreibe heut auch an Chorley, und will ihn darum fragen; auch an Mme. Moscheles ...' (Klingemann, 245).

30. D.V.: *Deo Volente* (God willing). In its issue of 26 September 1840, the *Athenæum* reported that Mendelssohn's 'Lobgesang' was the 'principal novelty' of the Birmingham Festival (757).

31. 'Reminiscenzen früherer glücklicher Stunden' (Moscheles, *Leben*, 1: 54).

32. 'Chorley und Klingemann kamen zu Tische ... Die beiden M. fantasiren nämlich zusammen über gegenseitige Themen und wenn ich sage, es war herrlich, schön, merkwürdig, so habe ich es doch nicht beschrieben; sieben Jahre lang hatte ich sie nicht zusammen spielen gehört, mein Eindruck war: es ist so schön, dass es der Mühe werth ist, sieben Jahre darauf zu warten' (Moscheles, *Leben*, 1: 54).

33. 'Beim Abschied zeichnet Mendelssohn noch mit der Feder ein ganzes Blatt voll Anspielungen auf die Erlebnisse der letzten Wochen in's Album der Frau, Chorley schreibt eine Erklärung in Knittelversen darunter, Moscheles einigen tiefbewegte Abschiedsworte' (Moscheles, *Leben*, 1: 58).

34. Moscheles, *Leben*, 1: 60. Schindler's *Life of Beethoven* (1841) was reviewed in the *Athenæum* on 13 February 1841: 123-5, and 20 February 1841: 150-52. In the issue of 13 February 1858, Chorley referred in passing to 'Herr Schindler's well-meant but stupid book' (215).

35. Schumann, *Tagebücher*, 3: 164.

36. 'Unter den Besuchen, die ich heute machte, war mir der bei Schumann's der interessanteste, weil mir die Frau eine Bach'sche

Fuge vorspielte' (Moscheles, *Leben*, 2: 64).

37. According to Hewlett, 'Her command of the instrument struck Chorley as "masterly", although "perhaps a little wanting in grace and delicacy"; but he was less favourably impressed with her husband's music' (1: 325).

38. 'Chorley war unwohl, musste im Hotel bleiben und Mendelssohn hatte die herrliche Idee (aus gutem Herzen entsprungen), ein Härtel'sches Clavier hinzuschicken, worauf wir ihm Schubert's Symphonie und meine grosse Sonate vorspielten. Nun ist Chorley besser und nach Berlin gereist' (Moscheles, *Leben*, 2: 66).

39. Chorley was sensitive to the contrast between Mendelssohn's warm hospitality and his own less expansive hospitality to Mendelssohn in England:

> I have been vexed half a hundred times, with thinking how little *I* could do for *you* when you were in England — owing to circumstances: but I think you understand my will to have been more active than my deeds — and I know few things that would give me greater pleasure than an opportunity of patching up the holes in my hospitality — You will give it us next year? ... Good bye & God bless you, & remember me very gratefully to Mme Mendelssohn, for all her kindness. Tell her how sorry I am always to seem so stupid & careless, when I am going away: — pray remember me very kindly, too, to the Davids. & believe me always Gratefully & faithfully yours, H.F.C. (Green Books, XII: 192)

40. Text as printed in Hewlett, 1: 327. There are minor textual variants between this and the version in the Green Books.

CHAPTER FIVE

The Forties: The Old Order and the Power of the Press

1 Music and Manners in France and Germany, 1841

Chorley and Henry Reeve liked life in Belgravia, a new, expensive, and fashionable part of town, but they were tired of their place at 9 Chapel Street, Grosvenor Place, and therefore in March 1841, hoping to find a more agreeable landlady, they moved a few blocks to the southeast, to No. 2 Wilton Street, near Eaton Square. As Reeve explained:

> Mrs. Smith's altercations with our servants were so frequent, and her presumption that we should remain *à tout prix* was so unpleasant, that we summoned up our strength last Monday, and in the course of a few hours hired a house — No. 2, Wilton Street, Grosvenor Place — for a twelvemonth, with option to renew the occupation. Rent, 180 guineas; which is what we pay now for part of a house. Furniture very good, handsome and abundant. Offices convenient. ... We are very well pleased to be on the sunny side of the street. ... [W]e have five bedrooms, one of which I shall convert, for the present, into a summer study. Our landlady, Mrs. Morris, is very liberal, and will do, or allow to be done, whatever we please; so that I may consider myself housed, I trust, for some time to come. (Laughton, 1: 144)

Chorley was busy writing during the move. In the new year 1841, he decided to write a book of travel impressions based on his autumn trips to the Continent. The initial idea of writing a book about music had been broached to Richard Bentley, publisher, as early as 1834:

> I am collecting some musical legends & traditions — & shall weave them up in various forms into as much matter as will fill about three volumes. If the book forthcoming have such success that you feel disposed to treat with me for them I shall be glad at your leisure to talk the matter over with you. I think I can make an interesting and singular series of papers from the materials I have

gathered. (MS, Wigan Archive Service)[1]

It was just as well that nothing came of this: by 1841 he knew far more about music than he had known in 1834,[2] and from his journals, his *Athenæum* reports, and memories of his autumn visits to the Continent Chorley constructed *Music and Manners in France and Germany*. He wrote to Mendelssohn about his new project on 31 January 1841. The letter shows his scruples about the delicate situation of becoming Mendelssohn's guest and personal friend, and then switching to the role of journalist, turning the private into the public — a 'nervous subject', as he termed it:

> I, too, have been very busy since the year came in: I dare hardly tell you in what occupation — perhaps Klingemann may have told you at all events, should any ... German friends chance to see what I shall give of *my impressions* — I hope they will find me clear of making a dishonorable & ungentlemanly use of the private intercourse with which I have been favoured. In all honesty — nothing could be further from ideas when beginning to keep a journal than the publication of all or any part of it. Enough of what is, to me, a nervous subject. —

Not surprisingly, several weeks later, after the book's publication, he wrote to Mendelssohn in June that he was exhausted:

> Though the date of your unanswered letter — the fifteenth of March — might seem to reproach me, — yet I make no apologies for not having replied to it earlier — because, without exaggeration, I do not think I have had one tranquil half hour since its arrival. For me, the season has been one of such work as I never knew before: I have been obliged to carry on a long piece of literary labour during the most occupied time; — to print as fast as I wrote & this with every distraction & engagement doubled, as it seemed. My mind, too, has been engaged to an unusual degree, with family affairs: in short, I have had as much to do, dear friend, as if I were a Doctor of Music, & the Director of the best instrumental Concerts in all Germany, to say nothing of composers!! (Green Books, XIII)

Dedicated to his brother, John Rutter Chorley, *Music and Manners* helped create for Chorley a European reputation as a discriminating critic and helped consolidate his influential position among English readers.[3] Chorley asserted that only one of the six journeys was taken specifically for the *Athenæum*, that is, 'with the slightest reference to Paternoster Row' (vi),[4] stating that the trips were 'strictly holiday ones' (vi).

He termed the trips 'rambles' (probably meant as an allusion to Edward Holmes's respected *Ramble Among the Musicians of Germany*, 1828).[5] The work indeed disclosed a rambling, discursive, whimsical sensibility ('That I retail this after dear Mrs. Nickleby's fashion is not the fault of Flibbertigibbet ...', 2: 64).[6] It portrayed a kind of fantasy image reached by a spiritual pilgrimage coexisting with, if not exactly parallel to, a whimsical stream-of-consciousness travelogue: the ideal goal of the musical travels was finally reached in Leipzig where a performance of Beethoven revealed the 'musical Germany of which I have so long dreamed' (3: 104). Musical France was revealed in its powerful Grand Opera — a great mixture of arts which, Chorley insisted, anticipated the future of European music drama.

The book's subtitle suggested its casual organization: — *A Series of Travelling Sketches of Art and Society*. Though it appeared in three volumes, the sketches were not designed to fit smoothly into a three volume format: rather, five 'travelling sketches' of France and of Germany straddled the three separate volumes:

Music and Manners in France

1. The Grand Opera of Paris (1: 3-205)

Music and Manners in Germany

2. The Brunswick Festival [1839] (1: 209-301)
3. Three Days in the Harz Country (2: 3-68)
4. Glimpses of Berlin (2: 71-249)

Music and Manners in France

5. Parisian Authorities (2: 253-302 and 3: 3-76)

Music and Manners in Germany

6. The Leipsic Fair (3: 79-127)
7. Two Visits to Dresden [1839 and 1840] (3: 131-82)
8. Notes on Nuremburg (3: 186-228)

Music and Manners in France

9. Parisian Contrasts (3: 231-90)

The informality of the *persona* freed the author not just to 'illustrate the present state of theatrical, orchestral, and chamber music abroad' (vii), but to comment on literature and painting as well, and to introduce paragraphs and whole sections which had nothing to do with music, nothing to do with literature or painting, and precious little to do with manners ('Three Days in the Harz Country', for example). The didactic, the whimsical, and the celebratory coexisted oddly, but comfortably.

Chorley wanted to convert the English to an appreciation of French Grand Opera, and wanted to celebrate the spirit of Mendelssohn working at Leipzig. Occasionally he was pleased to assume the role of Avenger, as when he reported on the poor playing of the overture to *Freischütz* at the

Berlin 'Schauspiel-haus' in 1839:

> I thought of Herr von Raumer's dictatorial demolition of
> our London music, and the sneers lavished by him in his
> English and Italian journals on all performances save Ber-
> lin performances — on all singers save Berlin singers, —
> drew my breath, and listened again. It was past doubt —
> the horns *were* lazy and false. Greater disappointment I
> have not often felt. (2: 85-6)

In fact, Chorley stated condescendingly, '[a]s regards classical opera in
Berlin, the age of lead has come on' (2: 141). Von Raumer was thus in no
position to complain about performance standards in London.

Chorley's first concern, in 'The Grand Opera of Paris', was to insist that
the French Grand Opera was unjustly neglected by the English. He complained that music-loving English visitors to Paris headed for the Théâtre
des Italiens, where they heard Grisi and Tamburini, just as they did at home
in London, 'but in a much smaller and shabbier *locale*' (1: 5). Meyerbeer
was the type of 'young France'; his operas needed to be *seen*, not just
heard — and seen in all the 'pride, pomp, and cricumstance [*sic*] which
belong to their representation' at L'Académie Royale (1: 45).

Thus, Chorley urged visitors from abroad to pay attention to the Opéra,
where one could be more impressed by the *mise en scène* than by the music
(1: 171-2). One could appreciate other great operas through their music
(*Tancredi*, *Barbiere*, *Fidelio*, *Euryanthe*, for example), but to understand
Grand Opera you had to *see* it, and you had to see it at the one theatre
capable of producing it: the Académie Royale. Only the Paris Opéra could
really put on *Robert*, *Guillaume Tell*, and, above all, the masterpiece of
Grand Opera (3: 167), *Les Huguenots*.[7]

The music at the Opéra was destined to be, in his view, the music of the
future. Chorley's hearing of *Les Huguenots* during his first visit to Paris
altered his perception of the potential of music drama. He assumed as part
of his professional obligation the task of enlightening the English public
about the direction which opera composition should take. The resources of
the French stage — action, singing, orchestra music, ballet, stagecraft —
combined in one overwhelming effect. And 'for effect, there is nothing
like' this opera (1: 192). Meyerbeer embodies new understanding of how to
present opera, for example, in his use of the chorus and concerted pieces:

> The manner in which the chorus is used throughout the
> full five acts of the musical tragedy distinguishes it from
> most operas I have ever studied. The plot of the drama is
> absolutely unfolded, not by recitatives and airs, but by the
> most elaborate concerted pieces. (1: 192)

Chorley summarized breathlessly (1: 192-204) how effective the situations in the opera were when seen staged, concluding that his recollection of *Les Huguenots* had the power of making it real, not remembered:

> I have found myself — every note of the music ringing in my ears as if I was listening to Falcon, Nourrit, and Levasseur — writing as of some real event which I had seen and heard, and not a mere dramatic presentment in a form which some still satirize as too absurdly conventional to be capable of producing the slightest deep emotion. It is too late after such a dream to come back with the lantern-light of small speculation to measure details, and examine peculiarities of structure. How far more gladly than describe such music, would I make Memory play it in the ears of my friend the reader! ... But it should be seen and heard in France; and I can hardly believe that the severest purist, the most earnest admirer of the serene tranquillities of the old school, could receive it, (and at least three hearings are necessary to its reception,) and not think a musical pilgrimage to Paris richly requited. (1: 204-5)

Chorley's critical fascination with the power of Meyerbeer's new kind of music drama and its effect on audiences affected his thinking and writing about the nature of opera for the rest of his career.

His focus next turned to the Brunswick festival of 1839. The main experience there was Mendelssohn's 'St. Paul', which the *Athenæum* had praised highly on the occasion of its English production in Liverpool (reviewed in the issue of 15 October 1836). The German performance caused Chorley to evaluate the work even more highly than before:

> Precisely at ten o'clock the performance began. I had heard the oratorio of 'St. Paul' two or three times before, but never so thoroughly enjoyed it. (1: 236)

Ten years ago in England he thought Spohr's 'Last Judgment' was fascinating, but it did not wear well. By contrast, Mendelssohn's work appeared to be a lasting masterpiece:

> How thrillingly expressed, by the multiplication of treble voices and wind instruments, is the celestial apparition in the scene of Saul's conversion! How ferociously real are the cries of the multitude at the stoning of St. Stephen! How melodious, in the sweet holiness of consolation, is the funeral chorus, "O happy and blest are they," when the proto-martyr is laid in his grave! (1: 239)

Then, serving as a transitional section, 'Three Days in the Hartz

Country' presented primarily a picturesque travelogue, without critical content. In the 'Glimpses of Berlin' Chorley announced that soprano Sophie Löwe, the idol of the Germans, was overrated. The operatic 'feud' between 'the Löwe' and 'the Fassman' was perceived as 'delicious' by scandal-loving Berliners (anticipating the tempest over the relative merits of Strumpf and Lederlung in the 'Pumpernickel' section of Thackeray's *Vanity Fair* a few years later). Still worse was Madame Grünbaum, though von Raumer praised her (2: 150). Chorley was struck by the disunity and factionalism of Berlin, the rampant 'spirit of intrigue and evil-speaking in Art' (2: 97). Not only were there 'general causes of disunion or egotism', but the Court had a bad influence. In short, '[e]very visit to the Berlin Opera left me more chilled and more disheartened than the last' (2: 142). The German repertory was a problem: Germans did not like their own operas, except those by Lortzing, which did not appeal to Chorley (2: 161).

He concluded the 'Glimpses of Berlin' with a report on the 'Huldigung' in 1840, where he eagerly anticipated Gluck's *Iphigénie en Tauride*. To value Gluck's operas highly was for Chorley a sign of a correct understanding of foundation of music drama, and so he was in 'a rhapsody of anticipation' (2: 239). But there was no life in the performance. Unlike the great Gluck performances still to come in the early 1860s back in London, these performances in Berlin's Schauspielhaus were ruined for him by unsuitable voices, that of Bader (Orestes) too old, that of von Fassmann (Iphigénie) out of tune. Chorley shared the audience's reaction to the performance: it was 'cold, and respectful, but unsympathising' (2: 244). The moral of this disappointment was that 'I made a covenant with myself never again to leave a certain pleasure for an uncertain opera eighteen hours off, though the name of Gluck, and the reputation of a metropolis at high festival-tide, conspired to beckon me' (2: 245). And so, back to Paris.

Prominent among the 'Parisian Authorities' whom Chorley discussed was the non-musical George Sand, Madame Dudevant, whom he saw at the theatre in 1837 (3: 5): she was impressive but somehow not entirely womanly, to an English sensibility. Still, Chorley saw extenuating circumstances: the falseness of French society and its recent horrifying political history:

> ... and shall we expect that, from a social chaos so wide,
> so deep, and so ancient, purity and beauty and order can
> spring, as by miracle, in the person of one who is no
> saint, but a self-willed and half-educated woman? ... At
> least, in the case of George Sand, — with the exception of
> a passage or two, such as the analysis of "Les Huguenots"
> I have translated,[8] where a vivid and penetrating spirit
> seizes what may have been the *arrière-pensée* of the composer, and sets it before us with a rare force and clear-

ness, — the whole of her poetical pages are given over to feelings rather than thoughts — to rhapsody rather than instruction — concerning Art. The balance and self-submission necessary for the thorough reception and firm hold of a subject so complex as Music, are wanting to her nature. (3: 21, 23)

She, like Berlioz, whom he met in 1840 (3: 25), was one of the modern iconoclastic 'enthusiasts', apt to be led astray from the path of true art. Berlioz, however, had already achieved some position for himself as critic and as musician:

The series of M. Berlioz' criticisms, if read carefully, would puzzle any poor student past cure. He hates particular rhythms, and particular movements, under particular moons. ... Gluck is set up as the only one prophet. ... Passages of sarcastic acumen, sharpened by personal feeling ... are oddly mixed up with citations from Shakspeare [*sic*], Oriental apostrophes, and epigrams which turn the thought entirely way from the primary object to the secondary influence. In short, M. Berlioz is a musician among the wits and rhapsodists, a wit and rhapsodist among the musicians. ... (3: 32)

Nevertheless, Berlioz never submitted to traditional instruction — he learned music 'in his own way' (3: 30). Thus, Berlioz's intellectual positions were reached in ways which seemed to Chorley odd and difficult to understand, even when he agreed with them. For example, Berlioz's 'Gluck idolatry' was in a sense shared by Chorley, but Berlioz's sound thinking in this respect was overshadowed, to Chorley's shocked disapproval, by his contempt for Handel, whom Chorley considered 'Gluck's nearest co-mate in music' (3: 32).

Chorley was much more favourably impressed with Franz Liszt. He quoted Liszt's obituary eulogy on Paganini from *La Gazette Musicale* which he termed 'of deeper import than I have found in any other *éloge*' (3: 36), partly because Liszt perceived that Paganini, though great, represented *egoism* in Art, being a 'selfish and vain character' (3: 42) rather than participating in the work of social transformation which is the artist's present calling. Liszt combined 'elevation of mind' and 'shrewdness of perception' (43), and was Chorley's favourite among the new musicians, though he too, because of his association with the 'Byron worshippers and the Hoffmann students', (3: 44) sometimes confounded the 'Beautiful' with the *bizarre* (3: 45). Alan Walker termed these pages 'a compelling account of Liszt's total command of the keyboard' (*Virtuoso,* 303).

Perhaps Chorley's receptivity to Liszt was influenced somewhat by the cordial personal relationship they had established through Henry Reeve in 1840. At any rate, he insisted that Liszt — though closely associated with the 'violent contrasts' of French romantic eccentricity — was a true musician:

> Many who have heard M. Liszt only once have been misled through the eye by the singularity of his appearance; and, prepared for what is unusual, on the strength of some sudden outbreak of Fantasy, have set him down at once and for ever as crazed. Because he brings a superabundance of fire and passion to the reading of works fiery and passionate, as the first movement of Weber's Concert Stück [which Chorley had heard him perform in London in May 1840], or Beethoven's Kreutzer Sonata, — illustrating their beauties (as Kean did Shakspeare's [*sic*]) with only too much force and vivacity, — they have forgotten the delicious calmness the artist could throw over music of a more tranquil character. Let me instance his playing of the *andante* of the same Sonata; or of Schubert's "Serenade" ... [or his] "Ave Maria." (*Music and Manners*, 3: 49-50)[9]

He conceded that the *Conservatoire* orchestra, of which the French were proud, was fine (a 'marvel of mechanical perfection', 3: 104). Nevertheless, 'my heart was not touched' (3: 70). Members of the audience 'were at heart cold' (3: 72) and, despite the 'rage' for Beethoven, did not really understand his music.[10]

Music and Manners then doubled back to Germany, for a description of the Fair at Leipzig. Chorley praised the subscription concerts as 'the most perfect expression of the musical spirit of Germany with which I have fallen in' (3: 99). The German orchestra at the 'Gewand-haus' played Beethoven's symphonies with complete musicality. The contrast with the mechanically brilliant Parisian *Conservatoire* orchestra was marked. Here finally Chorley found a land of music:

> As regarded those works of the Shakspeare of music, I felt, for the first time in my life, richly and thoroughly satisfied beyond reserve or question. ... Till, indeed, I heard the Leipsic orchestra, — my first love, the Brunswick Festival not forgotten, — I felt I had no right to say, "Now I am indeed in the musical Germany of which I have long dreamed." Had I not heard it, I should not have ventured to print the strictures upon that marvel of mechanical perfection, the orchestra of the Conservatoire. (3: 103-4)

He praised the violinist David, and Mendelssohn, but suggested that he must hold back what he could say about their achievements because he knew the men personally, and to discuss them personally violated his own sense of decorum:

> I could say more of Herr David's leading, as a thing in
> my experience entirely unique. I could dwell, too, upon
> the pleasant life he leads in his garden-house (the *beau-*
> *ideal* of a German musician's residence), spent in a con-
> stant interchange of good offices, musical and social, with
> his townsmen and strangers. ... But when a friend is in
> the case, self-restraint in the amount of praise should keep
> pace with fastidiousness of judgment. (3: 96-8)

His reticence about using personal revelations was even greater with Mendelssohn than with David:

> In his case, too, I feel that shrinking which makes it
> impossible, when with those one likes best and esteems
> the most highly, in good set phrase to rehearse their gifts
> and graces. (3: 98)

He could, however, at least speak freely of Mendelssohn's 'simplicity of heart' and 'integrity of purpose' (3: 98) and he agreed with those who said '[t]he boy came into the world upon a lucky day'.

In passing he recalled his visit to Robert Schumann and his reservations about Schumann's music (3: 126).

In 'Two Visits to Dresden' Chorley related how, during his visit in 1839, he 'first made acquaintance' with Weber's *Euryanthe* (3: 137), with Schröder Devrient in the title role.

> She was acting with all the old power and pathos that
> earned for her in England the title of "The Queen of
> Tears," and singing the terribly difficult music of the part
> with a force and freshness I found it totally impossible to
> account for, save on the hypothesis that some miracle had
> created her voice anew since she was last in London. (3:
> 140)

But it was in fact a tuning of the pitch somewhat lower than London's, and not a miracle, which accounted for the 'restored juvenility' of Schröder Devrient's voice (3: 141).[11] Tichatsheck's voice was the best voice in Germany for Adolar, though its future condition was in doubt since it was abused. In Chorley's view, Weber's talent was naturally adapted to plays like 'Winter's Tale', 'Cymbeline', and 'The Tempest' because he was 'the king of the mountain and faëry school' (3: 154), and was suited to 'romantic fantasy' (3: 154).[12]

In the second visit to Dresden (1840) Chorley was deeply stirred by the organ-playing of Herr Schneider on the Silbermann organ in the Sophien-Kirche. The church was empty except for Schneider and Chorley. After playing Bach's E-minor fugue, Schneider concluded his private recital by improvising — and 'the depth of his science was surpassed by the brilliancy of his fancy' (3: 172). Schneider's organ playing at the Lutheran church was as beautiful as the sound of an ageing castrato in the choir of the Dresden's Catholic church was repugnant: 'parcel squeak, parcel warble'. It 'had well nigh driven me back with disgust at its shrillness and its falsity'. The sound had 'that subtle union of piercing and oily tone which distinguishes an oboe' (3: 180).

In Nuremberg next, Chorley wandered the streets and ruminated, moved especially in St Sebald's cathedral by the organ chorale ('Ein Feste Burg') ('But what were all Meyerbeer's effects ... compared with the grandeur of this?', 3: 225).

In the final section, back in Paris, Chorley brought his book to a close by 'desultorily stringing together a few more of the contrasts and varieties of life and opinion' which he had set out to record. He noticed with pleasure a boy in the street picking out on his guitar 'Fleuve du Tage' (3: 248).[13] He contrasted his reactions to Versailles with those of 'Michael Angelo Titmarsh' (Thackeray) in the *Paris Sketch Book*.[14] He concluded his ruminations with praise for the French working people, even 'operatives of the very lowest class', and their potential for good influence on the nobility — witness Wilhem's singing classes for working men, and Hullah's adaptation of the techniques in England (3: 280). This kind of development, Chorley hoped, might lead to moral progress for the French nation, and the art of the workers might improve the character of the aristocracy.

> ... whereas the old Italians came to Art through Religion,
> the young French may come to Religion through Art; and
> the people humanise the nobility, in recompence for the
> corruption which the nobility formerly introduced and
> perpetuated among the people. (3: 290)

On 26 June 1841, the *Athenæum* printed a long two-part notice of the new book — *Music and Manners in France and Germany* (six and one half columns, pages 485-7, followed two weeks later by six more columns). It consisted almost entirely of quotations with only the slightest editorial comment, reminding readers that the book was from the hand of the author whose 'pleasant account of the Brunswick Festival, and letters from North Germany' had already been published by the *Athenæum*:

> Under these circumstances, that we may steer clear of all
> possible influences, we shall leave the writer to make his
> own way with the public; and if we are not very much

mistaken, he can say far more in his own favour than the
kindest critic could do. (26 June 1841: 485)

This was followed on 10 July 1841 (518-20) by more lengthy quotations,
largely about Meyerbeer and opera in Paris — including Chorley's dictum
that in order properly to 'relish' Rossini's *Tell*, 'it should be heard in Paris'
(520). The author of this elaborate scissors-and-paste notice made no
evaluation: 'We now leave the work to the judgment of the musical public
and general readers' (520).

Music and Manners was modestly successful, and added to Chorley's
reputation as a writer on music capable of discussing it within wider
cultural context of literature and art. It made a favourable impression on
Elizabeth Barrett, who referred to it more than once in her letters as rein-
forcing her belief that Chorley was a writer of great talent,[15] and on
Mendelssohn.[16]

In that same summer, 1841, Liszt was back in London after two
extensive tours through the British Isles.[17] The favourable impression made
on Chorley the previous summer in London was even more intense. Liszt's
personality fascinated Chorley, as he reported to Mendelssohn in a letter of
June 6:

> *Apropos* of Liszt: the long conversation we one day had
> about him has been again & again recalled to me. — Last
> year I was struck dumb by the playing: this year I am
> almost fascinated by the man: whose winning qualities
> have been strangely *brought out* (as the painters say) this
> season. When one considers his young life, & the
> miserably heated & feverish atmosphere he has breathed,
> when he was scarcely a boy — it is surely wonderful that
> there is so much to engage love & sympathy. — If it did
> not sound like a piece of desperate John Bullism, — I
> would say that I think *England has done him good*! I can-
> not believe that he will end his career where he is now,
> either in Art or in moral principle! (MS, Green Books,
> XIV, Bodleian Library)

After the season of 1841, once again Chorley set out on a continental
voyage. This time he was accompanied by Henry Reeve, with whom he
shared his London residence. He reported on his musical doings from time
to time in 'foreign correspondence' to the *Athenæum* (unlike his routine
work, anonymous week in and week out, these special reports were signed
'H.F.C.'). The first report was about an impressively staged Belgian 'La
Favorite', (2 September 1841: 733), then — with a few words on other arts
('To criticize painting and sculpture I have little pretension' [9 October
1841: 779]) — reported on a production of Marschner's uninteresting *Der*

Vampyr at Munich:

> Elaborately clever as is the composition, nay delightful in
> parts to the instructed ear, from its amount of contrivance,
> and reply, and orchestral contrast, and most carefully as it
> was performed by the best theatrical orchestra I have
> heard in Germany under Herr Kapellmeister Lachner's
> guidance, the heaviness and wearisomeness of the whole
> became almost intolerable; and as one massive concerted
> piece and unvocal *scene* after another "dragged its slow
> length along"[18] before an audience attentive, but cold, I
> was half tempted, in a moment of unjust and heretical
> forgetfulness, to think _____ right, who in the plenitude
> of whimsical paradox, declares Strauss to be the one only
> [*sic*] composer of modern Germany! (9 October 1841:
> 779)

In his report in the *Athenæum* the following week, he mentioned a singer
whose career he viewed with favour, Mrs Shaw, whom the Italians considered '*simpatica*', and Miss Novello, 'whose success, I hear, was great at
Padua' (23 October 1841: 811). He mentioned, too, composers whose
names 'have reached us in England', viz., Nicolai, Mazzucato, and Peri
(but no mention of Verdi). At La Scala the chief singers were Finklohr
('whom we rejected some years ago as unworthy to fill the post
provisionally assigned to her before Easter'), Brambilla (who 'sings and
acts far better' in Italy than in London), Guasco ('one of the many possible
successors to Rubini's throne'), and Varese ('more than respectable; but
feebler, and not so hopeful because not so young') (23 October 1841: 811),
with a praiseworthy chorus and orchestra: 'In short, I have received in La
Scala, that general impression of stability and resource, which is a *sine qua
non* with so far-famed an establishment, — a thing never to be found in our
opera at home' (23 October 1841: 812). Nevertheless, La Scala had no
worthy new works to perform: Mercadante's unmelodic *La Vestale*
(Spontini's was better), and *Catherine of Cleves* by 'the young *maestro*
Savj', which 'could hardly have lived to a second night, but for the fine
singing of Brambilla and Guasco' (812). Even Donizetti's *Regina de Gol-
conda* sounded fresh compared to these two operas. The Italians, unlike the
Germans, had ears only for their own country's music (812).

Privately, in a letter to Mendelssohn, Chorley outlined his detailed
itinerary:

> This year I had a charming journey: from Brussels to
> Treves, Frankfort (where I met Liszt & Miss Kemble)
> Heidelberg — Stuttgart, Munich — thence by the
> Tegernsee & the Achensee to Innspruck [*sic*] — Verona —

> Venice Milan — over the Splugen — Loire — Zurich —
> Strasburg &c. &c. down the Rhine home.

The party at Frankfurt and Mainz included Fanny Kemble, her sister Adelaide, 'our London friend Chorley, and the illustrious Liszt' (Kemble, 2: 122). Liszt and Adelaide Kemble gave performances together. The period must have been enchanting for the entire party. Fanny Kemble remembered it many years later:

> The time we spent on the Rhine during this summer afforded me an opportunity of almost intimate acquaintance with the celebrated musician who had persuaded my sister to associate herself with him in the concerts he gave at the principal places on the Rhine where we stopped.
>
> Our whole expedition partook more of the character of a party of pleasure than a business speculation; and though Liszt's and my sister's musical performances were professional exhibitions of the highest order, the relations of our whole party were those of the friendliest and merriest tourists and *compagnons de voyage.* Nothing could exceed the charm of our delightful travelling through that lovely scenery, and sojourning in those pleasant picturesque antique towns, where the fine concerts of our two artists enchanted us even more from personal sympathy, than the most enthusiastic audiences who thronged to hear them.[19]

Back in London, Fanny Kemble remained friendly with Chorley. (When Mendelssohn visited London in 1843 she remarked that she 'went to a party at our friend Chorley's, where dear Mendelssohn was, and where I heard some wonderful music, and read part of "Much Ado about Nothing" to them', *Records of Later Life*, 2: 291) and she later paid him a rather strained compliment: 'Mr. H. F. Chorley I believe to be a great friend of mine, and an uncommonly honest man, but I may be mistaken in both points' (Kemble, 3: 166). He was, at any rate, a friend of her artistry, and several times mentioned favourably in the *Athenæum* the readings she presented in her later life.[20] Reporting on the autumn 'English' season of 1841, Chorley hailed the debut of her sister, Adelaide Kemble, in *Norma* as an 'entire triumph' (6 November 1841: 860). The opera, moreover, 'is splendidly produced, the orchestra plays under M. Benedict's direction, as we never before heard orchestra play in an English theatre' (860).

As has been mentioned, the return from the Continent in the late autumn of 1841 also marked Chorley's return to solitary living, since his eligible bachelor house mate married Hope Richardson on 28 December (Laughton,

Reeve, 1: 173). Chorley moved yet again, sometime in late November or December 1841 — this time from Wilton Street to nearby No. 15 Victoria Square, Lower Grosvenor Place,[21] where he continued his active social life. It was this house which Elizabeth Browning termed 'enchanted', relying on a description given to her by their mutual friend John Kenyon (*Brownings' Correspondence*, 7: 110), and here Chorley remained until his final move to the little house in Eaton Square, ten years later.

The enchanted little house was a jewel case which set off not only his parties, but also, by contrast, his tendency towards solitary melancholy and brooding. Hewlett quoted from Chorley's journal a passage noteworthy for its focus on Chorley's inability to form relationships of lasting 'sympathy' with the very musicians and artists whose company he so eagerly sought:

> One gives out so much more sympathy to them than to those of any other class; one gets back so much less. They are not things for long leases! ... If one *could*, how much the best would it be to live totally alone! I think I have had to uncoil my tendrils so often, that I shall come to this before very long — to the smooth face which tells nothing, and the smooth heart which feels little! (Hewlett, 2: 29)[22]

Hewlett asserted that this passage was related to a vaguely described romantic disappointment caused by the marriage of an unnamed woman, believing that Chorley's feelings in 1841 were depressed 'consequent on the unexpected marriage of a distinguished *artiste* of his acquaintance, whose fascinations had tempted him to indulge in dreams which that event dispelled' (Hewlett, 2: 29).

There is, however, nothing extant, including the passage from Chorley's autobiography just quoted, which specifically indicates that Chorley had a romantic interest towards any woman. In this passage, the image of 'uncoiling my tendrils' appears to refer to emotional involvements with people, men and women, of the artist 'class' rather than to an unrequited love relationship with some particular woman. Possibly there was more specific evidence for a romantic attachment in the long sections of the manuscript 'Autobiography' not used by Hewlett. If so it would be interesting, but surprising.

Hewlett's account of Chorley's second romantic failure, in 1844, was also so delicately phrased that no certain conclusions can be drawn from it as to the depth of Chorley's emotional and/or erotic attachment, or disappointment:

> In 1844 occurred a second misadventure in love, more serious than the first — the rejection of what I believe was the only offer of marriage he ever made. As the lady is

> probably still living, nothing can here be added to the bare
> mention of the fact. Suffice it that, though the disappoint-
> ment was a very severe one, his subsequent relations with
> the author of it were frank and unembittered. (Hewlett,
> 2: 81)[23]

Whether or not Chorley wanted a wife, he certainly wanted human sympathy, and he complained bitterly about not having it. In an undated letter[24] to the publisher Richard Bentley, he wrote:

> There can be no objection to Miss E. knowing who had
> done his best for her: & I am truly glad that she is
> gratified. So *very little* encouragement comes to me from
> any side ...

Chorley took a 'peculiar and almost romantic interest' in Benson Rathbone, the namesake and nephew of his first real friend who died early. To this Rathbone's mother — wife of his friend's brother — he wrote on 27 March 1842, hoping 'to try and make him feel towards me as I did towards his namesake' (Hewlett, 2: 307). Chorley stated frankly that he was searching for an object of affection: 'I ... am endeavouring to cast about for occupation of some of one's best feelings among a younger generation, as I cannot bear the thoughts of the lonely egotism of middle age and the still more unlovely years which may succeed it, if the issues of life are not jealously watched' (2: 308).

Young Benson was allowed to visit Chorley, and relations between nephew and 'uncle' were cordial. A few years later, after a visit in April 1847 Chorley again wrote to Benson's mother: 'The sight of *your* Benson has made me so very wakeful, that I must relieve my mind ere I sleep, by telling you that it has given me a pleasure such as I fancied was past and gone for ever. I could have laughed and cried, after the first start, when Joseph brought in his name; for I have not seen him since he was a baby, and was not prepared for such a reminder of a face, and a blithe voice, and *ways* (though I don't know which), that I never forget for two days together'. Chorley wanted to have the pleasure of being 'to my own true friend's nephew and namesake what he was to me' (2: 308-9).

The physical reminder of the first Benson had been nearly overwhelming for Chorley: 'It seems to me as if not till this afternoon I knew how earnestly I must have loved and how closely treasured every remembrance of my one true friend' (2: 310). He saw himself as 'an uncle *extra*' to the 'new' Benson — 'be it for bed and board' or just companionship (2: 310).

Meanwhile, with the publication of his new novel, *Pomfret; or, Public Opinion and Private Judgment*, Chorley attempted to improve on the fortunes of *Conti* and *The Lion*. Henry Colburn published the three volumes in 1845 (Hewlett incorrectly stated that it was in two volumes, 2: 20). The new novel was neither better nor more successful than the previous ones. In *Pomfret* he created a secondary narrator, Paul Gray, fifty-six years old and growing deaf. Robert Browning wrote to Chorley that the *'framing round'* was 'charming' (Hewlett, 2: 26), but to most others it did not appear so. As a commenting narrator-observer of the story, Paul Gray's blandness contrasts with the emotional volatility of the romantic male, Walter Carew, who is romantically drawn first to Grace Pomfret, the narrator's niece and wholesome daughter of an English clergyman, and then to Helena Porzheim, the foreign opera singer (3: 43).[25]

At the novel's beginning, Walter Carew is engaged to marry Grace, but must wait until she reaches the age of twenty-two. Until then, Walter will travel and correspond with her. After various misunderstandings and plot twists, Walter Carew's affections shift to the gifted German singer, Helena Porzheim. She returns his affections. The self-abnegating Grace releases Walter to marry Helena. Relying on her private judgement while defying public opinion about a good match, she stays with her father:

> When remonstrated with on the score of destroying her own prospects ... — "Dear father," she would say, "... Let me keep with you, and comfort you; let us comfort each other against the world, and find some duties to perform. ... Let them say what they please about us. ..." (3: 306-7)

With bland Mr Gray as its 'author', the novel lurches amiably along, using multiple levels of narration: the religious scruples of Grace Pomfret's father form one narration — at the end of volume two he resigns from the clergy. The suitor's vacillation between two main love interests forms another narration, as Walter's long letters become the narrative-within-a-narrative. Letters are interwoven with comments on letters, with observation, reported conversation, and direct narration. These characteristics may account for Hewlett's belief that the novel's 'plan is as clumsy and incoherent as possible' (Hewlett, 2: 21).

The narrator attempts to create strands of internal structural cohesion: for example, the fathers of both heroines, the sweet Grace and the musical Helena, withdraw from their religions: Grace's father, Mr Pomfret, resists social pressures to remain a Christian clergyman; Helena's father, Mr Porzheim, follows social pressures to distance himself from Judaism. His family, however, is still Jewish, and therefore disadvantaged, in the eyes of Public Opinion. Allusions to Jews and the negative social consequences of being Jewish are numerous (though less so than in his final novel, *A Prodigy: A Tale of Music* [1866]): 'All the musicians are Jews' (3: 14).

Walter Carew, writing to Grace of his growing obsession with Helena refers to the scorn for Jews which, he realizes, informs most Public Opinion: 'She is Catholic — no Jewess, at least, as some one was saying' (2: 128). She is 'no Jewess' because her father 'was a Bonn Professor ... a good, dry, eminently tedious man ... [who] *had been* a Jew. The very words *had been* tell all — the abiding depth of the contempt and suspicion under which persons of his ancient faith labour' (2: 132-3).[26] That is, the daughter of a man who 'had been' Jewish but felt compelled by Public Opinion to change his religion, has a daughter who is 'no Jewess'. Walter Carew records, but does not share, the view of a German he met who praised a man in the following terms: 'a good man, a great artist (*Kunstler*): but pity it is that he is a Jew' (2: 134). The Professor's wife has high social hopes for her elder daughter, Diana, but the young German students believed, as Walter the letter-writer explains, that she was not their equal,

> ... merely because she had Israelitish blood in her veins. Miserable prejudice! — and among such brawlers for free-dom too, as the students of a German University! And Madame Porzheim knew this; she felt it with an aching disdain words cannot describe. ... Shrewd as the mother was in estimating her own position, she was wilful in mis-conceiving that of her child. A Professor's daughter, she thought, might marry any one. — She forgot the Jew's grand-daughter. (2: 136-7)[27]

At the novel's end, Paul Gray assures his readers that the hero will marry the singer, Helena. Do his readers wonder about other loose ends? The narrator begs off — 'Mine is no novel, I beg to remind them: but a few extracts from real journals, and a few pages of real family history' (3: 325). The ending's evasiveness is inept, but after the various levels of layered stories, letters, and long narrations leading nowhere it is unlikely that there were many readers left to notice.

2 Talent, Native and Otherwise

In the early 1840s Chorley was perceived as generally less friendly to native talent than the circle of critics around J.W. Davison. Davison's son commented:

> In the "Court Gazette," the "Musical Examiner" and the "Musical World," the claims of English musicians were advocated, at this time in a way which provoked opposition. Sterndale Bennett, Macfarren, Henry Smart, Mudie and Loder were the names to which the "native

> talent" force rallied. Jullien, Thalberg, and Costa were
> the more notable of the assailed foreigners. ... [Opposing
> the native talent school] were writers who supported one
> or more of the foreign musicians just named and who
> regarded the "native talent" cry as the claim for notice, of
> a small clique of English composers, a little mutual
> admiration society anxious for place and pelf. (Davison,
> 48)

Chorley was prominent among those who were not enthusiastic about the 'mutual admiration society'. Although his support for English musicians who met what he saw as European standards was as high as anyone's, he found fewer English artists meeting these standards than did the enthusiastic adherents of the native talent school. His private comments to Mendelssohn about the performer Adelaide Kemble and the composer Sterndale Bennett are revealing:

> ... though [Kemble's] voice is not nearly as good as some
> of the sisterhoods' [*sic*] — & she is a little fatter (to tell
> the homely truth) than a tragedy Queen ought to be — she
> is still *unique* in my knowledge of English artists. — Her
> success has thrown the native talent of England into fits
> ... as if they were ashamed of having, at last, a very great
> artist because she will not sing in operas that have no
> sense & meaning. But I think my dear countrymen grow
> more unaccountable every day and more & more mistake
> praise of themselves and abuse of every one else, for
> those principles of energetic action & study — that cost
> more self denial: but without which, there is no school —
> no Art! — Even Bennett, I think, *must* suffer at last from
> the extravagant praise which is heaped upon him by his
> *clique apropos* of any one else who is praised. I verily
> think, that if Beethoven could come back & write a new
> Symphony — it would be proved to be not half so good as
> Bennett's! — These things, sometimes vex me so much by
> their shallow folly [as?] to make me tempted to give up
> the matter in despair. (13 November 1841, Green Books,
> XIV, 202)

In Chorley's printed accounts of Kemble's singing, his emphasis was positive. He linked her performance at Covent Garden in December 1842 to the issue of 'native talent':

> During the career of twelve months on the English stage,
> ... Miss Kemble has habituated our play-goers, not merely
> to admit and enjoy the expression of passion in music (for

before her appearance, with the solitary exception of 'Artaxerxes,' no recitative opera had ever succeeded on the English stage), but to require of the artist impassioned action as well as musical feeling. Judged even by the standard of Pasta, Malibran, Schroeder, Grisi, Miss Kemble must maintain her own high place, whether as a singer or as an actress; but measured against her English predecessors she stands alone and supreme; as the one union of high dramatic and musical power which the annals of our stage record. (*Athenæum*, 24 December 1842: 1115)

Also in 1842, Macready sponsored a celebrated revival of Handel's *Acis and Galatea* at Drury Lane. Chorley was impressed, but not convinced that the revival was as significant for English opera as many were claiming. He began his notice

The first performance of Mr. Stanfield's 'Acis and Galatea' to the text of Gay and Shelley, and to music adapted from Handel's *Serenata*, and concocted by *Anonymous*, cannot be passed over briefly, whether as regards its brilliant success, or the influences on the progress of art which it is calculated to exercise. (12 February 1842: 149)

The production indeed was 'as a spectacle without peer in our English experiences' (12 February 1842: 149). The importance given to the scenery, however, offended Chorley, who complained that the focus should be on Handel. He complained about 'additional accompaniments' (e.g. addition of trombones to the overture), 'the substitution of a *contralto* for a tenor voice', and the interpolation of a scene with words from Shelley and 'the music by *Anonymous*' (149).

Chorley had more to say about this production the next week, using as a pretext his notice of a score of *Acis* published by D'Almaine & Company. He had only a few perfunctory words to say about the score ('we gladly embrace so seasonable an opportunity of returning to the work, the performance of which we noticed last week'), because he wanted to re-emphasize his disappointment with the production: the revival of the work should not be greeted as a major step in revitalizing English music theatre.

But we are told, that this revival of 'Acis' is intended to assist in the reformation of English opera: and the latter, it is generally admitted, has been partly kept in its present wretched condition by the absurdity of the subjects selected for musical illustration, or the undramatic manner in which they have been arranged. If this be true, what

> will be the amount of assistance derived from the course
> pursued by the Drury Lane management? In our opinion,
> the *galvanising* of concert-music, and the conversion of
> the scene-painter [Clarkson Stanfield] into the dramatist,
> are measures calculated to injure and to retard, rather than
> to strengthen and forward a cause, the real bearings of
> which are so essentially misunderstood by its noisiest
> advocates. (*Athenæum*, 19 February 1842: 172).

Chorley devoted three columns to Macfarren's *King Charles the Second* (*Athenæum*, 3 November 1849: 1112-13), produced at the Princess' Theatre, Oxford Street, under Maddox's management. He praised the music as 'masterly throughout' (1113), but took a dim view of the libretto by Ryan. Quoting passages to illustrate its 'trashiness', he deemed it 'rubbish'.[28] In his summary of the year's significant musical events, Chorley wrote that there had been 'no native appearance of any importance', then excepted ('perhaps') the production of this opera (as well as Catherine Hayes's great success in Ireland) (29 December 1849: 1340).

The native talent controversy continued to simmer, but by the late 1840s it was for the time being no longer in its 'active time', according to Henry Davison's retrospective:

> Under the auspices of Bunn, librettist and manager of
> Drury Lane Theatre, Wallace's "Maritana" was produced
> in November, 1845, and, a few months later, Macfarren's
> "Don Quixote" followed by Lavenu's "Loretta" and
> Balfe's "Bondman," while, towards the end of 1846,
> Loder's "Night Dancers" was produced at the Princess'.
> Still, on the whole, so far as English music was con-
> cerned, 1846 did not brilliantly compare with 1836. The
> effort which, in the earlier period seemed to have united a
> band of talented young men to assert for England her right
> to a place among modern musical nations, may be said to
> have already died out. The Society of British Musicians
> had lost its distinctive characters; its orchestral concerts of
> music by living British composers had dwindled into con-
> certs of the chamber music of composers of various
> nationalities and ages. The more conspicuous of the
> "native talent" band do not seem to have entertained any
> very affectionate respect for each other's genius.
> (Davison, 67-8)

For Chorley, the possibility that native British creative talent might take its place beside Rossini and Mendelssohn arose years later with the sudden appearance of Arthur Sullivan, a young composer with seemingly limitless potential to show the rest of Europe that great music could come from Britain.

When Benjamin Lumley took on the management of Her Majesty's Theatre in 1842, he intended to assert strong supervision over his performers. Soon, battle lines were drawn between him and stars of the 'old guard': Grisi, Mario, and Persiani. They were joined by the dissatisfied conductor Costa and supported by dissatisfied journalists, among whom Chorley was prominent. Lumley's first seasons glittered: extraordinarily popular brilliant ballets followed the operas, singers new to London were introduced (Ronconi, Frezzolini, Guasco, Favanti), and operas new to London, though Lumley grumbled that 'anti-Donizetti feeling [was] strong in England (the bigoted lovers of the old school having just then no one else to abuse, in default of the Verdi, who was yet to come)' (Lumley, 64).

Although Lumley remembered the season of 1842 as calm, turmoil was sensed by at least some observers. Fanny Kemble, keeping a watchful eye on the career of her sister, Adelaide, wrote to a friend on 6 May 1842:

> There has been a grand row at the Italian Opera-House, among the managers, singers and singeresses. Mario (Mons. Di Candia; I suppose you know who I mean) has, it seems, for some reason or other been *discharged*. Madame Grisi, who sympathizes with him, refuses to uplift her voice, that being the case; the new singeress, Frezzolini, does not please at all; and the new singer, Rouconi [i.e. Ronconi], isn't allowed by his wife to sing with any woman but herself, and she is a perfect *dose* to the poor audience. Lumley, the solicitor, manager of these he and she divinities, declares that if they don't behave better he'll shut the theatre at the end of the week. In the mean time, underhand proposals have been made to Adelaide to stop the gap, and sing for a few nights for them — a sort of proposal which does not suit her, which she has scornfully rejected, and departed with her tail over her shoulder, leaving the behind scenes of Her Majesty's Theatre with their tails between their legs. ... (Kemble, 2: 218)

Kemble was perhaps enjoying unreliable gossip: Mario was not fired and Grisi did not return for the summer of 1842 because in June she gave birth to a daughter (her second child, the first with Mario as father).

In the years immediately following the publication of *Music and Manners in France and Germany* Chorley frequently stressed two concerns. In the first place he insisted vehemently on the need for England's audiences to understand that the genius of opera had shifted to Paris — the Opéra. In the second place he proclaimed that the new Italian school of singing was deteriorating, in large part due to the vocal style considered appropriate by the composers following Rossini. Both these concerns were expressed without reference to Verdi, but they lay the groundwork for the intensity of Chorley's antipathy to Verdi's operas as Lumley began to produce them at Her Majesty's. The new Italian composers, he wrote, 'run a fair risk of destroying a school of singers', and to the success of a composer like Bellini could be attributed, as Fétis pointed out, the unpleasant and 'peculiar manner to which Mercadante and the younger school of his countrymen have addicted themselves' (1 January 1842: 15). On 19 March 1842, Chorley reported that Donizetti's *Gemma di Vergy* was not badly performed, but the music was 'its composer's feeblest, and the story, as one of the most improbable and sickly, which ever came out of the brain of enervated *libretto*-monger' (19 March 1842: 260).[29]

Generally Chorley did not mention his fellow journalists, but he made one of his infrequent exceptions for J.W. Davison, critic for *The Times* and other periodicals. Some of Davison's music had been published, and in some of his songs Chorley praised Davison's sensitivity to the text. Davison 'deserves to take his place among our classical song-writers in virtue of his setting of Keats's *In a drear-knighted December*' (1 April 1842: 300).

At Covent Garden, Miss Kemble in *Sonnambula* 'has never appeared to greater advantage' (9 April 1842: 323), while at Her Majesty's Theatre, the cast for *Lucia* showed the new spirit:

> The appearance of Ronconi in Tamburini's part, the substitution of Guasco for Rubini, amount to a first and serious inroad into that phalanx of consummate artists, whom other Italian singers, unable to find a place in London or Paris, have, with the satire of spite, called "*la vieille garde.*" (16 April 1842: 348)

But these were not bad singers. Ronconi was 'one of the manliest and least meretricious singers' today, although he did use 'the tremulous tone of the present mode (Paganini's solitary and worthless legacy to Art)' (348). Two weeks later, Frezzolini in Bellini's 'feeble' *Beatrice di Tenda* was criticized for her faults. 'How far some of them may be the inevitable consequence of the change of style which is passing over Italian opera music, we may possibly consider on some future day' (30 April 1842: 288). He continued the subject the next week:

> Whether, in any event, the new singers and the newest music of Italy could make themselves acceptable to the English public has been a matter concerning which we

> have always entertained grave doubts. It is clear, that,
> now, they have not even a chance. (7 May 1842: 411)

Ronconi was received more favourably than he deserved in *Torquato Tasso* ('the feeblest of Donnizetti's [*sic*] operas'), and Frezzolini, though possessing a beautiful voice, was misusing it: 'she chooses to consider it powerful, according to the acceptation of the word in modern Italy, and, therefore, strains it on all passages of emphasis, in a manner which gives pain rather than conveys passion ...' (14 May 1842: 435). The art of Italian dramatic singing 'in short, has gone down; and if we minutely notice *the how* of its decadence, it is for the warning of future managers, musicians, and librettists' (435).[30] Towards the end of the Italian season, Chorley warned that the new Italian music 'cannot, for all its dramatic capabilities, be allowed to take root in England' (9 July 1842: 612).

Against this background of dissatisfaction with the Italians, Chorley returned from time to time to his theme of the English neglect of French opera. A visiting German company at Covent Garden, giving some French opera in German translation, prompted him to rebuke the 'resolute determination [of English audiences] ... to *ignore* the claims and merits of French opera' (21 May 1842: 460). The Germans, of course, could not do justice to the demands of the works: 'Let no one, however enraptured he be with the *German Opera* performances of Monday evening, imagine that he has heard 'Les Huguenots' of Meyerbeer ... [which is] one of the most remarkable works of modern times' (25 June 1842: 572).

Lumley remembered 1843 as a 'glorious season' — 'the cabals of *la vieille garde* were in abeyance' (Lumley, 78). The ballet was about to enter its 'palmy days', and people 'today' (i.e. 1864) could hardly comprehend how important the '*danseuses*' were then (Lumley, 83). But for Chorley, '[t]he Opera-houses had come to an absolute dependance [*sic*] on Donizetti for novelties — the star of Signor Verdi not yet having risen on this side of the Alps' and therefore, not surprisingly, he found the season 'dry and unsatisfactory' (*Thirty Years'*, 1: 221). Still, the orchestra (thanks to Costa, for whom Chorley's admiration increased each season) 'had been worked up, by this time, into great beauty and European renown; and the chorus had, by the same able conductor, been made respectable, if not (as now) attractive' (*Thirty Years'*, 1: 229).

In 1844 Chorley fretted that the first night of Costa's *Don Carlos* was so 'poorly attended', and stated that he would defer reporting on the music till he heard it again, 'since one characteristic of all Signor Costa's compositions ... is high and minute finish' which can't be apprehended on one hearing (22 June 1844: 581).

His main example of the modern decline of singing was Favanti (the stage name for Miss Edwards), whom he pilloried at every opportunity, for example, her part in the first performance of Ricci's *Corrado d'Altamura*, a 'curiosity' rather than an 'attraction':

> That she was indignantly hissed by the stalls and the boxes, in spite of the attempts of pit and gallery to support her, is a fact we are obliged to record, as completing our justification for having declared the lady unfit for the position into which she was thrust. Great as was the ill-will stirred by our plain speaking, the real injury done to the *artiste* was by false friends and hollow praises, as the humiliation to which she was subjected on Saturday must now, we apprehend, have proved to her, though alas, too late! (17 August 1844: 757)

It was rumoured that Lumley had re-engaged her, a situation which Chorley believed supported his accusations of degraded standards.

In the 1840s some of the new faces in London were also old faces — faces of Chorley's mother and sister, who moved from Liverpool to London in 1845, settling in with Chorley's brother John in Chester Square. They were within reasonable walking distance of Victoria Square, where Chorley had been living alone since the marriage of Reeve in 1841. Of Mrs Chorley, Fanny Kemble spoke approvingly: she was 'the meekest and gentlest of human beings'.[31] Chorley often spoke of his sister with what Hewlett termed 'a suffusion of chivalric tenderness' (1: 219). About the time of her move to London, her health took a turn for the worse — she had some kind of problem with her spine — and from 1851 till her death in 1863 was 'a hopeless cripple' (Hewlett, 2: 82), though she continued social intercourse. Elizabeth Gaskell, for one, saw her and told Chorley in 1854: 'I *love* Miss Chorley' (Pollard, 278).

Other familiar faces belonged to musicians. Chorley stayed in touch with Mendelssohn. He was concerned about the impending change in Mendelssohn's career — the move from Leipzig to Berlin — and wrote on 6 June 1841:

> I love the scene of your late labours so much [Leipzig], that I hardly know how to reconcile it with my wish for you of the widest possible arena [Berlin] — And I think one hour of my kind friends at Leipsic & how sadly they will miss you: — and another, what pride & pleasure your family at Berlin will take in having you among them — an honoured & influential resident. — So that the King's invitation is like every other earthly prospect — a two-handled thing. For myself, I am very ambitious for my friends — & I am very willing you should lead a quiet life when you are twenty years older: — but it gives me extreme pleasure, I confess, to think of you wielding the

resources of a great metropolis, for the excellent & worthy purposes to which your life is devoted. How glad I am, that I am not called upon to decide for you: — being so nicely balanced in judgement, that I can sympathise with you, whether you choose the great or the little town. Your English friends are waiting for your decision with great anxiety. ... (Green Books, XIII, 256)

Later Chorley had harsh things to say in the *Athenæum* about Mendelssohn's relation with the court of Berlin: The King of Prussia was 'visionary'. 'His wisdom, however, fell short of his aim, because his personality and vanity were stronger than his wisdom' (19 September 1863: 360). With the King's strong support,

Translated Greek tragedies were to be revived and performed after the manner of the ancients, with choral and orchestral music by a modern writer. ... [But *Antigone* and *Œdipus*] remain so much dead matter, — at best representing a pleasure of which only the few and the gravely scholastic can partake in all its fullness. (360)[32]

A notice of the publication of Mendelssohn's 'Dix sept Variations Serieuses' appeared in the issue of 19 January 1842. This publication occasioned more praise for Mendelssohn who has a 'disdain of meretricious expression' (116). Chorley considered Mendelssohn's music grounded in the past (Bach and Handel) and at the same time originating the latest styles: 'The accompanied melody, which is the mainspring of all Thalberg's effects, though used at an earlier period by Weber, is, if we mistake not, first seen in its modern and attractive form, in some of Mendelssohn's works' (29 January 1842: 116).

Another characteristic is, that whereas Chopin's music seems peculiarly acceptable to the feminine sympathies, from the languor of its harmonies, and the delicacy of its forms, Mendelssohn's greater works are only to be grappled with by men. (*Athenæum*, 29 January 1842: 116)

This characteristic was caused by their 'physical solidity of touch', their 'total freedom from all the coquetries in which "the sex" delight', and the 'singularly fatiguing' hand positions they require (116). Privately, Chorley expressed his great interest in having more music from Mendelssohn in London:

We are now beginning to ask for *your* Second Trio! — Because, though it is all very well that you should write Greek Choruses for Kings to listen to — we are not the better for them! How much I should have like to have had

> a card to His Majesty's private theatricals that evening! —
> In spite of what you say about Berlin (turning most mali-
> ciously my weapons against myself) I cannot but believe
> that you are to do great things there — and I cannot but
> sympathise with the heart-felt pleasure it must give your
> family to have you among them (13 November 1841,
> Green Books, XIV, 202).

In 1844 Chorley welcomed Mendelssohn's *Lieder ohne Worte* (*Athenæum*,
11 May 1844: 435). Mendelssohn was guest conductor of the Philharmonic
that year. His conducting brought discipline to the musicians and evoked
from them earnest, committed playing, in Chorley's view, and, as Myles
Birket Foster put it, 'Nothing could be more harmonious than Mendelssohn's intercourse with the Directors' (*History of the Philharmonic*,
182). The programme included several vocal selections, as was customary,
sung by Castellan and Staudigl, Beethoven's *Leonore* Overture No. 1 (its
first performance in England, according to Foster, 185), Mendelssohn's A
minor symphony [No. 3] 'better performed and better relished than on any
previous occasion', Spohr's overture to 'Der Berggeist' and W.S. Bennett's
C minor *Concerto* (with Bennett as soloist).

> The engagement of Dr. Mendelssohn Bartholdy may be
> considered, we hope, as the commencement of a new era.
> It amounts, virtually, to a reconstruction of the laws of
> the Philharmonic Society — or rather, perhaps, an
> acknowledgment of weakness and insufficiency as must
> lead to reconstruction. (*Athenæum*, 18 May 1844: 461)

In two weeks, the orchestra is again commended for improvement ('We
shall soon be able to lay the finger on particular instruments, whose slovenliness was unperceived, in the days when all were slovenly', 1 June 1844:
506). Beethoven's violin concerto, with the boy Joachim, was enthusiastically received: 'Very few performers have come before us so satisfactory,
and for the future so brightly promising as this boy' (1 June 1844: 507), as
was Mendelssohn's 'Midsummer Night's Dream' music ('That no one can
write *scherzoso* music like our guest, all the world knows', 507).

The next week Chorley reported on a chamber concert given on 1 June
1844, 'planned by' Moscheles and Ernst. For decades he remembered the
playing of Thalberg, Moscheles, and Mendelssohn in Bach's Triple Concerto. It was Mendelssohn's playing in particular that struck him:

> This will be talked of as long as the far-famed Sontag and
> Malibran duett [*sic*], in the Philharmonic Concert-room.
> Which of the three players was the best we do not attempt
> to say; but we must have a word concerning the perform-
> ance of Dr. Mendelssohn, as the least familiar to London

> ears. When we hear him, we neither consider *tone*, nor
> any executive predilection, such as makes us listen for
> _____'s left hand, or _____'s shake, or _____'s chords.
> We are so subject to his musician-like command of the
> composition (not the instrument), so carried away by his
> animation and enthusiasm, never running wild for a
> chance bar or cadence — that details fall into their right
> places, namely, as subordinate to great interpretations of
> great thoughts. (8 June 1844: 533)

He called that performance to mind again twenty-three years later, in 1867, when the triple concerto was performed by a new generation: Clara Schumann, Arabella Goddard, and Charles Hallé (6 April 1867: 460).

The next Philharmonic concert in 1844 brought repeated complaints about the petty politics that interfered, but repeated praise, too, for its progress:

> An essay (not a note) might be written on the magnificent
> C minor symphony of Beethoven, as it was given on
> Monday. ... No one can be deaf to the progress the
> orchestra has made in subordination to the master mind of
> a great musician. This was again proved in the repetition
> of Dr. Mendelssohn's own Shakspeare [*sic*] music, which
> went with great spirit and precision. The other instrumen-
> tal pieces were Mr. W.S. Bennett's graceful and pic-
> turesque overture, 'Les Naiades,' and a very grim and
> interminable overture by Schubert, to 'Fierebras.' (15
> June 1844: 556)

On repeated hearing (especially during the 1860s at the Crystal Palace in Sydenham), Chorley came to find much of Schubert's music less grim and interminable.

Mendelssohn's conducting was painfully recalled to mind eleven years later when Richard Wagner was hired to conduct the Philharmonic, after Costa's quarrel with the management. In 1846, however, Chorley's worry focused on Costa himself. Chorley was alarmed that Costa might be appointed the conductor of the Philharmonic Society, and, when he was, Chorley criticized the appointment. Though Costa was perfect for opera, Chorley had no confidence that he was the right man to conduct the orchestral repertory. But after the first performance, he recanted. This was truly the 'commencement of a new era', as Chorley had remarked about Mendelssohn's conducting:

> Without unnecessary words of exaggeration, it may be
> stated as past question that the first Philharmonic Concert
> established Signor Costa in the foremost rank of con-

> ductors of classical music, and justified the directors in
> their choice. As we somewhat mistrusted the discretion of
> his appointment, it behoves us emphatically to say that we
> have heard no Philharmonic performance to compare with
> Monday's (March 16) (*Athenæum*, quoted in Hewlett, 1:
> 300)

Given Chorley's reputation for not changing his mind and for assuming an 'I told you so' position, this about-face is remarkable and almost unparalleled. Though some found Costa vindictive,[33] Chorley and Costa never had a falling out, and from that time on, Chorley's appreciation for Costa's conducting — symphony, opera, or oratorio — and his support for Costa's career never wavered.

Chorley was receptive, perhaps suprisingly so, to new music by Chopin in the 1840s, whose 'individual' style he noticed positively at the time of the publication of the 'Tarantella', the forty-sixth work of Wessel & Co.'s edition of Chopin. Though the piece at hand was dismissed as 'not one of its composer's happiest efforts' (1 January 1842: 19), it occasioned an extended analysis of Chopin's 'individuality', focusing on his 'fragility and delicacy'. One of Chopin's weaknesses was that, with some exceptions, he 'seems incapable of continuous effort'. Chorley commented on Chopin's 'peculiar harmonics'. These, 'at first acquaintance, so crude and ungracious in perusal',

> are things that must be felt, but which it is hard to des-
> cribe. At first, his constant use of the passing note in
> chords and combinations, will importune the ear, almost
> as an annoyance. ... By degrees, however, the listener
> will find, that constant uncertainty (to venture a seeming
> paradox) produces very nearly as much unity and com-
> pleteness of effect as a general certainty. (1 January 1842:
> 18)

These odd harmonies, a kind of clothing allowing at times 'old thoughts to pass muster as new ones' (18), were discussed as generally positive.[34]

At the end of the year he returned to the troubling 'odd harmonies'. Writing of the 'third ballad' ('New Publications', 24 December 1842) he observed:

> Chopin has hardly ever carried further his peculiar system
> of harmony than in this ballad; and the tenth and three
> subsequent pages will tax severely the faith and the
> patience of his admirers. Nothing but the nicest possible
> execution can reconcile the ear to the crudeness of some
> of the modulations. These, we presume, are too essen-
> tially part and parcel of the man, ever to be changed; but

> it is their recurrence, as much as the torture to which he
> exposes the poor eight fingers, which will hinder him
> from ever taking a place among the composers who are at
> once great and popular. (1115)

Chorley met Chopin in Paris (Hewlett 2: 95), and also when Chopin visited London in 1848. The publication of two of Chopin's waltzes (D flat major and C sharp minor) showed Chopin's real romance, according to Chorley, and the qualities of 'artistical significance and consistency, as well as an exquisite charm for particular listeners when in a particular mood' (6 May 1848: 467).

3 Chorley, Lumley, and Verdi

Although as early as 7 March 1840 Chorley had mentioned Verdi in passing (*Athenæum*: 194), the first substantial notice the *Athenæum* took of him came in August, 1844, six months before an opera by Verdi reached Her Majesty's Theatre. In it Chorley analysed Verdi's early operas — even though he had not seen them performed. He began by noting that Verdi was newsworthy:

> Recent occurrences and appearances having called the
> attention of our English public to the modern style, or
> rather no-style, of Italian singing, it may be as well for
> the critic to see what is doing in the world of Italian vocal
> composition; and, since the name of Giuseppe Verdi has
> begun to circulate widely as the *maestro* most likely to
> become popular, we avail ourselves of such opportunities
> as perusal of his compositions here published affords us,
> to offer a word or two concerning his operas. (*Athenæum*,
> 31 August 1844: 797)

Chorley then undertook two tasks, the first an analysis of what he considered the basis of all Italian opera, the second an analysis of how that basic principle applied to Verdi's works.

In general the basis for opera was melodrama — and all currently active composers seemed unable to understand that principle: Hector Berlioz, Richard Wagner, and 'Bellini's successors' (Donizetti and Verdi). Chorley sarcastically predicted that we may someday see without regret 'the Opera reduced to the shapeless recitative from whence it arose' (31 August 1844: 797).

After some transitional (and incorrect) biographical information ('It is not many years since Sig. Verdi was in this country'), Chorley moved to specifics about Verdi's music. Having examined several selections of

Verdi's music recently published in England, Chorley lamented that there was no melody, and that the works' 'varieties of forms' showed even less 'original fancy' than those of Pacini, Mercadante, or 'Donnizetti'.

Chorley's claim that Verdi's first operas had no original melodies remained basic to his criticism of Verdi for many years to come. Julian Budden's observation is here relevant: 'The idiom of the time was as narrowly defined as at any period in the eighteenth century, so that to a casual ear all composers seem to be quoting from each other'. Therefore 'Chorley accused Verdi of lacking originality and proceeded to ascribe to Donizetti what he thought to be Donizetti's, and likewise to Federico Ricci, Bellini, and Mercadante'.[35] Despite Verdi's poor melodic gift, Chorley found the concerted pieces were 'a shade worthier and more individual' than the other parts of Verdi's operas. Reluctant to seem approving, Chorley quickly pointed out that the striking effects had all been anticipated in Rossini's operas, and sniffed:

> We must note, too, that the progression of keys, in one movement, with a view to entireness in construction (a point till lately thought worthy of attention), is most curiously managed; unless some of the remarkable sequences are ascribable to transpositions on the part of the English publisher. Sig. Verdi shall have the full benefit of the doubt. (31 August 1844: 797)

Despite the reservations, the expressions of antagonism were somewhat tentative; the door of Chorley's mind remained perhaps half-open for Verdi. He granted Verdi a share of grudging admiration: 'There is a certain aspiration in his works which deserves recognition, and may lead him to produce compositions which will command respect' (31 August 1844: 797).

The first performance of an opera by Verdi in London took place in March 1845. Her Majesty's Theatre presented *Ernani* — about a year after the opera's premiere at La Fenice in Venice (9 March 1844) and little more than six months after Chorley's review of Verdi's scores in the *Athenæum*. Expectations for the season of 1845 were generally high, *The Times* commenting that 'Moriani and Fornasari are to appear before Easter, and as Easter falls early this year, the brilliant portion of the season will be of longer duration than usual' (17 February 1845: 5). Chorley began his notice by remarking enthusiastically that 'we do not remember so interesting a commencement of an opera season as that of this day week, when a new work by a new composer was executed by new singers; — and music, *maestro*, and vocalists alike stood the difficult test'. He added, 'By its length, which extends to four acts, its subject, and the treatment, it would seem as if the Italians are looking to the Grand Opera of Paris for their model in serious musical drama' (15 March 1845: 275). For Chorley, of course, the Grand Opera in Paris was the right model to emulate.

He brought from the performance the concerns similar to those caused by his reviewing some of Verdi's published scores six months earlier: Verdi's lack of originality, his ability to construct interesting 'concerted' music, and his disturbing treatment of voices. Verdi's 'free use' of other composers' music was noted, but there was some attempt at originality, too — 'a disposition to study new effects in the concerted music. ... Signor Verdi's choruses are spirited: they move'. Nevertheless, in his writing for voices, Verdi's 'uncouthness of interval' is 'ruinous'. 'The soprano part is perpetually above the stave. ... To make matters worse, the orchestra is for the most part at full strength — very frequently fortissimo, leaving the poor *prima donna* no choice, save scream or pantomime'. Composers no longer have the 'slightest right to complain of the short-lived date of the voices of the present generation' because it is 'their own ruthless ignorance' of how to write gratefully for the voice which is causing the decline in the level singing. Under the circumstances, the quality of singing by Angiolina Bosio (Elvira), Moriani (Ernani), Fornasari (Don Ruy Gomez), and Botelli (Don Carlos) ranged from adequate to good (15 March 1845: 275-6).[36]

Looking back on these 1845 London performances of *Ernani* in *Thirty Years' Musical Recollections*, Chorley focused on his later fixed antipathy towards Verdi, rather than his initial mild scepticism: the opera

> was received with curiosity rather than sympathy. To myself, it gave hopes which have not been justified by its writer's subsequent operas, more popular though they have been. His style, for a moment, struck the ear by a certain rude force and grandeur. How vulgar these have seemed to us, owing to reiteration, will be presently dwelt on. (1: 256-7)

By way of contrast, the reaction of *The Times* to this season's *Ernani* was representative of those who found Verdi somewhat intriguing: Verdi's work (to judge by melody alone) 'is not yet equal to the better works of Donizetti. There is in him, however, something of character ... that gives promise of better things. Lumley has done well to introduce him'.

In October 1845, the *Athenæum* printed 'Foreign Correspondence' from Trent, which stated:

> One word more: the new opera of Verdi's is to be 'Il finto Stanislao' — what I heard of 'I Lombardi,' I liked, according to its order. But more, perhaps of the Man of the Hour, in another letter. (4 October 1845: 969)

And from Milan, the same month:

> So far as regards public favour, the ball is at Signor Verdi's foot. How must Rossini laugh sardonically at

> seeing Bellini and Donnizetti [*sic*] rapidly taking their places on the shelf, whence he himself is beginning to be removed *as a classic*, for the sake of this noisy new comer! ... — Signor Verdi being the most desperate tearer and taxer of his singers who has yet appeared. I think the characteristics of his music are easily mastered; amounting to a certain largeness of outline and *brio* in his slow concerted music, — a picturesque feeling for instrumentation, and a curious absence of fresh melody. Almost all his *cabaletti* proceed by the starts and stops and syncopations, which Pacini introduced so happily, and wore threadbare: since the device ... quickly becomes predictable. ... (21 October 1845: 1034-5)

Judiciously, Chorley noted that Verdi's writing 'bespeaks a certain ambition' and that Meyerbeer, too, is 'originally unmelodious' (1035). But the balance tipped against Verdi:

> It seems to me that unless Signor Verdi presently exhibits a few more varieties than the perpetual strain after an exaggerated climax, which is the main idea of all his concerted music, and the formal piquancy of his airs, — his reign will hardly last longer than ... but I have bound myself over against prophecy. (25 October 1845: 1035)

Later in the autumn, Chorley briefly called his readers' attention to a new opera to be performed at Dresden, 'a new musical drama' by Richard Wagner: 'Der Tannenhaüser' [*sic*] (1 November 1845: 1059). As there was at first with Verdi, there is some tentative positive interest, reported in 'Musical and Dramatic Gossip' the next week:

> Mr. Wagner's opera of the 'Tannenhaüser', mentioned last week, was given, it seems at Dresden, on the 21st ultimo, with the most brilliant success. The composer was called for at the close of each act, and treated, on his arriving at home, with a torch-procession and a serenade. To avoid falling into the misleading tone of the foreign journals on such occasions, let us remind the reader that the tests of a musical success are permanence and circulation. (8 November 1845: 1085)

But it was another ten years before Chorley began to realize the threat which Wagner was to present to the music's future. For now Wagner was nobody, but Verdi was a real threat to standards.

After the summer season of 1845, Lumley, like Chorley, went to the Continent. One of his purposes was to negotiate with Verdi about the possibility of his writing an opera for London. Although London's reaction to *Ernani* did not prove that Verdi would be a draw, Lumley was apparently confident that the next opera by Verdi would be a greater curiosity than the previous one (the success *Nabucco* was then enjoying in Paris augured well for its London chances).[37] Some of Verdi's business dealings with Lumley at this time are preserved in the *Copialettere*, edited by Gaetano Cesari and Alessandro Luzio. We know that Verdi's irritation with his publisher Giovanni Ricordi had reached a crisis, and Verdi signed a contract on 16 October 1845, binding himself to write two operas for Ricordi's rival, Francesco Lucca.[38]

Emanuele Muzio was Verdi's pupil, companion, secretary, and idolater: from him (especially his letters to Antonio Barezzi) we learn a good deal about Verdi's negotiations. On 27 October 1845, Muzio wrote to Barezzi about the amusing foreigner who had arrived in Milan while Verdi was out of town:

> As soon as Lumley heard about the outcome of *Nabucco* he came from London along with Escudier [the French publisher], to sign up the Signor Maestro for next spring. Not finding him in Milan, they went to Clusone, where he was [visiting Countess Maffei]; but as they were on their way there, he was coming back, so they keep running after him till they find him. They thought he was in Busseto, and wanted to go there directly. It is very likely they will sign him up for London, with a third more than the fee he would receive in Italy, plus lodging, because there two little rooms cost twenty francs a day. (Garibaldi, 227; translation from William Weaver, *Verdi*, 164-5)

When Lumley and Verdi got together at last, the negotiations seem to have gone smoothly; at any rate we have Muzio's excited report to Barezzi two days later (29 October 1845) that the engagement was agreed on ('Il signor Maestro è proprio scritturato per Londra, ieri mattina'). Verdi was to write an opera a year for ten years ('volevano che si obbligasse per 10 anni!!! e dare un'opera per anno!', Garibaldi, 232).[39]

Meanwhile, back in London, in its issue of 11 October 1845, the *Illustrated London News* reported to the English on the sensational soprano Jenny Lind, saying that she would be making her English debut sooner or later at Drury Lane under the management of Alfred Bunn. It added that 'most liberal offers have also been tendered to her by Mr. Lumley's agents for Her Majesty's Theatre' (233). Although Lind had in fact contracted with Bunn to appear at Drury Lane in English language performances of Meyerbeer's *Feldlager von Schlesien*, she changed her mind and decided not to come to England for the season of 1846. On 18 October 1845, she wrote to Bunn asking to be released from her contract.

Bunn's reply was to threaten legal action against her.[40] For the season of 1846 there was to be no Verdi opera written especially for London, and no appearance of Lind either under Bunn's management at Drury Lane or under Lumley's at Her Majesty's. Jenny Lind was the singer of the day; Verdi was becoming the composer of the day. The groundwork for a complicated Lumley-Lind-Verdi-Mendelssohn-Chorley connection was being laid.

In 1846 Chorley's attitude toward Verdi's music changed from intermittent open-mindedness to complete hostility, and the success, even the continued existence, of Her Majesty's Theatre under Lumley was threatened by the establishment of a rival Italian opera company at Covent Garden comprising many members of Lumley's own company. The leading defectors were Persiani and her composer husband, and Grisi and Mario.

On 17 January 1846, Chorley considered Verdi's newly published *Sei Romanzi*. Headed 'The Verdi Mania', the review took the position that Verdi was all bad. 'We are led to pay more attention to this newest of Italian *maestri* than his merits demand, from the circumstance that, bad or good, his Operas contain certain elements of popularity. ... How long Signor Verdi's reputation will last, seems to us very questionable'. This became Chorley's characteristic approach (taken in the 1860s for Schumann and Wagner, too) — to warn repeatedly that Time will soon obliterate the false artists. Already some listeners note that Verdi's rhythmic tricks in *Nabucco* have been 'found out', and that 'little or nothing remains: little science — no melody' (17 January 1846: 73).

Fuel to the fire was the new conductor at Her Majesty's: Chorley's much admired Costa was replaced by Michael Balfe. Both Costa and Balfe sent strongly-worded letters to the press (*Athenæum*, 31 January 1846). This action occasioned a list of grievances against Lumley's administration enumerated by Chorley: 'We will thankfully concede that the Opera orchestra and chorus are better now than ever before. In all other respects, however, the Opera has deteriorated year by year since it came under Mr. Lumley's control' (31 January 1846: 128).

From the grievances, Chorley was moved to support the establishment of a rival opera house: 'Our contemporaries now tell us that Covent Garden is forthwith to be arranged as a second Italian Opera House. ... [W]e cannot but consider such a project as hopeful, and an inevitable result from the course pursued at Her Majesty's Theatre' (31 January 1846: 129). *The Times* countered a few days later: 'It appears, on inquiry, that the scheme of opening Covent Garden Theatre as an Italian Opera-house, far from being established, is a mere matter of conjecture' (*The Times*, Friday, 6 February 1846: 4). Throughout the season of 1846, Chorley harped on the poor artistic standards of the opera house, and fifteen years later, in *Thirty*

Years' Musical Recollections, he recalled:

> It would serve no good turn ... to recall the green room
> tales and their contradictions, which agitated those who
> are concerned in such matters. — It is enough to have
> lived for a while in the cauldron of Scandal, without stir-
> ring its waters afresh. (2: 4)

It was Chorley's contention that most other journalists during the late 1840s belonged to Lumley's 'army of trumpeters in the Press who play in any key the manager pleases' (*Athenæum*, 17 June 1846: 665). Chorley was joined by Gruneisen, writing anti-Lumley pieces in the *Morning Chronicle*, but he believed that too many journalists whitewashed or ignored problems of management: 'There was no record of failure. ... The so-called power of journalism had never a greater rebuke than in the downfall of Her Majesty's Theatre — day by day described as unparagoned in the splendour of its performances, and as enjoying a well-deserved prosperity!' (*Thirty Years'*, 1: 279).

The reception of Lumley's season of 1846 in the popular press seemed to bear out many of Chorley's claims that the press was on Lumley's side. Regularly in *The Times* and elsewhere there are formulaic phrases about the brilliance of the house ('crowded to excess with rank and fashion', followed by the names of some of the more prominent members of the audience, especially titled ones). When Lumley brought out two more operas by Verdi, *Nabucco* and *I Lombardi*, the press received them favourably, for the most part. *The Times* praised the 3 March opening night of *Nabucco* (presented as *Nino* 'in conformity with the feelings of the English as to the unsuitability of Biblical subjects for theatrical representation'), noting that 'the work was received with a stronger feeling of approbation than has been displayed on the production of any new Italian opera for a long time' (*The Times*, 4 March 1846: 5). The scenery and production values were the best ever at this theatre; the appearance of the house was both 'gorgeous' and in 'good taste'. For *Nino* a 'run' is 'confidently predicted' (4 March 1846: 5). The *Illustrated London News* found it 'characterized by merits of the highest order' (7 March 1846: 162). *Nino* was praised even more fervently in the next issue: a 'splendid chorus' here, a 'glorious burst of harmony' there, 'charming melody' everywhere, and a 'splendid crescendo' which was 'grandly effective'. The unison in 'Va Pensiero' gave the piece a 'wild simplicity of character' that was especially appealing (14 March 1846: 175). The critic (presumably George Hogarth) liked *I Lombardi* better each time he saw it, especially the 'concerted pieces' (*Illustrated London News*, 23 May 1846: 341). The critic for *The Times* (presumably J.W. Davison) affirmed that 'the success is unquestionable' (13 May 1846: 5)

Chorley attacked with sustained severity. Of *Nino* he wrote: 'But with every sympathy in favour of a new style, and a new master, our first hearing of the "Nino" has done nothing to change our judgment of the limited nature of Signor Verdi's resources' (*Athenæum*, 7 March 1846: 250). Verdi's occasional effective passages were ruined because there was not enough contrast: everything was too noisy (just as Rossini had been in the 1820s and earlier to the ears of such listeners as Mount Edgcumbe, but this was not a parallel that Chorley drew). Later in the season, *I Lombardi* was even worse: 'more tawdry in instrumentation than either "Ernani" or "Nabucco" and less substantial in idea'. Grisi was uncomfortable in the role of Giselda because 'happily for the world, she was not trained in the unmitigated screaming in which Young Italy delighteth' (16 May 1846: 507).

Chorley's opposition to Lumley's management extended beyond issues relating to Verdi. Lumley's proceedings 'up to this point, entitle the season of 1846 to be called the most meagre in interest of any during the last twelve years' (25 April 1846: 434). A little later, after a performance of *Barbiere*, he noted the consequences of Costa's departure: 'The orchestra is now more frequently before or after the singers, than with them' (2 May 1846: 459). And after major last-minute cast substitutions: 'Those who have watched the courageous downward progress of the management of our Italian Opera, assuredly *should*, by this time, be almost beyond the reach of further surprise' (27 May 1846: 530).

Lumley perceived his relations with the press to be generally good (Lumley, 72), but believed that those who opposed him were motivated by personal spite. He was angered by 'press critics, who desire exclusive privileges, and when refused dip their pens in the bitterest gall' (128). It was his relations with his singers that he focused on: the problems had begun under his predecessor, Laporte, and inevitably got worse because Lumley wouldn't capitulate. The singers whom Lumley termed the *vieille garde*, or the cabal, or the 'clique', were power-mad (Lumley, 9, 14, 134, *et passim*). This clique had temporarily triumphed in 1840 when Laporte replaced Tamburini with Filippo Coletti and members of the audience under the sway of the cabal responded with the 'Tamburini riots', prompting the re-engagement of Tamburini. To substantiate his claim, Lumley asserted that when Grisi — at the centre of the clique — was absent from the company in 1842, Tamburini was replaced without scandal by Ronconi (Lumley, 35).

During the 1846 season the only members of the old guard singing at Her Majesty's were Grisi (with Mario as a relatively new member of the old guard) and Lablache, and Lablache was in no way rebellious. Lumley saw himself, nevertheless, as sinned against by the power-mad singers.

Two people close to the turbulence left accounts decades after the events which in some ways overlapped. Willert Beale, a manager himself, noted that Lumley quarrelled with Giuseppe Persiani, more noted as husband than as composer, because he did not want to produce Persiani's opera: 'To that quarrel, and to a reserved, autocratic bearing towards his artists, may be traced all the rivalry against which Mr Lumley had subsequently to contend' (Beale, 1: 43). In the recollection of C.L. Gruneisen, Lumley

> to this day [i.e. 1869] according to his book, dwells on a monomania that he was ruined by a cabal. His error was in supposing that ballet was in the ascendant over opera, and to uphold the former, he sacrificed the latter.[41] The Tamburini and Persiani secessions were only the prelude to the projected dismissals of Grisi and Mario; the schism with Costa was another fatal miscalculation. ... Mr. Lumley's downfall was chiefly owing to his infatuated belief in the power of the press. He conceived newspaper journalism to be omnipotent. Hence his neglect of the stage and his attention to the newspaper people before the curtain. ... Mr. Lumley relied on the press, and was ruined by the press. Had he acted solely on his own unquestionable abilities, and had he not listened to those advisers, now dead and gone, whose basis of action was in turn corruption and intimidation of journalists, he might at this moment [1869] have been still the ruler of the Haymarket Opera House. (Gruneisen, 5)

In this heated climate, Lumley had several plans for a successful season: the possible return of Rubini, a possible ballet on the subject of Faust to be written by Heinrich Heine, and a new opera by Verdi, *King Lear* (Lumley, 142-3).

The *Athenæum* printed a letter from Lumley complaining about Costa in the issue of 7 February 1846. In the same issue, Chorley announced that 'the opera to be written by Signor Verdi for Her Majesty's Theatre is said to be on the story of "King Lear"'. Chorley was sceptical: 'As it is an opera *to be* written, let us point out to all concerned, the risk of selecting a story in which the female interest is subservient' (7 February 1846: 157). On 2 May 1846, the *Athenæum* announced that it had wind of bad news for Lumley: 'It is generally rumoured that the opera "written expressly for London" is not to be expected this year' (459).

Lumley was to be disappointed in all his hopes: Heine's ballet, Rubini's return, Verdi's opera — each was cancelled or postponed. 'As evil fortune would have it', Lumley recollected in his *Reminiscences*, 'about this time Verdi's health gave way; he was unequal to the arduous task, and the opera was not forthcoming' (142-3). In fact, in January 1846, while Verdi was in Venice preparing for the first performances of *Attila*, he did become ill

(Cesari and Luzio, 16). It was not unusual for Verdi to have various symptoms of illness while he was preparing a new opera; his illness the previous years had delayed the production of *Alzira* at San Carlo in Naples (Cesari and Luzio, 9-12). This time the recuperation period dragged on longer than ever before. Some wondered whether the long convalescence was partly a psychological necessity: he was not really ready to write the opera for London and needed a pretext, though Frank Walker disputed this possibility as 'impertinent' (147). Whatever caused the illness and the prolonged recovery, an opera for London was out of the question. From Milan, Verdi wrote to Lumley on 9 April 1846, with the bad news:

> Signor Lumley,
>
> I know that the news I am about to give you will not be unexpected, namely that because of the illness suffered in Venice, I am not able to come to London, and still less to write the opera there. This same day Signor Lucca will send you two medical certificates given him, which will authenticate things. You cannot imagine how distressed I am to have to renounce the honour of writing for London. My health is improving so slowly that it makes me incapable of even the slightest occupation, and I am forced to remain here idle, scrupulously following a medical cure until it is time to go to Recoaro to drink the waters, etc. … I hope that this inconvenience will not cause any harm to our relationship, and praying you to respond with two lines about the matter, I style myself with all respect yours faithfully. (Cesari and Luzio, 20-21; trans. of first paragraph from Weaver, *Verdi*, 165-6)

Lucca forwarded this letter to Lumley in London, enclosing a medical certificate from Dr Giacinto Namìas of Venice (22 March 1846) and another from Dr Gaspare Belcredi of Milan (6 April 1846) (Cesari and Luzio, 19). From Lumley came two letters — sympathizing, but urging Verdi to reconsider. In the first (14 April), Lumley hoped that Verdi would still come, for the change of scene and the brilliance of the London season would do him good.[42] A month later, he wrote again with news of the great popularity of *I Lombardi*, proposing a non-medical cure: the enthusiastic English applause awaiting him.[43] David Kimbell noted that Lumley's first letter displays 'effusive and insensitive breeziness' (*Verdi in the Age of Italian Romanticism*, 193), but it could just as easily be said to display the dignified but understandable desperation of a manager about to lose one of the main novelties of a season in trouble. For Lumley, Verdi's illness could not have come at a worse time. Verdi himself, though, insisted that the trip was off, writing on 22 May that 'the natural curiosity to see an extraordinary city like London, my self-esteem, and my self-interest would be sufficient motives not to delay the execution of my contract with Signor Lucca. But my health prevents me, and I have a need for absolute repose' (Cesari and Luzio, 22).

Muzio, too, was disappointed that the London trip was off. Lucca had offered to pay his expenses as a travelling companion and 2000 francs. But, as he wrote to Barezzi on 14 May 1846, if Verdi could not go, so be it: rather than have Verdi suffer — to the devil 'with all the money in the world, because to me he is dearer than the whole universe!' (Garibaldi, 245).

Lumley, during his post-season visit to the Continent, pursued Jenny Lind in earnest, knowing that she was determined not to honour her contract with Bunn at Drury Lane.

Chorley, too, was interested in meeting Lind, and naturally went through Mendelssohn to do so, writing him from the 'Hotel d'Angleterre. Frankfort' on 18 September 1846:

> Do for once, my dear Mendelssohn, *'if you cannot be decent, be as decent as you can'*! Here I arrive last night, the 17th — no *Lind* — no *you*: — no line for *me*. But I hear she is coming here next week — so I shall go to Stuttgart on Sunday: & return here on Saturday, the 27th *expressly to hear the Lady*. — Now won't you give me a line to her (that is, if you think we should suit) which may excuse my presenting myself to her — I don't want to *stare*: still less to force myself ... on any one because I am, unhappily, a journalist. So if I don't find a note from you which will justify me in waiting on her, here, (*Hotel d'Angleterre*), tomorrow week — the 27th (one has to be precise about dates, when dealing with such *punctual people as you*) I will do my best to enjoy the talent in public: & give up the other pleasure. I hope you had a good journey from England — which will encourage you in another good journey *to us* — & that you have have [*sic*] found Madame Mendelssohn & the dear children well.
>
> (Baal peculiarly silent)
[here Chorley inserted a short musical
quotation from the chorus to Baal in
'Elijah': 'Hear and answer'] Prestissimo.
Affly yrs
H.F. Chorley

Pray give my kindest regards to Mme Mendelssohn & remembrances to David. (Green Books, XXIV)

In a few days, Chorley was ecstatic about Lind — more so than he ever was after she came to London, writing to Mendelssohn again from Frankfurt (Sunday, 4 October 1846).

> I am old & wicked (every *demisemiquaver* in London will swear to that!) but I hope not yet quite ignorant, nor stupid: & after a fear of disappointment, I hardly know how to describe, laughed & cried like a child again, with a sort of pleasure, which reconciles me to long dreary intermediate years of existence, when I begin sometimes to fancy I can hardly be human: so hard seems life, & so unkind the world! Thank you for a very *very* intense pleasure: I was so disturbed last night, that I was obliged to write to Mlle L[ind] — before I went to sleep: & to-day I do so, to you as a sort of 'afternoon service' — not quite so dangerous, I hope, as the one we sat through at Liège. — I heard the lady in the 'Fille du Regiment' & shall stay for 'La Sonnambula' & 'La Vestale'. But will you let her go on singing translated works? — I have seen her, too, twice, but having here no party[?] of matrons to vouch for my 'pristine purity', we are obliged to be so ceremonious that I sit on the edge of my chair & make speeches — & visits ten minutes long — when I should like to stay as many hours. ... — In short, it is an odd and pleasant change, to be here quite[?] alone & unknown, with such a very rich pleasure at intervals. — I shall stay till Thursday evg. or Friday morning: — & then go to Paris. — She says *she will not* [?] come to London. — What opera schemes have been proposed to you? has any one ever thought of the 'Bernstein Hexe' as a subject. It seems impertinent to offer a hint, but is not meant as such, by
>
> Yours aff^{ly} & gratefully
H.F. Chorley

Mendelssohn did not pursue Chorley's suggestion that he set Meinhold's novel.[44] For her part, Lind announced on 6 October 1846 to her friend Madame Birch-Pfeiffer that she was going to Vienna to sing in Meyerbeer's *Feldlager von Schlesien* — 'and all the more, because it has fallen through in London [with Bunn]' (Holland-Rockstro, 2: 3-4). She ended her letter with an indication of the direction in which her thoughts were moving: 'Lumley (the Director of the Italian Opera in London), what has he not offered! And what an amiable man he is! He came here; but I have sent him to Italy, to look for a singer there. But, he still hopes to get me; and, if you should hear that I have really gone mad, I may then go to London'

(Holland-Rockstro, 2: 4). Three weeks later, it was definite, as she wrote her to close friend, Madame Wichmann, from Munich on 27 October 1846:

> Now let me tell you that I am going to London: and that Mendelssohn alone was able to induce me to do so. For you know what confidence I place in his advice; and, beside that, things have really so shaped themselves, that I can clearly see that God Himself has so ordained it — and, against one's destiny, one can do nothing. (Holland-Rockstro, 2: 6)

Mendelssohn in his long letter to Lind dated 31 October 1846, mentioned that he had a number of reservations about her contract for London: she should have agreed to eight performances a month, not ten, and 'something ought also to be altered on the score of money'. But, he added, 'all this must, I believe, be looked upon as settled, now and for ever, since you have signed', and he strongly supported this step in her career and predicted that 'you will be greeted, in England, musically and personally, with such love, and jubilation, and rapture, as has seldom fallen even to you' (Holland-Rockstro, 2: 7-8). In the same letter Mendelssohn told her of the frustration he was feeling about the opera libretto Madame Birch-Pfeiffer was supposed to be writing for him:

> ... I will also write to him [Lumley] once more about the *libretto*, and press him on the subject.
>
> This brings me back to Madame Birch-Pfeiffer. ... I foresaw, long ago, that she would find a thousand and one excuses for not writing a *libretto* at all.
>
> ... I should indeed be glad if I could soon, in accordance with my most hearty wish, write something dramatic — and especially, for you. Of what I can do in that way I will neglect nothing; of that I assure you; for I should at all times have gladly written dramatic music, but now more gladly than ever. And then I have a secret foreboding, which tells me that, if I do not attain to the composition of a fairly good Opera, *now*, and *for you*, I shall never accomplish it at all. But, on that point again, I entertain a regular Turkish fatalism — that, if it never happens, it never was to happen, even though I may have done all that I could do to bring it about. And that, I am doing. So I shall be content if we meet again in this life, be it with, or without an Opera. (Holland-Rockstro, 2: 9-10).

News of Lumley's contract with Lind was clearly important for Verdi. 'God Himself' told Lind to accept; Verdi was probably more persuaded by pounds, shillings, and pence. He wrote to Lumley on 11 November 1846, that he was willing to compose an opera for London: he must have the right to choose the best artists in the company, among them Lind and Fraschini (Cesari and Luzio, 30). He mentioned the subject again in a letter to Lucca on 2 December, and again on 3 December, telling Lucca moreover that he had finished about one third of *Masnadieri* (Cesari and Luzio, 33-4). If Lumley would agree to the opera and if he would give Verdi the pick of the company, specifically Lind and Fraschini, then a contract for the following season was on again.

Verdi's earlier ideas — either Shakespeare's *Lear* or Byron's *Corsair* would have seemed more obviously suited to the interests of an English audience than another version of Schiller's *Die Raüber*. Mercadante's version (*I Briganti* in 1836) had not pleased. So Lumley's pleasure in getting Verdi to sign the contract was somewhat muted. 'Verdi now offered his "Masnadieri"', Lumley recalled in his *Reminiscences*, 'and with this proposal I was obliged to close' (192).

In 1847 the battle against Lumley's house begun so forcefully the year before came to its crisis. The most relevant issues for Chorley were: the place of Verdi in the repertory, especially Verdi's new opera, the position of Jenny Lind as a golden-age singer, the existence or non-existence of a new opera by Mendelssohn, and the viability of a new, rival company of Italian Opera at Covent Garden performing in direct competition with Lumley's company in the Haymarket.

Lumley had announced in his prospectus that 'The celebrated Dr. FELIX MENDELSSOHN BARTHOLDY will likewise visit England, and produce an opera expressly composed for her Majesty's Theatre, the libretto founded on the *Tempest* of SHAKESPEARE, *Miranda*, Mademoiselle JENNY LIND' (quoted in *Morning Chronicle,* 12 April 1847: 6). By 13 February Chorley was asking his readers rhetorically: 'what became of the promise of Meyerbeer, with his "Camp de Silésie" — what of Verdi with his "Robbers" — what, even, of the one substantial hope of the theatre, Mdlle Jenny Lind?' (*Athenæum*, 13 February 1847: 179). He wondered 'whether even, any *libretto* has been accepted' by Mendelssohn (179). About a month later he announced: 'It is now, too, known beyond mistake — Dr. Mendelssohn's letters, which we have seen, being our warrant — that there will be no "Tempest" this year: there having been (as we mentioned some weeks since) no engagement on the composer's part to produce such a work' (20 March 1847: 315).

Lumley had a clear conscience about Lind's Miranda in Mendelssohn's *Tempest*. He recalled bitterly that 'both these reports [Lind's engagement and Mendelssohn's opera] were denied with singular acrimony by the Covent-Gardenite sharpshooters of the pen — and yet both were substantially true' (Lumley, 159). From Milan Lumley had sent Mendelssohn a letter with an enclosed libretto for the projected *Tempest* on 12 November 1846 with the following comment: 'I hope you will be satisfied with its general arrangement of course there must be changes in it — dependent on your wishes and feelings — and the effects you wo^d like to produce' (Green Books, XXIV, 133, Lumley to Mendelssohn). Lumley said that Mendelssohn did not write to him until 21 February 1847, to say that the opera would not be ready (167).

In April, Chorley entered the picture as a potential librettist himself: in a letter to Mendelssohn dated 22 April 1847, T.F. Beale enclosed a twenty-page sketch for an opera based on *The Winter's Tale* — 'I find my friend Mr Chorley through emotions of delicacy abstained from mentioning the subject of his libretto to you' (Green Books, XXV, 239, T.F. Beale to Mendelssohn). Chorley, too, had a clear conscience about his accusations, as he clearly remembered, several years later: 'I passed the last three days of August, 1847, beside Mendelssohn at Interlachen in Switzerland and heard first-hand Mendelssohn's irritation at the "unauthorised use of his name" in announcing "*The Tempest*"' (*Modern German Music*, 2: 388).

Meanwhile, Her Majesty's Theatre was presenting what amounted to an early Verdi festival: *Nino* [*Nabucco*], *Ernani*, *I Due Foscari*, and *I Lombardi*. These were not calculated to sweeten Chorley's irritation with composer or manager. 1847 began with a fresh attack on Verdi, occasioned by a letter he printed from an anonymous reader stating that *I Due Foscari* was successful in Paris, and adding: 'I think it much to be regretted that you should, for some incomprehensible reason or other, *systematically* decry a composer who, with many defects, has great merits ... On the whole he is far superior to all the living composers' (*Athenæum*, 2 January 1847: 24). Chorley printed the letter in order to have the pleasure of replying. Verdi 'represents the extremes of that extravagant school of writing which, under pretext of dramatic effect, has all but ruined the singers of Italy'. Verdi '*tears* his voices' and uses 'trombones in unison with the voice, — no matter what the subject'. His melody is 'simple and clear plagiarism of the most worn-out commonplaces of modern composers' (2 January 1847: 24).

These views are similar to what in a way had become almost a consensus of much press opinion: it is clearly exemplified by the following excerpt from the *Examiner*:

> Of original melody, there is scarcely a bar to be found in his entire works. Nay, he perpetually repeats himself. ... His erudition, such as it is does not take him far, and he goes back to his darling unison. His merit — and every fresh opera confirms this opinion — is his feeling for the drama which his music is to illustrate. ... His attention is directed not merely to his principal vocalists, but to the choruses, which form, as it were, the substances to his

> drama; and he elaborates these, not so much by "writing," as by balancing masses of sound of different quality, one against the other. (*Examiner*, 16 May 1846: 308)

Chorley's position was closely related to this one, except that he took everything in an entirely hostile way, emphasizing the severity of the melodic failings, de-emphasizing the excellences of the dramatic interest, and adding a note of fury over Verdi's writing for (or against) the singers' voices.

The contempt for Verdi spilled over to general sarcasm directed at Her Majesty's Theatre. Costa's replacement was derided for his conducting of *Norma*: 'Mr Balfe in the last impassioned scene *outstamping* the drums, by way of keeping matters together' (19 June 1847: 653).

On 6 April 1847, the new and much-discussed 'secession company' opened at Covent Garden its first season with Rossini's *Semiramide*. The performance was a great success, with cabalist Grisi in her prime and Marietta Alboni in a tremendously successful debut as Arsace. Chorley recognised the orchestra as 'unquestionably the best ever assembled in England ... and the general *ensemble* ... [is] something never heretofore attained by any Italian performances in this country' (10 April 1847: 394). The 'ensemble' aspect of the performances at the new house elicited extensive press comment. The details about the composition of the orchestra in the notice from the *Illustrated London News* are revealing:

> To eulogize the band too strongly would be impossible. Costa has achieved a most important improvement in the balance of instruments; by adding to the strength of the stringed ones, the braying of brass has been balanced. We never heard such first violins for brilliancy, and the luscious tones of the tenors and violoncelli, and the power and crispness of the double-basses, were quite as delightful ... and we rank the Covent Garden band as now the first in the world. There are fifteen first violins, with Sainton at the head; fourteen second, with Ella; ten violas, with Hill; ten violoncelli, with Lindley; nine double-basses, with Anfossi; with the usual complement of wind instruments [for a total of eighty players].

Covent Garden presented two operas by Verdi in 1847. In *Ernani* Alboni sang Charles the Fifth. Had the substitution of contralto for bass happened at Her Majesty's Theatre, Chorley might have been less accommodating: at Covent Garden he confined himself to noting that 'such experiments ought not to be made by a management professing itself careful of musical integrity' (10 July 1847: 737-8).[45] *I Due Foscari* manifested 'sublime' acting from Ronconi (and not bad singing), but in general the opera 'strengthens our judgment of the utter worthlessness of the music' (26 June 1847: 683).

On 2 June 1847, Muzio arrived in London and reassured Verdi that Jenny Lind was indeed going to be singing in the new opera; Verdi arrived on 5 June (Phillips-Matz, 214). Muzio reported that the singers at Covent Garden were 'all enemies of Verdi's music' (Garibaldi, 336; Muzio to Barezzi, 29 June 1847), and, while he granted the excellence of Grisi and Mario in *I Due Foscari*, was sure that they refused to perform it more than twice because of their jealousy. Costa, moreover, was a Neapolitan and 'since they are jealous, proud, and neither able to do good things nor sing well, they do not want others to do well either'.[46]

Verdi arrived and conducted the first performance of *I Masnadieri* at Her Majesty's. Muzio wrote to Barezzi on the day after the premiere that 'the opera create a furor' — the orchestra, singers, and press reception: everything was 'beautiful' (in Muzio's English: 'bietifol') (Garibaldi, 344).

The opera was received with great applause on the first night. It was, however, not really a success, and was never revived in Victorian England. Ivan Turgenev, then on his first of several visits to London, saw the opera and wrote to Pauline Viardot-Garcia that it 'had a very nice little fiasco' (*Turgenev and England*, 10). Queen Victoria confided to her journal that the music was 'very inferior and commonplace' (quoted in Godefroy, *Dramatic Genius of Verdi*, 1: 164). Chorley told his readers that 'we take it to be the worst opera which has been given in our time at Her Majesty's Theatre' (24 July 1847: 795) and later, in *Thirty Years' Musical Recollections* he insisted that it was 'perhaps [Verdi's] most paltry work' (1: 296).

Even Lumley, who had gone to so much trouble for so long in order to take credit for this premiere, did not choose to defend it. In his *Reminiscences* he noted that, although it was given 'with every appearance of a triumphant success', it was in fact a failure, not just in England but also in Italy.[47] Lumley's comment on Verdi's use of the great but very fat bass, Lablache, has been quoted often: 'Lablache, as the imprisoned father, had to do about the only thing he could not do to perfection — having to represent a man nearly starved to death' (193). But according to Gruneisen in *The Morning Chronicle*, Lablache's portrayal of Maximilian Moor was a redeeming feature of the evening: his character 'was the only one commanding the sympathies of the audience' (23 June 1847: 5).

The Times greeted the opera with a long, respectful notice, citing points of similarity with Schiller's play, and pointed out that the world of 'rank and fashion' was in attendance. The critic's only negative remarks were calculated to reflect well on Lumley: 'Whatever opinion may be entertained of the merits of this opera, this fact is certain, — that the manager in its production has acted in a manner worthy of the director of such an establishment' (*The Times*, 23 July 1847: 5). The *Illustrated London News* reported that 'the opera was highly successful' (24 July 1847: 58), but the critic of the *Examiner* did not think that the opera had much chance of 'living beyond the occasion' (24 July 1847: 469).

Verdi intended to negotiate a very high price for his future services at Her Majesty's. To Clarina Maffei he wrote on 17 July 1847 (five days before the premiere): 'It is true that they have offered me 40 thousand francs for an opera and that I have not accepted. But do not be amazed, because it is not an excessive sum and if I were to return I should want much more' (Cesari and Luzio, 459). Verdi conducted two performances of *I Masnadieri*, then, leaving the conducting to Balfe, left for Paris to begin preparing for a production there of *Jérusalem*. From Paris on 2 August 1847, he wrote to Lumley expressing his willingness to write an opera a year for the next three years (Cesari and Luzio, 43) for 90 000 francs each season.[48] Lumley's reply was polite but evasive. No contract was offered.

'The English will not have Verdi', Chorley insisted in his review of the season (28 August 1847: 917). Furthermore, suggesting reservations about Lind, Chorley warned that her attraction might not continue. 'So end our labours, then, with regard to the most fatiguing season in our experience' (917). Verdi, of course, was not the only interesting issue that fatiguing season. Jenny Lind's voice no longer produced in Chorley unqualified rapture, as it had in the autumn of 1846. With Norma, she had slipped. Not only Chorley rushed in to criticize. Davison's *Musical World* recorded: 'Tuesday, June 15th, will long be remembered as the epoch of Mdlle Jenny Lind's first failure in England' (4 September 1847: 566). Norma was 'not only out of her sphere, but beyond her strength' (566). Grisi's performances of the role were the standard against which Lind was faulted. A maidenly Norma would not do. Earlier Chorley had railed against Bellini, along with Donizetti, but in the future he implicitly accepted *Norma* as part of the basic repertory, as a worthy vehicle for Grisi.[49]

In a way, the competition between the two opera houses served the interests of the audiences, who were offered various dazzling attractions. Edmund Yates remembered that younger opera-goers shifted their allegiance to the new house; older opera-goers remained with Lumley.[50] In Chorley's opinion, the second season of the battle between the two houses showed that Her Majesty's Theatre was still a victim of the star system: 'The season, in short, has been nothing more or less than Mdlle Lind's second season, — less brilliant, of course, than her first' (*Athenæum*, 28 August 1848: 861). At any rate, he added, London's opera houses, unlike those on the Continent, had not been silenced by revolutions and 'the workings of Republicanism, Communism, and the other *isms*' (861).

At Covent Garden, *Les Huguenots* finally came into its own with Mario, Viardot (Valentine), Castellan, Alboni, and Tamburini. The orchestra and chorus matched those of the Opéra in 1836. The season of 1848 finally established French Grand Opera as 'particularly congenial to the taste of the wide English public' (29 July 1848: 755), after years of Chorley's insistence on its significance to deaf ears. At last the English embraced Meyerbeer's opera, in this unprecedentedly gorgeous production, with the 'utmost enthusiasm' (732). It was 'admitted beyond contradiction to be the most important operatic production of the last ten years' (22 July 1848: 731).

When Grisi took up the role of Valentine from Viardot, Chorley said she was 'wonderful', marvelling that her acting, 'at the present stage of her career … argues a power for which even we were unprepared, — highly as we have always rated her' (26 May 1849: 553).

In *Le Prophéte* no one could take Viardot's place. Her great success at the Opéra (reported in the *Athenæum*, 21 April 1849: 418) was repeated in London. 'Verily, Madame Viardot Garcia, as the Mother of the Impostor, was well worth waiting thirteen years for' (*Bentley's Miscellany* 25 [May 1849]: 523). Fides was a part 'which Meyerbeer has so strengthened for her use, that few besides her will do wisely to attempt it' (524). In general, 'This new opera by Meyerbeer *is* worthy of its predecessors' (522).

When 'the Swedish lady' reappeared in 1848, it was with 'every sign of unabated popularity', but to Chorley's ears her voice seemed 'somewhat coarsened since last year' (*Athenæum*, 6 May 1848: 468). Hector Berlioz, not having Chorley's opportunities to hear her, wrote bitterly to another journalist, Morris Barnett, threatening to take vengeance on Lumley:

> After the article I did for Mr. Lumley in the 'Débats' two years ago, and took so much trouble to get inserted, I had a right to expect a certain amount of civility on the part of that sublime impresario. When I went to London, he sent me a ticket for Her Majesty's Theatre every evening when it was empty … [but] as soon as Mlle. Lind began her performances, I could not gain admittance. … If Mr. Lumley thinks that such behaviour is proper, he is strangely mistaken. … ['Money grubbers' like Lumley] had better not treat writers so contemptuously, especially those they may have need of, for they know perfectly well how to put them in their place one of these days.
>
> This, my dear Barnett, is strictly between ourselves. I don't want to complain or let it even be suspected that I pay the least attention to these managers and their little ways. (quoted in Ganz, 66)

Lind made fewer appearances during 1849, the third season of the war. Chorley found Lumley's conductor, Balfe, a target for ridicule: In *Ernani* 'the orchestra and chorus were more than usually noisy, coarse and unsteady. We wish Mr. Balfe would prevail upon his foot and his *bâton* to perform *piano*. On Saturday the two out-thumped the great drum' (31 March 1849: 339). Looking for another draw to equal or at least approach Lind in popularity, Lumley brought back Sontag. Although she had retired from the stage to marry Count Rossi, the revolutions of 1848 ruined the Rossi fortunes and Sontag again became a breadwinner. Chorley was generally impressed at the return of this important singer from the past, wondering whether she could now survive, given 'the rapid and extreme mutations of opera during the last twenty years' (7 July 1849: 701). On the whole, he was favourably impressed. 'Time — to use the poet's phrase — has treated the lady like a lover, not like a destroyer' (14 July 1849: 723). Bringing with her return 'associations, recollections, and fantasies', she moved him to exclaim that 'the sunny geniality of tone from F to F is a rarity',[51] and that her success recalls 'the glorious days of the Opera' (724).[52]

At the end of 1849, Chorley relayed to his readers hopefully a report from Naples that Verdi-*mania* was in decline (22 December 1849: 1313).

4 Modern German Music

When John Ella presented Schumann's piano quartet at the Musical Union, Chorley commended him for being the first to present a new composer to the musicians of England, but was cool to the work. He called readers' attention to his comments in issue 886 of the *Athenæum*. Schumann's position in Germany was 'somewhat analogous to that of M. Berlioz in France', and if this work were characteristic, 'he falls back among the second rate', despite puffs in the 'German press' (1 April 1847: 345). The real battle against Schumann, however, was not waged until the 1860s, when Clara Schumann began making regular recital tours to England and when the Crystal Palace began programming Schumann's orchestra music on a regular basis.

In 1854, thirteen years after he published *Music and Manners in France and Germany*, Chorley issued a substantially altered two-volume reworking of it. He omitted all of the material about music in France. He retained much of the old material about Germany, and added new German material. Too different from the original to be a second edition, it was renamed *Modern German Music*. The old passages remained to shed light on artistic life 'previous to the year of confusion, 1848' (Preface, 1: [vii]), and, as in *Music and Manners*, he chose to include not only musical matters, but background relevant to the 'time, place, and society' in which the music was produced (1: ix).

In volume one, the most significant new section deals with Chorley's knowledge of Wagner's operas in the early 1840s — 'In 1840, Herr Wagner was not openly revolutionary; being in composition apparently an imitator of the least amiable peculiarities of Herr Meyerbeer' (1: 348). His discussion of Wagner is one of the earliest and fullest published in English:

> The cardinal fault in the new manner of composition (or decomposition) which has produced fruit so little satisfactory, may not solely arise from Herr Wagner's perversity and poverty in special gifts combined. It may be a necessary consequence of the times we are living in, and of the ferment which is brewing around us. ... History must now be as amusing as a romance — romance must be as profound as a history. ... There must be a story, inner meaning, mystical significance — intellectual tendency. (1: 368-9)

Most of the new passages are the four sections which form a large part of volume 2:

1. a consideration of Spohr (2: 77-96), whose music exercised a 'temporary charm over most lovers of German art' which generally led to 'a gradual disenchantment with respect to them' (2: 78).
2. a discussion of music in Vienna, most significantly Schubert, not well known in England until the Crystal Palace concerts in the 1860s (2: 132-207). Schubert's listener 'becomes blanked by long, weary passages of constructive *remplissage*, in which it would seem as if the composer had gone on simply because he did not know how to change the inspiration' (2: 206). Nevertheless, with Schubert's passing Vienna lost its 'light of creative genius' — 'the old priests are gone, and there are no new ones to fill their places' (2: 207).
3. a discussion of music in the Rhineland: Cherubini, Beethoven, the Bonn festival of 1845 and Beethoven's influence, good and bad, and Jenny Lind's continental performances before her arrival at Her Majesty's in 1847 (2: 211-380).
4. a discussion of Chorley's visit to Mendelssohn in Interlachen for three days in August, 1847, shortly before Mendelssohn's death, and an account of the discussions they had about the current state of European music (2: 383-418). During this visit, Mendelssohn told Chorley that he did not expect to live long, but Chorley brushed such foreboding aside.

For Chorley, and for many others, 'Germany and German music are gravely, perhaps irreparably, changed by the untimely death of Mendelssohn' (2: 384). But no sooner 'was he cold in his grave' than Germans were questioning his stature, and trying to put in his place 'an idol no worthier of exaltation than Herr Schumann' (2: 402). In assessing Mendelssohn's lasting worth here, Chorley singled out numerous works for special mention or discussion, among them string quartets, the 'Melusine' and 'Meerestille' [*sic*] overtures, the violin concerto, movements from the symphonies, the choruses to *Athalie* and *Oedipus*, songs, and *Lieder ohne Worte*.[53]

Modern German Music appeared in two volume format published by Smith, Elder, and Company in 1854. Its dedication page read: 'To the Memory of Departed Friends, these pages are gratefully and affectionately dedicated'. In its preface, Chorley noted that 'a portion of it appeared' already in *Music and Manners in France and Germany* (1841). Characteristically Chorley declared that the basic nature of his critical opinions has not changed for many years:

> It has been my fortune (or *misfortune* as may be) to
> undergo very few conversions with regard to Music and
> its masters, I hope that I know more than I did — but I
> have not come to like what I disliked then years ago, or
> the reverse (ix)

The *Athenæum* gave it a four-column notice (15 April 1854: 462-3). J.W. Davison, the reviewer for the *The Times*, condemned it in a significant and long-remembered denunciation, ridiculing it especially for being an old book 'which fell dead from the press' in its earlier appearance as *Music and Manners in France and Germany* (1841) (*The Times*, 25 April 1854: 8), and ridiculing its author as one who considers himself not only 'the model-critic of the press, a critic of critics as well as of musicians — a phoenix among reviewers' but also 'infallible':

> He must have been born innately infallible, with an organ-
> ization incapable of receiving false impressions — his
> mind a sheet of white paper, upon which nothing but
> eternal truths could be written. (8)

Chorley's complacent-sounding pronouncement that he has had 'very few conversions' with respect to his opinions about music is an example not of steadfastness, but of foolishness, according to Davison. He was not good on 'Glück' [*sic*], Mozart, and Beethoven; he was too hard on Spohr and too easy on Liszt, since 'it is useless to anathematize Herr Wagner and Herr Schumann, if Dr. Liszt, their inventor and their prophet, is tolerated'. Although Davison conceded some worth to the passages about Mendelssohn, in general the book was poor:

> In recapitulation we may say, that, where Mr. Chorley's
> criticism is intelligible it is a *galimafrée*, hashed up out of
> the leavings of others; and that where it is not intelligible,

it is the strangest, most grotesque, and "freakish" (a
favourite word of the author) kind of criticism that was
ever applied to art and artists; that, in short, to cite a
well-known judgment, "what is good in the book is not
new, and what is new is not good." (*The Times*, 25 April
1854: 8)

Chorley's hopes for a favourable reception were dashed. *Modern
German Music* records a more important disappointment than that,
however. His long-nourished hope that his name might go down in history
linked with Mendelssohn's as joint creator of a masterpiece was ended by
Mendelssohn's sudden illness and death. Mendelssohn had been looking
over Chorley's draft of a scenario for an opera based on *The Winter's Tale*.
During their brief vacation encounter in Switzerland in 1847 that hope had
not yet been dashed:

> He then went on to talk over other Shakspearian subjects;
> in particular "The Winter's Tale;" a sketch from which
> had been laid before him: — this seemed in some degree
> to have engaged his liking. "Something very merry," said
> he, "could be made with *Autolycus*." ... "We have no one
> in Germany who can write opera books," Mendelssohn
> continued. "If Kotzebue had been alive ... *he* had ideas!
> ... Well; I must do my best with 'Loreley,' for Geibel has
> taken great trouble with the poem. We shall see." And
> then, again, he broke off suddenly, and put his hand to his
> head. "But what is the use of planning anything? I shall
> not live." (2: 390-91)

A few weeks later, Mendelssohn was dead.

Notes

1. The letter is undated, but Chorley included his return address — 5
    Stafford Row, Pimlico — which indicates that the letter was written
    before 1838, when Chorley and Henry Reeve decided to share a
    house at 9 Chapel Street, Grosvenor Place. The mention of the 'book
    forthcoming' is presumably *Sketches of a Sea Port Town*, which Bent-
    ley published in 1834. Bentley published none of Chorley's other
    books during the 1830s.
2. From 1836 to the end of his life, Chorley visited to the Continent
    almost every autumn. He generally used these annual holidays less for
    relaxation as for as opportunities for hearing new music and new per-
    formers. For someone who became increasingly prone to dwell on his
    ill health and semi-invalid state, he found surprising reserves of

energy on many of these trips for itineraries that would exhaust the healthiest sportsman. As Hewlett noted,

> ... in spite of his weak *physique* he would undertake these expeditions at any season, and sometimes at a moment's warning. Long night-journeys in the most pitiless of weather and unaccommodating of conveyances, interruptions of pre-arranged plans of travel and needful seasons of repose, were cheerfully submitted to if Music were the siren that summoned him. His Continental journals abound with evidences of a vagrancy that any one unacquainted with his motive would naturally ascribe to the restlessness of disease. Having settled down, to all appearance, for a week at Leipsic, he suddenly emerges at Berlin, lured by the report of a performance of Gluck. From Dresden he hurries off to Paris on a similar errand. ... (1: 302-3)

Chorley's ears and his enthusiasm were both at their freshest during his first six visits to the Continent — in 1836, 1837, and 1839 he travelled to France; in 1839, 1840, and 1841 to Germany. These visits formed the background to *Music and Manners*.

3.   Mendelssohn wrote to Chorley from Berlin on 7 September 1841 that the book was available in Germany, but he had not yet seen it:

> Strange enough it is that I have not yet been able to get it, and do not know anything beyond what I saw in almost all the German papers, which I found this spring at a Leipsig [*sic*] coffee-house. There they had translated your fine fluent English in their own hackneyed style, one this bit, and one the other; and they all like and praised it very much, and gave outlines, as they called it, of the whole; but of course that conveyed only a very limited and weak idea of your work to me, and I long the more to read it by myself and in the shape in which it was meant and written. (Hewlett, 1: 342-3)

François Joseph Fétis had *Music and Manners* (and Chorley's later book, *Modern German Music*) in his library, according to the catalogue published in 1877 by the Bibliothèque Royale de Belgique. Fétis's *Biographie Universelle* (2nd edn, 1883) commented: 'Un jugement juste en ce qui concerne l'art, et des observations originales exprimées avec esprit, distinguent cet ouvrage de beaucoup de publications du même genre' (286).

4.   In 1839 the *Athenæum* published 'foreign correspondence' reports, two from Berlin, two from 'Leipsic', and one from Brunswick,

printed in the issues of 5 October, 26 October, 2 November, 9 November, and 16 November 1839. All except the first were signed 'H.F.C.' In 1840 came a 'foreign correspondence', 'The "Huldigung" at Berlin' (31 October 1840: 867-8), another 'Foreign Correspondence. Nuremburg, October 31' published 14 November 1840 (906-7), and still another 'Foreign Correspondence. Paris November 15' (28 November 1840: 947-8). All three were signed H.F.C.

5. In discussing 'The Court and the Opera' at Berlin, Chorley referred to the 'agreeable author' of the *Ramble Among the Musicians of Germany*, without naming him (*Music and Manners in France and Germany*, 2: 141). Later, still unnamed, he was termed 'my pleasant predecessor' (and again identified as 'author of the "Ramble"') (2: 217). Chorley's obituary of Holmes singled out the *Ramble* for praise (*Athenæum*, 5 November 1859: 605).

6. In Dickens's *Nicholas Nickleby* (1838-39), Mrs Nickleby was portrayed as good-hearted but addle-headed.

7. Compare Blaze de Bury's later assertion: 'Paris, je le répète, est devenu le centre de l'opéra moderne, et cela non point à cause du plus ou moins grand nombre de chefs-d'œuvre qui s'y sont produits, mais uniquement parce que c'est à Paris qu'a pris naissance le nouveau système de drame musical qui régit le monde. ... *Guillaume Tell*, *Les Huguenots*, *la Favorite*! opéras français, d'auteurs allemands et italiens' (43, 45).

8. Chorley's translation of part of Sand's *Lettres d'un Voyager* was in the first volume of *Music and Manners* (177-86).

9. Chorley noted Liszt's 'strong feeling for all music that is peculiar by its nationality' (the Tarantella, the Waltz, the Polonaise, the Mazurka, etc.). Chorley's own early essay on national music, 'A Few Words Upon National Music' appeared in *Conti the Discarded*, 1835 (2: 301-17).

10. 'Somehow or other, what I heard seemed as far from the real deep-felt delivery of Beethoven, as the occasional "*Superbe!*" and "*Magnifique!*" of the audience, discharged in proper places, is from the real praise which the music demands. ... [T]hey do their best to approach these mighty works, but the achievement is above them and beyond them' (3: 70-71).

11. 'My ear has not that singular decision which retains a memory of tone, independent of pitch — a positive faëry gift belonging to the highest order of musical organisations; and it did not occur to me that the cause of Madame Schröder Devrient's apparently renovated clearness and purity might lie in the flat diapason of the orchestra. It is so, however; the Dresden band being nearly half a tone lower than any I have ever heard. But this flatness threw over the whole performance of a powerful and brilliant orchestra, most carefully directed by Herr

Reissiger, a languor' (*Music and Manners*, 3: 140).

12. Chorley's sharp ear for musical influences called attention to the similarity between the duet in *Euryanthe* ('Hin nimm die Steele mein') and a 'motivo' in Rossini's *Tancredi*. To him, the similarity illustrated the difference between plagiarism and imaginative creativity: 'But if the harshest construction is to be put upon coincidence, the plagiarism is amply atoned for by the grace, variety, and intense expression of the second part' (3: 151). The connection between this phrase and *Tancredi* had perhaps recently occurred to Chorley, since he did not mention it in his 1840 *Athenæum* notice of the performance of *Euryanthe* at the Prince's Theatre. At that time he called attention to the same phrase simply by asking: 'where [is] there an Italian illustration of "*Gioja*" or "*Felicità*" more rapturously entrancing that the "Hin nimm die Seele mein" of the re-united lovers, in the second act?' (6 June 1840: 461).

13. 'Fleuve du Tage' was a song known in England as well as France: Thackeray alluded to it in *Vanity Fair* (1847) as appropriate for a simple but good-hearted young woman to sing (chapter 21). Geoffrey and Kathleen Tillotson in their edition of the novel pointed out that it was simple enough for 'the merest beginner' (201).

14. Thackeray's dismal description was true, but 'not the whole of Versailles as I have know it. ... there were signs of life, as well as tokens of decay, at Versailles, when I first visited it in 1836' (3: 263).

15. For example, she wrote to Mitford: 'Then I like the Music & Manners, & Mrs Hemans's Memoirs, & much besides' (to Mitford, 25 March 1845, *Brownings' Correspondence*, 3: 138).

16. Chorley wrote to Mendelssohn on 13 November 1841: 'Many thanks for your good natured disposition with regard to my book. It was completed in such a whirl wind — being entirely constructed in the midst of our fullest season, & published *to be eaten hot* (like our muffins in a morning) and so very much has happened since it appeared, that it seems to me like a thing of past times already' (Green Books, XIV, 202).

17. For a discussion of these English tours, see Allsobrook.

18. 'A needless Alexandrine ends the song / that, like a wounded snake, drags its slow length along'. Pope, *Essay on Criticism*.

19. Kemble's judgement of Liszt's genius was not entirely favourable: 'Liszt was at this time a young man, in the very perfection of his extraordinary talent, and at the height of his great celebrity. He was extremely handsome; his features were finely chiselled, and the expression of this face, especially when under the inspiration of playing, striking grand and commanding. ... Liszt became, at the very opening of his career, so immediately a miracle, and then an oracle, in the artistic and the great world of Paris, that he was allowed to

impose his own terms upon its judgment; and suffering himself the worst consequences of that order of success, he achieved too early a fame for his permanent reputation. A want of sobriety, a fantastical seeking after strange effects; in short, the characteristics of artistic *charlatanerie*, mixed themselves up with all that he did, and, as is inevitably the case, deteriorated the fine original gifts of his genius' (Kemble, 2: 125-7).

20. On 21 January 1860, Chorley wrote, 'we are glad to see that Mrs. Fanny Kemble has been again reading at Boston, in "the States," with her usual success and unimpaired power' (100), and on 17 November 1866, in 'Musical and Dramatic Gossip', he informed his readers that 'Mrs. Kemble, every true lover of Shakspeare [*sic*] will be glad to hear, is again giving dramatic readings in the provinces' (651).

21. The move can be dated by the heading of Chorley's letter to Mendelssohn on 13 November 1841, written from Wilton Street but with the notation: 'in future 15, Victoria Square, Lower Grosvenor Place' (Green Books, XIV, 202). He commented: 'I should be ashamed to look at your letter with its date of *September the seventh*, had I not good reasons to give for my delay in answering it. First I did not return home till the middle of October from the Continent, and since then, I have been in a perpetual and most unexpected hurry. — I found Reeve ... on the point of being married immediately — which compelled me immediately to seek out another resting place and the result of a very unprofitable search has been my taking a house on my own account: furnishing the same &c. &c. — My sole & unassisted self — so that my correspondence has confined itself to cabinet-makers, upholsterers &c. &c . ... I long to show you all my little house & how wise a travelling bachelor can be in the chapter of chairs & tables — remember me when you are charitably disposed' (Green Books, XIV, 202).

22. Hewlett referred to, but did not quote, one of Chorley's travel journals describing a friendship about which only the following is known:

> One diary chronicles his extreme delight at meeting in Leipsic with an American gentleman, Mr. Perkins, 'young, handsome, and rich, who has come out from home resolutely to work out a career in art, with the hope of doing good to his country by its agency when he goes back.' With this gentleman, who devoted himself to the study of music, 'with very many requisites for the task,' Chorley subsequently became intimate, and, I believe, supplied the words for a cantata composed by him. (Hewlett, 2: 300)

Mr Perkins was possibly Charles Callahan Perkins (1823-86), the Bostonian art patron who was in Leipsic studying art sometime around 1846 or not long after. I cannot explain Hewlett's allusion to a cantata by Perkins and Chorley.

23. E.M.W. Tomlin suggested that Chorley was later in love with Mamie Dickens, to whom he bequeathed an annuity of £200 (Tomlin, 448). Although Tomlin inferred from this legacy a possible romantic attachment to Miss Dickens, it might also be seen as a evidence of 'family' feelings associated with his devotion to Charles Dickens in the 1850s and 1860s. Writing to Mrs Fields on 3 May 1872, Georgina Hogarth mentioned it matter-of-factly: 'You saw, no doubt, by the papers that he left Mamie a substantial remembrance of his regard for her and his gratitude to her dear Father in the form of an annuity of £200'. Hogarth then added that it was an 'acceptable addition to her income and she is glad to have it' (MS FI 2706, Huntington Library, San Marino, California).

24. Written in the 1840s: the return address was 15 Victoria Square, where he lived from 1841 to 1852. MS, Wigan Archives Service.

25. There are numerous musical allusions, e.g. to Rossini's *Otello* (1: 177), Donizetti's *Belisario* (1: 183), to Schroeder-Devrient (1: 79), Malibran (1: 108, 110, 118, 123, 127, 188, etc.), Pasta (1: 196), and to Mercadante's *I due Illustri Rivali* (2: 226 and 228). Chorley generally referred to this opera as '*I due* ...' instead of '*Le due*'.

26. Another character, Golstein, is 'a very Shylock, resolute to have his pound of flesh' (2: 130). Public Opinion spreads various accounts of Helena Porzheim's origin: she is said to be the 'daughter of a noble family somewhere in Austria', or 'niece of a Jew rope-dancer', or 'sister of a Madame Huttenbrenner' (3: 43).

27. The Professor dies; Prince Caspar seems on the verge of marrying her daughter Diana. The Prince's mother has other ideas. Appearing unexpectedly, and mistaking Helena for Diana, she announces that her son will not lose face 'because of an intrigue with a Jewess of Bonn' (2: 165) since 'there is no legal marriage betwixt such as he and such as you!' (2: 166). She has come to buy her off. When Prince Caspar absents himself, Helena turns to the stage to earn money for her mother and sister.

After this story of Walter's about the Prince's inconstancy, Paul Gray, formerly the novel's narrator, re-imposes himself as storyteller. Gray's story will eventually put the correspondent-hero in a situation parallel to the Prince-villain of the story-within-a-story (i.e. Prince Caspar's love for Diana doesn't last, just as Walter's love for Grace didn't last). But the situation is also different, since the ethical English hero remains willing to marry her, out of duty.

28. Chorley's criticism of libretti was not confined to English operas. The 'stories' of *Don Giovanni* and *Figaro*, for example, 'are obsolete, puerile, and not dramatically interesting' (*Athenæum*, 4 May 1850: 483). Nevertheless, Chorley noted that *Don Giovanni* had achieved 'canonization in England' (7 August 1858: 177).

29. His sensitivity to "mismanagement" was always great. He cited a complaint in von Raumer's *England in 1841* about a performance of *Don Giovanni* in 1836 (loud prompter, numbers omitted, and others interpolated) in order to show that von Raumer is 'a witness in support of an opinion we often expressed in 1836, as to the mismanagement of our Italian Opera' (*Athenæum*, 2 April 1842: 289).

30. For a while, Chorley reported positively on the success of early success of Mrs Alfred Shaw, who, 'between two Italian engagements, has been making a foray into Germany, with brilliant success' (12 February 1842: 149).

31. Kemble added that Mrs Chorley was confused by Mrs Grote's appearance at one of Henry's parties. She turned to her son and asked 'Henry, my dear, who is the gentleman in the white muslin gown?' (Kemble, 2: 65).

32. See also Eric Werner, 'Komponist in Königlichen Diensten', *Mendelssohn*, 398-420, and Michael P. Steinberg, 'The Incidental Politics to Mendelssohn's *Antigone*' in Todd, *Mendelssohn and His World*, 137-57. For Eduard Devrient's discussion of Mendelssohn's work in Berlin, a city which he came to regard as 'prison' (252), see Devrient, 212-56. In *Modern German Music* (1854), Chorley censured the King of Prussia for not encouraging Mendelssohn more actively to write an opera for Berlin:

> Some royal wish of seeing a German story set by a German composer, might have persuaded Mendelssohn to abridge the time of hesitation which he had allowed to elapse before he attempted opera-composition as a man, and might have recorded the present King of Prussia's reign in the history of Art, by some great, enduring, and universal work, which should have been to the theatre what 'Elijah' is to the sacred concert room. (*Modern German Music*, 1: 288)

Mendelssohn had written to Klingemann in London on 24 January 1841, asking advice about accepting an invitation to Berlin, requesting that he share the information with no-one, not even Chorley or Moscheles: 'Der neue pruss. König hat mir nämlich vor einigen Monaten die brillantesten und vorteilhaftesten Anerbietungen nach Berlin machen lassen' (Klingemann, 258).

33. In the 1880s, for example, Henry Mapleson remembered him as 'des-

potic' (Mapleson, 1: 126) and 'remarkably vindictive' (2: 284); the more favourable view was that he was 'a splendid disciplinarian' (Foster, 193). For discussion of Costa's reforms see Ehrlich (70-76).

34. Davison in *The Times*, by contrast, was generally hostile to Chopin's music, though he wrote a fulsomely laudatory pamphlet published by Wessel in 1843. In addition to publishing Chopin, Wessel and Stapleton employed Davison at this time for their house journal, *The Musical Examiner* (1842-44).

35. 'Verdi and the Contemporary Italian Operatic Scene', (Weaver and Chusid: 86). For discussion of Verdi as apparent 'borrower' see Dean and Lippman, passim. For aspects of common musical language see 'Donizetti's Operatic World' and 'Donizetti's Use of Operatic Conventions' in Ashbrook's *Donizetti and His Operas*, 207-82. Around this time, however, the opera amateur in New York, George Templeton Strong, heard Verdi's melodies as distinctive, recording in his diary for 2 December 1848:

> [Verdi's] melodies, original or not, have distinctness and character. ... He never ventures on the dignity of repose, but puts on all the steam he can raise, and keeps up a ceaseless torrent of forcible-feeble emphasis, passion, and vehemence till one is weary of him as of an author who deals only in italics, large capitals, dashes, and interjection marks.
>
> This is certainly true of *Ernani*, the only production of Verdi's that I know much about. (quoted in Lawrence, 520)

36. Fifty-five years later, George Bernard Shaw too complained about Verdi's misuse of voices, writing in *The Anglo-Saxon Review* (March 1901) that 'until Boito became his artistic conscience he wrote inhumanly for the voice and ferociously for the orchestra. ... He practically treated that upper fifth as the whole voice, and pitched his melodies in the middle of it instead of the middle of the whole compass, the result being a frightful strain on the singer' (Reprinted in Shaw, 414-15). Chorley had second thoughts about his initially positive reaction to Fornasari: in *Thirty Year's Musical Recollections* he complained: 'That sensibility and excitement which gave to Signor Fornasari's first appearance a false air of genius, dwindled, flattened, and faded — night after night — part after part. The tremulous quality of his voice, (that voice of young Italy, bad schooling, and false notions of effect), became more monotonous and tiresome than the coldest placidity could have been' (1: 228).

37. Several favourable French press reports were reprinted (in Italian translation) by Garibaldi (227-31).

38. Lucca in fact published *Attila*, *Il Corsaro*, and *I Masnadieri*. Verdi's relations with Lucca deteriorated rapidly. 'With me he has been insensitive, boorish, and demanding' (Verdi to Piave, 14 January 1848, Luzio, 2: 350).

39. For English accounts of Verdi's dealings with Lumley and the journey to London (based primarily on the material in Garibaldi and the *Copialettere*) see Frank Walker, 158-63; Budden, 1: 318-22; and Kimbell, *Italian Romanticism*, 190-207.

40. See Holland and Rockstro, 1: 228-36 and 290-98. They stated that in 1845 Lind was not contemplating singing at Her Majesty's instead of Drury Lane, even thought Bunn and others thought that was her real intention.

41. For Lumley, the 'palmy days' of the ballet were 1844 and 1845, more generally the entire decade. Edmund Yates said Lumley staked everything on the ballet, even more than on Jenny Lind: 'It was to his *ballet* that Mr. Lumley looked for his principal attraction, independently of Jenny Lind' (1: 179), adding '[a]nd well he might; for surely neither before nor since was that style of entertainment brought to such a pitch of perfection' (1: 179).

42. 'C'est avec un vif regret que j'ai appris votre maladie au moment ou je comptais avoir les plaisir de vous revoir ici presque immediatement. Je suis bien aise d'apprendre que vous y portez le soins que requiert une organisation aussi sensible que celle d'un genie créatif comme le vôtre. Veuillez agreer l'expression de toute ma sympathie. ... Je suis sûr que le changement de scène et une visite à Londres pendant une saison aussi belle et aussi prospère (je n'en ai jamais connu de plus brillante à notre Theatre) vous fera plus de bien que tous les remedes imaginables' (Cesari and Luzio, 20-21).

43. 'J'espère que cette nouvelle [the success of *I Lombardi*] vous fera plaisir et qu'elle agira si efficacement comme antidote à votre indisposition, que vous viendrez ici en prendre une bien plus forte dose en forme d'applaudissement; ce qui ne peut vous manquer' (13 May 1846, Cesari and Luzio, 22).

44. Vincent Wallace's *The Amber Witch* (libretto by Chorley after Meinhold's novel) was performed by Mapleson's company at Her Majesty's in 1861.

45. Muzio recorded matter-of-factly that in London there was no difference between contralto and bass ('A Londra contralto e basso è lo stesso') (Garibaldi, 337).

46. 'Da un *Naopoletano* la Lynd non si poteva sicuramente aspettare delle belle cose, giacchè essi sono invidiosi, superbi, e non potendo nè fare belle cose, ne cantar bene, non vogliono neanche che gli altri facciano bene' (Garibaldi, 343).

47. That it was a failure in Italy does not seem to be strictly true, as is

suggested by the list of printed librettos published in 'The Verdi Archive at New York Unversity: part II' (Chusid, Jensen, Dauy, 31). As late as 1870 Escudier wrote Verdi about a successful French revival of the opera, *Les brigands* (Casale, 10, note 7).

48. Phillips-Matz commented that 'Lumley did not answer at once; Verdi made other commitments; and the proposed future collaboration came to nothing' (Phillips-Matz, 219). Presumably Lumley would not have been eager to enter into a contract with Verdi on such terms at this point.

49. The Lind-Grisi short-lived rivalry in 1847 as Norma evoked many reactions by non-musical journalists. Albert Smith, in 'The War of the Normas', wrote:

> Now glory to La Diva, who still reigns the queen of
> song;
> And glory, too, to Costa — may he wield the bâton
> long. ...
> For ill-advised was Jenny, when she thought to reach
> the throne
> Of that unrivalled songstress who made the part her
> own.
> (Smith, *Wild Oats*, 218)

Another devoted theatre-goer, Edmund Yates, also remembered Lind's performance as inferior to Grisi's:

> The next time I heard Mdlle. Lind was from the same coign of vantage [i.e. the third row in the gallery], about a month later, on her first appearance in *Norma*, and, as this performance was attended by the Queen in state, I had equal difficulty in getting in. ... The performance itself was unquestionably a failure: the adherents of the theatre tried to talk about a "new reading" of the character of the Druidical priestess; but the public would have none of it; and it was generally allowed that Grisi's Norma remained untouched.
> (Yates, 1: 178-9)

50. Fashions in dress also had significance in the musical politics of the theatre war. Yates remembered that at Covent Garden 'it was the fashion of the younger men to wear, in evening dress, black ties, in contrast to the large double-folded white cravats which were *de rigeur* at the Haymarket house' (Yates, 1: 180).

51. In a discussion of Viardot, Chorley emphasized that this octave was the 'natural basis of every *soprano* voice' but in many singers it was 'weak, or toneless, or uncertain' (*Bentley's Miscellany*, July 1848: 38).

52. For a negative view of Sontag's voice, see Thackeray's letter to Adelaide Kemble (Mrs Sartoris) about the condition of her voice in 1850, when he heard her in Paris:

> I went to hear Sontag whom the polite world received with immense kindness, but what I admired most was some of the girls of the Conservatoire singing just a few notes by way of a chorus to one of her songs. O how much fresher their voices were than hers! O how much better it is to be young than to be anything else, ever so good, or clever, or rich! ... It doesn't do to have a 'beautiful voice, considering'. ... (28 March 1850, Ray, 2: 655-66)

53. Mendelssohn's brother wrote to Klingemann that Chorley's notices in the *Athenæum* of Mendelssohn's death had pleased him; they were simple, true, and deeply felt ('Der Chorleysche Aufsatz gefällt mir sehr wohl, und ich bitte Dich, ihm meinen aufrichtigen Dank zu sagen, daß er sich meiner bei dieser Gelegenheit erinnern wollte. Er ist einfach, wahr und tief gefühlt' (10 December 1847, Stolzenberg, 184).

CHAPTER SIX

The Fifties: in Mid-Career

1

The 1840s ended and the 1850s began with Chorley dissatisfied and disturbed by personal and professional changes. His main musical concerns in the 1850s were the decline of singing standards, Verdi's new operas, the legacy of Mendelssohn and Meyerbeer, the disappointing productions of the native English composers, and the disappointing reception given by English audiences to his new discovery, Gounod. In this period he widened the range of his literary activities: not only did he publish novels and reviews of novels, but he also attempted to succeed as a playwright.

C.W. Dilke had resigned the editorship of the *Athenæum* in 1846. His successor, T.K. Hervey, resigned in 1853. Under their successor, William Hepworth Dixon, the *Athenæum* lost some of its influence for a time, and Chorley's professional working environment was less sympathethic than it had been.

Other changes came in the form of losses: Chopin, who had played at parties in Chorley's house, died in October, 1849. Chorley's obituary in the *Athenæum* appeared 27 October 1849. In keeping with his belief that Chopin's sensibility, unlike Mendelssohn's, was feminine, he termed Chopin's genius 'as original as delicate' (1090). From Paris, Turgenev wrote praising his sympathy for Chopin: 'votre article sur Chopin dans l'Athenaeum m'a fait beaucoup de plaisir; je crois qu'il est difficile d'être à a fois plus sympathique et plus juste: c'est ainsi qu'il faut parler des morts' (6 November 1849).[1]

In November, in a letter to Richard Bentley, the publisher, Chorley proposed to write several musical articles of 'anecdotes and recollections' — his idea prompted by 'the death of poor Chopin — to whom I was much attached' (Monday, 5 November 1849; MS, Wigan Archives Service). The article on Chopin (evidently the only one of the several proposed which was actually written or published) appeared in February 1850 (185-91). In it, Chorley termed Chopin 'one of the most graceful, delicate, and original artists' who ever wrote for the piano, one whose works provided 'enchantment' (*Bentley's Miscellany*, 185). He instructed his readers in the meaning of Chopin's rubato as a key to understanding the composer:

> The left hand of the player is never to be out of *tempo*:
> the right hand may almost always (save in the case of

some distinctly formal instrumental figure) indulge in *tempo rubato*. Again, whereas other pianoforte masters insist on the equality of the fingers — in spite of the anatomical lock and key put by Nature on the motion of the third digit, — Chopin provided for their inequality: wishing, as he once told me, so far as was possible, to develop, not to destroy, the individuality of each member of the hand. (*Bentley's Miscellany*, 187)

Chopin's best interpreter was Liszt, when Liszt was 'dreaming' at the piano (188).

Chopin managed well the transition from the circle of Madame Dudevant (George Sand) in Paris to the lion-chasing salons of the Mrs Leo Hunters of London,[2] and Chorley concluded the article with touching reminiscences of Chopin's 1848 season in London, when he was so tired and ill that he had to be carried upstairs. At times he looked 'fifty when he took his place [at the piano]', but he was transfigured by playing the piano and looked 'twenty-five when he quitted it' (*Bentley's Miscellany*, 189).[3] Despite his illness he played at the London Polish Ball for charity, though 'hardly one of the audience cared when he began, or knew when he ended' (190). 'His death leaves us almost without a composer for his instrument meriting the name' (191). Hewlett (2: 95) reprinted Chorley's memorial sonnet.

CHOPIN

Like to the murmur of a weary stream,
   Like to the dance of yellow leaves that fall
   Fantastically slow, — like to the call
Of spirit to far spirit in a dream,
Thy music — save by times, when joyous theme
   Of clarion-note blown from a castle wall,
   Or pageant dance for Southern carnival —
Bade through the shadow pomp and pleasure beam.
   Years wore, and years — and paler burned the light,
And lower, softer breathed the dying song;
Thus fainteth day, gray willow-banks among,
   So gently that we know not when 'tis night.
   O, who dare mourn the loss of our delight,
Pain was so earnest and Decay so long!

In the autumn of 1850 there was further loss when Chorley's friend George B. Maule died unexpectedly in a road accident between Barcelona and Valencia (Hewlett, 2: 48). They had taken trips to the Continent together. Little is known about him; he 'left no mark by which the world will remember him' (Hewlett, 2: 47), but his death was a blow to Chorley, who recorded in his diary for 28 September 1850: 'We travelled three times together, and his face in my house often supplied the face of one of my own family. ... Travelling will never be to me the same thing again; for to him I largely owe my little experience on this subject...' (Hewlett, 2: 49).

Elizabeth Barrett continued to be concerned for Chorley's well-being. She wrote to Mary Russell Mitford on 9 January 1850, expressing concern about his depression, his seeming inability to live up to his potential, and his dissatisfaction with life and his career:

> Tell me, — do you hear often from Mr Chorley? It quite pains us to observe, from his manner of writing, the great depression of his spirits. His mother was ill in the summer — but plainly the sadness does not arise entirely or chiefly from this cause. He seems to me over-worked, taxed in the spirit. I advise nobody to give up work; but that Athenæum-labour is a sort of treadmill discipline in which there is no progress, nor triumph — & I do wish he w^d give that up & come out to use with a new set of anvils & hammers. Only of course he couldn't do it, even if he would, while there is illness in his family. May there be a whole sun of success shining upon the new play. (*Barrett-Mitford Correspondence*, 3: 289).

Three months later she returned to the subject, after the production of his play *Old Love and New Fortune*, commenting that his early promise remains sadly unfulfilled:

> We have heard from Mr Chorley who seems to have received very partial gratification in respect to his play, and yet prepares for more plays ... I cannot help thinking that he might achieve other sorts of successes more easily & surely. Your criticism is very just. But *I* like his 'Music & Manners in Germany' better than anything he has done — I believe I always *did* like it best — and since coming to Florence, I have heard cultivated Americans speak of it with enthusiasm, yes, with enthusiasm. 'Pomfret' they w^d scarcely believe to be by the same author. I agree with you that it is a pity indeed for him to tie himself to the wheels of the Athenæum, to *approfondir* [grow deeper into] the ruts . . what other end? (30 April 1850, *Barrett to Mitford Letters*, 3: 297-8).

While Barrett was concerned that Chorley was wasting his talents with journalism and playwriting (her private support for his talent coincided with his frequently expressed public support for her genius in the *Athenæum*),[4] Chorley was indeed engaged on a new novel: *Roccabella: A Tale of a Woman's Life*.[5] He intended to dedicate it to Charlotte Brontë as his contribution to the 'question so passionately referred to in "Jane Eyre" and "Shirley"'. But 'losses' and 'discouragements' in the first years of the 1850s caused him to set the novel aside. For a time it rested alongside his never-completed study of the nature of genius.

In the summer of 1850 Chorley assumed the editorship of *The Ladies' Companion*, on Mrs Loudon's retirement (Hewlett, 2: 6). (It is not clear exactly why Chorley took over the editorship from Elizabeth Loudon, or why he relinquished the editorship).[6] Like the *Athenæum*, Bradbury and Evans's periodical *The Ladies' Companion At Home and Abroad* was published every Saturday. It sold for 3d per copy. Each of the 27 issues comprising volume I (29 December 1849 through 22 June 1850) carried a subtitle: 'Edited by Mrs. Loudon, assisted by the most eminent writers and artists'. In her opening issue, Elizabeth Loudon wrote a statement of editorial policy, stating that the journal marked a change in the focus of her career — '… hitherto, my name has been only known in association with gardens and flowers' (29 December 1849: 8). The issues edited by Loudon mixed literary studies (Mary Cowden Clarke's *Shakspeare* [*sic*] *Studies of Woman* in seven parts), short stories and sketches, serialized novels, poetry, cursory notices of opera and other entertainments in London, and information about gardens, sewing, and general household concerns. Loudon's work was intended to serve 'a higher aim' (29 December 1849: 8), assisting women with such 'mental cultivation' as was appropriate to perform her 'duties'. The emphasis on mental cultivation was pronounced.[7]

The tone of the editorial in the first issue of the second volume of *The Ladies' Companion* signalled a change in emphasis away from the intellectual: fashion and 'the season' received greater emphasis as part of woman's world of duty.

> The return of Her Majesty to town on the 17th of June, and the daily chronicle of festivities for which our Sovereign's re-appearance has been the signal, in the form of drawing-rooms, balls, concerts, &c., revive speculations, for which this journal is perhaps the properest medium of utterance. — In whatsoever proportions the graver rights and duties of life are adjudged and distributed, to Woman, beyond all dispute, belongs the casting voice in social usages and manners. (29 June 1850: 8).

Chorley's editorials (none signed or initialled) were discursive and allusive. Gone were Loudon's focussed examinations of women's educational and working situations; the new editorials sometimes reprimanded, and scolded women for being scolds. Those on women's involvement in Protestant-Catholic religious controversy, for example, asserted that 'She [Woman] has too glibly argued matters' (30 November 1850: 360). Woman should return to being 'the Prop, not the Bellows. ... We would entreat her to refrain from swelling the tide of wrath by ejaculation, which is not reason, — and by emotion, which is partly temperament' (360).

As one would expect, Chorley's literary acquaintances contributed: eight essays on pets by Mary Russell Mitford appeared in the course of the first volume. (These later were expanded into *My Literary Life*, which Mitford dedicated to Chorley, but for whom 'this book would never have existed'.) Mrs T.K. Hervey contributed several short sketches and several poems. Geraldine E. Jewsbury's novel, *The Sorrows of Gentility*, was serialized in thirteen parts between 7 September 1850 and 30 November 1850. Mary Howitt, Chorley's acquaintance from the Friends in Liverpool days, published several of her own poems and one translation from Fredericka Bremer. The *Companion* no longer published George Hogarth on musical subjects: in his place H.F. Chorley signed 'Domestic Music and Fashion' (6 July 1850: 30-31) in which he repeated Hogarth's counsel that amateurs should stay away from music meant for Grisi, Sontag, Viardot, and Lind. He also signed 'Domestic Vocal Music: Limits and Hints' (17 August 1850: 126-7) and a two-part essay, 'Counsels to Contralto Singers' (19 October 1850: 270-71 and 30 November 1850: 383).

Chorley's novella, *The Story of a Bouquet*, written under his pseudonym 'Paul Bell', was published as the journal's lead story beginning in the first issue of the second volume (29 June 1850: 1-4) and was concluded in twelve chapters spread over four consecutive issues. A few months later Chorley serialized another novella anonymously: *Kate's December: A Tale of Mystery in Nine Chapters*.[8] Also scattered throughout volume two were eight of Chorley's poems, all signed H.F.C.

There were three short notices of new music in volume two. One was a positive notice of Schumann's *Album für die Jugend* (7 September 1850: 175). Though unsigned, it is probably Chorley's, despite its praise for a composer he normally condemned. It attributed good qualities to the piano pieces because they were *not* characteristic of their composer:

> Herr Schumann, the most mystical of mystical composers
> for the adult — a sort of Emerson among the musicians —
> has condescended, for the sake of beginners, to be as
> simply pretty, as charmingly clear, and as neatly charac-
> teristic, as if he had never puzzled grown folks. (7 Sep-
> tember 1850: 175)

With volume three (1 February 1850 through 1 July 1851) the characteristics of the periodical shifted again: it was now a monthly — with more fiction and a coloured full-page illustrations, either a fashion plate or an illustration to a story. Mary Russell Mitford continued her essays on poets — American Poets (O.W. Holmes) and Female Poets (Joanna Baillie, Catherine Fanshawe, Miss Susanna Blamire, and Mrs James Gray [Mary

Anne Browne]). Other contributions came from William and Mary Howitt and Mrs T.K. Hervey. Chorley praised his own long established favorites (Mendelssohn, Barrett Browning) and his recent discovery, Gounod. The review of Gounod's sacred pieces performed at Hullah's monthly concert in January presented him as a composer on the verge of great acclaim. Those who criticized Gounod, wrote Chorley, had a vested interest in doing so, or were unable to appreciate novelty. The audience 'was powerfully, incontestably moved' (1 February 1851: 45). Chorley went on record with a predication of Gounod's significance:

> In short, it will be a most disagreeable surprise to us,
> should the world fail to hear of him "loud and long," as
> one of the most original, most sincere, and most elegantly
> expressive of the poets who have ever spoken their poetry
> in Music. [signed "H.F.C."] (1 February 1851: 45)

The publication by Ewer and Company of Mendelssohn's *Heimkehr aus der Fremde (Son and Stranger)* was noted; the work was recommended for amateur performance 'in a small theatre, or even in a large drawing room' (1 April 1851: 141).

Not only did Chorley as editor welcome contributions from his friend Mary Russell Mitford, but he also recorded his admiration for her in his article, 'Female Poets: Mary Russell Mitford. By the Editor' (1 May 1851: 155-9). It consisted largely of an excerpt from Act 1 of Mitford's unperformed drama, *Otto of Wittelsbach*, and was a mark of esteem from one unperformed playwright to another.

The *Ladies' Companion* reviewed Barrett Browning's *Casa Guidi Windows* and Hawthorne's *House of Seven Gables* in the issue of 1 July 1851 (pages 244 and 245). Chorley's 'conviction' that Mrs Browning was 'supreme among the poetesses of England' was reinforced by 'her latest and best poem'. He quoted from it lines which were 'almost Shakspearian in their force and universal beauty' (244). His only reservation was his imperfect sympathy for her political views on Italy. Chorley considered the subject 'more complex' than she did (he had already begun writing his novel *Rocabella*, in which he satirized gullible English supporters of European revolutionary causes). The review was unsigned.

In the short notice of *The House of Seven Gables* in the *Companion*, Chorley stressed the importance of Hawthorne's fiction in general, commenting that 'our recommendation' discovered his talents nearly twenty years ago (1 July 1851: 245). In the *Athenæum*, he identified himself 'as having introduced Mr Hawthorne to the English public' (24 May 1851: 547). Hawthorne's early works had indeed interested Chorley, as Hewlett indicated:

> For the creative genius of Hawthorne he had always
> entertained the highest admiration, and was proud, as I
> have already noted, of having been the first English critic
> who drew attention to its manifestation in the "Twice-
> Told Tales." The novelist's subsequent works had
> received his lavish praise. both in public and private;
> especially the "Scarlet Letter," which he commended to a
> friend at Liverpool as "the most powerful and most pain-
> ful story of modern times — the only tale in its argument
> in which the *purity* overtops the *passion* ... It has struck
> me prodigiously; and I think will end in taking a very
> remarkable place among stories of its quality." (Hewlett,
> 2: 108-9)

This long sustained support for Hawthorne in the *Athenæum* began as early
as his 1837 review of *Twice Told Tales*, and in his notice of *The Wonder
Book*, he remarked that 'it is fifteen years since we began to follow him in
the American periodicals' and to call his work to the attention of British
readers (17 January 1852: 81).

The marked file of the *Athenæum* attributes a number of reviews of
Hawthorne to Chorley:

1. *Mosses from an Old Manse* (8 August 1846: 807-8)
2. *The House of Seven Gables* (24 May 1851: 545-7).
   Chorley is particularly interested, 'as having introduced
   Mr. Hawthorne to the English public' (547), a point
   also stressed in the notice in *The Ladies' Companion* (1
   July 1851: 245).
3. *The Blithedale Romance* (10 July 1852: 741-3) (the
   issue's lead review)
4. *Transformation; or, The Romance of Monte Beni* [*The
   Marble Faun*] (3 March 1860: 296-7)
5. *Our Old Home* (3 October 1863: 428-30. 'A more
   charming, more unpleasant book has never been written concerning England than this ... [it shows] surprisingly bad temper' 428).[9]

Although Chorley was often enthusiastic about other novelists' books, to
other critics' music criticism, perhaps not surprisingly, he responded more
often with correction or reproof. For example, when George Hogarth published a revised version of *The Musical Drama* as *Memoirs of the Opera* in
1850, Chorley's review tried to correct some of the work's mistaken principles. Hogarth believed, incorrectly, that for opera after Rossini, 'the music
is everything, the drama nothing'. In fact it was the other way around,
insisted Chorley. In general, although these were 'agreeable volumes',

Athenæum readers were cautioned that Hogarth had produced 'no complete manual or memoir' (11 January 1851: 58).

He was unimpressed with the work of the one musical journalist who was also a prominent composer: Berlioz. For example, despite his commendation in 1852 of Berlioz' treatment of the orchestra in *Romeo and Juliet*, his review in 1856 of Mary Cowden Clarke's translation of Berlioz's *A Treatise upon Modern Instrumentation and Orchestration* focused on what Berlioz did *not* know about the musical instruments: Berlioz thought harps were properly termed orchestral instruments (instead of solo instruments), and he thought organs had five manuals — true only of the 'ferocious, shrieking old French organs'. This misunderstanding perhaps accounted for his dislike of the organ's use with orchestra, and it exposed what Chorley considered shocking ignorance of Handel's music. 'It is not from such a measure of experience that the great treatise of instrumentation of the nineteenth century is to be written'. Finally, Berlioz did not know how to write for voices, witness his 'repulsive leap of a ninth' in the 'Cinq Mai' Cantata, which he cited as a model! In short, 'we do not consider him complete, calm and self-postponing enough to be of high value as a teacher' (*Athenæum*, 1 November 1856: 1343).[10]

For his fellow authors of opera libretti, Chorley seldom had a good word. Chorley's concern for the principles of libretto construction showed in his many severe comments on operatic libretti. In explaining why only two of Mozart's operas still hold the stage (*Don Giovanni* — which had achieved 'canonization in England' already[11] — and *Figaro*) he stated that the stories of the others 'are obsolete, puerile, and not dramatically interesting' (*Athenæum*, 4 May 1850: 483). Writing of Rossini's otherwise exemplary *Guillaume Tell*, he complained that '[t]he opera-book contains almost every fault that an opera-book can contain' (10 April 1852: 410). He joined the universal chorus of condemnation for Bunn's translations, remarking in the Musical and Dramatic Gossip column of 1 May 1852, of the English *Fidelio*: 'When the appearance and acceptance of such *perversions* are possible, who can wonder that English persons of education avoid listening to operas in English ...' (497). Of Spohr's setting of *Faust* he wrote: 'the story is one unfit for music, unless it be treated in the commonest melo-dramatic form' (17 July 1852: 780).[12]

Another great loss came in the autumn of 1851. While Chorley was out of the country, his mother died. Her death was followed by no change in the pattern of his life except that in the following year, he purchased the house in which he lived for the rest of his life: 13 Eaton Place West. Like the places he had shared with Reeve, it was in Belgravia, fashionable and newly developed, with street after street of expensive and spacious residences behind dignified, cream stucco façades. Spacious residences except for Chorley's, that is. The estate agent showing the house to Chorley made a comment about its narrow staircase. 'Never mind', Chorley replied to the astonished agent, 'I shall require a very narrow coffin' (Hewlett, 2: 217). Charles Hallé called it 'the tiniest in London perhaps' (Kennedy, 118). He visited it often, meeting there not only musicians, writers and even future chief justices (Alexander Cockburn and J.D. Coleridge),[13] and described it as 'real gem' (118). Hewlett remembered its richly decorated interior this way:

> The dining-room, to which dark paper and curtains, a tall antique cabinet in carved oak, a projecting *armoire*, filled with old china, books on each side of the window, and some specimens of Etty, Turner, Patrick Nasmyth, and other artists, gave a certain air of sombre quaintness; the recessed landings, and the miniature double drawing-room, bright with white and gold, formed singularly attractive reception-rooms for a bachelor with a large acquaintance, while the "chamber in the wall," as he used to call his tiny spare bed-room, was big enough for the lodging of any guest who was more than an acquaintance. (Hewlett, 2: 217)

2 Gounod: The Discovery

Chorley announced Gounod's genius to the English reading public in 'Musical and Dramatic Gossip' for 26 January 1850. He predicted there on good authority that a great new composer was about to emerge in France (107). Not long after that, Viardot introduced Chorley to Gounod, and Chorley reacted as if thunderstruck, recording in his journal for March, 1850: 'It was great pleasure to me in Paris to add to my list of sensations Gounod, of whom the world will one day hear as *the* composer, or else H.F.C. is much mistaken' (Hewlett, 2: 94). That same month in the *Athenæum* Chorley announced that the 'new composer' — as we know from 'private information' was writing an opera for the *Opéra*, to be performed in next winter's season (23 March 1850: 321).

Again in the issue of 27 April 1850, Chorley mentioned the French 'composer of extraordinary distinction and promise' (259). Gounod is mentioned by name in the issue of 22 June 1850, where the 'Gossip' mentioned that he won a prize for composition ten years ago at the *Conservatoire* and that in his new opera there would be a principal part for Viardot.

Gounod sent Chorley some sacred choral works, hoping he could get them performed (MS letter cited in Huebner, *Gounod*: 34); Chorley obligingly urged John Hullah to agree to perform them. This created awkwardness, as Frances Hullah explained, since Chorley was more certain of their genius than was Hullah. As Hullah's wife later recalled, Chorley,

> having found 'a new composer, Gounod by name,' wished to secure him a hearing rather on trust, Mr. Hullah preferring to wait till he could call on Gounod in Paris, where he meant to pass his next Easter vacation. Fortunately he was able to agree with Mr. Chorley in his estimation of Gounod, though he wrote somewhat cautiously: 'I carried off four compositions from Madame Viardot's house ... Of these things it is difficult to speak confidently. A great original musical genius is such a creation that one is slow to come to any conclusion. That the pieces I have seen and heard, in a way, are thoroughly workmanlike is their least praise; perhaps their most extraordinary quality is their simplicity.' (Hullah, 57)

Chorley, of course, shared none of Hullah's tentativeness about Gounod's genius. Personally, too, he was flattered by Gounod's fervent attentions. Gounod wrote to him (as 'mon bon, bien cher, excellent ami') on 11 October 1850 with news about the progress of *Sapho* and the revisions it was undergoing; he charged Chorley to keep this all confidential.[14] By December, Gounod was addressing Chorley as 'mon bien cher ami et frère'.[15]

When Hullah performed four pieces by Gounod at St Martin's Hall in January, 1851, Chorley announced in the *Athenæum* that 'we augur a career of no ordinary interest for M. Gounod' because he has 'a genius at once true and new' (18 January 1851: 89).

In the same year, Chorley joined Viardot, Turgenev, and others hovering around Gounod in Courtavenel as he put finishing touches on *Sapho*. For three days Chorley was part of the process of creation. Gounod wrote to Turgenev that *Sapho* 'feels that she is surrounded by grandmothers, godfathers, godmothers ...'[16] Though French critics saw it as a *succès d'estime* (Huebner, 33), Chorley told *Athenæum* readers that its production was 'one of those events which mark a period in Art', the opera 'justifying to the fullest every opinion expressed and every prophecy put forth respecting him' (19 April 1851: 436). It received a single performance at Covent Garden in August. Chorley said the critics presented 'a chaos of unmitigated dispraise and hopeful admiration' (16 August 1851: 882). The 'dispraise' came certainly from *The Times* and the *Musical World* ('a work more full of pretention and more empty of merit we never heard');[17] the hopeful admiration came mainly, it seems, from Chorley. He insisted that Gounod's opera 'entitles him to a place among the most eminent living composers' (882). Later, in *Thirty Years' Musical Recollections* (1862), he termed it

the 'best *first* opera ever written' except *Fidelio* (2: 153), and complained
about being alone in his early recognition of Gounod's genius:

> Though "Sapho" was well received by the audience ... the
> wrath and ridicule outpoured by most of the censors of the
> press, were too vehement and curious not to be put on
> record. The event has not justified the sagacity of those
> who jeered at and assailed the music, and who declared
> that any expectation invested in its writer was only so
> much sheer hallucination. (2: 156)

In the *Athenæum's* 'New Publications' column, 6 August 1853, Chorley
commented that Gounod's *Méditation sur le Premier Prélude de Piano de
S. Bach* ['Ave Maria'] was 'an inspiration' and was 'the rage' in Paris
(947). Later this combination of Gounod's ingeniously sentimental melody
with Bach's first Prelude from the *Well Tempered Clavier* became the rage
in England, too. When Gounod's next opera, *La Nonne Sanglante*, failed at
the Opéra in Paris in 1854, Chorley — while not predicting future success
for it — insisted that it had much 'admirable' music, and that — given the
'luckless and impracticable story' — its 'failure cannot be accepted as
decisive' (28 October 1854: 1308).

Chorley's interest in Gounod's potential to become a great composer
intensified. In 1856 the New Philharmonic Society, with Benedict as conductor, performed Gounod's second symphony 'with great care and spirit'
(26 April 1856: 527). The symphony was 'behind its time', a quality which
was not its weakness but its strength, since the example of Mendelssohn
demonstrated how contemporary genius could take 'retrogressive' forms (26
April 1856: 527):

> [G]ratitude is owed to the *New Philharmonic Society* for
> its having brought out unfamiliar works, such as the two
> Masses by Cherubini, — for its having enabled the
> Londoner to form some judgment, "for better for worse,"
> on the peculiarities of M. Berlioz, — for its having
> afforded to English writers that helping-hand for which
> they are always crying, and of which they never seem
> able to avail themselves, — and now, for being "first
> foot" (as the Scotch say) in producing one of the latest
> works of a composer to whom the world is beginning to
> turn, for present pleasure, and with hope for the future.
> (26 April 1856: 527)

Chorley's review of this symphony is unusually important in understanding the perspective from which Chorley assessed potential additions to the
canon. Its assumptions about Beethoven, Mendelssohn, and issues of
influence-borrowing-plagiarism illustrate not only Chorley's reaction to

Gounod's artistry specifically, but also to contemporary symphonic music in general. In his eagerness to persuade, Chorley revealed underlying principles more articulately and expansively than usual:

> We have been always at variance with those who hold that Music can only be continued by destruction, and who maintain that, to be new in symphonic writing, it is necessary to begin where Beethoven ended, — forgetting that subsequent to the close of his career and the diffusion of his last works, such events have taken place as the disinterment of Bach and the acceptance of a genius in Mendelssohn, entirely distinct from Beethoven's, and, in some sort, retrogressive. Such preachers of strange doctrine must be greatly discomfited by such a work as M. Gounod's Second Symphony. New it is, though not modish; — fresh in feeling and clear in idea, though as regards profession of discovery, not more audacious than Haydn's later and Mozart's earlier Symphonies. (527)[18]

Gounod was primarily, but not exclusively, the focus of Chorley's attentions when he considered the possibility of French music as pointing the right direction to Europe. For example, a few months after his review of Gounod's second symphony, he returned from a visit to Paris with praise not only for Gounod but also for Louis Théodore Gouvy:

> The faith, which we have for some years expressed in France, as in a country likely to yield sane and sound musical composition in the form of symphonic music, gathers strength with every subsequent visit. (10 January 1857: 57)

Saint-Saëns, too, was French in the best sense:

> Among the younger Frenchmen there is M. Camille Saint-Saens, with some of whose orchestral music we had the other day an opportunity of making a partial acquaintance. He, too, has ideas, and a way of his own, which are neither Italian nor German. ... We should be glad to hear any instrumental compositions as unmistakeably English as the symphonies, overture, and *intermezzi* of these gentlemen are distinctively French. (10 January 1857: 57)

In 1858 Chorley commented in regard to Gounod's first Symphony that 'The *Crystal Palace Concerts*, again, show that the music of M. Gounod is making its way, as all true things will do, resistlessly; — no matter by whom the barriers put up' (20 March 1858: 378). There was a long, number by number analysis of the score of Gounod's 'Solemn Mass' in the issue of 10 April 1858 (472-3).

At the *Opéra* in Paris, he reported that the revival (though 'with mutilations') of *Sapho* with Désirée Artôt (11 September 1858: 337) was successful. Better still, Gounod's next opera, *Le Médicin malgré lui*, performed at the Théâtre Lyrique, was heard 'with an amount of pleasure hard to overstate' (25 September 1858: 403). Gounod seemed to be coming into his own as a dramatic composer. At this time Chorley, disgruntled with the Opéra, was quite positive about the thriving state of performances at the Théâtre Lyrique, and was a keen supporter of the 'consummate singing' of its prima donna, Marie Caroline Miolan-Carvalho (7 November 1857: 1396). Therefore it was not surprising that, after *Le Médicin*, Chorley looked forward to the promised new opera *Faust* 'with great interest' (25 September 1858: 403).

Faust came to assume central importance in Chorley's writings during the 1860s. When Chorley reported on its first performance, with Miolan-Carvalho as Marguerite at the Théâtre Lyrique, he wrote proudly about his own prescience: 'In 1851 the name of M. Gounod was unknown, save to some half-a-dozen persons' (26 March 1859: 428). Chorley predicted, as he had earlier about *Les Huguenots*, that it was only a matter of time before English audiences would take it to their hearts. For him, *Faust* was the legitimate heir of the French Grand Opera tradition, which he had supported since the 1830s, and was the long-wished-for alternative to the wild 'music of the future'.

Chorley hoped that Gounod would set his version of *Winter's Tale*, with Viardot as Hermione. In 1847, Mendelssohn had chosen not to set Chorley's libretto. Sadly for Chorley's intermittent hopes of riding to fame on another man's coat tails, nothing came of this project with Gounod, either.[19]

3 The Italian and French Schools

The view of the 1850s emerging from Chorley's weekly journalism — generally confirmed by his retrospective view in *Thirty Years' Musical Recollections*, had several broad outlines: 1. French Grand Opera had finally achieved its proper place in London (thanks in no small degree to Chorley's far-sightedness), 2. the Royal Italian Opera at Covent Garden under Gye's management was justly triumphing over Her Majesty's Theatre in the Haymarket, still under Lumley, and 3. Verdi had regrettably solidified his grip on English audiences through the popular *Rigoletto-Trovatore-Traviata* trio. Although each of these operas was susceptible to the sort of formulaic abuse Chorley lavished on their predecessors, there were some occasions when he was grudgingly impressed by these operas, especially *Trovatore*.

In 'Musical and Dramatic Gossip' for 5 January 1850, Chorley printed the report that *Luisa Miller* was 'very coldly received' at Naples (26). The next week's 'gossip' announced that the report of the failure had been contradicted, but he quoted 'a Naples correspondent' to confirm it (12 January, 1850: 51). *I Puritani* was reported as 'dead', — neither Lind nor Sontag being able to revive it — and Chorley contrasted this short lived success with the opera whose importance he had proclaimed, *Les Huguenots*, which was still 'of first-class interest' (16 March 1850: 292). Mayer's *Medea*, revived with Parodi, was dead, too, and Chorley wondered how even Pasta 'could now impose upon the world music so monotonously mediocre as this' (16 March 1850: 291).

In March 1850, the two houses began their seasons: the Royal Italian Opera commenced 'brilliantly' with 'an admirable performance' of *Il Franco Arciero* (i.e. *Der Freischütz*, with recitatives by Costa), though Chorley remarked in *Thirty Years'* that it was 'relished by others more than by myself. German music and Southern words do not agree' (2: 121). Her Majesty's Theatre revived *Nino/Nabucco* (with Sims Reeves and Parodi) to Chorley's fervent wish: may that be all for now of Verdi's operas — 'their popularity in England is not on the increase' (23 March 1850: 320). The time for French opera (imported in Italian translation) had finally arrived — and Tamberlik's debut in *Masaniello* at the Royal Italian Opera in *Masaniello* was well received (6 April 1850: 378).

Although Catherine Hayes and Sims Reeves were singing *Lucia* well at Her Majesty's Theatre, 'how long will singers continue to be so distressingly fond of this sickly work?' Moreover, 'the Haymarket band is by many degrees worse than it was in 1849' (6 April 1850: 378). Sontag's voice in *Don Pasquale* at Her Majesty's Theatre, though small, showed 'delicate vocal brilliancy' but Donizetti is passé, 'our English taste being now set towards grand Opera' (13 April 1850: 401). Similarly, the new tenor in *I Lombardi* at Her Majesty's Theatre, Beaucarde, 'has a tenor voice of the most beautiful quality possible' and has 'a triumph'. Too bad he did not sing 'other music than that of the newest Italian destructives — which, we trust, and believe, will never take root in England' (27 April 1850: 458).

While Grisi and Mario were praised in *Les Huguenots* at Covent Garden, Sontag at Her Majesty's Theatre was 'overparted' in *I Puritani*, 'that most exhausted of operas' (11 May 1850: 513).

As Alice in *Roberto il diavolo* Grisi astounded him: 'There are few facts in the annals of music comparable to this Lady's entering upon grand French opera after so many years of practice in the dramatically slighter Italian school'. Only Viardot was better (25 May 1850: 562). Chorley quite shifted his opinion, one of the few times he did, when he wrote *Thirty Years'*, saying of the *Alice* of Grisi, whom he termed 'the most resolute of Opera-Queens to retain her throne by trying at everything which every singer had done', that 'a more complete mistake was never made' (2:129). By contrast, *Lucrezia Borgia* at Her Majesty's Theatre provided yet another occasion for commenting on the waning golden age of singing:

> Madame Frezzolini is possibly the most attractive and finished specimen extant of the songstress dear to and destroyed by Verdi; and the present plight of her voice, its former even beauty considered, may wisely be taken to heart by all *cantatrici* who find the new school, so called, easy and seductive. (25 May 1850: 561)

Viardot's excellence in the French school was celebrated on the occasion of her appearance as Fides in *Le Prophète*: 'we can but advisedly record a triumph which is unique in our recollections of the stage. — The whole opera goes infinitely better than last year' (22 June 1850: 668).

The production of *Moise* at Covent Garden in 1850 was of the revised version: 'the composer seems to have been aware that it contained some of his most glorious music. …The new introduction and the new *finale* to the third act' were new to London audiences in 1850 (*Thirty Years'*, 2: 124-5). The new matter is 'magnificent': 'what can be said that is too high in praise?' (125). Dazzled by Tamberlik's high notes, Chorley wrote in the *Athenæum* that his 'C sharp in chest-voice … claims a record as the most amazing feat which we have ever encountered in our experience of tenors' (20 July 1850: 772).

Halévy's *Juive* with Viardot as Rachel was performed at the Royal Italian Opera this season, and *La Tempesta* at Her Majesty's Theatre. Chorley treated both respectfully. *La Juive* is 'the best French ware of the second class' (*Thirty Years'*, 2: 131), as well as 'M. Halévy's best serious opera' (*Thirty Years'*, 2: 129); and the libretto to *The Tempest* was by Scribe ('the French as not to be trusted with Shakespeare', 2: 114).

The season of 1850 verified that, in general, London opera audiences were lucky: 'it is past doubt that the public gains by the rivalry, in the variety and excellence of the artists summoned' and in 'energy' (31 August 1850: 931). The '*ballet* appears to have been tacitly abandoned, — even at *Her Majesty's Theatre*' (931), and, in general, the quality of performances at Her Majesty's 'has been lower than in former years, the orchestra more slovenly, and the chorus coarser' (931).

After the season, Chorley kept his concerns before his readers in the 'Musical and Dramatic Gossip' columns. About Meyerbeer's continental reputation, for example, he wrote:

> Let critics, anti-Meyerbeerish or anti-Israelitish, or hyper-mystical, rail as they will, the popularity of the 'Prophète' has spread like wildfire throughout Germany. (7 September 1850: 956)

It was reported from Trieste that Verdi's *Stiffelio* 'pleased less' than *Luisa Miller*, which itself 'pleased very little. In fact, it was obvious that such acceptance as Signor Verdi finds can only be based on the absence of any better composer' (7 December 1850: 1288).

The earliest mention of *Rigoletto* seemed to be in the issue of 5 April 1851, in the 'Musical and Dramatic Gossip' column:

> 'Rigoletto,' Signor Verdi's new opera, founded on 'Le Roi s'amuse,' is described as poor in melody and entirely deficient in concerted pieces. The composer, however, is said to have made less noise with his orchestra than on former occasions. (387)

Later that autumn, the report from 'foreign correspondence' was that 'never, surely, was opera more ignominiously received' than was *Viscardello* (18 October 1851: 1097). 'Yet', Chorley added, 'the opera is by no means its maker's worst, — ... in particular, the treatment of the orchestra in a night-duett, betwixt two men, pleased me. ... But the staleness and common-place of every *motivo* is only equalled by its ugliness' (1097). In 1861, in *Thirty Years' Musical Recollections*, Chorley recalled the hostile Roman audience at that performance: 'I have never heard an opera more furiously hissed than was "Viscardello" (the Papal version of "Rigoletto") at Rome, in the year 1851: although that work is now everywhere' (2: 291).

Periodically, Chorley criticized the management of the opera houses, but the subject was no longer treated so obsessively as it had been in the mid-1840s. Moreoever, these 'asides' were not always directed at Lumley, who, indeed, was commended for his production of Halévy's *La Tempesta* in 1850 and in 1851, on the production of Thalberg's *Florinda* (although Scribe's '*libretto* is not a good one'). Chorley commented that the opera's 'production is in the highest degree creditable to the management of Mr Lumley; whose resolution to try novelty merits all honour, — whether the novelty be esteemed by the public a blank or a prize' (5 July 1851: 724). Nevertheless, during Lumley's troubles in 1852, Chorley was not sympathetic: the troubles were 'the necessary consequence of the measures of bad management steadily pursued' (29 May 1852: 611). And despite Gye's presentation of Gounod's *Sapho* at Covent Garden, Chorley was stern with him: 'we cannot hold Mr. Gye's to have been a satisfactory season' — and, 'Feeling, as we do, that the Covent Garden standard has been of great importance to art, we cannot see it depreciated without words of warning earnest and early' (30 August 1851: 933). At the end of the season of 1852, Chorley again criticized Gye: 'There are time and material for the retrieval of lost character in future seasons, should the management please. If it should not, — the theatre must go the way of so many other theatres, and perish of mistakes in its management' (28 August 1852: 923). A year later, noting that Piatti, the cellist, and Bottesini, the bass player, had not been re-engaged for the orchestra and that the *programme* was unsatisfactory, Chorley compared Gye's future to Lumley's past: 'If Mr. Gye begins thus early to play Mr. Lumley's game, he is certain to meet with Mr. Lumley's fate; and that after a briefer reign ...' (26 March 1853: 393).

That season, Mr Lumley's 'game' had reached a barrier: when his house closed, it did not reopen. Harold Rosenthal attributed to Lumley a series of problems beyond his control:

> First there was the lawsuit over Johanna Wagner, then the non-arrival of Sontag; then rumours that Balfe was going to resign, and that Lablache, Cruvelli and Gardoni all wanted to leave. In the event the public lost all faith in the management and by the end of the season Lumley was virtually bankrupt. There was to be no opera at Her Majesty's for the next three summers. (Rosenthal, *Two Centuries*, 100)

Lumley believed that many of his problems were caused by his 'Italian Opera speculation in Paris' (*Reminiscences* 322), asserting that the Parisian *Coup d'Etat* of 2 December 1851 destroyed the fortunes of Italian Opera (325). Chorley, however, believed that Lumley's own management failures were behind the closing of the house:

> But, it must be stated that one cause of wreck and disaster was the desertion of the theatre, owing to the systematic deterioration of its musical performances, — for which the temporary frenzy (the word is not too strong) excited by one wonder [Lind], offered no equivalent. (*Thirty Years'*, 2: 195-6)

During the closing of Her Majesty's, Covent Garden, that bastion of French Grand Opera, presented Verdi's popular new Italian operas. *Rigoletto* arrived in May, 1853. The quartet in the opera's last act, the 'gem of the opera', was 'deservedly *encored*' (21 May 1853: 625), and *Rigoletto* was pronounced the only success with the public of the 'disappointing' season (27 August 1853: 1018). Finally, Verdi

> took some real hold of our public. It is by some spoken of as Signor Verdi's best work. — I have always found it dull, dismal, and weak. ... One excellent piece, however, "Rigoletto" does contain — that quartett, in which while the libertine *Duke* and *Maddalena*, the assassin's sister and decoy, are toying within the wretched hovel, the

daughter and the father are shivering in the storm without. This is most ingeniously and effectively combined. — Further, the *Duke* has a popular song, the frivolity of which is not misplaced; and on these two numbers — on the coarse but forcible horror of the revolting story, and on the exceeding fitness of the actors to their parts [Bosio, Mario, Ronconi] — may be ascribed such favour as "Rigoletto" has gained in England. (*Thirty Years'*, 2: 196-7)

Chorley's notices of the final years of Grisi's career began in 1853 when he stated that the her New York engagement was to be taken as an indication of her retirement (27 August 1853: 1018), but on 15 October he retracted the news about America (1233) and in his yearly reflections on the season just passed, expressed doubts as to whether Grisi was really retiring at all (17 June 1854: 757). His irritation with her for not retiring, or rather for repeatedly retiring and then reappearing, increased (the next year he noted disapprovingly that Grisi 'unwisely, we think, reconsidered her determination [to retire]; and will appear for a few more "farewell" nights', (19 May 1855: 593). By contrast, he was so pleased with Bosio at this period that he considered a *Barbiere* at the Royal Italian Opera with her, Mario, and Lablache 'worthy of the best days that are gone' (13 May 1854: 596), and when Bosio sang Gilda a few nights later, Chorley found that her 'exquisite singing' helped to 'make endurable Verdi's weak "Rigoletto", — which opera has been revived with success'. (27 May 1854: 659). 'Musical and Dramatic Gossip' for June 3, 1854, mentioned the 'first of [Grisi's] twelve farewell performances ... in her favourite part of *Norma*' (694).[20]

In 1855, *Trovatore* joined *Rigoletto* as a major public success. At the Royal Italian Opera, Chorley momentarily forgot that Verdi's operas ruined voices; they did not ruin the voices of Ney [Bürde-Ney], Viardot (especially), Tamberlik, and the promising Graziani. About *Trovatore* Chorley was more positive, or at less negative, than he generally was about Verdi: 'The beginning of the second act, the concerted piece at its close, and the entire fourth act, are his best operatic music' (19 May 1855: 593). In his overview of the opera season, written a few months later, he stated simply that '[t]he fourth act of "Il Trovatore" has advanced Signor Verdi's reputation here as a composer' (11 August 1855: 930).

The somewhat grudging concession that Verdi's operas might have some worth was interesting coming from Chorley. He returned to this possibility in *Thirty Years' Musical Recollections*, in his ambivalent commentary on *Trovatore's* popular success in the season of 1855:

> Signor Verdi this year, at last, arrived at his real popularity in England — not equalling that of Bellini, but surpassing that of Donizetti — by the production of his "Il Trovatore," — the work among his works in which his best qualities are combined, and in which indications scattered throughout earlier productions present themselves in the form of their most complete fulfilment. ... [It contains] a quintessence of all that Signor Verdi has derived, combined, and originated; with something of his own. ... One of the points in "Il Trovatore," — which may be found worthy of remembering ... is Signor Verdi's essay at vocal Spanish gipsy colour The chorus of waifs and strays opening the second act has an uncouthness, — a bar or two of Oriental drawl, — before the Italian anvils begin, — which must remind anyone of such real gipsy music, as can be heard and seen in Spain. ... No melody really exists among those people, — and the wild cries which they give out could not be reduced to notation, were it not for the dance which they accompany.
>
> There is much more in the "Miserere" scene — a picturesque beauty, and an originality not to be doubted or denied by anyone to whom the stage speaks — though the leading phrase of the concerted piece might never have been found, had not there been an apparition scene in "Semiramide," in which Signor Rossini had shown how terror might be told in rhythm. ...
>
> [T]he charm of "*Il balen*" must wear out in time. ...
>
> Possibly, too, "Il Trovatore" has already lost that popularity, in all its fulness, which its music enjoyed for awhile [*sic*]. There is no returning to the work as a whole, for reasons already indicated — the essentially superficial and showy nature of its effects. (*Thirty Years'*, 2: 218-23)

Thus, Chorley deemed the initially impressive *Trovatore* effects 'already exhausted' (*Athenæum*, 6 July 1861: 25). But in 1855 he was not yet tired of those effects: with Ney, Viardot, Tamberlik, and Graziani, the opera 'could be heard from time to time without repugnance, and the fourth act with pleasure — when it is given so well as at Covent Garden' (19 May 1855: 593).

In a notice of Rossini's *Conte Ory*,[21] which opened the Royal Italian Opera season for 1855 'pleasantly', Chorley commented on the patchwork nature of the music ('How many of the pieces may belong to Signor Rossini's 'Viaggio a Rheims' is not to be told, — but the opera has in no respect the air of a piece of patchwork' [21 April 1855: 466]), and on the high quality of the music: '... to think of what Italian music has sunk to since it was written' (466). By way of illustration of this point, when *Ernani* was performed by the Royal Italian Opera at Covent Garden, Chorley reverted to his 'it's just a passing phase' approach to Verdi: 'Time merely increases our conviction that, in England and France, the operas of Signor Verdi only pass because there is nothing else', The time was ripe for a better composer to come along and easily 'sweep them away to the limbo of forgotten frenzies' (5 May 1855: 528).[22]

This season Chorley welcomed Meyerbeer's 'new' work, 'L'Étoile du Nord', as a 'triumph' (21 July 1855: 847), another vindication of his own perspicacity fifteen or so years earlier, when he attempted to convince his readers that in Paris Meyerbeer was creating a new and exciting kind of music drama. As on other occasions, Chorley took pleasure in pointing out that those earlier works were now, at last, firmly established in the repertory:

> Operatically, the past has been the Meyerbeer week at Covent Garden. Three of the composer's grand operas have been given five times during seven days, — 'Le Prophète' for the first time this year on Tuesday. Madame Viardot never acted the part of *Fides* with more spirit, or sang it with fuller, finer voice, than on this occasion (4 August 1855: 907).[23]

In the following week's 'Musical and Dramatic Gossip' he noted that the English were now 'constant' to Meyerbeer (11 August 1855: 930) but continued to demonstrate '*over*-constancy' to operas like *Norma* and *Lucrezia Borgia* (930). This complaint may have reflected not so much his dislike for the operas themselves as his irritation that Grisi continued to sing those roles instead of retiring gracefully: 'Considering the state of Madame Grisi's voice ... we hope she will stop reappearing', he wrote (28 July 1855: 880), and added the following year, 'we are sorry to see' that Grisi was advertised to reappear in the season of 1856 (2 February 1856: 144).

On the whole it seemed that opera was faring better in London than in Paris in the mid-1850s. Chorley was no longer entirely convinced that they ordered things better at the Paris Opéra.[24] When Chorley commented on *Semiramide* at Paris in the autumn of 1854 he deplored the 'dismal people' of the chorus, the 'feeble' orchestra, and the 'parsimony' shown in the scenery (14 October 1854: 1236). A far cry from the hey-day of the 1830s, when he urged his readers to travel to Paris where alone they could comprehend the power of grand opera.

At the beginning of 1855, the *Athenæum* reprinted in condensed form an article by d'Ortigue in the *Journal des Débats* about the first performance of Berlioz's 'L'Enfance de [*sic*] Christ', which 'seems to have created a real sensation in Paris' (6 January 1855: 23). Although Chorley wrote the words to part of this piece, he seemed uninterested in it, and his few references to it seem perfunctory, though not entirely dismissive.[25]

All in all, the year 1855 had been a remarkable one: the fourth act of *Trovatore*, which 'has advanced Signor Verdi's reputation as a composer' (11 August 1855: 930); Meyerbeer's presence for the production of 'L'Etoile', Wagner's controversial appointment to conduct the Philharmonic; and Berlioz's reappearance in London to conduct the New Philharmonic.

During the winter months of 1855-56, Chorley frequently noticed the performances of Jenny Lind-Goldschmidt, now a concert rather than an opera singer, and he continued to regard her with some ambivalence. On one occasion he wrote that 'Now, too, her voice is at its best' (15 December 1855: 1471), but on another he asserted that her singing was 'strenuous' (5 January 1856: 18). Her oratorio singing was excellent in *Elijah* (22 December 1855: 1504), better even than in the *Creation* or the *Messiah* (22 December 1855: 1504 and 5 January 1856: 18). Although she now sang works requiring little virtuosity, she could still dazzle with, for example, a chromatic scale 'ascending to and descending from E altimissimo' (12 January 1856: 47). Nevertheless, at her second concert, Chorley had never heard 'her upper octave so strained', and predicted that 'at any moment the period of decay may arrive'. Chorley reported the rumour that 'Madame Goldschmidt will sing again at *Her Majesty's Theatre* this spring. In this, however, we do not place credit, imagining it merely a tale encouraged by those who desire to see that opera-house re-opened' (26 January 1856: 111). And re-opened it was, and with Benjamin Lumley again at the helm, though of course without Lind, whose farewell to opera was indeed permanent.

The event that precipitated the re-opening of Her Majesty's Theatre was a fire at the rival theatre. After a ball on Wednesday, 5 March, Covent Garden Theatre caught fire about 5 a.m., and burned completely, fortunately with no loss of life. During the ten years of its existence, it had presented 'performances of a perfection, as regards their orchestral and choral execution, hitherto unheard in England' (*Athenæum*, 8 March 1856: 304)[26] The company decided to give performances that season at the Lyceum. Lumley took advantage of his opportunity.

Her Majesty's, newly opened after three years, soon found *La Traviata* a tremendous draw, with Piccolomini as Violetta; her success (along with the other seasonal sensation, Johanna Wagner as Bellini's Romeo) cheered Lumley and distressed Chorley. After Chorley had the opportunity to look over the printed score of *Traviata* he reported that it was 'written in the composer's later manner; — grouping with his "Rigoletto" and "Trovatore" without being equal to the latter opera' (3 May 1856: 562).[27] He also reported, but disapproved of, Piccolomini's popular success: 'never *was prima donna*, in our recollection, received with such a positive storm of rapture' (31 May 1856: 689). Although she did not approach Sontag or Lind as a vocalist — no fioratura, no trill — 'the audience seem enraptured by Mdlle Piccolomini' (28 June 1856: 817). Chorley explained that the subject matter of *Traviata* was inappropriate:

> The taste for what is morbid, already shown by Signor Verdi in his acceptance of 'Le Roi s'amuse' as subject for an opera, must have led him to 'la Dame aux Camélias' as text for another work, since musical temptation in the story there is none. Consumption and song can only be conciliated on the argument that everything which is said and suffered can be set to *cavatinas* and duetts. This is obviously untenable. Wit has no interpretation by chord and counterpoint, to touch one extremity of drama — physical pain as little, to indicate the other. The slow pulmonary death of the Lady of Pleasure, when accompanied by an orchestra, is more repulsive to us than when it is gasped, sighed, and fainted to its dying fall, by Madame Doche, the original Camélia Lady. Having protested against this wresting of Music into the illustration of what is coarse, literal, and distressing — in remonstrance against all false employment of a lovely art, whether the falsifier be Signor Verdi in the choice of subject, or Herr Wagner in his manner of setting the subject chosen — a few words will complete our sketch of the tale of 'La Traviata.' (31 May 1856: 688-9)

His protest was aimed at the inappropriateness of linking music to 'slow pulmonary death', and he found himself himself in the odd position of defending Verdi by refusing to join a moral crusade against portraying a prostitute sympathetically on stage. Though he found Verdi's music 'trashy' (16 August 1856: 1503), as he had so often before, he maintained that the crusade was hypocritical, or at best naïve. To his friend Charlotte Cushman, the American actress, he wrote sceptically on August 16: 'Have you heard of *The Times* taking a moral fit *apropos* of "La Piccolomini"?[28] And he asked at the end of the season in the *Athenæum*: 'But is so sudden a wakening-up of censorship altogether fair? ... that it is not the only opera having a *morbid* libretto our opera history for the last quarter of a century must prove' (16 August 1856: 1023). Intensely disliking the Violetta of the moment, Piccolomini ('the prettiest *prima donna* who can *not* sing' [16

August 1856: 10-23]), but not supporting the moral crusade against the opera, Chorley's notices carefully distinguished between appropriate and 'silly' reasons to dislike *Traviata*.

> We understand that Mdlle. Piccolomini's 'La Traviata' in the provinces has been, in certain cases (as at Birmingham), a success of empty benches, and a triumph at which no ladies chose to be present. This is silly and inconsequent, if it be a protest directed against the morals of the opera by audiences who have stomached former abominations, musical and dramatic, of equal flagrancy. If, however, it be read as indicating provincial estimation of the worth of the singer or the artist, it is wise and well, and too much publicity cannot be given to the failure. (6 September 1856: 1123)

On other occasions Chorley protested the double standard at work in the 'movement' against *Traviata*'s immorality:

> The movement is absurd because inconsistent; but such inconsistencies are as old as plays and publics. The great situation in [Costa's] 'Malek Adhel,' of a nun clinging to a crucifix as shelter from the persecutions of mundane love shall be applauded to the echo, while the selfsame combination in Sir Edward Lytton's drama of 'La Vallière' shall be hissed from the boards. Our tragical audiences rejoice over funeral processions in 'King Richard the Third,' 'Romeo and Juliet,' 'Hamlet,' (the last with a quarrel in the grave, above the corpse!) — in 'Duchess Eleanour' [Chorley's own play] the sight of catafalque and pall shall raise great wrath. 'La Favorita' and 'Lucrezia' shall pass among operas, 'La Traviata' shall be singled out. This is all very silly. ... (25 October 1856: 1314)

It was a relief for him to turn from Verdi's operas to Costa's oratorios. Though some considered Costa to be the foreign enemy of native talent, Chorley, as always, supported him, asserting that his oratorio, *Eli* as performed at the Sacred Harmonic Society, was one that 'may take root among our accepted oratorios' (23 February 1856: 241) and reporting that the second performance was even more warmly received than the first (1 March 1856: 272). *Eli* was repeated at the summer choral festivals, and the performance at the Bradford Festival, with Clara Novello, Viardot, and Sims Reeves, 'was only one degree less fine than the Birmingham one of the same Oratorio' (6 September 1856: 1122), achieving 'entire success for the work and its composer' (1122).[29]

For Chorley, the most enjoyable performances of the season of 1856 were those being presented in an new and unusual venue: the Crystal Palace at Sydenham, where 'Opera Concerts' were being presented 'to an enormous audience' — indeed, 'half London' seemed to turn up at Sydenham for the performances (14 June 1856: 752). 'Every one, we repeat, seems to enjoy these suburban festivals — performers included' (12 July 1856: 871-2). The relaxation and good humour which these performances evoked helped him find something good once again to report about Grisi, after much sniping:

> The freshness and brilliancy, too, of Madame Grisi's voice were too remarkable to be overlooked by honest chroniclers ... proof that ... the late afternoon of those who have made themselves competent is brighter than the full morning of those who are incomplete. ... (19 July 1856: 902)

By 'those who are incomplete' Chorley meant singers like Piccolomini and Johanna Wagner, dredged up by Lumley to fool the new generation of opera goers into applauding mediocrity, and thus to create the 'appearance of popularity': neither woman, indeed 'deserves the name of singer' (2 August 1856: 968). This must be said in 'defence of what is good and true' (968). Lumley had learned no lessons from his earlier failure. The false puffing and the pressure on journalists to celebrate these mediocrities as success recalled the battles between the theatres at the time of the opening of the Royal Italian Opera at Covent Garden: 'the song of triumph was never louder in misrepresentation of its misdeeds, even in the days that are gone' (968). Gye, by contrast, was comfortably back in Chorley's favour, temporarily — with Lumley to compare him with. He 'weathered his difficulties sensibly and courageously' at the Lyceum, where Bosio and Nantier-Didiée 'have advanced in favour' and where 'Madame Grisi and Signor Mario have had fewer "bad nights" than they must have had in a larger theatre, and in M. Meyerbeer's operas' [which were not produced that season] (2 August 1856: 968). Later, during an autumn season at Drury Lane, Chorley recorded his amazed pleasure at Grisi's assumption of Donna Anna, 'the force and freshness of which were astounding: the best performance of the part by her that we have witnessed for many years past' (22 November 1856: 1439).

Gye's season of 1857 was again at the Lyceum. Continuing irritation with Piccolomini and Lumley's puffery at Her Majesty's Theatre perhaps contributed to Chorley's ongoing re-evaluation of the current state of Grisi's singing. When she and Mario appeared in *Trovatore*, Chorley's re-awakened awe for the recently-scorned voice carried over to his uncharacteristically positive writing about Verdi:

The tenor was in his best voice. ... The performance, however, of the new *Leonora* was more remarkable still, since the part is tremendous in its demands on the voice, — a long as well as an arduous one. In what magic caldron the lady has had a dip we know not, but on Thursday she was marvellous from first to last; equal to the music, — without stint, strain, or sacrifice, flinging out those rich high notes which of late years she has used so charily — as though she had found some spell which makes Time roll back, and was resolved that this new part should be her most brilliant one. We remember nothing comparable to the renovated force, purity, and lustre of her voice. Her appearance was magnificent — her acting, especially in the "Miserere" scene, impassioned and touching. With these artists, in such high order — supported by Signori Graziani and Tagliafico, and Madame Didiée [Azucena] — 'Il Trovatore,' as Verdi's best opera, may prove to the Lyceum what 'Les Huguenots' was to Covent Garden. We have rarely witnessed a more stirring performance, — we have rarely to record a case of more genuine and well-merited triumph. (15 April 1857: 540)

During the continuing popularity of *Traviata*, there was finally an alternative to the despised singing of Piccolomini at Her Majesty's: at the Lyceum, Gye's company presented it with Bosio and Mario. 'The audience seemed as rapturous over this unpleasing drama as over the excellence with which its music was executed' (23 May 1857: 669).

Long a lover of Gluck's operas, Chorley at this time began to promote them vigorously. There was an encomium in the *Athenæum* of December 15, 1859, in which he compared Gluck favourably to Mozart, Gluck's operas being 'fresher, more forcible, and more dramatic'. The new interest in Gounod and the revival of interest in Gluck augured well for the future of foreign music drama in London:

There are few names more perpetually in the mouths of our musicians and writers on music than the name of Gluck; few composers less understood or really known. Four years ago, on the publication of Herr Schmid's valuable Biography [*Athen.* No. 1450] [i.e. 11 August 1855], an endeavour was made to bring the subject more tangibly and more clearly before English *connoisseurs* than it had of late been brought; but the interest may, at best, be said to have smouldered. There is now a stir among the ashes. 'Orphée' is drawing its crowds in Paris. 'Iphigenia in Tauris' will be performed in Manchester early in the year.

... In this country Gluck has suffered by the exclusiveness
of our admiration of Mozart. Yet, that Gluck's operas, in
spite of their remoteness of theme (belonging to the
academical taste of the times during which they were written), are fresher, more forcible, more dramatic, than
Mozart's, we venture to maintain; and that the younger
man drew not a few of his inspirations from the elder one
is, at least possible. (15 December 1859: 819-20)

4 Native Talent Again

In 1850, the correspondent for the *Athenæum* in Berlin wrote of Viardot's
triumphs there in *Les Huguenots*. But Chorley commented that the Germans
were cold, and had bad taste: 'Verily, the Von Raumers and other such
high-flown tourists ... will do well ... to refrain from again sneering at our
wretched taste in England' (4 May 1850: 483).[30]

Chorley himself continued to be perceived by others as one who sneered
at native talent. For example, in 1853 he wrote in the 'Musical and
Dramatic Gossip' column:

A rumour reached us the other day of yet another musical
society about to be founded for the encouragement of
"native talent," in the formation of which Sir Henry
Bishop and Dr. Bexfield are concerned. Really, this same
"native talent" of ours reminds us of the lady in Currer
Bell's "Shirley" who was always "composing herself." —
Every English body has been always "encouraging it,"
since the year 1834, when "the British Musicians"
assembled. Yet, what has it hitherto achieved? (26 March
1853: 393)

In a later 'Musical and Dramatic Gossip' column he noted serious problems
at the Royal Academy of Music: 'Rarely has an institution existed worse
administered'. It was 'organized (to use a word by courtesy) in accordance
with the fancies of dilletantism' (29 July 1854: 948). Henry Lunn[31]
responded in a letter in the next issue, defending the RAM on the grounds
that it raised the tone of British musical life (5 August 1854: 975), and
Lunn wrote again, this time attributing the appreciation of Beethoven and,
to a degree, of Bach, to better standards of musical education today, which
were partly attributable to the influence of the RAM (26 August 1854:
1047).

The next year Chorley continued to discuss the English appreciation of
English music. He objected to 'a show of paying attention to native talent'

made by Wagner during his season at the Philharmonic when Wagner had Charles Lucas conduct his own Symphony #3 in B flat at the fourth concert on 30 April:

> [Charles Lucas's Symphony was] written some twenty years ago ... for the *Society of British Musicians*; — and in those days, by certain critics, like all the music there produced, "borne up to the skies" with raptures as loud as the American praise of Herr Wagner, and vitriolic contempt launched against those who refused to accept such exercises as revelations [for example, Chorley himself]. (5 May 1855: 528)

Chorley then asked rhetorically, 'What has that society done for British compositions? 'Young England' began 'as a dependency of Germany', he asserted, and Young England seems stuck (528).

At the end of the remarkable year 1855, when both Wagner and Berlioz were conducting English orchestras, Chorley reiterated his belief that England needed a new composer:

> Those who, with us, deny Herr Wagner and his works, and who only accept M. Berlioz and his contrivances as *extras*, ought (did they desire life for their art as earnestly as pupils for themselves) to turn attention down new channels of healthier interest, provided by their own ingenuity. "The cry," in short, is for a composer; and the times are singularly propitious for the appearance of one. (29 December 1855: 1539)[32]

In the autumn of 1856 there was so much operatic activity that Chorley, tongue in cheek, wondered whether London might return to the eighteenth-century schedule of 'fashionable' operas seasons in the autumn, and seriously he maintained that, thanks to some extent to changes caused by the railways, there was now a large potential audience for opera presented in English:

> Surely, "the moral" may be deduced that our great London public is waiting and wanting opera-music, and that the time is ripe for the establishment of an Opera in English, were the enterprise only taken in hand wisely and by competent persons. The materials exist. Our home composers are "dying for an opportunity." A repertory of foreign works, totally unworn, could be easily drawn out; and fair performance would, apparently, bring vast, and, it may be presumed, remunerating, audiences. (1 November 1856: 1344)

Looking back over the year 1856, Chorley suggested that not much of great significance had happened in English music — he mentions 'the *cantatas* by Messrs. Macfarren and Hatton, and an overture by Mr. C. Horsley' (27 December 1856: 1614). When Hatton's cantata, 'Robin Hood', (with text by G. Linley) and Macfarren's cantata, 'May-day', had been first performed during the summer at the Bradford Festival, Chorley's tone was condescending:

> The *cantata* [*Robin Hood*] pleased us, and, from its absence of affectations, deserved to please. To consider it, however, as a work by which a musician takes rank, or establishes a style, or which displays any extraordinary amount of thought, science, or variety, is impossible. (30 August 1856: 1090)

and

> Is it useless once more to tell Mr. Macfarren that were he to exercise more selection in his first phrases, and knew where to condense, he might yet gain the universal and cordial acknowledgment as a composer, which, till now, he seems to have been thoughtlessly or perversely bent on denying himself? (6 September 1856: 1122)

Instead of chastising the English composers in his 1856 retrospective, however, Chorley predicted better things for the future: 'Barren in some respects as the time appears, it may be, so far as England is interested, seed-time, to be followed by a plenteous harvest' (27 December 1856: 1614).

That harvest, contrary to the expectations of many supporters of native talent, was not to be embodied in Sterndale Bennett, for whose work Chorley 'does not seem to have entertained much admiration' (Davison, *Forty Years*: 69). Chorley was at this time somewhat exasperated with Bennett, at least partly because of their collaboration on *The May Queen: A Pastoral*:

> It is possible that at the Leeds Festival Prof. Bennett's May-*Cantata* will be produced. This he is known to have had in hand for many years (as the Author of the words desires us to state), long before Mr. Macfarren's justly successful Cantata to Mr. Oxenford's verse, was brought forward. (1 May 1858: 569)

When the cantata was performed, Chorley could only record (as the 'anonymous' reviewer who had also written the text) that '[i]t is as impossible for us to pass any judgment on either the subject or the words of 'The May Queen' as it was on those of Mr H. Leslie's Biblical *Cantata* [*Judith*]' (11 September 1858: 338). He confined himself to remarking, as almost every Victorian interested in music said or wrote at one time or another, that Sterndale Bennett should 'write more frequently' (338).[33] When the score of *The May Queen* was published it was again noted that criticism was 'impossible' because of the reviewer's share in the work (11 December 1858: 765). A couple of months later, Chorley was slightly less taciturn: 'The success of this *Cantata*, as a piece of English concert-music, is without a precedent in our recollection' (19 February 1859: 260).[34]

Chorley wrote *Judith*, 'A Biblical Cantata', for the Birmingham Festival of 1858; Henry Leslie composed the music. Chorley took all the words from the scripture, though he borrowed the name of Judith's attendant, Amytal, from Metastasio's *Betulia Liberata*. Interestingly, Chorley asserted in his printed libretto that, unlike most stories in the Bible, this one was concerned with the individual action, not with its universal application. He chose not to write a cantata with a moral:[35]

> I cannot present the words which follow without some explanation. — It occurred to me while considering the story of "Judith" with reference to music, that, whereas in the Testaments, Old or New, there is hardly a single episode without its moral of large application — the Apocryphal histories stand on narrower ground; being mainly picturesque legends — narrated as such. Thus I have treated the Widow of Bethulia, as belonging to the world of special tradition, not of universal instruction. This is a legend of the heroine who availed herself of her beauty "to answer a fool according to his folly" — who conceived herself empowered to deal subtly with a brutal invader, "for the exaltation of Jerusalem," and for the deliverance of a beleaguered people. It is no lesson. ('Introductory', *Judith*)

Letters to Charlotte Cushman and Charles Santley at this time were full of his excitement over Viardot's participation in the performance and his expectations for success. He hoped Cushman would attend:

> As to "Judith" — I should feel secure of its success, were not my fingers in the fire — But I cannot conceive anything grand[er] than her declamation: — she was here this day week. ... — & I cannot conceive anything grander. (15 August 1858)[36]

To Santley he wrote about Viardot's appetite for hard work:

> I am held fast here, by work & feel very much exhausted: but there's no use in saying so. I think "Judith" will turn out very well. M^{de} V. was here — at her part, for 7

hours, one Sunday — the first full rehearsal was on
Monday: very satisfactory.[37]

Chorley's collaborations were notorious for being rocky and potentially
explosive. When Leslie changed some of the music for *Judith*, some of the
words, too, were altered. Chorley mentioned his irritation in print: 'a matter or two have been added to the text (not, we are requested to state, by
the original arranger of the words)' (i.e. Chorley himself) (12 March 1859:
363).[38] In this case as in many others, his efforts on behalf of 'native
talent' resulted in disappointment.

5 German Talent Again

After Mendelssohn's death, British critics generally continued to see him as
representative of the best in composition. Chorley was especially concerned
to guard the flame of his reputation, both by reminding readers of his
excellence, and by deploring indications that he was insufficiently
appreciated. These, especially in Germany, with the increasing attention to
the 'music of the future', happened more and more frequently.

In a four-column report on music in Weimar, Liszt's piano concerti were
termed too difficult for anyone but him to play (14 September 1850: 981).
Wagner's *Lohengrin* was described: 'the band has intelligible and vivacious
services to perform' but the voice parts were senseless (981). From Paris it
was reported that the overture to *Tannhäuser* was judged 'overcharged,
baroque, and extravagant' (7 December 1850: 1288), which, Chorley
reminded readers, was the way he had described *Lohengrin*'s music, a few
weeks earlier.

English friends of Mendelssohn were committed to setting up a scholarship fund for students. Jenny Lind sang a benefit at Exeter Hall for the
fund, but Chorley noted sourly in June 1851 that money raised by her singing was not matched by German funds (28 June 1851: 692).

Webster's production of Mendelssohn's Singspiel, *Heimkehr aus der
Fremde*, was presented at the Haymarket Theatre as 'Son and Stranger' in
1851. 'More warmly no production could be received by a crowded house',
and it was well prepared by Mellon (*Athenæum*, 12 July 1851: 744).

In November, 1851, the *Athenæum* gave Liszt's book, *Lohengrin et
Tannhäuser de Richard Wager* a three-column review. The reviewer was
sceptical of Liszt's claims on Wagner's behalf — for example, he noted that
labelling of 'peculiar orchestral phrases' for characterization was not very
advanced, citing as other examples Meyerbeer's Marcel (*Huguenots*) and
Weber's Eglantine (*Euryanthe*). Musical 'romanticism' was here defined by
its current practitioners: Berlioz in France, Wagner and Schumann in
Germany.

Schumann came in for a small, perhaps begrudging bit of commendation for *Album für die Jugend*, whose publication was noticed in the issue of 27 March 1752 (361). And in the same issue Berlioz was commended for his orchestration. He was warned that he must not 'underrate *matter*'. The performance by the New Philharmonic Society of *Romeo and Juliet* 'has again convinced us of the supremacy of M. Berlioz in the matter of orchestral colouring' (362).

Chorley was only occasionally surprised, but it is interesting to note the few times when his critical evaluations changed and the very opera he disliked one season proved delightful the next. *Il Flauto Magico*, for example, in 1851 was 'oppressive' — 'and this not solely because of the unintelligible dullness of the story' (12 July 1851: 743). In 1852, however, it 'seemed on Tuesday evening to hit the taste of the opera goers' and the opera was 'as warmly enjoyed as in 1851 it was respectfully endured' (and 'Mdlle Zerr as the *Queen of Night* excited more than the olden wonder and applause by her little *rococo* squeaks in *altissimo*. These, however, are Mozart's fault, not hers') (15 May 1852: 553).

Using the introductory phrase Chorley frequently chose when announcing his own works, he wrote that 'We are requested to state that a second series of "Music and Manners in Germany", by Mr. Henry F. Chorley, is in preparation' (26 June 1852: 788).

In August, 1852, there was half a paragraph of defiant reaction to Wagner's 'Death of Siegfried' (that is, the libretto) and its 'lengthy preface': 'we do not fear that the disease will infect many valuable members of society, spread wide, or last long' (7 August 1852: 853). But that was, in fact, exactly what was feared. Only two weeks later, the *Athenæum* acknowledged its fear that the disease might become contagious: 'Herr Wagner's one claim on notice is, the attention which he has excited among a few generous and romantic, but easily-bewildered thinkers ...' (21 August 1852: 901). A few months later a performance of *Tannhäuser* was damned again, in 'foreign correspondence' for 1852: Though the legend is 'attractive and haunting', its small musical interest — for example, the end of Act Two, after the 'sermons' — is welcome only by comparison with what precedes it. 'How low must the opera-goer be brought when he can think of Verdi with complacency and longing!' (18 December 1852: 1399). 'There is comfort, however, in thinking that beyond Herr Wagner in his peculiar manner it is hardly possible to go' (1399). 'Musical and Dramatic Gossip' reported in May 1853 that Wagner's Nibelungen project was to be in four poems, commenting that this 'Babel-building' would of course not succeed (21 May 1853: 626).

Schumann was generally connected in Chorley's mind with Wagner: both composers were fantastic, undisciplined and 'diseased'. About this time, John Ella began to introduce Schumann's music into his chamber music programmes. When Ella presented the E flat major Piano Quintet in March of 1853, Chorley reacted: 'in three of the four movements the ideas are worn and stale, not to say frivolous' (26 March 1853: 391). In 1854 the Philharmonic presented Schumann's Symphony in B flat. Altogether it was 'robust in places, but in places, also, very ugly, and throughout crude in colour and thick in texture. ... Here, we imagine, it may never be wanted again' (10 June 1854: 724). In the 'New Publications' notices the next month, Chorley comments on *Thirteen Scenes of Childhood*, an English issue 'of one of the earliest, most pleasing, and most precious works of its strange composer' written before he 'perversely wandered off into *Fog*-land' (29 July 1854: 947). He noted also the publication of the march from Wagner's *Tannhäuser*, describing it as 'patchy' (948). More disappointment was expressed at the verbosity of Dr Schumann's four volumes of 'musical criticisms and speculations' (4 November 1854: 1346)

Although Chorley's crusade against Schumann's music belonged mainly to the 1860s, when it came to be performed frequently at the Crystal Palace and elsewhere, there were significant signs of Chorley's hostility much earlier. Already in 1841 he had expressed strong reservations about Schumann in *Music and Manners in France and Germany* (1841) and a decade later Chorley reprinted this passage in *Modern German Music* (1854) with significant alterations. For one thing, the text was slightly shortened by omitting entirely the phrase labelling Schumann 'the German Berlioz', and the comment on Schumann's talent in the footnote was considerably expanded to lament that, in the intervening years, the talent had not lived up to its promise. To the original footnote in the 1841 text he added strictures about the decline of Schumann's talents and the decadence of the taste which applauded his music:

> It was said, in 1839-40, that Herr Schumann had declared his resolution of writing a work which should outdo Beethoven's Ninth Symphony. Since that time, he has produced largely: and admirers have gathered round him asserting that he has entirely fulfilled the above tolerably ambitious resolution. It appears as if the usual order of affairs has been followed in his case; as if extravagant mysticism, assumed to conceal meagreness of idea, had given way (as the composer grew older and more impatient to secure popularity) to a dullness and heaviness of common-place, little more acceptable, not in the least more beautiful, and certainly less amusing. Opera, *Cantata*, Symphony, Quartett, *Sonata* — all and each tell the same story, and display the same characteristics — the same skill of covering pages with thoughts little worth noting, and of hiding an intrinsic poverty of invention, by

grim or monotonous eccentricity. There is a style, it is true, in Dr. Schumann's music — a certain thickness, freaked with frivolity — as mastery which produces no effect — a resolution to deceive the ear, which (as in the case of certain French composers) ends in habituating the ear to the language of deception; and spoils the taste without substituting any new sensations of pleasure. — Up to the present period Dr. Schumann's music may be said to be submitted to rather than generally accepted in Germany. A general acceptance, I must think, would imply a decadence of taste even more rapid than that which has taken place since the above sketches were made. — 1852. (*Modern German Music*, 2: 52-3).[39]

More opposition to Schumann's music was expressed in Chorley's notice of Clara Schumann's performance of *Carnival* on her second recital of the season, Tuesday, 17 June 1856. The programme notes discussed the nature of the Society — the 'Davidsbündler' — and Chorley objected:

Now, as it is with pictures, so also is it with music. Those works of Art of which nothing can be made unless some *Hamlet* stands at our elbow to teach us what is "whale" and what is "ouzel," are shows or sounds good only for a *Polonius*, but for no one of a more manly intelligence. (21 June 1856: 786)

It infuriated Chorley that self-styled German crusaders against Philistines took credit for their contributions to Art and ignored the significance of Mendelssohn:

Nevertheless, at the time when these poor and dreary trifles were written, — in criticism of contemporary German music and its direction, — there was still living and labouring in, *and for*, Germany, with all his heart and soul and strength, a certain man called Mendelssohn; "dry and empty" (to repeat the jargon of a sect), because his compositions, being pure music, stand in need of no historical or mystical explanation; and because, having studied his art as a science, he could not be other than "correct." — Well, he has his fame, which is increasing; and these 'Davidsbündler' have made their noise ... So let it be; but if these things are to be thrust upon us, — if no warning will be taken — no consideration understood, — we must speak the plain truth, in protection of the modest and the half-instructed. (21 June 1856: 786)

The next week, the New Philharmonic Society performed Bartholomew's English translation of Schumann's *Das Paradies und die Peri* — in the presence of Queen Victoria — with Lind-Goldschmidt, whose 'voice was more fatigued and unequal than we have heretofore heard it' (28 June 1856: 816). The arrangement for conducting was odd: Sterndale Bennett was the conductor, but Clara Schumann sat 'in the orchestra' and 'guided the conductor, and gave the *tempo* Philharmonic to the *solo*-singers. ... It is unmanly to have put her thus in front of the battle' (816-17). It was an 'attempt to force success for a bad work' (816):

> [T]o return to the subject, after having years ago discussed the composition, and again in 1855 ... is an ungrateful task. ... Like other so-called innovators, Dr. Schumann is essentially as trivial in idea and as poor in resource as the most intolerable of the "Philistines." (816)

Sterndale Bennett's son reported that it was 'coldly received' (*Life*, 248).[40] John Edmund Cox later claimed that the audience at this unhappy performance would have received *Das Paradies* with 'vehement demonstrations of derision' had not Queen Victoria been in the audience.[41] Like Chorley, Cox claimed that Lind's voice at this time — already 'worn and strained' — seemed 'more fatigued and unequal' than ever. The idea of seating Madame Schumann on the stage, as if a kind of meta-conductor, may have been well-intentioned but appeared ludicrous, implying that Bennett was incompetent to steer the chorus and orchestra through a work 'extravagant, whimsical, and unintelligible, overloaded with caprice, and totally devoid of the ghost of a melody' (Cox, *Musical Recollections of the Last Half Century*, 2: 304).[42] In general, as Cyril Ehrlich noted, the critical notices of this performance were 'for once, unanimous, and arguably the worst in Philharmonic history' (*First Philharmonic*, 105).

On 5 July 1856, Chorley stated that Clara Schumann, though 'among the greatest female players', was 'past her prime' and would not 'do wisely to adventure a second visit to England' (843) — and perhaps some resentment for Jenny Lind's attempts to 'force success' for Schumann caused Chorley to acknowledge her farewell concert curtly: 'Madame Goldschmidt will be little missed from the world of Art' (5 July 1856: 843).[43]

Reviewing Schumann's 'Slumber Song' ('Schlummer-Lied') in the 'new publications' column of 26 July 1856, Chorley used his keen ear for noting influences and similarities to temper praise with condescension:

> The pleasant effect of this *notturno* was mentioned not long since, when it was introduced to us by Madame Schumann. The melody, as we then said, is preferable to the generality of melodies by its composer. Where lies the original? The first bars coincide almost note for note with

the favourite tenor song, "If with all your hearts," in 'Elijah.' (26 July 1856: 935)

Continuing to commend the concerts at the Crystal Palace in Sydenham, Chorley occasionally expressed his antipathy towards Schumann almost genially:

> The *Crystal Palace* at Sydenham bids fair to become a haunt of musical importance; not merely in virtue of Handel Festivals and Opera Concerts (both of which rank in the class of accidental luxuries), but because of the established concerts given weekly there. This is, in part, owing to the right placing of the right man, — Herr Manns, the conductor, ... but in part, too, owing to some enterprise in the selection of music. For instance, we were glad to go thither on Saturday last to hear Schumann's Symphony in D, which (whether it be liked or disliked) ought to have been brought to judgment at our *Philharmonic* (or Artists') concert long ere this. ... The work struck us as containing fresher and more marked ideas than distinguish many of Schumann's other works. ... We may never "be adhesive" (as the American lady said) to this music; but are grateful for every new opportunity of forming, or *re*-forming, a judgment. (2 May 1857: 572-3)

Occasionally performances of Mendelssohn provided respite from the intrusion of Schumann into the repertory. Balm to his soul was the Sacred Harmonic Society's performance in January 1857 of Mendelssohn's music to Racine's *Athalie*, for the first time in London since 1849,[44] along with Rossini's *Stabat Mater*.[45] It was 'excellently performed', the text read by Mr Phelps, and the women soloists Clara Novello, Lemmens-Sherrington, and Charlotte Dolby. Chorley believed that all composers could profit from studying *Athalie* and the two court commissions, *Antigone* and *Oedipus*:

> For the public one opera would have been a greater boon than these three contributions of music to classical tragedy. — By the professor they cannot be studied too closely nor praised too highly as examples of genius working freely within strange trammels and triumphing in its work. (31 January 1857: 154)

A passing comment in 'Musical and Dramatic Gossip' for 12 July 1856 reported on a prize scholarship given to young Arthur Sullivan: 'The first election of a Mendelssohn scholar in our London *Academy of Music* took place on Thursday week, the successful candidate being Master Sullivan, a boy belonging to the Chapel Royal' (872). Master Sullivan proceeded to study in Leipzig. In a few years Chorley began to report with increasing enthusiasm on his progress as a composer. In the 1860s, as the threat from the music of the future increased, Sullivan was to become the greatest of Chorley's hopes that a new composer — and an English one at that — would be worthy of the legacy of Mendelssohn.

6 Wagner the Conductor

In 1855, both Wagner and Berlioz conducted in London, Wagner the Philharmonic and Berlioz the New Philharmonic. Wagner's engagement was particularly controversial and, for many, unwelcome. As George Hogarth tactfully put it in his history of the Philharmonic Society, Costa 'unexpectedly declined to accept the renewal of his engagement which was offered him, and the Directors after much an anxious deliberation, offered the appointment to Herr Richard Wagner, by whom it was accepted. The choice did not eventually prove a happy one' (107). Hogarth's language was temperate, and his reviews of Wagner's conducting in *The Illustrated London News* and *The Daily News* were among the more accepting.[46] J.W. Davison, in his notice of Wagner's first appearance as conductor of the Philharmonic in *The Times*, pointed out that 'Herr Wagner was about the last person in the world that any one would have dreamt of as successor to Mr. Costa' (14 March 1855) — and certainly the last person Chorley deemed worthy to succeed him.

The reasons for Costa's resignation went back to 1848, when Costa and Sterndale Bennett had a falling out over the correct tempo in one of Bennett's overtures. For the next several years, Costa believed himself to be thwarted and frustrated in various ways, finally resigning just before the 1855 season. Berlioz hoped to get the engagement, but had already been engaged by the New Philharmonic, which would not release him from the contract. Mr Andersen, principal of the seven directors, went to Zurich 'and engaged Richard Wagner' (Davison, 163). Wagner's supporter Ferdinand Praeger assumed credit for the appointment: 'I was Wagner's first and sole champion ... It was through my sole exertions that the Philharmonic Society in 1855 offered Wagner the post of conductor'.[47]

Of course, as early as the mid-1840s Chorley had known Wagner's name, and had even heard some of his music. Ten years earlier for his *Athenæum* readers he had reprinted (with some scepticism) German press reports of the success of 'Der Tannenhaüser' (1 November 1845: 1059). In those days Liszt, energetically promoting the career of the young Wagner, expected that Chorley would join the cause and wrote to Gaëtano Belloni from Weimar on 14 May 1849 that Chorley could be useful:

> ... here is what we [Wagner and I] have decided to do and

> what must be accomplished. First of all, to present a
> great, heroic musical work, whose score was completed a
> year ago, *in London and in English*. Chorley especially
> will be very helpful to him in this undertaking. (Walker,
> *Liszt*, 2: 114).

Twelve days after Liszt's letter, Chorley obligingly asked his readers: why
not *Tannhaüser* in London? Liszt's *feuilleton* in the *Journal des Débats*, he
remarked, 'is naturally provocative of English curiosity' (26 May 1849:
553).[48]

Although Wagner was not to become one of Chorley's causes, Liszt's
production of *Lohengrin* did draw Chorley to Weimar in the summer of
1851. He was thus one of the few English journalists who could discuss the
new composer from actual experience.

In 1855 Chorley took a hard line when reviewing the engagement from
his end-of-the-year retrospective position:

> Never were wreck and ruin more notably expedited by
> perverse and jealous folly than by the engagement of Herr
> Wagner, and his evolutions and extravagancies at the head
> of what *was* our best orchestra. Instruction, too ("with a
> difference") is to be got from the *New Philharmonic
> Society*, which has *not* taken root among our institutions,
> in spite of its having hung itself on Charity, and of having
> had the assistance of Mr. Berlioz as conductor for two
> concerts.

Chorley wrote contemptuously that some New York newspapers had
characterized the concerts as successful:

> Those who desire to learn how Herr Wagner, like "a sec-
> ond Daniel come to judgment," has, at last, shown the
> ignorant Londoners which way music should go, — with
> further particulars of his unprecedented triumphs in this
> city, — are referred to certain American Art-journals, in
> which these facts and feats are gloriously chronicled,
> together with many hard and cutting things concerning
> wicked British journalists, who have been deaf to Herr
> Wagner's charming. (5 May 1855: 528)

This was the hostile tone that later critics often complained about, or
ridiculed, as exemplifying mid-Victorian provincialism. Francis Hueffer,
for example, regretted that on the day after the first concert (12 March
1855) 'most of the daily papers came out with a shower of abuse, which
was echoed in the weeklies, notably in *The Athenæum*, and continued
without any abatement during the entire stay of Wagner in London' (Huef-

fer, 50). And Adam Carse recorded that after each London concert 'the puny critics revelled in their opportunities of abusing Wagner's conducting' (Carse, 356), which was a failure 'measured by the Mendelssohnian standard' (360). Ridicule directed at Chorley and Davison struck the following generation as poetic justice: since they 'had no end of fun in ridiculing Wagner and his admirers in former years; now that the tide has turned, have we not a right to a little fun at their expense? The comicality of the criticism will, like good wine, still further improve with age ...' (Finck, 1: x). Chorley's reviews revealed to Ashton Ellis 'a man of naturally, or at least chronically bad temper' (Ellis, *Wagner*, 5: 183):

> As Chorley appears to have been the solitary London critic who had heard a note of Wagner's music prior to the Spring of 1854, it is to him and his tirades in the *Athenaeum* that must be attributed the sneering antagonism with which the master was greeted even before his arrival in England. (Ellis, 5: 424)

Praeger named four publications as having the greatest power to influence public opinion about music: the *Musical World* (Davison), the *Sunday Times* (Joseph Bennett), *The Times* (Davison), and *Athenæum* (Chorley) (Praeger, 264-5). Praeger sent notices praising Wagner to New York journals, generally more receptive to Wagner than English journals; from time to time the London papers commented on the absurdities of the reports in New York papers.[49]

Ernest Newman's explanation for Wagner's hostile reception by English critics was somewhat less contentious than that of the nineteenth-century perfect Wagnerites: 'The trouble [with the London critics in 1855] was that they were men of ordinary intelligence brought face to face, for the first time in their professional lives, with a contemporary phenomenon that was extraordinary, and failing to see how much bigger it was than themselves' (Newman, 2: 463).

Chorley's notices were indeed unsympathetic. Here is his initial welcome to the new conductor:

> Nothing could be much more familiar to the Philharmonic orchestra than the "full-pieces" selected to inaugurate Herr Wagner's appointment as Conductor for the year. These were Haydn's Seventh Grand Symphony, Mendelssohn's Overture 'The Isles of Fingal,' Beethoven's "Eroica" Symphony, and Mozart's Overture to 'Zauberflöte.' — Nothing could be stranger than the performance. — The violins were rarely together. The pauses in Haydn's *andante* were very long pauses, and every *forte* was a *fortissimo*. Mendelssohn's Overture was

hurried and muddled, without ease or undulation, — and Beethoven's Symphony was a fatiguing piece of exaggeration, stuck full of fierce *sforzandi* and ill-measured, *rallentandi*. Further, Dr. Spohr's *Scena Drammatica*, got through heroically by Herr Ernst, was as badly accompanied as *solo* could be, — while the hackneyed *trio* from 'Cosi fan tutte,' 'Soave sia il vento,' would have gone utterly to sleep had not Madame Novello (who was in very fine voice) kept it in motion by giving the time with her head to the conductor. Was it worth while to affront the profession in London and to send a deputation to Zurich for no better result than this? — Spirit Herr Wagner indisputably possesses, — but of his sense as a reader of great compositions by great masters Monday's concert gives us a poor opinion: — and it remains to be seen how far his fits and starts will be able to impress our orchestra should he be intrusted with the production of any unfamiliar music. — The room was thinly attended. (17 March 1855: 329)[50]

In the second performance of the season (26 March), Wagner conducted Mendelssohn's violin concerto and some of his own music from *Lohengrin*. Chorley was outraged by both, for different reasons:

A case of more discreditable scrambling through well-known music — period and place considered — is not in our recollection. The accompaniment, too, to Mendelssohn's *Violin Concerto*, played by Mr. Blagrove, was positively bad, in spite of the affectation of care given by the withdrawal of the *ripieni* instruments from the *solos*. ... He has, as a critic (unless we mistake) "finished up" Mendelssohn, having described him as a man "who, having nothing to say, said it elegantly." As a transcendental conductor — having nothing to do with such music — he did that nothing with due bustle and pretension. (31 March 1855: 385)[51]

And the transcendental music on the programme, not surprisingly, was not worth the advance puffs:

Except, in short, for the stir which has been made in the matter, and the empiricism with which the music was recommended in the *programme*, these specimens of "composition for the future" would hardly have been worth a line of analysis for any intrinsic novelty or merit they possess. (385)

Chorley painstakingly listed the borrowings and influences he heard. In the introduction to Act I of *Lohengrin*,

> the idea, if idea it be, recalls a phrase used by Weber in 'Euryanthe', and another used by Halévy in his 'Guido'. This is dressed out by a division of the violins and the employment of them at the *altissimo* notes of the scale, so as to produce an impression of singularity rather than sublimity. Thus also, M. Félicien David and (in his 'Attila') Signor Verdi have described dawn effects by the orchestra; thus M. Jullien has, more than once, fitted out a sunrise, for one of his descriptive Quadrilles. ...

As for the epithalamium (the wedding march), it was 'petty and pretty', as if 'M. Adam had flung it off'. (31 March 1855: 385)

7 An Author in Search of an Audience

Chorley's turn as a dramatist came in 1854. Ever since the mid-1840s Chorley had been trying without success to get two plays performed: *Archibald* (later given the more interesting title of *Old Love and New Fortune*), and *Duchess Eleanour* (drafted in 1846 and finally performed in 1854). Both plays were elaborate, five-act 'Elizabethan-revival' verse dramas, the first a comedy, the second a melodrama/tragedy written with Charlotte Cushman in mind for the title role.

In 1844,[52] after reading *Archibald* in manuscript, Mary Russell Mitford encouraged Chorley warmly:

> Between crying and excitement, I never closed my eyes all night, and can hardly see out of them to-day:. ... I have to entreat that you will let her [Elizabeth Barrett] see "Sir Archibald." She is most desirous of the favour, and will esteem it as it deserves. You could hardly have a reader of more true sensibility to beauty, or more thoroughly willing to admire all that is sweet, and true, and tender, in you especially, of whom she has heard so much ... I can think of nothing but that play. I am as sure of a high success as I should have been with [Knowles's] "Virginius," or [Schiller's] "William Tell," or [Tobin's] "The Honeymoon" — the three greatest plays of this century; yours is better than either. Be sure to tell me what Macready says. (quoted without date, Hewlett, 2: 18-19)

Barrett was apparently willing to read the play, but was not sure that Chorley really wanted her to, as she noted in her letter to Mitford on 19 June 1844:

> I conclude by persisting in being a little restless about the comedy, . . & by fearing (by fits) whether you may not have taken for granted M[r] Chorley's courtesy for *a friend of yours*, to be real cordial liking for the plan of my reading his work. [... Therefore] if there sh[d] be the slightest gesture of retreat, . . interpret it aright, & *for my sake* do not say a word more. My opinion, as an opinion, is worth nothing with regard to theatrical matters, you are well aware; and certainly it cannot be worth seeking. (*Brownings' Correspondence*, 9: 24)

A few weeks later, the play had not arrived, and Barrett wrote Mitford that 'I am *not* surprised that it has not come, . . & you cannot reasonably reproach me for a want of astonishment' (9: 43). The play languished, presumably unread by Barrett or anyone else, for a few years: then it seemed for a brief period that *Archibald* might indeed be performed, and Chorley wrote excitedly to Charlotte Cushman on 15 February 1847:

> Well, but my news — which will not be very shortly dismissed. — I told you — did I not? that I had sent "Sir Archibald" to M[r] Phelps, through the medium of a friend. — Well I now hear, that M[r] P — will try the play — & that I shall shortly receive more tidings thereupon. At all events, such a recognition, seem'd[?] a step towards opening the door, — won't I caper, if I once get in? — [53]

This came to nothing, however. Not until Monday, 18 February 1850, did the Surrey Theatre stage it — now under a new title: *Old Love and New Fortune*. The *Athenæum* reported that it 'was successfully produced'. Moreover, it 'is written with remarkable care and point, and at times the dialogue rises into poetic fervour': On the other hand, much in the review was lukewarm: 'Too much action is supposed to pass in the intervals between the acts', the reviewer complained.

> The incidents chosen for the vehicles of this main interest are ingeniously contrived — though they, and the motives, are not always produced with sufficient clearness. ... The "old loves" are all ultimately reconciled to the "new fortunes." — So many circumstances are with difficulty reconcileable in a five-act drama, — but Mr. Chorley has effected their agreement with considerable art. ... The audience were more than ordinarily attentive; ... [and at

the end] called for the author.

The play was 'well acted and well received', though performances were perforce suspended until the 'needful licence' was obtained (*Athenæum*, 23 February 1850: 211).

The text of the play, published by Chapman and Hall, was the occasion for another notice in the *Athenæum* the following week, together with the characteristic long excerpts. It should now have 'a better reception ... than even that which it obtained from a theatrical audience' (2 March 1850: 230). In Chorley's 'constructive powers' there were 'certain deficiencies'. The review's conclusion was an encouraging recognition of potential for future achievement: 'Our quotations will show what has been realized by the new dramatist, and what may be expected from him when he shall have mastered the technicalities of his art' (231).

Chorley was more optimistic than customary about his future prospects. Although the theatre, oddly, had neglected to secure a licence for the play and therefore had to shut down for several nights until one was procured, Chorley felt they had presented his play well and was elated by the audience response. His exuberant letter to Cushman, 7 March 1850, who was at that time performing in New Orleans, recorded his elation:

> I never saw a piece better put on the stage — more evenly acted. — The house was pretty well filled with just five and twenty people in it who knew my name (*twelve* of whom must have paid) — since I totally declined all packing processes, as totally impossible to me. — The same evening "The Noble Heart" by Mr Lewes came out at the Olympic — so none of the press came to me — since he had been round, &c:&c:&c:&c:&c:&c:&c: ... When all was over & the success sure, & I called for — by pit & gallery — *violently* — then I *did* get nervous: — but still strong in the satisfaction that I had made people cry & laugh & like me — who could have no *preoration* (as we say in France) in my favour — ... On the Tuesday some of the *big-wigs* of the press had come, & had poured tepid water on the play: — they could not ignore its having pleased, but not one would say so for four days: — *The Times* "couldn't make out what it was about &c:&c:" ... I have had kind words & praise on every side. ... I wish you could have seen my play.

He was also emboldened to request that Cushman commit herself to the role of Duchess Eleanour:

> Under these circumstances, I write to you as you would to me ... had you "the wooden ladle" & *I* "the silver

> spoon."[54] — Supposing that you still esteem "the
> Duchess" as highly as of old — is it unfair to wish that
> you should make her your own thoroughly? —
>
> Tho' she will one day thrive — this will never happen
> till you have played the part so entirely was it calculated
> for you — & as I believe that such transactions are
> habitual in our world — I feel that I can ask you ...
> without any fear of our good understanding & old friend-
> ship being disturbed; or without shame in so doing ... I
> have learned much of my trade while putting "Old Love"
> on the stage — & should revise & retouch "The Duchess"
> throughout, ere it is acted. ...[55]

And three weeks later Chorley confided (anonymously) to his readers in the
'Musical and Dramatic Gossip' column:

> Letters from the United States confirm the tidings of the
> golden harvest reaped by Miss Cushman in her own
> country, — so magnificent, we are told, as to tempt the
> Lady to protract her American tour — her intention still
> being to return to England. It is understood in dramatic
> circles that a tragedy "expressly" written for Miss Cush-
> man has been for some time in her hands, only waiting
> for a fit opportunity to be represented. This now may pos-
> sibly be found (as befell Mr. Lovell's 'Wife's Secret') on
> the other side of the Atlantic.

Before *Duchess Eleanour* was performed, however, Mr Wigan, manager
of the Olympic, put on 'The Love Lock', suggested by Carlyle's translation
of Tieck's story, 'The Runnenberg' (Hewlett, 2: 126). Its failure on 13
February 1854, as Chorley recorded in his journal, was 'dismal enough. ...
I have witnessed more than one scene of the kind, but I think I never saw
disapprobation more violent' (Hewlett, 2: 127).

Duchess Eleanour followed the dismal failure a month later, at the
Haymarket Theatre on 13 March 1854. The first performance was successful, but the second performance was not. Dixon reviewed it for the
Athenæum (18 March 1854: 348). Mr Buckstone wrote Chorley that 'you
have shown so much dramatic power in your dialogue, that, with a more
natural and a better subject, I would not hesitate to produce another play
written by you' (Hewlett, 2: 142).

Chorley's friend, Mary Russell Mitford, wrote to the Reverend Hugh
Pearson about the failure of two of Chorley's plays so close together. Chorley had just reviewed her *Atherton* coolly:

> Ah me! Retribution fell upon him very shortly in two
> columns and a half of the "Times'" best thunder-bolts,

> which, as he can never expect again such promotion as to
> have two plays fail in a fortnight (inasmuch as managers
> will guard against that species of danger), is about the
> severest vengeance that could befall him. (Mitford, *Let-*
> *ters*, 1872, 2: 214-15)

Chorley commented in a note, after seeing for the first time Mitford's less
than supportive comments:

> Regarding the failure of both [plays], there is something
> to be told, time and place befitting. That of the tragedy
> was brought about on its second performance — after its
> having been received with favour on the first night — thus
> reversing the fate which has attended the production of
> some among the plays which still keep the stage — I
> retain the letter, as containing one of the temporary *spirts*
> of temper, — from which not the most just or generous
> woman who writes "to the moment," is secure — advert-
> ed to by me in an earlier page. Such are so many mere
> passing clouds. ... (Mitford, *Letters*, 1872, 2: 124-5)

In 1857, *Duchess Eleanour* was briefly resuscitated in a manner more
surprising than pleasing. Chorley ended his 'Musical and Dramatic Gossip'
for 23 May 1857, with a report of its performance in Boston:

> One of the curious accidents to which English productions
> in print are liable, is announced in a late account of
> American theatricals, published in one of the Sunday
> papers. "This evening," says the paragraph, "Eliza Logan
> produces (at Kimball's Museum, Boston) a tragedy
> originally written for Miss Cushman, by Mr. H. F. Chor-
> ley, but which has been re-constructed and re-written
> especially for Miss Logan, and entitled 'The Duchess.'"
> The author empowers us to say that this process of re-
> construction and re-writing, for better for worse, has been
> done without his knowledge or consent. (670)

Chorley wrote several more plays, manuscript copies of which are held by
the British Library, but no more were performed.

In 1855 Sir William Molesworth died. In the same year Mary Russell Mitford died. Chorley's letters gave evidence of a continuing depression. On
16 August 1856 he wrote to Charlotte Cushman:

> Well: may it be very long before you have as heavy a
> heart, as your poor old correspondent this Saturday night,

has — I have no business to write, perhaps, when I am in such plights, but, perhaps, you will forgive it, when you remember, how few living creatures are left, to whom I dare or can (or will) discuss my dolours, whether in French or English.[56]

Taking leave of Cushman before she visited Rome in 1856, Chorley wrote to her on 14 November asking that she perform a sentimental pilgrimage for him. His early supporter from Liverpool days, the dedicatee of his first novel, *Conti*, was buried there:

> The name in the English Burial Ground at Rome is
>
> > Margaret Lace,
>
> > or M[rs] Ambrose Lace of Liverpool
>
> She died there in 1853 — and I should like to have a leaf — or blade of grass from her grave: — for in her, I lost my oldest, kindest & most intimate friend. — It is weak work relic-gathering — but the greater part of my life is filled with thoughts of the dead & gone; & I don't indulge the weakness often.[57]

On Sunday, 15 August 1858, he wrote to Cushman that he was 'utterly alone'; in that state one feels 'one has nothing to lose: & so is perhaps, as free, as a human creature can be, to devote such little life & spirits as are left, to objects & affairs which have no reference to one's own personal happiness or unhappiness'.[58]

The most intimately revealing expression of his dissatisfaction with life was the elaborately self-analytical letter he wrote on 2 February 1859, to Wentworth Dilke. In it he probed more deeply than is usual into his recurring nostalgia, loneliness, and depression, trying to see whether Dilke believed anything could be done about it.

> Dear Wentworth,
>
> I called on you the other day to trouble you about a very dull subject, my own affairs. A few words on paper will perhaps best explain my meaning. I have been feeling, for the last few years, that things are not quite as they should be with me. I do not mean as to worldly circumstances, since, so long as I can work as now, I can live quite as well as a man need do in my situation; and though I have had a rather unusual share of ill-luck, I have no pinch for the present, no fear for the future. But I am living too much alone. Such family intercourse as I have is entirely confined to my poor sister, and that is neither supporting nor cheering; and I find my life beginning to weigh so heavily on my nerves and spirits, that I cannot

go much further without some attempt to right myself. What I should like would be to find some little occupation which brought me more into contact with companionable and intelligent people. My intercourse with the musicians does not fill this want, since in that I *give* much, and receive only in return as much as suffices for the necessities of my position before the public. Thus it has occurred to me to ask you whether, in some of all these ramifying art-designs, schools, museums, &c., &c., I could not be made of use; since I do not think that my knowledge (especially on all lower matters connected with decoration, &c, &c.), or my experiences of what exists here and abroad, are less than those of many who appear to succeed and to give satisfaction; and I fancy that I might be able to turn them to account, without losing my hold on my own peculiar public, which I think I may say, without vanity, is now very strong, though neither gainful nor refreshing. I think I need not say to you that I would undertake nothing that I could not accomplish; still less, that I am not afraid of work; but I feel the necessity of a relief from a state of things brought about by a singular number of deaths, changes, want of ability on my own part to push myself forward, and my painfully solitary position as the last of a family, with no living younger relative to look to, and no creature within reach to whom I can speak of what passes in my mind. You will see that this letter is one requiring no answer (I feel secure of your good-will); but if occasion should serve, do not forget its contents. Let me again repeat that it is no money-pressure that makes me trouble you. When I cease to be a journalist I can make up £400 a year, on which I can dream out my old days abroad; and should I survive others of my family, that income must be increased. Thus I cannot, I trust, be misunderstood, while I must also beg you to excuse my prosiness, in explanation of a tale and a situation other than cheerful, or perhaps much longer tenable by, Yours ever faithfully, Henry F. Chorley. (Hewlett, 2: 294-7)

Although Chorley described himself as isolated and alone, in fact old friends still remained in the 1850s and a few new friendships developed, too, though in some cases we have only fragmentary glimpses of them. Around 1858, for example, Chorley wrote (to 'dear B.' in Liverpool) about an outing. He identified his companion 'E' as a 'new acquisition', one who 'has taken to' him:

> On Friday we were but four men in the drive to Syden-
> ham (with the Sims Reeves and Miss Cushman to dinner).
> I took down E____, a new acquisition — one, though not
> up to Maule (who ever will be?), who is more in that
> style — solid, superior, gentle, and gentlemanly — than
> any one I have lately met — a man of deep learning in
> Oriental matters, who has taken, too, to me. (Hewlett,
> 2: 219-20)

His friendship, too, with his 'nephew' — that is, the nephew of his old friend Benson Rathbone, also named Benson Rathbone, remained a consolation to him. On 29 December 1855 Chorley wrote to Benson: 'You would not find it easy to believe how often and how affectionately I think of you and your happy household, unless you had gone through my discipline of loss, and lived to see almost everything fail you on which you have placed reliance' (2: 311).

The most significant of the new relationships in the 1850s was his friendship with Charles Dickens. Dickens made Chorley feel welcome at Gad's Hill, treating him like an honoured member of the group of family and friends with which he surrounded himself after his separation from his wife in 1857. Chorley responded with gratitude. In his will, Chorley termed himself one who was 'greatly helped' by Dickens.

In 1836, long before they met, Dickens — in one of the *Sketches by Boz* ('The Streets: Night') — mentions a stout bass singing 'The brave old oak' (or 'Hoak', as the singer has it), a song composed by Edward J. Loder to Chorley's words.

Chorley loved Dickens's novels, from *Pickwick* to *Our Mutual Friend*. Although during the 1830s and 1840s he did not generally review Dickens's novels for the *Athenæum*,[59] he read them, knew them thoroughly, and quoted from or alluded to them frequently in his own writing. In *Music and Manners in France and Germany*, for example, he alluded to 'the minute and graphic writer of "The Old Curiosity Shop"' (1: 96). Further on in *Music and Manners* he characterized some of his own rambling prose as written 'after dear Mrs. Nickleby's fashion' (2: 64), and he reported from Berlin on a performance of the 'low comedian' Beckman in Raimund's *Der Bauer als Millionair*, confessing that its humour escaped him just as the Wellerisms in *Pickwick* would escape a German (*MMFG*, 1841, 2: 154). The *Ladies' Companion*, too, made frequent reference to Dickens's novels.[60] In the late 1840s, writing in *Douglas Jerrold's Shilling Magazine* under his 'Paul Bell' pseudonym Chorley alluded to Mrs Nickleby and Mr Lillyvick, to Miggs from *Barnaby Rudge*, to Miss Tox from *Dombey*, and others. ('Pope, Pipe, and Progress: A Peep at North Italy', 7 [January-June 1848]: 176). And he enjoyed occasional more elaborate Dickensian arabesques:

> 'Tis the finest thing in the world to have won a classical
> reputation. Well did dear Mrs. Jarley know the value of
> the adjective![61] But tell us, what *is* German Opera? ... a
> *Frau Harris*? concerning whose very existence soberer
> controversialists than *Betsy Prig* may propound grave
> doubts? [*Martin Chuzzlewit*] Hardly so. ... ('Musical
> Notes for May by Tartini's Familiar', *Bentley's Miscel-
> lany*, June 1849: 645)[62]

It is not certain when the two men met, though they seem to have
become close friends in 1854. E.W.F. Tomlin suggested they may have
met first in the 1830s at Lady Blessington's gatherings at Gore House:
(434-48); perhaps they met at Harrison Ainsworth's, who also knew them
both,[63] or perhaps through Dilke, who had been friendly with the Dickens
family since he and Dickens's father had both worked in the Naval pay
office early in the century.[64]

According to Dickens's daughter, Mamie, the acquaintanceship blos-
somed into friendship when in 1854 both found themselves working for the
same charitable cause. They took a liking to one another immediately and
their friendship developed to the extent that throughout the 1860s there was
a real bond of intimacy between them. In a letter to Henry Hewlett, Mamie
Dickens recalled their friendship and the positive effect it had on Chorley's
spirits:

> I can't exactly tell you *when* my father first knew Mr.
> Chorley, but a great may years before he became intimate
> with him. About the year 1854, my father was much
> interested about getting a pension for two literary persons,
> friends both of his and of Mr. Chorley. He then wrote to
> Mr. Chorley on the subject, and he — always ready to do
> anything good and kind — exerted himself a great deal in
> the matter. This business brought them a good deal
> together, and from that time till my dear father's death,
> they were fast friends. Mr. Chorley used to come con-
> stantly to Gad's Hill, used often to invite himself, and was
> always most welcome. People who were in the habit of
> seeing him only in London would hardly have known him
> at Gad's Hill, I think. He was a brighter and younger
> being altogether there. (20 August 1872; quoted in
> Hewlett, 2: 236-7).

By 1855 Chorley was inviting Dickens to his house for supper. Dickens frequently accepted Chorley's hospitality, as did his daughters Katie and
Mamie, and reciprocated it.[65]

It was convenient to get to Dickens's country house from London by train from London Bridge railway terminus, a short walk from Dickens's *All the Year Round* office in Wellington Street, Covent Garden. Travel time was approximately an hour from London into Kent as far as Higham, one stop before Rochester; from the little station there it was a short carriage ride to Dickens's spacious house, Gad's Hill. Later (in the 1860s) one could leave London from Victoria Station, not far from Chorley's house in Eaton Place West, and get off at Stroud — Rochester Bridge Station (Hewlett, 2: 234) or from Charing Cross Station, even closer to *All the Year Round* than London Bridge.

Charles, Mamie, and Kate Dickens came as guests to dinner parties in Chorley's little house. Chorley was as flattered and honoured by his special relationship with Dickens and his family as he had been with Mendelssohn. His sense of loyalty came into play too: as he had been defending Mendelssohn from revisionist criticism in the years following his death, so he found Dickens, already being criticized as the shadow of his former self, also in need of support and defence. Some were saying that the Saint of Christmastime, the good old Dickens, canonized for his humour, had died and a dry, burned out simulacrum had replaced him, continuing to write increasingly dreary serials. Chorley, however, found much to praise in Dickens's later novels: 'This novel shows progress on the part of its writer in more ways than one' he wrote about *Bleak House* in a lead article (17 September 1853: 1087). *Great Expectations* 'can be charged with only one fault; — that of being too short' (13 July 1861: 44). *Our Mutual Friend* 'is one of Mr. Dickens's richest and most carefully-wrought books' (28 October 1865: 570). Dickens, in turn, found Chorley pitiable and lovable. Peter Ackroyd suggested plausibly that Chorley's view of himself as a 'disappointed man who thought he had failed in life' brought out Dickens's 'instinctive care and sympathy' (Ackroyd, 911).

His major narrative effort, however, went into a new novel which he had started ten years earlier, lain aside, and now finally finished: *Roccabella*. Ever supportive, Dickens told him it was 'a very remarkable book indeed. ... [While reading it] I knew myself to be in the hands of an artist' (Hewlett, 2: 161).

Other friends made less positive comments. Frederick Lehmann recalled a conversation he had with Chorley in 1859 about the 'political novel' he had just finished. Lehmann's prediction that it would have 'ulta Tory' ideas was not far from the mark:

> [Chorley] never loses a chance of showing you his immense importance, his in fact being the *'unglückseliger Atlas'* on whom the world rests,[66] the fountain of knowledge and advice to which all throng. He took occasion to tell me during the sitting, that he had just finished a politi-

cal novel called *Roccabella*, begun in 1849. He has
deposited in it his experience of Refugee life and I suppose his ultra Tory ideas. It will come out immediately.
(*Ancestors and Friends*, 206)

Chorley published the novel as a tale told by Paul Bell, a persona he
began using in 1845 while writing numerous short articles for *Jerrold's
Shilling Magazine* between 1845 and 1848. For those articles he took the
pen name of a fictitious businessman who was 'a descendant of
[Wordsworth's] Peter Bell the Potter' (*Shilling Magazine*, January-June,
1845: 124).[67]
The novel shows how 'a woman's life' can be dedicated to high causes
— to improving the world — and how it can be twisted and exploited by the
unscrupulous Reds, who will take advantage of that impulse to Reform.
These members of the continental secret societies, plotting to overthrow
their governments, are cowardly, foolish, and truly without principles.
Thanks to the gullible (for example, their well-intentioned English supporters), they continue to make trouble:

> ... the secret societies of French, Italians, and Germans,
> existing in the capitals of Europe — and suffered to exist
> not merely by the ignorance of despots, and the con-
> nivance of police ministers, but by the folly of those wise
> men whose dream it has been to overturn society, and to
> extripate [*sic*] wrong from the face of the earth (2: 83).

The first person narrator, Mr Bell, is a plain, good hearted, roast beef
Englishman. His relative, Rosamond, is bored with life in Liverpool and
dissatisfied with her lot as a woman. She exclaims to Mrs Bell, 'What is
there that a woman could not do, if she would — supposing she had only
half the privileges of men?'
Rosamond's tiresome English husband dies and leaves her £2000 a year
to live on, but his will, like the dead hand controlling Dorothea Brooke in
Middlemarch, stipulates that the annuity will cease if she remarries. She
does remarry — Roccabella, a dashing Italian revolutionary, who makes
romantic promises of social improvement:

> [W]hat a new era was opening! — what life! what pro-
> gress! what enlightenment! what brotherly love for all the
> human race! There were to be no poor any more! no
> unhappy marriages any where! no more inequalities of
> fortunes, because no more injustice! "Ah, my Rosa-
> mond!" was the conclusion, "it is a proud thing for you,
> as an Englishwoman, to have lived to assist in carrying
> out such noble schemes of freedom and reform!" (2: 4)

They move to Paris, where Rosamond associates, reluctantly, with people such as Agricole Delbar, the artist who paints her portrait as Judith. The revolutionaries meet, awaiting the Angel of Deliverance, as the narrator describes with sarcastic contempt:

> The peoples were ready to rise; the oppressed nationalities had filed their fetters with such a patience of misery, that the first movement would snap them, and liberate the prisoner for ever! They would hear great news from every country. ... England, too — cold, conventional, practical England — they would hear, was at last stirred, had at last been tortured into generous and vindictive action, by the exactions of a bloated, and perverse, and bigoted aristocracy. (2: 107-8)

But Agricole murders Roccabella, the revolution fizzles, and the reader is repeatedly reminded that Rosamond's idealism is worthy of a better cause than the 1848 uprisings. Mr Bell muses sadly, 'O, poor Rosamond! ... She always *did* want misery; and now it is let loose on her with a vengeance' (2: 222). And when Mr Bell travels from England to Paris towards the end of the novel, he remarks on the futile destruction caused by the revolutionaries and their hopeless uprising, and on the anger aroused in sensible people by the foolish rabble rousers who cause such suffering. Mr Bell angrily comments:

> [One] *will* break out when he hears the political trader in blood and brains, whose cant is a "principle," whose personality is self-interest, and whose operation on the spirits of other men ends in agony, destitution, torture, and "endless weeping" to them, and in general disappointment to himself — talking by quiet English firesides and among tender-hearted and generous English women, of such days, and of such scenes. ... (2: 296-7)

Chorley used some of the themes and situations which George Eliot later was able to transform with mastery. For example, Chorley's Rosamond is a character not unlike Dorothea Brooke, one yearning to make a difference to the world, accustomed to 'giving up', and searching for an appropriate role in a society where reform and reformers are not always what they appear — but Chorley presented the character one-dimensionally, simplifying it numbingly into a cliché-ridden caricature.

The story assumed two points of view, Mr Bell's as well as the 'omniscient' narrator's. The narration of Chorley's previous novel, *Pomfret*, made some attempts to reconcile and rationalize various points of view. In *Roccabella*, however, it seems to have been an arbitrary decision to create a narrative voice which is not only a minor player in the story but also its alleged 'author': the voices of the two narrators do not differ in their disapproval of revolutionary causes in general, and of Italian revolutionaries in particular.[68]

In the 'Dedicatory' section of *Roccabella*, Bell termed himself 'the eldest-born of the Phantom family' of Currer, Ellis, and Ashton Bell and stated that it was originally his intention to dedicate the book to the author of *Jane Eyre* and *Shirley*. But since Charlotte Brontë died between the time he first suspended work on the novel and the time he resumed work, a new dedicatee was required. No other change of plans was needed, though, since Chorley's perspective had remained fixed in time, and 'in resuming a labour long laid aside, I did not find that I had any words to unsay; ... it has been my lot to find few things bad which I found good — no matter how many years ago — or *vicé versâ*' (*Roccabella*, 'Dedicatory', 1: iv).[69]

He decided to dedicate the book to the author of *Aurora Leigh*, 'one whom I have long held to be the most distinguished of women gifted for poetical authorship whom England has ever produced.'

Feelings about Italian politics had been high in the late 1840s, when Chorley began writing the novel; for the Brownings at least, they were higher still by 1859. Elizabeth Browning wrote, 'I never will forgive England the most damnable part she has taken on Italian affairs, never' (Irvine and Honan, 365).

The Brownings had, by chance, seen the *Athenæum*'s notice of *Roccabella* and had made a note to themselves to read it. But they were surprised to learn that the novel's author, Paul Bell, was their friend Chorley:

> It is strange — 'Roccabella' is *the* book — We saw a review of it in your Athenæum, & never once thought of you — Who could have supposed that a conferedate would be treated so lightly? ... Yet neither of us had a notion, by dream or vision, that the author was a dear friend of ours, & that moreoever our own personal vanity was dearly interested in what he had written.
>
> Dear Mr. Chorley, I feel as if I could *thank* you for not being of the politics of your *Guild*. (1 November 1859)[70]

Hewlett rightly considered the dedication 'a grave error in judgment' (2: 167), since the novel suggested that English supporters of Italian revolutionaries were misguided, like Rosamond Westwood, or laughable, like Porphyria Tatt. It was singularly insensitive for Chorley to expect that the author of *Aurora Leigh* would be gratified by the dedication of a novel whose purpose was to satirize both revolutionaries and their supporters. By thanking him in advance for 'not being of the politics of your *Guild*', Mrs Browning showed that she had no idea how hostile Chorley was to her own politics.

The Brownings read *Roccabella* carefully. Then Mrs Browning wrote Chorley a remarkable letter. Diplomatic, tactful, and potentially conciliatory, she did not concede the slightest validity to the novel's implication that support for Italian revolutionary causes was best left to cads and fools. Bluntly she disagreed with the tenor of this 'novel with a purpose'. At the same time, she was resolved to avoid quarrelling with Chorley, if at all possible:

> My dear friend — I thank you with all my heart for your most graceful and touching dedication, and do assure you that I feel it both as honour & as pleasure.
>
> And yet, do you know, Robert says that you might peradventure by the dedication of your book to me, mean a covert lecture . . or sarcasm . . who knows? Even if you did, the kindness of the personal address would make up for it. Who wouldn't bear both lecture & sarcasm from anyone who begins by speaking so? Therefore I am honoured & pleased & grateful all the same — yes, and will be.
>
> But dear Mr. Chorley, you don't silence me, notwithstanding. The spell of your dedication hasn't fastened me up in an oak forever. [...] The whole truth is not here — not even suggested here — and let me add that the half-truth on this occasion is cruel.
>
> One thing is ignored in the book. Under all the ridiculousness, under all the wickedness even of such men and women, lies a cause, a right inherent, a wrong committed. [...] You evidently think that God made only the English [... and that] Truth, generosity, nobleness of will & mind, these things do not exist beyond the influence of the Times newspaper and the Saturday Review [...]
>
> Well, I have lived thirteen years on the continent, and, far as England is from Italy, far as the heavens are from the earth, I dissent from you, dissent from you, dissent from you.
>
> I say so, and there is an end. [...] Dear Mr. Chorley, Robert & I have had true pleasure (in spite of all this fault-finding) in feeling ourselves close to you in your book [...] Don't say it's the last novel, you who can do so much [...]. Very affectionately yours, Elizabeth B. Browning. (25 November 1859; Kenyon, 2: 350-52)

Charles Dickens and Robert Browning also wrote Chorley long and detailed responses to *Roccabella*. Robert Browning stressed the sufferings of the Italians (Hewlett, 2: 169-74). Dickens, while agreeing that Italians do 'have the faults you ascribe to them (nationally, not individually)', urged nevertheless that it were better not 'to exhibit those faults without referring them back to their causes' (Hewlett, 2: 165; also *Nonesuch Letters*, 3: 148-50). Nathaniel Hawthorne and his wife also sent letters of appreciation (Hewlett, 2: 166-7).

The *Athenæum* paid *Roccabella* cursory attention (24 September 1859: 396-7); William Hepworth Dixon wrote a few comments followed by more than a column quoting the novel's description of Princess Morgenstern. 'Those who like the specimen given will send for the quaint and impassioned book from which we have drawn it' (397). Though some of the secondary characters were interesting, the main characters failed to engage Dixon:

> For this wayward, foolish woman, so egregious in her devotion to a bad man and so fearfully punished for her absurdities, we do not care a rush; though we admit that readers more susceptible and sentimental may find for her some pity, and even some excuse. Neither do we care much for the handsome scoundrel who carries her away. ... (396).

Perhaps the publishers had little expectation that the book would sell: Robert Browning wrote 'I never see you advertised' and marvelled that the *Athenæum* could dismiss its own writer so summarily: 'What a notice that was in the "Athenæum"!' (Hewlett, 2: 173).

Chorley might have wondered whether anyone beside Dickens, the Hawthornes, and the Brownings read *Roccabella*. Although the jinx of Chorley's name on the title page was gone, the novel sold no better as 'Paul Bell's' work than it would have sold as Chorley's.

Notes

1. Quoted from MS in Fitzwilliam Museum, Cambridge, in Waddington, 'Turgenev's Relations With Chorley' (29).
2. Mrs Leo Hunter hunts celebrities in Dickens's *Pickwick Papers*, Chapter 15.
3. Wilhelm Kuhe remembered that Chopin's 'figure was attenuated to such a degree that he looked almost transparent; indeed, so weak was he that at a party given about that time at Chorley's when my wife was present, he had to be carried upstairs, being too feeble to walk' (Kuhe, 113).
4. It was, however, Hervey, in "Our Weekly Gossip" (1 June 1850: 585 and 22 June 1850: 662), not Chorley, who suggested that she be

appointed poet laureate, according to the marked copy. A few years later Chorley greeted the publication of *Aurora Leigh* with mixed feelings, criticizing 'the huge mistake of its plan' (22 November 1856: 1427) while asserting that its author was 'the greatest poetess of any time' (1425).

5. Completed and published in 1859 under the pseudonym Paul Bell, it was dedicated not to Brontë but 'to the author of "Aurora Leigh"'. 'I never thought to finish this tale. But the humour came back not long ago, and (for better, for worse) the history is here brought to a close' *Roccabella*, 'Dedicatory', iii.

6. I believe that the journal's change of editorial policy under Chorley probably contributed to a decline in readership, which in turn contributed to its merger with other fashion magazines. Auerbach, however, stated that under both Loudon and Chorley the journal's editorial policy was 'appealing to its readership' (128) up to the time of its editorial merger in 1852 with *The New Monthly Belle Assemblée* and *The Ladies' Cabinet of Fashion, Music, and Romance*, which was 'the most archaic and traditional of the three' (123).

7. The duties were domestic for a married woman. A single woman's duties were 'less clearly defined' (8), though they often included assisting in the household of a married relative. Still another duty, especially for rich women, was 'lending a helping hand to such of their own sex as may be in poverty or distress' (8) — women struggling because of 'the premature death of their fathers or husbands'.

   Chorley apparently contributed nothing to the first volume. 'Music as an Accomplishment' (5 January 1850: 17-18) echoed Mrs Loudon's editorial statement about the *Companion*'s goals ('Music is peculiarly a female accomplishment') and was signed George Hogarth. The first volume's single notice labelled 'Music' — reviewing the opening of the Philharmonic season on 2 March (16 March 1850: 175) — was signed 'H.H.' Seven papers on 'The Cultivation of the voice' were signed 'F. [Frank?] Romer, Esq.'

   In the final issue of volume I, Loudon's editorial remarks, 'A Few Words on the Condition of Woman', concerned the 'class of maligned and despised females' known generally as 'old maids' (406). In fact, she wrote, 'a single life need not necessarily be an isolated one; there is work for all, there is love for all' (22 June 1850: 407) (authorship presumed to be Loudon; not signed or initialed 'J.W.L.'). Another editorial concern of volume I was 'How Should Girls Be Educated' (16 March 1850: 168). The topic was continued (23 March 1850: 184, and 6 April 1850: 216). All three were signed 'J.W.L.' (18 May 1850: 328).

8. 7 December 1850: 369-71; 14 December 1850: 385-8; 21 December 1850: 401-4; and 28 December 1850: 417-19. Years later Chorley

called attention to this work in a letter to the editor of the *Athenæum*:

> The following is from a correspondent: — "As there
> has been talk in your columns about the original idea of
> 'The Merry Widow,' and reference made to Madame
> de Girardin's admirable 'La Joie fait Peur,' — a writer
> having perhaps fewer readers than the Italian priest had
> hearers whom he addressed as 'Pochissimi Signori,'
> may be allowed to raise his voice and say, that a tale
> entitled 'Kate's December,' published in 1850 in 'The
> Lady's Companion,' [*sic*] is nearer to the new play
> than Madame de Girardin's story turned backwards.
> There was the blind mother, and the daughter who hid
> the bad news, and went to balls, in order to spare
> suspense to her family. The hero of my tale, though,
> was a brother, not a husband. I may add, that the tale
> would never have been written, had not such an
> instance of real heroism occurred within the circle of
> my own friendships. All the persons, however, were
> already gone, or far away in 1850, whom allusions
> then, or disclosures now, could annoy, had their names
> been told. PAUL BELL." [i.e. Chorley] (*Athenæum*,
> 28 February 1863: 303)

9. Chorley's review of *Transformation* praised Hawthorne's sensitivity
    to the sheer beauty of Italy, but with the characters he was less
    impressed than he had been with those in *The Scarlet Letter* and *The
    House of Seven Gables*. The review drew a letter of protest from Mrs
    Hawthorne about Chorley's comparison between Hilda and Phoebe in
    The House of Seven Gables:

    > For indeed and in truth Hilda is not Phœbe, no more
    > than a wild rose is a calla lily. ... I am very much
    > grieved that *Mr. Chorley* should seem not to be nicely
    > discriminating; for what are we to do in that case? ... I
    > utterly protest against being supposed partial because I
    > am Mrs. Hawthorne. (Leamington, 5 March 1860,
    > quoted in Hewlett, 2: 110-11)

10. Despite these strictures, the *Athenæum* remarked in Berlioz's
    obituary:

    > Perhaps the most useful labour of Berlioz' life was the
    > compilation of his 'Traité d'Instrumentation et d'Or-
    > chestration Moderne.' His own strong point was,
    > unquestionably, writing for the orchestra, and on this
    > subject he spoke with the authority of a master.

(*Athenæum*, 13 March 1869: 376)

11. *Athenæum*, 7 August 1858: 177.
12. Chorley tended to be indifferent or hostile to performances of Spohr's works. The next year he wrote that the revival of *Jessonda* at the Royal Italian Opera was not 'dramatic'. It was 'lugubrious, sickly, and mono-chromatic' (13 August 1853: 969).
13. Hallé said Chorley 'was a man of strong views, fearless in his criticism, perfectly honest, although often and unconsciously swayed by personal antipathies or sympathies' (Kennedy, 118).
14. 'Je vais aussi faire un grand changement que nous venons de decider avec Madame Viardot: c'est *l'ode* de Sapho au 1er acte — je crois, nous croyons tous les deux, elle et moi, que l'effet n'en est pas sûr comme *ode lirique*, comme morceau de concours et de représentation *d'apparat*. Je vais tâcher de trouver quelque chose de plus brillant. (garde toute cette confidence pour toi seul)' (MS, Fitzwilliam Library, Cambridge University).
15. Gounod to Chorley, 31 December 1850. MS Fitzwilliam Library, Cambridge.
16. MS Biblioteque National, quoted in Huebner, 30.
17. *Musical World*, 16 August 1851, quoted in Fitzlyon, 274. *The Times* reported on Gounod's characteristics: 'want of melody, indecision of style, ineffective treatment of voices, inexperience in the use of instruments, accompanied by an affectation of originality disclosed in strange and unsuccessful experiments, excess of modulation ... [&c]' (quoted in Fitzlyon, 274). For French criticism, see Huebner, 33.
18. He continued:

> Let us enter a little into particulars. — After a few bars of simple and stately introduction, the *allegro*, in E flat 3/4 time, starts spiritedly on a subject, which is a real one, inasmuch as every phrase in it has form and meaning. In its opening and measure it will recall, per-haps to others besides ourselves, that waltz by Mozart, long known in England as the "Queen of Prussia's," — but there is no plagiarism, and we merely allude to the remembered tune for description's sake. The subject is handsomely displayed, and not, as modern fashion is, exposed and snatched away ere the second subject is introduced. This is a long, sweeping passage of melody, fascinating in its flow and orchestral treat-ment. The *allegro* (in short) moves; the second part grows from the first naturally, yet not tritely, — for M. Gounod is a true Frenchman in his determination to satisfy the ear by disappointing expectation, and there

is more than one happy example of delicate, yet unexpected, modulation, such as we do seldom find among German or Italian writers of the classical period. The close of the movement is bold, but good and arresting. The *larghetto* (in B flat, common time) is a delicious movement. There is a touch at its commencement, and in two subsequent bars a positive reminiscence of the *adagio* in Beethoven's Ninth Symphony, but this is only transient; and the conduct of the movement, and all its forms, figures and ways are no more *alla* Beethoven than they are Haydn*ish*. The episode in the middle of the movement is graceful, and excellent as a relief. The *scherzo* in G minor is no less marked in its leading phrase, restless, almost sullenly stormy in its rapidity; — not *scherzoso*, — and thus mis-named, till the pastoral *trio* comes in G major, with its gracious *musette* effect, giving the desired relief. The *finale*, in E flat 2/4, is the most individual, and possibly, the best of the four movements; — in this different from the generality of modern *finales*, which are too apt to show the weakness, in idea, of a composer, however he may try to mask the same behind the devices of fine writing. The theme has the seizing piquancy of an *air de ballet*, without being either operatic or impertinently frivolous. In its sustained and arch vivacity this last movement approaches nearer Beethoven's *finales* than any modern music we recollect, save it be Mendelssohn's *Saltarella*. We may speak of this Symphony again, and meantime must repeat that, its period, its country and its parentage considered, it has fulfilled our expectations, and those, as the readers of the *Athenæum* are aware, were not small. It was very well performed and cordially received. (26 April 1856: 527)

19. Lehmann, *Ancestors and Friends*, 206.
20. A singer of the golden age just before Grisi, Henriette Sontag, died at this time while on tour in Mexico. Chorley's obituary in the issue of 15 July 1854, reminded readers that her initial success was in the days of Pasta and Malibran; years after she retired her life had been 'sacrificed', since the reversal of fortunes of the noble Rossi family, into which she married, prompted her to return to the stage to earn money for her family (880) in a second autumnal career before a new generation of audiences.
21. Chorley spelled the opera's title '*Conte* Ory' here and in *Thirty*

Years', 2: 218; but *'Comte* Ory' in *Thirty Years'*, 2: 251.

22. Edward Bache wanted to write operas and study in Italy. Alfred Mellon wrote to him (27 June 1854) asking: 'What does Chorley say, or Simpson? ...' (Bache, 39). In a letter to his parents, 30 July 1854, Edward wrote: '... and I have written to Mr. Palgrave Simpson and Mr. Chorley, asking their advice. They advise me most strongly not to go to Italy to study, but to go in a year or two's time to travel if possible' (40). Chorley's advice that Bache travel, not study, in Italy, was consistent with his scepticism about musical standards there in the 1850s.

23. He sounded a favourite theme a week later: 'Very pleasant has been the enthusiasm [for Meyerbeer] to ourselves, — in part because we recollect how some eighteen years ago those few among us who wrote in praise of M. Meyerbeer's 'Huguenots' — then in its young glory at the *Grand Opéra* of Paris — were criticized by their English contemporaries, as people whose brains had been disturbed by the desire of running after any outlandish novelty. Yet, though we are slow to move, when moved we English are constant' (11 August 1855: 930).

24. 'We have month by month written the story of the decay of the *Grand Opéra* during many years, conceiving that theatre to be the most interesting musical theatre in Europe. ... A completely new spirit must be infused into the *Grand Opéra* or it will sink into utter ruin' (8 November 1856: 1378).

25. For example, in 1867 he wrote:

> The Trilogy, 'L'Enfance de [*sic*] Christ,' by M. Berlioz (the second part of which contains his most rational music), has been given at Lausanne. (*Athenæum*, 30 March 1867: 428)

Berlioz dedicated part two of the work to John Ella.

26. Perhaps the most interestingly written of all the 'operatic' articles in Charles Dickens's *Household Words* is Albert Richard Smith's 'Theatrical Ashes', 13 (22 March 1856), a meditation on the great Covent Garden fire, which seemed to signal that the recently started company would have to give up. Smith lamented the 'really miserable end of a such a splendid building':

> If it was fated to be burnt down, the fire should have burst out — provided all could have got away — in the last scene of le Prophète, with Mario singing the drinking song, surrounded by his beautiful bacchantes, as the flames began to lap and twine about the gilded doors and costly draperies of the palace of Munster. (218)

As an appropriate memorial to the house, Smith imagined an operatic allegory in the form of a statue representing staples of the current operatic repertory:

> I would have a souvenir of the late theatre also in the market-place. It should have a fountain, the basin supported by Norma, Don Giovanni, Dulcamara, Valentine, Maffeo Orsini, and Fides; and on top I would have a statue, suggested by the antique, of Mario sitting amongst the ruins of Covent Garden. (220)

For the final household word on the burning see John Hollingshead's 'A Phantom Theatre', about the rebuilding of Covent Garden, *Household Words*, 17 (8 May 1858): 484-6.

27. Three years earlier Chorley had published a second-hand report of the notorious first night of *La Traviata* in Venice: 'it may be told that "La Traviata", the latest opera by Signor Verdi, written for Venice, has failed utterly: — the failure being frankly accepted as such by the author in a letter addressed to the *Gazetta Musicale* of Milan' (2 April 1853: 426).

28. MS, Cushman Collection, Library of Congress.

29. In 1859 Chorley dedicated his *Handel Studies* to Costa, in part 'because you have done England good service in the point of music'. These studies are mainly sketchy impressions of the *Messiah* and *Israel in Egypt*, written hastily with 'no scientific pretension' (4).

30. Similar irritation emerged in Chorley's 'Musical and Dramatic Gossip' column on 30 August 1856, where he maintained that the projected monument to Handel should be on English soil, and that money should be raised in Germany as well as England for its support: 'The Mendelssohn Scholarhip is not the only case in which German Reverence has said "Do let us dip into England's purse!" the while clasping her own strong-box tight. ... They profit by us — they respect our probity, — but they love us little, and esteem our judgment less' (1090).

31. Lunn was later editor of the *Musical Times*, 1863-87.

32. He continued:

> In France (as has been duly noted), M. Gounod is beginning to make a figure as one who will be heard; in Germany, something to sustain the old credit of the land may be found in the works of such conservative writers as Herren Emil Naumann and Reinthaler: — but, in England, with the exception of Mrs. Bartholomew's 'Nativity,' Mr. H. Smart's opera, and Mr. Howard Glover's *Cantata*, there has been absolutely nothing. (9 December 1855: 1539)

He identified three main areas of significant musical activity in England in 1855: 1. Lind-Goldschmidt's concerts, 2. Three operas at the Royal Italian Opera — *Conte Ory*, *Trovatore*, and *L'Étoile*, and 3. Costa's *Eli* at the Birmingham Festival (1539).

33.   Chorley complained that Sterndale Bennett did not compose enough music. 'Why are we not to hear of some new work by Dr. Bennett? He might have taken for his device the aloe which flowers once in a hundred years' (*Athenæum*, 7 January 1860: 23).

34.   He announced another collaboration in a similarly impersonal way: 'It has been said that at one of its concerts during the coming season a secular *Cantata*, by Mr. Lindsay Sloper, will be produced, — the words to which are by Mr. Henry F. Chorley' (27 November 1858: 690).

35.   He may have in the back of his mind his use of the character Judith in *Roccabella*. In volume 2, Chapter 4, 'A Red Evening', Rosamond is persuaded to impersonate Judith for a *tableau*. The reaction from the 'small group of spectators' is: '*Brava! brava!* ... How she will smite him, not wholly for the sake of Israel, but in contempt of his love, and in redemption of herself from the abasement of having feigned to listen to it!' (2: 90).

36.   MS, Cushman Collection, Library of Congress.

37.   MS, Liverpool Record Office (undated), 920 SAN 1/5.

38.   This situation anticipated two later controversies: one occasioned by changes made by Sims Reeves and other singers to Chorley's translation of *Faust* in 1864, another occasioned by Benedict's request that Joseph Bennett revise Chorley's words to *St Peter* in 1870.

39.   In 1848 Chorley commended Ella's Musical Union for 'being the first to bring a new composer to judgment', but he scorned the puffs from the 'German press'. If this work was characteristic of Schumann, 'he falls back among the second rates ... (as we pointed out some four years ago)' (1 April 1847: 345). Schumann's position in Germany was 'somewhat analogous to that of M. Berlioz in France' (345).

40.   Bennett had voted against Costa's appointment as conductor of the Philharmonic Society in 1846 and relations between the two musicians deteriorated dramatically. Chorley was not pleased that Bennett succeeded Costa as conductor for ten seasons from 1856-65. According to Bennett's son, 'Bennett's friends, acquaintances and pupils appear to have agreed unanimously that he felt little or no love for Schumann's music' (Bennett, *Life*, 341).

41.   Cox called Lind's voice 'more fatigued and unequal than it had ever been before' (*Recollections*, 2: 304) — echoing Chorley nearly word for word, as he often did. Joseph Bennett remarked that Cox, who wrote for *Bell's Weekly Messenger*, was not a 'critic of distinction' (*Forty Years of Music*: 13).

42. Bennett conducted *Paradise* again on 5 March 1866, with Parepa instead of Lind, as the first concert of the season (Foster, 290). It was still received with hostility (Ehrlich, *First Philharmonic*, 110).

43. Lind continued to sing publicly from time to time until as late as 1883, and Chorley's irritation simmered down. For example, his report of a concert given by *The Society of Female Artists* in 1861: 'Here Madame Goldschmidt was to be heard, and liberally; her services never being given by halves. — Never during her career did she sing in better voice nor with finer finish than on Thursday. She has benefited by repose. ... Why she should not still enter on a career, without inordinate *prestige* or pretension, as the first living *soprano*, but with success enough to keep warm the heart of any female artist, rests with her own will to decide' (*Athenæum*, 6 July 1861: 24). For a summary of Lind's public appearances in England and on the Continent after her retirement from opera see Holland and Rockstro, 2: 431.

44. At the time of the 1849 performances of *Athalie*, Chorley discussed the work for readers of *Bentley's Miscellany*, noting that it was not well understood by members of the Philharmonic audience. 'Musical Notes for March by Tartini's Familiar', 25 (April 1849): 409-11.

45. Belleti and Sims Reeves joined Novello and Dolby for the Rossini:

> Probably a larger amount of beauty does not exist within the same musical space than is contained in Signor Rossini's 'Stabat' — the last and most gorgeous Italian composition of its order. ... Whether the 'Stabat' has been ever more nobly executed than on Friday week may be doubted.

46. Hogarth wrote:

> We do not ... feel able to pronounce an opinion of it [Overture to *Tannhäuser*]. Before this can be done it must be heard more than once; and we believe it will produce an effect in a theatre ... which can never be given to it in a concert-room. According to our present impression, it wants form, symmetry, and that clear rhythmical melody which ought to be found in every description of music. Where there is a melodious phrase, it is generally overpowered and lost in a mass of intricate accompaniments. There are things in it, however, which must at once strike the hearer as beautiful ... and the whole piece certainly shows, like the music of Berlioz, a great command over the resources of instrumentation. (*Daily News*, 16 May 1855: 5)

and

> Mendelssohn's Symphony in A minor, the "Scottish Symphony," was played with powerful effect, though the times of some portions of it were not altogether the same as those given by Mendelssohn himself. Probably M. Wagner never heard him conduct the symphony. An author's own reading, of course, must be the best; though we confess that M. Wagner's ideas, when the were different, did not always displease us ... In the overture to *Leonora*, likewise, the time was occasionally pressed and relaxed in a manner to which we have not been accustomed; but our impression was that these licenses, as they are deemed, heightened the fire and vigour of this incomparable overture. (*Daily News*, 29 May 1855: 2)

After Wagner's final concert, Hogarth remarked diplomatically: 'Whatever differences of opinion may exist among our critics as to the peculiarities of his style as a composer, there can be no question as to his genius and attainments, or as to his high position among the musicians of the age' (*Daily News*, 28 June 1855: 2).

47. Praeger, ix. Praeger was considered by some later commentators vainglorious and self-promoting.

48. This mention of Wagner is likely to be simply a coincidence, rather than a direct or indirect response to Liszt's plan (Liszt was specifically interested in introducing *Lohengrin*, not *Tannhäuser*).

49. To illustrate the absurdities, Chorley printed quotations side-by-side: one quotation, reprinted from the *New York Musical Review and Gazette*, alleged inaccurate reporting in the *Athenæum*; beside it, another quotation reprinted exactly what the *Athenæum* had published. The comparison of the two quotations was presented for the benefit of 'all such home and foreign readers as understand English' (11 August 1855: 931).

50. The programmes for all the concerts were listed in Foster, 241-4, Davison, 166-74, and Newman (less fully — 'the minor pieces being omitted as being of no interest to-day'), 2: 461-3. Wagner's reception by the London press was discussed by Ellis, 5: chapter 2.

51. Compare George Hogarth's more generous assessment of the excerpts from *Lohengrin*:

> The English public had, for the first time (for we do not take into account one or two lame attempts to play one of his overtures), a specimen of Herr Wagner's qualities as a composer. A fragment of a dramatic work, transferred from the theatre to the concert room,

is necessarily heard to disadvantage, being deprived of
the scenic spectacle and action. ... Wagner's music,
however, deprived as it was of these essential acces-
sories, had a great effect, and a most favourable reception. It was found to have much breadth and clearness,
flowing and rhythmical melody, and marvellous variety
and richness of instrumentation. ... (*Daily News*, 27
March 1855: 6)

52. Barrett's letter of 19 June 1844, quoted below, was apparently written
not long after Mitford's letter to Chorley. Hewlett dated the letter
simply as 'anterior to 1846' (2: 18).

53. MS, Cushman Collection, Library of Congress.

54. An allusion to the full title of Dickens's *Martin Chuzzlewit*: '... showing, moreover, who inherited the fancy plate, who came in for the sil-
ver spoons, and who for the wooden ladles.'

55. MS, Cushman Collection, Library of Congress.

56. MS, Cushman Collection, Library of Congress.

57. MS, Library of Congress; quoted in part, with some variants, in Stebbins. Despite depression, he continued to write and publish works in
addition to his regular journalism. In the *Athenæum* (13 December
1856: 1505 and for 20 December: 1543) George Routledge and Company listed in its full page advertisement for new publications *Faery
Gold for Young and Old*, 3s 6d, 'edited' by H.F. Chorley and
illustrated by W. Harvey. This children's book had a casual origin:
Chorley was 'sauntering down one of the galleries in Bordeaux, in
search of a book to read on the railway' and came across tales from
Savinier Lapointe, with a preface by Béranger expressing enthusiasm
for the work. Chorley found that he shared the enthusiasm (*Fairy
Gold*, vi). The title page termed Chorley the 'editor', but Hewlett
suggested that Chorley wrote the 'paraphrased translation' (2: 175).

58. MS, Cushman papers, Library of Congress.

59. An exception was *A Christmas Carol*, reviewed by Chorley on 23
December 1843. Another exception, according to Marchand (304)
was *Martin Chuzzlewit*, reviewed 10 July 1844: 665-6 (Marchand
cites his source as Ley, 285; the marked file does not give attributions
for 1844).

60. References, for example, to Miggs (*Barnaby Rudge*) 30 November
1850: 360 (editorial); to Mrs Wititterly (*Nicholas Nickleby*) 17
August 1850: 126 (signed article); and to Miss Lucretia Tox (*Dombey
and Son*) (unsigned column, 'Mrs. Grundy's Commnon-Place Book')
1 May 1851: 189.

61. Repeatedly over several decades Chorley alluded to Mrs Jarley's
remark in *The Old Curiosity Shop* that waxworks are not real at all
but 'calm and classical'.

62. Attribution from *Wellesley Index*, 5: 151.

63. As Antonio Gallenga attested: 'I knew ... William Harrison Ains-
     worth, at whose house I frequently dined with a lot of friends, and
     where I met Mr Henry Chorley' (Gallenga, 2: 105).

64. 'The Dickenses and the Dilkes have been friends from the beginning
     of the century to the present day; Mr. Dilke's father and Mr. Charles
     Dickens's father were in the same office under Government' (Dilke,
     1: 71). See also Forster, 1: chapter 2.

65. See, for example, Dickens's letter to Mrs Gaskell, *Nonesuch Letters*
     2: 622. The seventh volume of the Pilgrim edition of Dickens's letters
     records no letters from Dickens to Chorley.

66. Lehmann alluded to Chorley's self-pity in his reference to Heine's
     poem, as set to music by Schubert, 'Der Atlas': ('die ganze Welt der
     Schmerzen, muss ich tragen' — 'I have to bear the whole world of
     sorrows').

67. 'Paul Bell' wrote the following for *Douglas Jerrold's Shilling Maga-
     zine*:

> volume 1 (January-June 1845)
>> Paul Bell in Account Current with William
>> Wordsworth, Esq., Laureate (124-9)
>
> volume 4 (July-Decemnber 1846):
>> August Visions (325)
>> Columbine at Court: A Christmas Fancy (528)
>> Feasts and Funerals: A Homily for the Middle
>> Classes (406)
>> Sumptuary Presumptions (136)
>
> volume 5 (January-June, 1847)
>> Heads and Tails of Families
>>> 1. The Discipline of the Dableys (35)
>>> 2. Slagg's Patents (123)
>>> 3. A Religious Subject (313)
>>> 4. My Lame Boy's Tastes (414)
>>> 5. A Young Head Upon Old Shoulders (538)
>
> volume 6 (July to December, 1847)
>> Little Gentlefolks; or, Shows of the Season (141)
>> November Clouds and Counsels (414)
>> Pound and Penny Bribery (204)
>> The Prince and the Philibeg (537)
>> The Season out of Season (45)
>
> volume 7 (January-June, 1848)
>> Arbor Libertatis; or, Freedom's May-poles. An
>> Extravaganza (400)
>> Fashions (and Fugitives) for March (331)
>> The Keep-Out Tax (203)

> Pope, Pipe, and Progress; a Peep at North Italy
> (171)
> The Small Sins of London (21)

68. This attitude is consistent with views he was publishing elsewhere under the name 'Paul Bell' in the late 1840s, for example, 'Pope, Pipe, and Progress; a Pccp at North Italy', *Jerrold's Shilling Magazine*, 7 (1848): 171.

69. A reminder of unchanging views already cited ('I have not come to like what I disliked ten years ago, or the reverse' *Modern German Music*, Preface, 1: ix) and an anticipation of *Thirty Years' Musical Recollections* (1862), when he 'found no discrepancy betwixt past and present judgments worth adverting to' (Introduction, 1: xi).

70. MS, Boston Public Library, Department of Rare Books and Manuscripts, Mss. Acc. 12b.

CHAPTER SEVEN

Final Years at the *Athenæum*: 1860-68

1

At the beginning of the 1860s there were a number of people whom Chorley counted as friends, notwithstanding his complaints about being alone and friendless. In addition to Dickens, whom he visited frequently at Gad's Hill, there were Frederick and Nina Lehmann, whom he visited at Woodlands, their house in the northern London suburb of Highgate. Dinners or other social gatherings at this time might also include Prince Galitzin, whose private labours on behalf of Russian music Chorley commended,[1] Virginia Gabriel,[2] Lady Molesworth, Chief Justice Alexander Cockburn, Robert Browning, George Grove, Henry Reeve, Mr and Mrs Bancroft, the actors, and, of course, musicians — among them Hallé, Costa, Joachim, and Mrs Sartoris (Adelaide Kemble), who was often in the company of her adoring Frederic Leighton, the artist. Edward Dannreuther recalled that 'whomever he invited was *somebody*', and the conversation was usually about everything *except* music, since Chorley ('very wisely') 'declined to talk shop' (*Musical Times*, 1 October 1898: 650).

At times, Chorley's conviviality could be very lively. Lehmann wrote to his wife about a party at Hallé's where Chorley 'had drunk the elixir of life just in the right quantity last night and was wonderfully youthful and frisky' (Lehmann, *Memories*, 227). After the party, Chorley and Lehmann walked home together 'as far as the corner of Park Lane'. Chorley's pontifical manner both amused and slightly irritated Lehmann:

> He had recently made Holman Hunt's acquaintance at Gad's Hill, and was very much struck by the notion that he paints Christ from his own face. In 'The Light of the World' there is certainly some similarity. He quite hugged this discovery, as you know he does everything which he thinks he has found out. (*Memories*, 228)

Holidays on the Continent still held his interest and occasionally offered a delightful surprise. Most memorable and enjoyable was a visit to Sicily, when, after seeing Palermo for the first time in October, 1860, Chorley wrote to his young friend, Virginia Gabriel, a long letter expressing his delight. 'See Palermo and pray you may live to see it again!' he exclaimed.

> I find it beyond my dreams & it has been my dream for

> many years, else should I never have dragged my weary
> heart & failing body [illegible] ... I never had till now
> quite as much colour as I wanted on a landscape I
> had the strange sort of feeling which does not come very
> often in a lifetime — *What have I done to deserve seeing*
> *such beautiful things?* I am afraid this place will make me
> unfaithful to Venice ... (8 October 1860)[3]

Indeed, he babbled so much of Palermo to his English friends that it became a private joke among them. Nina Lehmann, writing to her husband that she visited and liked St Jean de Luz, added that she meant 'to swear by it for the future, and pity people who haven't seen it, as Chorley did about Palermo' (Lehmann, *Memories*, 185).

The next year, 1861, brought still another memorably happy holiday journey: this time to Spain in the company of Frederick Lehmann. When he heard that Lehmann was going to take a holiday in Spain Chorley said (to Lehmann's astonishment), 'That sounds very nice. I don't mind if I go with you' (Lehmann, *Ancestor and Friends*, 208).

The self-invited Chorley began his holiday by visiting Gad's Hill on his way to meet up with Lehmann. As so often seemed to happen there, the man often considered frail and sickly by many, including himself, felt younger and stronger at Dickens's house. Dickens was known for taking extraordinarily long walks as a matter of routine. During Chorley's visit this time, Dickens was moved to walk twenty-two miles. To everyone's astonishment, including Dickens's, Chorley matched his host step for step. Dickens wrote to Wills, the sub-editor of *All the Year Round*, that after twenty-two miles 'at my pace' Chorley seemed none the worse, and he added: 'I stood amazed, and have ever since remained in that attitude' (31 August 1861, *Nonesuch Letters*, 3: 232). He then proceeded to Biarritz, where he met up with Lehmann, whose letters home to Nina about vacation life with 'dear old Chorley' show that he and Chorley turned out to be good travelling companions (*Ancestors and Friends*, 208-9).

Despite these good times, during some periods of the 1860s Chorley may have spent more time with alcohol than with either his work or his friends. At these times the 'elixir of life' showed a less charming side. Mamie Dickens observed Chorley at a play one night in 1864 'dead drunk', for example. She related the events of the evening to Mrs Lehmann:

> He was long past speech, and it is Dickens's idea that he
> has been in this state all the time he has been alone at
> Biarritz. That is his *idea*, you know. At dinner he
> couldn't speak, so the three Dickens's talked to each other
> without minding him. I need not write all the misadven-
> tures. He got to the theatre alone somehow, went into Mr

> Oxenford's box and fell on the floor ... [Later, he] grad-
> ually recovered *slightly*. (*Ancestors and Friends*, 212)

His friends were saddened and, to a degree, offended by such behaviour. Less sympathetic observers ridiculed him with gusto, and in at least one case publicly. In 1862 he was the target of a long satirical poem, *Musical Cynics of London*, by George Linley.

> From some lone swamp, some noxious spot of earth,
> Where only pois'nous reptiles have their birth,
> This Thing, corrupt in body as in mind,
> A walking Upas, pest of human kind,
> First crawled to light, devoid of soul or heart,
> Foredoom'd to act the spiteful Cynic's part.
> Some may remember when to London came
> This awkward stripling, zealous for a name,
> A crop-eared Puritan, of slender sense,
> Of little learning, though of great pretence;
> With pocket-money savings got together
> To serve in time of need, or stress of weather,
> With eager longing to increase his store,
> To ape the pedant, though unskilled in lore. (page 1)

To Linley, Chorley's position in London musical circles was attributable not to his merit but to corruption. He ridiculed Chorley's dinner parties ('Who would not thank the Gods for an invite / To be the guest of such a Sybarite?' [page 3]), his appearance, and his high-pitched voice:

> We hear the orange-woman's cry
> In yonder quiet street,
> Reminding us of Chorley's voice,
> So high, and yet *not* sweet. (6)

Linley compared Chorley to the much ridiculed 'Poet Bunn' — to Bunn's advantage:

> Compared with Chorley, it is *no* mis-nomer,
> 'Tis *not* pseudonymous to call Bunn — Homer! (12)

He also attacked Chorley as a public drunk, anticipating Mamie Dickens's private letter, and a self-important bully. Once, for example, Chorley was asleep and snoring loudly at a concert. Therefore, Linley claimed, 'the Superintendent of the room, naturally enough, imagined that some drunken fellow from the streets had gained entrance'. On waking, the drunken fellow unrepentantly 'squeaked, with a voice something like an Indian yell, "*Do you know who I am?*"' (Linley, footnote to page 9).

Professionally, the beginning of the 1860s presented Chorley with an operatic repertory that he had tired of, at least temporarily. He expressed his hopes in January 1860 that the new year would bring a new direction in the operatic repertory. There were too many nights of the same old operas, *Lucrezia Borgia*, *Norma* and *Les Huguenots*. Grisi was partly to blame, since every time she announced that she was 'positively' retiring, the operas with her principal roles were repeated. Instead of these, Chorley recommended unhackneyed works like Mozart's *Seraglio*, Gluck's *Orfeo*, and Auber's *Domino Noir*. Since it was becoming difficult to find enough singers 'capable of doing justice' to *Zelmira* and other 'less-known' operas of Rossini, perhaps Verdi, now retired at his 'Sabine Farm', would now apply himself studiously and produce 'better artistic, not *quasi*-amateur music' in the future (7 January 1860: 23).

If the operatic repertory seemed somewhat stagnant at the beginning of the 1860s, the new decade did bring a new direction in poetry. Elizabeth Barrett Browning's *Poems Before Congress* appeared in March 1860. *Athenæum* readers had been given a foretaste of its political content the previous autumn, when the *Athenæum* printed 'A Tale of Villafrance, As Told in Tuscany' (24 September 1859: 396). Chorley was not receptive either to that sample or to the other poems in the collection. How best address Napoleon III? Mrs Browning's poem termed him:

> Emperor
> Evermore

Moreover, like Christ, 'he might have had the world with him, / But chose to side with suffering men, and had the world against him when / He came to deliver Italy' ("Napoleon III. In Italy": 413-16).

It is possible that Chorley, irritated (perhaps unconsciously) by Elizabeth Browning's lack of sympathy for the politics of his *Roccabella*, was paying her back by responding negatively to the new political poems. On the other hand, it is equally likely that Chorley, like the other English reviewers, simply didn't like them. Dorothy Mermin suggested plausibly that 'he finally lost patience with her deviation from the kind of womanliness he admired' (Mermin, 234). 'It must first be remarked that Mrs. Browning's Art suffers from the violence of her temper. Choosing to scold', Chorley asserted, 'she forgets how to sing' (*Athenæum*, 17 March 1860: 371). Years before, he had warned readers of the *Ladies' Companion* not to scold — this advice applied to lady geniuses, too.

Although Elizabeth Browning had prepared herself for hostile criticism from English reviewers, she was still annoyed — and particularly so with the formerly devoted Chorley. Robert Browning's pithy phrase for Chorley's review was 'cat scratch'.[4] Yet it was as difficult for Chorley's imagination to sympathize with the spirit of the politicized verse in *Poems before Congress* as it was for either of the Brownings to respond favourably to the spirit of 'ultra Tory' satire of revolution in *Roccabella*. Chorley remained faithful to his belief in the poet's established talent: 'her old friends and admirers can but thank the Gods for her poetry, and leave her politics to those who have stomach for them' (371). He concluded his review by maintaining, though grudgingly, that she is

> here, as before, a real poetess, — one of the few among the few, — one who has written, in her time, better than the best of English poetesses, — and proves the same on this occasion, by taking to its extremity the right of "insane prophet" to lose his head — and to loose his tongue.

From Elizabeth Browning's perspective, one of the most acutely irritating aspects of her book's reception was the misunderstanding some reviewers had that the last poem in the collection, 'The Curse', was about England, instead of the United States. Its place in a work otherwise about Italy and the European 'Congress' of 1860 contributed to the confusion. Chorley shared the mistaken impression, even though his review actually quoted ten stanzas from the poem, including:

> Because yourselves are standing straight
> >In the state
> Of Freedom's foremost acolyte,
> Yet keep calm footing all the time
> On writhing bond-slaves,— for this crime
> >This is the curse. Write.
>
> Because ye prosper in God's name,
> >With a claim
> To honor in the old world's sight,
> Ye do the fiend's work perfectly
> In strangling martyrs,— for this lie
> >This is the curse. Write. ...
>
> Go, wherever ill deeds shall be done,
> Go, plant your flag in the sun
> >Beside the ill-doers! ...

Terming the poem 'a curse to England', Chorley wrote that it was a 'terrible assumption of vain-glory, that those whom the poetess curses must be accursed', and he regretted that this fact 'seems to be lost in the blaze of her own infallibility' (*Athenæum*, 17 March 1860: 372).

Elizabeth Browning wrote a letter to the *Athenæum*. Both Brownings were disappointed and irritated that, instead of publishing her letter, the journal published a brief notice that the verses

> in her 'Poems before Congress,' entitled 'A Curse for a
> Nation,' are levelled — not against England as is
> generally thought — but against the United States; not on
> account, she now tells us, of any remissness on the Italian
> Question, but on account of the Negro Question. Every
> English reader of Mrs. Browning will rejoice in this
> assurance. We may be allowed to ask, in extenuation of
> our own hasty and incorrect inference, — why a rhyme on
> Negro Slavery should appear among 'Poems before Con-
> gress'! (7 April 1860: 477)[5]

The Brownings assumed that it was up to Chorley to decide whether to
print the letter. Browning wrote her last letter to Chorley a few weeks later.
In it, she was again building bridges and reconciling their differences: '*I
was wrong in taking for granted that the letter which referred to your
review was entrusted to you to dispose of, — and you were not right in
being in too much haste to condemn a book you disliked, to give the due
measure of attention to every page of it*' (2 May 1860, Kelley and Hudson,
8: 327-8)

After this sharp, hurtful acrimony, it was a relief for him to turn to
Mendelssohn, a well-understood composer, and to a particularly glorious
performance of his *Elijah* at the Crystal Palace, Sydenham, with Costa conducting and Parepa, Sainton-Dolby, Palmer, Sims Reeves and Belletti singing.

Seldom had Chorley been more stirred by a performance, seldom more
eloquent. Unusually, in his notice he seemed conscious of the religious con-
notations of the concept of 'canon' as it blended with the concept of
'standard repertory' — the music Mendelssohn wrote made for us a 'heaven
on earth', and the composer, now canonized as a kind of artistic saint, was
gratified by the offerings of those who, in paying worthy tribute to him,
were, in a sense, worshipping him:

> There is on record the career of no musical artist, creative
> or executive, which can be compared with that of
> Mendelssohn, as regards love, hope, joy, success,
> prosperity, intellectual cultivation, immediate recognition,
> — all that makes a heaven on earth. ... When has a death
> been so mourned? It might be almost said that the love of
> survivors has shown itself in passionate excess, as regards
> his music, — in this country at least, — so unceasing has
> been the reference and return to it. The enthusiasts in
> England could be numbered by hundred — what do we
> say? — by thousands, who will not admit that an
> uninteresting note or a weak bar is to be found in any

music bearing his name. — Never were concert compositions more incessantly played and sung. Never has a great
work (not an opera) been so instantaneously placed on its
high pedestal as 'Elijah' in England. — The celebration of
yesterday week, if regarded with these considerations,
may be characterized as unique. It was one for all those
who knew and loved Mendelssohn (and who that knew
him did not love him?) to take part in, and to recollect
with no common feelings. "How he would have enjoyed
it!" was ever present as a thought. ...

Such a day is so full of memories, yearnings, affections, running throughout all its beauty as a sweet though
mournful undertone, — that to record its event coolly is
not an easy task. But it must be tried; — unless for record
rhapsody were to be obtruded. ...

... [B]y no one else before the world save Signor Costa
could such a performance have been conducted to a close
with such smoothness and precision. ... Later in the evening the moon got up, and the [Crystal] Palace was illuminated, and the Torch Procession emerged from among
the trees, winding round the great central fountain — the
mixture of fire, water, coloured vapour, with a lovely
May-night for canopy and background — the dim thou-
sands of spectators capriciously dispersed, and the charming landscape features of the Sydenham garden, — making
a scene not to be forgotten. We cannot close the above
notes of it without repeating "How he would have enjoyed
it!" (12 May 1860: 656)

Later that autumn, he mentioned the farewell concert of Clara Novello,
singing 'with unimpaired powers'. Chorley was now better disposed
towards her powers than he had been seventeen years earlier when he wrote
to Mendelssohn in May 1843 that she was 'a very bad tempered failure, as
might have been predicted' (Green Books, XX). He regretted her decision
to retire, assuming, of course (with Grisi's apparently never-ending career
in mind) that the decision would not be revoked — 'should hers prove a
case of retirement, not followed by a return' (24 November 1860: 717).

At the end of the year, Balfe's new English opera, *Bianca, the Bravo's
Bride*, conducted by Mellon, was received enthusiastically by the audience
at the Royal English Opera, Covent Garden, but equivocally by Chorley.
Although Louisa Pyne was 'singing at her very best' and Harrison doing
'his utmost', Chorley characteristically was disappointed in Palgrave Simpson's libretto: 'Especially do slackness of language in dialogue and halting
versification jar on the ear in serious opera. ...' Moreover, Chorley found

the cheerful concluding soprano *rondo* dramatically 'forced', though 'audaciously pretty and brilliant'.[6]

> ... [I]t remains to be proved, whether ... [*Bianca*] will keep the stage as his 'Bohemian Girl,' and (on the Continent) his 'Four Sons of Aymon,' have done. (8 December 1860: 797)

A few weeks later, Chorley reported the death of Alfred Bunn, a central figure in English opera of the 1830s. Many of his obituaries during these years were sentimental and nostalgic. Bunn's death, however, was reported coldly:

> The death of Mr. Bunn, the well-known manager, playwright, and author, which took place suddenly, at Boulogne, last week, claims a line here. He was active and energetic, but unscrupulous and unwise in all the three characters; and thus, though hard working, and, after his coarse fashion, zealous to catch "the town," he did not succeed, because he did not deserve to do so. (29 December 1860: 916)[7]

2

In 1862 Chorley wrote and published a masterpiece, *Thirty Years' Musical Recollections*. It chronicled a kind of allegorical struggle between operatic Good and Evil — order, disorder, and order restored — which Chorley thought had taken place in London between 1830 and 1859. Dedicated to his friend, Mrs Lehmann, the narrative had an autobiographical subtex, since Chorley played a role as combatant as well as historian. In the 1840s, during the middle years of the recollections, Benjamin Lumley took over the management of the Italian Opera at Her Majesty's Theatre in the Haymarket. He flattered the consumers, audiences of 'rank and fashion', but abused his performers and manipulated public opinion by means of alliances with foolish and weak journalists. Flattered by his attentions, these unscrupulous journalists proclaimed falsely that all was well with artistic standards. Thus a crisis arose. Worthy singers led by Grisi, Mario and Persiani fled with Michael Costa, their conductor, from Her Majesty's Theatre in the Haymarket. They established the Royal Italian Opera at Covent Garden in order to create a reformed temple of lyric drama. Although the management of the new Royal Italian Opera at Covent Garden changed, the valiant singers and conductor laboured on. Lumley counter-attacked, with Jenny Lind's English debut as ammunition. By far the most popular singer of the time, Lind was his defence against the betrayal and defection of the old guard. But after only three seasons, Jenny Lind bade farewell to opera. Lumley's theatre limped on for a few more seasons, then burned down. Rebuilt, it burned again. In 1859, the final year of the thirty years of 'recollections', London had one Italian opera company, Chorley's narration ended, and poetic justice had been done.

The hero of this story was Henry Fothergill Chorley, the vigilant journalist. Other journalists, lulled by Lumley's self-promoting lullabies, nodded. He, however, correctly identified and fearlessly publicized the artistic problems at Her Majesty's Theatre. Courageous and modest, he wrote no falsehoods and expected no accolades.

Chorley located the beginning of the struggle in 1840 (the year of the Tamburini riots): 'In 1840 the Opera management, which for half-a-dozen years had gone on from strength to strength, began to change its plans, and to show symptoms of uneasiness, decomposition, and pretext' (*Thirty Years'*, 1: 176). Laporte left and in 1842, when Benjamin Lumley assumed the position of manager, Chorley's hostility intensified.[8]

If Chorley had written *Thirty-Five Years' Musical Recollections*, or *Thirty-Six Years'* or *Forty-One Years'*, the story would have been more complex, chronicling not only a revival of the fortunes at Her Majesty's Theatre in the Haymarket, but also a temporary role reversal which found Covent Garden in the late 1860s, under the management of Frederick Gye, in danger of becoming the 'bad' house. Michael Costa, the conductor, became dissatisfied with Gye, as he had been at Her Majesty's with Lumley. Chorley once again backed him: 'Can there be any idea on the part of the management of playing over again the mistaken game so signally lost by Mr. Lumley at Her Majesty's Theatre?' he asked his *Athenæum* readers. (19 October 1867: 505).[9]

Thirty Years' is by its nature the kind of book one can casually pick up and put down, a semi-reference work, organized year by year. When not berating Lumley, it meanders and rambles. Hewlett, who was not especially musical, and who was generally not very comfortable with Chorley's musical writing, did not imagine that this book was to remain Chorley's firmest claim to permanent significance as a writer. He simply observed that it was better than it seemed: 'The formal method in which he has arranged his subject, and the unusual slovenliness of his style in this book, have probably deterred many readers from doing it justice' and have occasioned an initial sense of 'repulsion' in many readers (2: 205). But Hewlett did not understand: the book found an audience which Chorley's other books never did. Ernest Newman wrote that the work represented 'Chorley ... at his best' in his introduction to a 1926 edition of the work (xv): '[T]here can be no question of his competence as a judge of the old schools of Italian opera and Italian singing' (xv). Newman stressed Chorley's authority to speak on issues such as vocal ornamentation, issues presumed to be dead when Newman wrote:

> Who to-day, for example, can understand the old passion
> for "ornaments" in vocal music? ... We of to-day are
> inclined to think that these ornaments were only evidence
> of the bad taste of the singers and the tyranny imposed by
> them upon audiences. ... (vii)

A more fundamental reason for the book's endurance as an archetypal opera saga is that, despite its meandering, it vividly relates a melodramatic narrative of inexorable poetic justice. That story gives the book a central intensity and narrative energy.

As the chronicle moves methodically from year to year, readers are presented with many small essays which examine the canonical status of various singers and composers, frequently covering all or much of their careers, not just the portion of their career relevant to the specific year, and not always immediately relevant to the larger good-vs-evil structure. This kind of wheels-within-wheels narration, which adversely affected the success of most of Chorley's fiction, actually strengthens the authority, and reinforces the interest, of his operatic history.

Many of these 'interrupting' essays are separately titled, and their immediate relevance to the specific year during which they are discussed varies. For example, the essay 'Opera Goers in 1834' follows, naturally, the description of the 1834 season, and the discussion of Alboni comes, naturally, in 1848, the year she made her debut as *Arsace* in *Semiramide* at Covent Garden. In the essay on Giulia Grisi's career (affixed to the year 1836, two years after her debut), Chorley's discussion covers twenty-five years. The tone of the narration, becoming unstuck from its year-by-year frame, illustrates how the book developed a kind of double narrative, simultaneously present and past:

> While I am writing, in May, 1861, the vision of all her
> glory, so long protracted, is rapidly passing from the
> stage. The hour of her parting with her subjects has come.
> It is hardly in the course of possibility, that any such
> phenomenon as a career like hers in this country will be
> witnessed by the chronicler — if such should be — who,
> thirty years hence, would carry on the tale of Foreign
> Opera in England. (*Thirty Years'*, 1: 116-17)[10]

Interesting, effective, and characteristic, this style moves readers back and forth between the specifics of year-by-year narration and grander overviews. The complexity of the specific details notably enriches the simplicity of the basic fairy-tale. The intensity of the critic's engagement with lyric drama enlivens both small details and sweeping generalizations.

Among the subjects treated in the essays is Chorley's admiration for

Gluck's operas. Since Gluck was not performed in London during the period covered by the book, Chorley brought him in by the back door, as part of the essay on Viardot which followed his account of 1848, the year in which Viardot appeared at Covent Garden as Fides in Meyerbeer's *Le Prophète*. In this context, Chorley discussed the revival of Orphée, in Berlioz's reworking. Presented in Paris in December 1859, it was fresh in his mind (and he had discussed it in the *Athenæum* on 14 January 1860). He wrote that the interpolation of the often-discussed '*bravura*', spectacularly sung by Viardot at the end of Act 1, 'was sanctioned by Gluck, though the music is Bertoni's, or Guadagni's — at all events, not his own' (2: 59), and he noted that it made no great impression in 1860 at Covent Garden because it was sung by someone else.[11] Gluck is not only a great, and greatly under-appreciated, dramatic composer. He is also 'as truly Lord and King of serious musical Drama, as Handel is of Oratorio' (2: 55-6).

Chorley did not refer to his own previous written judgements about musicians in writing these recollections, whether in his books or in the *Athenæum*. Instead, he based his account on his memory and recollections at the time of writing, 1861, satisfied that doing so would not produce contradictions. After all, he believed that his opinions almost never changed, or needed to change, as he had stated in the preface to *Modern German Music*, the dedication to *Roccabella* and again now: 'It has been gratifying to me, on comparing these pages, after they were written, with the notes thrown off at the time, — to have found no discrepancy betwixt past and present judgments worth adverting to' (*Thirty Years'*, 1: xi).

For once, the *Athenæum* gave one of Chorley's books a long and enthusiastic notice.

> To us, who love the art and honour the artist, pleasant are
> the memories of old sounds and old singers; and grateful
> are we to one who, like Mr. Chorley, carefully records
> and pleasantly recalls them. (31 May 1862: 715)

Occupying almost three pages, spreading across eight columns, the review by John Doran, author of many *Athenæum* reviews during the 1860s, quoted long sections from the book approvingly. Doran compared the book to an earlier text of theatrical reminiscences:

> We do not know that we can better indicate the plan and
> the spirit of this book than by saying that it reminds us of
> that part of Colley Cibber's 'Apology' in which, after
> enumerating the 'companies' of his day, he names the
> pieces they played and then passes judgment, in his
> admirable way, upon the actors. (715)

Although Wagner was only a peripheral concern in *Thirty Year's Recollections*,[12] he figured prominently, and ominously, in the *Athenæum* reports at this time. 1861 — a few months after publication of *Thirty Years' Musical Recollections* — was the year of the notorious *Tannhäuser* fiasco at the Opéra. Chorley relished it. He had prepared his readers for the opera's failure months in advance. In a report on 'German Bath-Concerts' (at Wiesbaden and Baden-Baden, 1 September 1860: 296-7) he wrote:

> There [in Carlsruhe], it may be recollected, Herr Wagner's 'Tristan' was to be produced last year. It was put in rehearsal; but after many weeks of laborious study, was abandoned as too uncouth — too little like music to be endured — or learnt. His day, we believe, and for the interests of Art, *hope*, is done in his own country. Whether he will revolutionize Paris, under Imperial protection, remains to be seen. (1 September 1860: 297)

In the same issue, in 'Musical and Dramatic Gossip', he mocked Wagner's lack of integrity as shown by his willingness to give Paris the ballet it always demanded:

> The German admirers of Herr Wagner are considerably puzzled just now to know what to do about the consistency of the author of 'Oper und Drama,' — the man who denounced all concession as so much claptrap. ... Thus, after Herr Wagner's Spartan and self-asserting diatribe, this quiet acquiescence in attempting to popularize a composition which might else offer too little to satisfy the sprightly and dance-loving public of Paris is indeed instructive, by way of warning to all theory-spinners, self-praisers and haranguers, if the rumour be correct. As historians bit by bit of the smartest controversy which has occurred in music since that betwixt Gluck and Piccini, we cannot over look the rumour, nor the chagrin which it has caused among the sincere disciples of a prophet who is supposed to be yielding to "French influence." (197c)

Tannhäuser's production was delayed at Paris because 'Herr Wagner's music is not to be learnt at a short notice; — so that Paris may possibly have to wait till All Fools' Day ere this ninetieth [*sic*] wonder of the world is revealed to it' (26 January 1861: 126).

Finally the new '*no*-music' was presented (23 March 1861: 402). Not even the presence of royalty and a 'brilliant assemblage' of Wagner's supporters could silence the audience (402). Chorley could not be there to witness the confirmation of his predictions of failure, but

> So far as some half-score of accounts from public and pri-

> vate sources can justify belief and announcement, there is
> small doubt that the failure has been entire, —
> extraordinary and, it may be fancied, conclusive. If this
> be true, so ends — and ends well — one of the most fla-
> grant attempts at forcing forward what is spurious and
> false recorded in the history of Art. — Not a stone had
> been left unturned to compel or cajole a success in Paris
> for Herr Wagner. Money had been liberally shed in the
> cause; a twelvemonth's intrigue and contrivance brought
> to bear on influence; a time unprecedently [*sic*] long for a
> work which had been performed already, had been
> devoted to preparation. All in vain — and most deser-
> vedly in vain. No doubt allowance is to be made for
> antagonism stirred by Herr Wagner's paraded disdain of
> the music which preceded his attempts, and by the
> extravagant ardour of his partizans. But be such allowance
> greater or less, the work brought to judgment remains
> intrinsically bad, ... [and] we are glad, for the sake of
> Art, that the verdict has been so condemnatory. (402-3)[13]

The next year, 1862, brought Verdi's humiliation at the hands of the
commissioners of the London Exhibition. They rejected *Inno delle Nazione*
on the grounds that they had commissioned a march, not a cantata.
Mapleson saw Verdi by chance once day, disappointed by the com-
missioner's actions. 'I at once cheered him up', remembered the manager of
Her Majesty's Theatre 'by telling him I would perform it at Her Majesty's
Theatre if he would superintend its direction, Madame Tietiens undertaking
the solo soprano part' (Mapleson, 1888, 1: 43).[14] Chorley was one of the
commissioners. Not surprisingly, he defended the propriety of their actions.

> Of the new German, English and French music performed
> at the opening of the Exhibition, we have spoken else-
> where. — That Italy has been unrepresented on the occa-
> sion, has not been owing to any neglect of the Com-
> missioners, but to the proceedings of the representative of
> Italy. Having been requested early in last July to compose
> a grand march for the festival, about the second week in
> last month he forwarded a *solo* with *chorus*, written for
> Signor Tamberlik to sing; there being notoriously no *solo*
> possible or advisable at such a time and in such a place —
> of course, under such circumstances, the delay in for-
> warding the contribution rendered re-consideration or
> application elsewhere impossible. — The Commissioners
> had no alternative, and the land of music had no new

utterance in the day's chorus, owing to the mistake made by the most popular of its living musicians. (3 May 1862: 454)

The accusations of unfairness to Verdi rankled, however, and Chorley returned to them the next month:

The Commissioners have been charged with offences happily not committed. ... It was only at the last moment that the representative of Italy put it out of the power of any one concerned to receive an alternative for a work utterly useless and unfit for its position. Let this matter be put on record for the last time. The statement is necessary, in reply to those who have commented on fabrications, not facts; and who appear delighted to raise a storm on an occasion where all should, and *might* have been harmony. (14 June 1862: 798)

After all this, Chorley's negative remarks on the music of *Inno delle Nazione* — when it was finally performed — were anticlimactic:

Signor Verdi's '*Cantica*' (so his musical contribution to the Great Exhibition is styled) has just been published by Messrs. Cramer & Co. We are satisfied that now, when the fever of party excitement is over, there can be but one feeling in regard to the composition — and that, taken on its own showing, it is not a favourable specimen of Signor Verdi's talent. (21 June 1862: 830)

Many people were also incensed that Costa refused to conduct William Sterndale Bennett's composition for the Exhibition. Chorley again had an explanation exculpating the commissioners (and Costa) from reproach. No insult was intended, he wrote.

There have been misunderstandings abroad on the subject of the English music, and the conductorship of it, which a few words will put an end to. In July last Signor Costa was expressly retained to take charge of the foreign music *alone*, and those who turn to the *Athenæum* of the 20th of that month will find the following announcement: — "Dr. Bennett has been applied to (as we hold was fitting) to compose the music for the Great Exhibition of 1862, and to conduct his own composition (as was no less fitting)." Nothing else could have been done without offering a slight to the English conductor of the Philharmonic and Bach Societies, and the Leeds Festival. — In a correspondence betwixt Signor Costa and the Commissioners, which has been published, the latter fully and distinctly bear out the facts as above. (3 May 1862: 454)

3 The Performers of the Future

Before Chorley coasted into retirement, there were still performers and composers whose careers he hoped to assist or to damage. On the whole, he was less engaged with, and less passionate about, the voices of the new generation than those he had heard at the start of his career. The 1860s were years for evaluating Tietjens (or Tietiens), Artôt, Orgeni, Cruvelli, Fioretti, Penco, Miolan-Carvalho, Vilda, and the new 'Queen of Song', Patti. He wrote about Tamberlik, Giuglini, and Mongini as well as Mario's continuing prominence. The great days for mezzo and contralto women's voices, however, seemed mostly in the past, and basses, too, had caused little stir[15] since the retirement of the great Lablache, though Formes was still singing. All of these singers, and dozens of others, elicited reactions at times dismissive, at times approving.

Although for Chorley the golden age of singing was almost over, he could still become excited by great new voices, especially if they were his discoveries. In the 1860s the full sunshine of Chorley's consistently approving smiles beamed not on a soprano but on an emerging English baritone from Liverpool, Charles Santley. Chorley had high hopes for him, one of which was that Santley would figure prominently in a popular reassessment of Gluck's operas. When Hallé conducted Gluck's *Iphigenia in Tauris* at the Free Trade Hall in Manchester in 1860, it was Gluck's dramatic genius which, in the first place, prompted Chorley's enthusiastic endorsement:

> It is rare that we have been allowed to feel so unalloyed a sensation of mixed excitement and satisfaction, as while listening to the splendid and successful musical performance of Gluck's 'Iphigenia in Tauris,' at Manchester (11 February 1860: 212)

But he was also stirred to enthusiasm by the singers, especially Santley, who 'has made another step higher, in his rapid ascent, as *Orestes*' (212).

The opera came to London, in Chorley's translation:

> The *Athenæum* must be historical rather than critical, with regard to the concert-performance of Gluck's 'Iphigenia' on Wednesday evening, with the English words by Mr. H. F. Chorley, under the direction of M. Halle. ... [Santley] improves from month to month. ... The success of the work ... was, apparently, decisive. The performance, we understand, will be shortly repeated. (23 June

1860: 861)

Chorley's crusade for Gluck reached a high point just two years before he retired from the *Athenæum* in response to performances of *Iphigenia in Tauris* at Her Majesty's Theatre in 1866. He praised it to the skies, then, in two of the following weeks, returned to the subject, in order to emphasize not only Gluck's greatness, but his potential popularity, as the following excerpts from each of the three reviews show:

> Granted adequate execution, Gluck's operas are not more dead than are 'Lear,' 'Hamlet,' 'Julius Caesar,' 'Coriolanus.' The life of eternal truth and beauty is in them; and when properly expressed and interpreted, this must strike home to the hearts of all who like something more stately than 'La Traviata,' and something more solid, whether in story or in song, than 'Martha.' (12 May 1866: 641)

The review of the repeat performance at Her Majesty's Theatre noted that it was 'fully attended' despite competition from Patti at Covent Garden: 'Greater beauty of classic form cannot be dreamed of, — greater power of passion was never put forth. ... But enough, for the hour, of a study, and of our earnest desire to rectify what has long seemed to us a sentence most narrow and illiberal, and, as such, unworthy of our enlightened country' (19 May 1866: 678-9). After the third performance Chorley still found himself drawn to analyse and, if possible, proselytize on Gluck's behalf:

> The genuine interest excited by the performance of 'Iphigenia' increases, and signally so among the artist-class of listeners (which may be said to include the most refined connoisseurs). ... Signor Arditi's orchestra does its work excellently. No apology is needed, for speaking of this opera a third time, so earnest is our desire to set in its right light a masterpiece of music, by one to whom our pedants (who, true to their pedantry, never take the trouble of really studying a subject) have turned "a cold shoulder." Mr. Mapleson cannot be too warmly thanked by those who think as we do. (9 June 1866: 776)

Looking back, Santley viewed these performances in 1866 from a coolly different perspective: '[W]e did our best' for *Iphigenia*, he conceded, 'but it did not prove attractive, and was only played three nights. There are fine bits in it, but to me Gluck's music is tedious; and, judging from experience, the public is much of my opinion' (*Student and Singer*, 241-2).

Santley's career reached a high point of visibility and success with his performances of Valentine in *Faust*, both the initial performances in Italian at Her Majesty's Theatre in 1864 and the performances of Chorley's English translations at the same theatre in 1865. For help along the road that led to this success, he acknowledged Chorley's support freely in his reminiscences. In these he relates how Chorley visited him while he was living in Italy, introduced himself, and persuaded him that he was better off returning to England to make a career than staying in Italy. Back in England in 1857, Chorley took Santley under his protection, and Santley's family was appropriately grateful. Santley's father wrote on 8 October 1856 asking whether Santley should or should not accept an (unspecified) first engagement, hoping that Chorley 'will be kind enough to give him the benefit of your advice & experience. ... I presume to trouble you on this head through the kindness you have already shown & the sympathy & interest you have expressed in reference to my dear lad'.[16]

Chorley frequently asked Santley to dine with him, and tried to further his interests by urging Hullah to engage him. Hullah auditioned the young baritone and, though not seeming to be enthusiastic about his voice, engaged him for the part of Adam in Haydn's *Creation*. Before one of his concerts, at a private dinner (at Chorley's house again) he met Manuel Garcia, the important singing teacher (brother of Viardot and Malibran). He also secured three engagements at Crystal Palace concerts, as well as a few other concerts in and around London. After the first of the Crystal Palace concerts, Santley attended, reluctantly (out of a sense of obligation and 'duty') Chorley's 10 o'clock after-concert party, where he met his future wife, Gertrude Kemble, also a singer.

In return for helping Santley's career behind-the-scenes, Chorley exacted artistic obedience:

> [M]y friend and monitor, whose kindness and generosity
> bound me to study his wishes, insisted upon my selections
> being submitted to him for approval. One song in particu-
> lar, which I was anxious to sing at the Surrey Gardens, he
> rejected with indignation, and told me if ever I sang it he
> would cut my acquaintance. (*Student and Singer*, 145)

In November 1857[17] Chorley invited Santley to dinner: 'I dine at 5 1/2. — & should be very glad to see you. — I can only look after you in a distant & *round-about*-way — but as I am honestly anxious for your success, I should not like you to feel solitary on the day of your first trial in London, if I can avoid it. — If you would not like to dine here, have no scruple in saying so. — but as you don't begin till late, you may like to see a friendly face before you begin, — & so, do what will make you most comfortable.'[18] Soon afterwards, Santley's grateful father wrote from Liverpool:

> to thank you from my heart for the warm interest you

have evinced for him & invaluable aid & above all for your I must say parental consideration in cheering him up for his trial — I cannot express in language what I feel therefore will not attempt it — I shall remain your debtor as long as life lasts — and trust that he will feel the same obligation. ...[19]

Chorley summoned Santley abruptly to his house late one night in December 1857 to meet and sing for Costa.[20] It was an important connection for Santley's career, as Chorley's excited tone suggested:

My dear M[r] Santley. —

... Costa has been here: — & I am afraid that tomorrow, I have not a moment of time for you — When I tell you that he wants me to take you to him on *Tuesday & that he has undertaken in the most cordial manner — to help — &* that he wants to hear you *very early in the week* you will see the importance of our having a word or two. — The Birmingham arrangements are not yet made. Indeed the good chances seem to multiply ...

The next summer Chorley's chatty letter of 19 August 1858, to Santley, vacationing in Devonshire, provided still more 'parental' guidance of the kind that defined their relationship:

I will not dwell on other matters which make me feel very melancholy & much discouraged just now, since they only relate to my private affairs & feelings. — I am sorry to hear that Miss K's cold is no better *yet.* ...[21] I *hope*, that in spite of music & of courtship, you will still continue a course of time & thought for that steady general cultivation in things a little beyond the precise sphere of your own art. — which nevertheless will add to your power by ... giving refinement and reality to every conception. You should always have some good book in reading — if only you can read a couple of pages a day. Everyone is pleased with your success, & wishes you well — You must live up to their expectations.

With Chorley's support, Santley was well positioned to make his own way. The introduction to Hullah, Garcia, and, especially, Costa had been helpful. During the 1860s Santley often sang engagements with Costa, and was the first Elijah in Costa's oratorio *Naaman*, presented at the Birmingham festival of 1864.

Santley created principal roles in Chorley's *Amber Witch* (The Commandant), and his translations of *Iphigenia* (Orestes), *Dinorah* (Hoel), and

Faust (Valentine). The critic who seldom changed his mind, never changed his mind about Santley: by 1863 Santley was generally mentioned in the *Athenæum* as simply the best 'baritone and bass singer that has been in England since the memory of man — an artist accomplished in every style and school of music' (19 September 1863: 378). There seems to have been no falling-out with Santley, personally or professionally; the notices of his performances in opera and oratorio were consistently laudatory, with only minor exceptions.[22] In turn, Santley, in his reminiscences published in 1892, amply acknowledged Chorley's help with his early career. Nothing he published, however, suggests that he reciprocated the warmth of Chorley's affection in those years.[23]

With Santley's career well launched, Arthur Sullivan next occupied the role of the 'dear boy' whose career in its early stages was to be greatly aided by Chorley's behind-the-scenes support.

A new world of singing began in 1861, two years after Chorley's *Thirty Years'*. Mario was still singing as though 'the world was all before him where to choose' (*Athenæum*, 6 July 1861: 25),[24] but the protracted series of 'farewell' announcements by Grisi had weakened her standing as the reigning Opera Queen. Finally, in 1861 (the year she turned 50), Grisi's London farewell seasons came to an end when she made her last appearances as a member of the Royal Italian Opera at Covent Garden. That season, while one Queen was singing her final roles, there appeared, as if providentially, the new Queen to succeed her, Adelina Patti.

Still in her teens, Patti had been performing in the United States for years to great acclaim; as early as 1852 she had been billed as 'La Petite Jenny Lind' (Cone, 28). Chorley had conscientiously mentioned in his columns several times in the past year or so that she was reputedly a great singer,[25] Indeed, the year before she came to London he reprinted extravagant praise for Patti from the *New York Musical Review and Gazette* mockingly, in order to expose it as hyperbolic foolishness: 'Some readers may be amused by the following criticism on the new singer in detail ...' (28 January 1860: 140).[26] She was only one of many names reputed by the foreign press to be great. As it happened, the reign of the young singer who arrived from New York with little fuss proved even longer than Grisi's.

In the week before Patti's first appearance at Covent Garden, Chorley was more interested in Grisi's impending retirement than Patti's debut:

> [A] rumour may be mentioned floating about in the cor-
> ridors, to the effect that Madame Grisi is bound, under a
> penalty, not to sing in London for five years after the pre-
> sent season. This enforcement of her vow of farewell
> (supposing the tale true) amounts to something painfully

like humiliation.[27] — On Tuesday, Signora Patti, a young lady who has principally sung in America, if, indeed, she be not a native of "the States," is advertised to appear in 'La Sonnambula.' (11 May 1861: 638)

Patti's appearance as Amina on Tuesday evening, 14 May 1861, created enthusiasm in the audience which grew mightily as the evening progressed. Of that debut Chorley wrote a few days later:

> Mdlle. Patti, on Tuesday night, was, from first to last, greeted with applause as rapturous as attended the best of her predecessors. Bouquets (a rare sight at Covent Garden, when even an established favourite is in the case) broke out in a thick shower at the end of her first air. The house seemed determined to pass an unanimous vote that she was perfect. On Tuesday, Mdlle. Patti struck us as a singular combination of youth and maturity. Her appearance is not unpleasing; her figure is girlish; her voice is already developed to its utmost, if not already fatigued. A blind man might have fancied it the property of a singer past her prime. It is a high *soprano*, well in tune, reaching easily to E flat *in alt* — powerful enough for any theatre; more flexible than fascinating. Her shake is clear and brilliant. She seems to prefer *staccato* changes and ornaments, and, according to the fashion of the day (when the fashion of worn-out singers is to complain of the height of the pitch), she obviously delights in astonishing her public on the topmost notes of the scale. As an actress, she appeared to us composed rather than full of feeling. What she did was elegant and unaffected; not always, however, appropriate. (18 May 1861: 669-70)[28]

Patti's popular success with the audience at Covent Garden had been immediate and dazzling. As if in response, Grisi rose to Patti's challenge and left London cheering as the ageing queen of song sang her final performances of Norma, Lucrezia Borgia, and Valentine. Chorley was moved:

> Madame Grisi seems determined that her last should be her best nights. Not only her dramatic passion, but the state of her voice too (from time to time) are amazing. Why need people talk of retirement, if, as Time advances, they would yield somewhat of that old, absolute, monopolizing power with which *Statira*, in the plenitude of youth and beauty, kept the stage against all rival *Roxalanas*? (9 June 1860: 797)[29]

Davison, too, immediately realized that the season was extraordinary, containing both 'the last performances of an artist of long-established celebrity' and 'the first performances of a new comer of almost unexampled youth and promise' (*The Times*, 20 May 1861: 12). During the performances of *Don Giovanni* that summer, when the two sang together in the same opera, with Grisi as Anna and Patti as Zerlina, it was as if the crown of prima donna assoluta was being handed on to its rightful heir.[30]

To Chorley's ears, Patti possessed the vocal potential to disappoint as much as the potential to develop into a thoroughly satisfying singer; for the first few seasons she sang Chorley seems from time to time dubious about the permanence of her success. When she appeared as *Lucia*, for example, the week after her debut, Chorley noted faults and warning signs, Her voice seemed tired; perhaps her career would be short:

> Meanwhile, Mdlle. Patti is more intensely the fashion than any singer who has till now sung at Covent Garden; — and (a fact honourable to all concerned) her vogue has owed nothing to such preliminary measures as made every one of Mr. Lumley's *Cynthias*, — whether a Lind or a Parodi, a Sontag, a Cruvelli, or a Piccolomini, — applauded on her arrival with the same frenzy, and praised with the same superlatives, by acquiescent critics. ... The fatigue of her voice was more evident there [i.e. in *Lucia*] than in 'La Sonnambula.' Its tones were frequently not agreeable — now and then out of tune. (1 June 1861: 734)

This month Chorley also published in Dickens's weekly, *All the Year Round*, an article discussing and evaluating various noted sopranos who had sung Amina in London — among them, Malibran, Persiani (the best, if one is 'considering the part musically' [321]), Lind, Sontag, etc. In the concluding paragraphs he turned his attention to Patti, 'the youngest Amina of all', by whom London audiences, 'without a single note of prelude or preliminary trumpet', have been excited. Patti is an Amina who may 'set Europe on fire' ('Amina and the Mill-Wheel', 29 June 1861: 323).[31] In August, however, Chorley found fault with Patti in *Il Barbiere*, perhaps as irritated by Gye's puffs as by Patti's faults. Why did Gye 'force honest people to declare that the new Rosina is not so good as Malibran, Viardot, Sontag, Madame Grisi, and half a score of her predecessors less famous than they?' She sang in 'questionable tune', and apparently in questionable taste: interpolating a '*bravura*' by Wallace in the lesson scene was surely a 'mistake' (3 August 1861: 159).

During her first seasons in London, the sniping continued, and during the next season Chorley found more reason to predict vocal trouble ahead:

> Royal Italian Opera. — Mdlle. Patti's performance in the

> weak and repulsive opera of 'La Traviata' shows, as a
> piece of acting, advance on the personation of last year.
> ... A more unlovely and diseased subject was never
> chosen for music. From the temper of Monday's audience
> (large as it was) we might draw hope that the morbid pop-
> ularity of this bad opera is on the wane. As regards her
> singing, the power gained by Mddle. Patti since last year
> tells to good effect in Signor Verdi's music; but the ear is
> increasingly struck by an increased painfulness of tone,
> which, if carried a little further, will be anything rather
> than welcome. (7 June 1862: 752)

Other critics expressed some scepticism about the condition of her voice, too, despite the continuing acclamation of the public.[32] In 1862 Chorley wondered querulously, 'How is Mr. Gye to mount his operas, great or small, with a deteriorated troop and one "star"?' (12 July 1862: 57).

These moments of sniping were choice examples of Chorley in the role of curmudgeon; yet they did not completely represent his considered view of Patti's career. After the first two or three seasons, we read more and more frequently of Chorley's enthusiasm for Patti's voice. When other favoured sopranos (Orgeni and Artôt, for example) made their London debuts later in the decade, Chorley was careful to urge that Covent Garden should use them well as artists and to note that, of course, they could not displace Patti (not that there was any chance that Patti would have allowed herself to be elbowed aside).[33] At the Handel Festival at the Crystal Palace in 1865, Patti 'surprised us by her gentle devotional sincerity, by the purity and largeness of her musical reading of Handel's ample and stately phrases' (1 July 1865: 25). The next season Patti's Marguerite in *Faust* caused Chorley to exclaim with delight that 'it would be difficult to sing better than Mdlle. Adelina Patti does at present' (4 August 1865: 153). Her singing was found wanting only when compared to the legendary golden age of Italian singing in Chorley's youth. The greats of that era were by now increasingly forgotten, or deemed uninteresting and irrelevant, by the new generation of musicians and audiences mired in decadence. Indeed, to prove the decadence of Italian singing, only a few months before his retirement from the *Athenæum* Chorley cited 'the disproportionate success of Mdlle. Adelina Patti (a minnow where Tritons have been), simply because she is a prepared vocalist' (28 December 1867: 901).

4 The Music of the Future and the Canon

In the 1860s Chorley's writings implicitly supported, and explicitly argued on behalf of, a canon of established composers. Handel, Mozart and

Beethoven were the three 'great classical masters' (*Athenæum*, 7 July 1860), and to them he generally added Gluck and Bach. In dramatic music, *Faust* continued the tradition of *Les Huguenots*. Bellini and Donizetti were rather tolerated than celebrated, and Verdi was still resisted. Rossini and Mendelssohn were established masters, while Wagner and Schumann[34] shared responsibility for infecting European musicians and audiences with the unwholesome 'music of the future'. Arthur Sullivan showed promise of being England's alternative to the decay.

Believing that Gluck was among the undeservedly neglected operatic composers, Chorley assumed a mission in the 1860s of promoting his music. Santley's early career had helped that cause to a degree, but the real source of energy prompting a Gluck revival was Paris, where Berlioz's interest in Gluck easily matched Chorley's. More than other any single event, performances in Paris by Viardot of Berlioz's version of Orphée at the Théâtre Lyrique proved to Chorley that Gluck could be re-inserted into the contemporary operatic canon. The career of Viardot culminated with this role, which was a greater popular success than anyone had anticipated. After the first performance on 18 November 1859, there were many more performances of the opera with Viardot over the next three years.

> But we cannot dream of any fulfilment of such desire more consummate than is to be found in the Orpheus of Madame Viardot. There is nothing on the modern musical stage that can approach it; there has been nothing on the musical stage of any day than can have surpassed it. As a piece of acting, it must take rank with the *Medea* of Pasta, with the noblest antique creations of Rachel or Madame Ristori. ...
>
> The *bravura* at the end of the first act would be an utterly hopeless attempt for any one else now singing. The well-known "Che faro" ... becomes what it was meant to be, — a wail of bitterest desolation and woe. ... Madame Viardot has never been in fuller possession of her vocal powers than she is now, after "a run" of an opera, dependent for its effect so largely on her sole self. The other parts in 'Orphée' are fairly cast; the orchestra and chorus, which have been carefully drilled under the superintendence of M. Berlioz, are good; the stage appointments (as is the rule of M. Carvalho's theatre) are liberal, and in the finest artistic taste. ...
>
> But no lover of what is loftiest, most real, and, withal, most beautiful in dramatic music, can fail to find one of the satisfactions which occur too rarely in a lifetime in Gluck's 'Orphée,' as now given at the *Théâtre Lyrique* (14

January 1861: 58-9).

Orphée, performed of course in Italian as *Orfeo*, came to Covent Garden in July 1860. With Czillag instead of Viardot in the title role, however, its impact seemed less powerful than it should have been.[35]

At Dudley House, Lord Dudley presented a private concert performance with Viardot as Orphée, as well as private performances of *Iphigenia in Tauris*.[36] Chorley, who normally reported only on public events, made an exception for these evenings and wrote enthusiastically about both composer and singer:

> Though it is not our wont to trespass on private entertain-
> ments, there are cases that justify an exception being
> made: such as the three concert performances of Gluck's
> operas, — two of 'Iphigenia,' with English text [by Chor-
> ley] and English singers [with Charles Santley, Sims
> Reeves, and Tietjens, who was not English], and one of
> 'Orphée,' — with Madame Viardot, given in the same
> house, within the week. Even without stage accessories or
> action, the effect of the last was something unparalleled,
> and must be dwelt on, if only to substantiate what has
> been said in regard to the disadvantages under which the
> opera has been heard on the Italian stage in
> England. Further, in reference to rumours which have
> been circulated during the past spring, it should be put on
> record that the gifted artist, whose singing so moved and
> electrified her audience, has never been in fuller posses-
> sion of her vocal powers than on Monday last.
> (*Athenæum*, 21 July 1860: 101).[37]

When *Alceste* was performed in Paris in October 1861, Chorley was again excited by Viardot's performance and by Gluck's music. The production 'is intrinsically the most important and interesting event in the musical year 1861; one which may — must — lead to others of the kind in Paris' (19 October 1861: 516).[38] *Alceste* too was successful, although it did not match the popularity of Orphée.

Barely 42 years old, Viardot's career on the Paris and London operatic stage came to an end. But Chorley's fascination with Gluck was independ-ent of Viardot's advocacy. In 1866 the production of *Iphigenia in Tauris* at Her Majesty's Theatre was wholly satisfactory: 'A better *Orestes* could not be desired than Mr. Santley', and Tietjens, at whose voice Chorley often sniped, 'is heard to her best advantage in this music' (12 May 1866: 642).

Gluck's position in the repertory was, of course, by no means the only example of Chorley's determination to influence what was to be received and what rejected. The existing canon during the 1860s was in flux, sometimes in turmoil, as events during this decade slowly altered the accepted canon of the standard repertory.

The degenerate tendencies of the 1860s, as Chorley saw them, centred on music variously termed wild, modern, and rhapsodical, composed by musicians of 'young-Germany' and those under their influence. The same people who affected to criticize Mozart, Beethoven, Weber, and 'yawn at' Mendelssohn had the audacity to 'dream and scream over some piece of absurdity by Schumann, or defend the monstrosities of Herr Wagner' (*Athenæum*, 19 September 1863: 359).

Henry Chorley and James W. Davison were generally seen as the most influential critics of the mid-1860s.[39] Others of note included George Hogarth, Henry Smart, Charles Lewis Gruneisen, Desmond Ryan, Howard Grover, and Henry Sutherland Edwards. As a group the writers, including Chorley, welcomed the growing importance of the Crystal Palace concerts, despite Manns's too frequent performances of Schumann's music (Wyndham, 44, and Graves, 135, 170.)

Joseph Bennett in *Forty Years of Music* (1908) divided the critics of the 1860s into two groups — the J.W. Davison group, to which he himself had belonged as a young man — and the independents, mainly Chorley. As he put it:

> They [musical critics of 1865-70] consisted of a central group presided over by James William Davison, of the *Times*, and an outlying set, each man moving independently in, so to speak, his own orbit. Among these, Henry F. Chorley held a prominent place. Chorley wrote various books, which [can be consulted, and] are of far higher authority on the subject of his eccentric personality than I can pretend to be. Indeed, I had no personal intercourse with Chorley, nor did he, on his part, seek to be acquainted with his brothers of the pen. But Chorley was an interesting character, albeit exclusive. He had a special faculty of putting nasty remarks in very small paragraphs, with the inevitable result of making himself obnoxious not only to those for whom they were intended, but also to their sympathisers amongst the public and in the press. He was a man of strong likes and equally powerful dislikes. (9)

Bennett cited these two journalists, Davison and Chorley, as the two most important music critics. Though they published their criticism anonymously, their identity was not really a secret. The two men did not socialize, or even particularly like one another, but, in general, they agreed intellectually on the broad outlines of the canon and they set the tone for the other journalists. Davison was by this time arguably the more influential of the two, writing not only for specialized musical publications, the *Musical Examiner* and the *Musical World* with their relatively small circulations, — but also continuing to write for *The Times* which, by the mid-1850s, had an enormous circulation — over 50 000 readers daily, more than ten times the readership of its nearest rival, the *Daily News*.[40] Moreover, as Bennett asserted, Davison's influence was felt indirectly in the writings of a circle of younger journalists gathered around him.

By contrast, Chorley wrote mainly for the *Athenæum* which, under William Hepworth Dixon's editorship from 1853 to 1869, had lost some of its prestige to its newer weekly competitor, the *Saturday Review*. H.R. Fox Bourne believed that Dixon's 'encouragement among his contributors of the strong expression of likes and dislikes frequently grounded on nothing worthier or safer than *personal friendships* or animosities, or subservience to publishers and advertisers, caused its steady deterioration from year to year' (*English Newspapers*, 2: 313-14). The strong expression of likes and dislikes, of course, had characterized Chorley's writing on music since the 1830s, and he maintained vigorously that much of Beethoven's late music was a kind of bad influence on later composers, that Schumann was not the successor to Beethoven, and that Mendelssohn was Schumann's superior.

August Manns's enthusiasm for presenting works by Schumann, Brahms, Schubert,[41] and late works by Beethoven as routine parts of the repertory at Crystal Palace at Sydenham played a major role in the adjustments being made to the standard classical repertory. As Schumann's music became part of London concert life in the 1860s (particularly at the Crystal Palace concerts), Chorley's sustained antipathy acquired notoriety and, in the view of some, too much influence. His friend, Frederick Lehmann, for example, commented in unpublished *Reminiscences* that Chorley 'cordially disliked Madame Schumann (whom, by the way, he always called "the shoe-woman"). There can be no doubt that by his ignorant but constantly expressed detestation of Schumann's music he for many years prevented that great composer from becoming properly known and appreciated in this country' (R.C. Lehmann, *Memories*, 230). It was related in a letter of reminiscence by Ernest G. de Glehn to Henry Saxe Wyndham that Sullivan visited the Glehns soon after moving back from Leipzig:

> Henry Chorley, the critic, an old friend of my mother's, was there, and [Franklin] Taylor [Sullivan's fellow student at Leipzig] was invited to play. He announced that he would like to play us some new works of Schumann — on which Chorley burst out that nothing would induce him to listen to Schumann, and when the rest of those there insisted, he went out and sat in the hall while Taylor

> played. (Wyndham, *Sullivan*, 250)

Along the same lines, Charles Graves related this (presumably apocryphal) anecdote: 'Mr. Chorley ... made it a point to the end of his life to walk out of the concert-room at the beginning of the second movement of Schumann's [piano] Quintet, to mark, it is said, his high disapproval of a certain chord in the eighth bar!'[42]

Sometimes Chorley's reviews took the form of passing sarcasm, as when Chorley commented on 18 February 1860:

> Another advance towards the "music of the future" was made at the Sydenham Concert on Saturday, where overtures to 'The Bride of Messina,' by Schumann, and to 'Benvenuto Cellini,' by M. Berlioz, appeared in the *programme*. (244)

On 11 May 1861, in the 'Musical and Dramatic Gossip' Chorley wrote: 'At the *Musical Society's* Concert, on Wednesday, Schumann's Symphony in B flat, the most reasonable and pleasing of his orchestral works with which we are acquainted, was given' (638). But on 29 June 1861, Chorley wrote that at the Musical Art Union Pauer played Schumann's concerto, a 'pretentious and confused work. ... [T]here is not an idea in this *Concerto* by Schumann which is not trite and shallow' (868).

Chorley protested that some were now calling not Schumann but Mendelssohn 'shallow' (868). On 31 August 1861, he wrote angrily:

> The perversity of the Germans in musical iconoclasm has reached the pedestal of Weber's statue. ... The same people who swallow the recitatives of 'Tannhäuser' and the cacophonies of 'Lohengrin,' — who exalt Schumann above Mendelssohn, — who pity *grandpapa* Haydn, and who, among the works of Beethoven, deify Beethoven's aberrations, — are trying to cry down Weber. There is no turning back the stream of the great river Folly, but in the storm of its own violence it runs itself dry ... (290)

On 5 April 1662, after a Crystal Palace concert, Chorley wrote:

> The band, too, did its best for Schumann's Symphony in B flat, without bringing us nearer to any cordiality in accepting the music. Let people make what they will of it, it is music (to our strong conviction) belonging to a time of decay. ... (470)

One of the most extensive discussions of Chorley's reasons for disliking Schumann was printed in the issue of 17 January 1863. In the section 'New Publications' Chorley reviewed with exasperation the score of Schumann's

Mass for a Four-part Chorus, with Orchestra, Op. 147, No. 10 of his Posthumous Works (Leipzig, Rieter-Biedermann; London, Ewer & Co.). As he often did, Chorley expressed his irritation at those who praised Schumann at Mendelssohn's expense:

> We cannot ... consent to "enter on the list" of great composers a man so deficient in melody, so licentious as to impurity in harmony, so imperfect in technical skill, and so frequently false in expression, as Schumann. It is a treason to beauty, to truth, to knowledge, to represent him (as Germany is now disposed to do) in the light of Beethoven's continuer — as the man in the depths of whose poetic genius the shallow and correct works of Mendelssohn are being rapidly swept out of sight to their right level, as so many mediocrities. Why, even in any one of the few posthumous Quartetts by the composer of 'Fidelio' (so disastrously appealed to as models and points of departure), there are more of the delicious "thoughts which create thoughts," by seizing and charming the ear, than in the entire mass of overwrought and morbid composition by Schumann which we are invited to digest. ... (91)
>
> Schumann starts his "Gloria" on a group of notes, rather than a phrase, so artfully contrived as to mystify the ear as to the key (C major): — this is obviously a darling notion with him, since it is repeated obtrusively again and again, without any reason, save that of the writer's obstinacy. ...
>
> Nor is there anything more grotesque in music than will be found in page 45, on the phrase "sedet ad dexteram Patris, et iterum venturus est cum gloria." The leap to the last word, and the scream on it, may belong to the future; but if they be accepted as sufferable, all art and reverence of the past must thenceforth and for ever be abolished. ...
>
> The character attempted in this journal eighteen years ago of Schumann as a composer, stands before us clear and emphatic as the character which we repeat to-day. The driftings of fashion hither or thither — the allowances claimed for want of new idea, miscalled progress — the vacant desire for change (as if change implied novelty), have little influence over those who cannot see that crooked is straight, that a broken nose is as seductive as a feature chiselled by Phidias, or that a flat surface implies

more relief than one including clear lights, pure half-tints, and deep shadows. As a specimen of vacancy and platitude, claiming for themselves the honours of profound thought and choice wisdom, it is hard to fancy anything more remarkable than this Mass by Schumann appears to us. (92)

The next month, Chorley was a little less vituperative about a performance of Schumann's music at the Crystal Palace Concerts:

The 'Overture, *Scherzo*, and Finale,' by Schumann (Op. 52) were played, if we recollect rightly, many years ago, at one of the Philharmonic Concerts. The *suite* is one of the clearer and more pleasing of its author's compositions. ... Suffice it to say, that though the peculiarities to which we object are tempered in this peculiar work, they are to be felt there. ... (21 February 1863: 268)[43]

He was stirred to wrath again, however, when Edward Dannreuther played the piano part in Schumann's piano quartet in E flat major:

This is no music for us; nor shall we ever become reconciled to the hardihood of ugliness which is therein paraded by way of originality. ... [Dannreuther played well] in spite of the uncouthness of the work on which his labour was wasted. He will do well, however, save when presenting himself before a young German audience, to eschew Schumann's music, for that has as small chance of establishing itself in England as it had in 1848, when this very quartett was introduced by Herr Edward Röckel (*Athenæum*, 'Musical and Dramatic Gossip', 20 June 1863: 817).

Never before had music been under such serious threat of disease and decay as it now was. Antipathy towards the 'music of the future' — chiefly the music of Schumann and Wagner — thus permeated much of Chorley's writing during his final years at the *Athenæum*.

Chorley's attempts to thwart the acceptance of the music of the future were not all published in the *Athenæum*. Somewhat surprisingly, Dickens's mass circulation weekly journal, *All the Year Round*, also provided a home for some of Chorley's articles on music. In 1864 Dickens published 'Old, New, and No Music', a two-part article in which Chorley denounced the music of the future.[44] In it Chorley lumped together Schumann, Liszt and Wagner as part of the same unwholesome phenomenon, and he criticized the so-called regeneration of German music currently being discussed in continental intellectual circles. He noted sarcastically that the Germans considered it 'new and noble to represent music as something which music never was and never will be — an expression of political feelings ... of a defiant and exclusive nationality, frowning at one country, scowling at another, sneering at a third, ignoring a fourth' ('Old, New, and No Music', 22 October 1864: 261).

For the readership of *All the Year Round*, Chorley reiterated the same premises he stated and re-stated in his weekly *Athenæum* columns: Some of Beethoven's music — though 'sublime' — had been a bad influence, setting an example of 'mischief' to succeeding generations of 'idle dreamers and theorists' (261), particularly in the late works. The main responsibility for the false 'regeneration' of music, however, lay with Wagner, whose talent and promise had deteriorated from the mildly interesting *Flying Dutchman* and *Tannhaüser* to the deplorable *Lohengrin* and the 'insolent' theorizing of *Oper und Drama* (263).

Dickens wrote to Wills about this article on 8 October 1864: 'I've gone through the No. carefully, and have been down upon Chorley's paper in particular, which was "a little bit" too personal. It is all right now, and good, and them's my sentiments too of The Music of the Future' (Dickens, *Letters*, Nonesuch edition, 3: 339).[45]

There are two more long articles printed in *All the Year Round* in which Chorley specifically attacked the music of the future even more vehemently:

1. 'German Opera and its Makers' in three parts (8 July 1865; 573-6, 15 July 1865: 583-7; and 22 July 1865, 607-11)
2. 'Depths and Heights of Modern Opera' (9 October 1869: 450-54)

These articles were intensely concerned with opera as art, not simply popular entertainment. Their publication in Dickens's family magazine suggested that Dickens had come to view opera as a subject worth serious didactic treatment, and considered *All the Year Round* as an appropriate outlet for such discussions.

The articles treated the issue that was increasingly assuming a position of importance in European musical life: nationalism — the relative significance and merits of the Italian, French, and German traditions. Both articles maintained that, contrary to general English opinion, the real home of nineteenth-century music drama was France. Accordingly, they denounced the German 'music of the future', most particularly Wagnerian opera, because it threatened the continued healthy development of opera. As the titles indicated, the subject matter of the articles was quite varied;

both, however, discuss the 'music of the future' controversy which was beginning so thoroughly to shake nineteenth-century European thought. The intellectual tenor of the articles reflected a consistent point of view, and internal evidence suggests that they are probably by a single hand, Chorley's.[46]

'German Opera and Its Makers' was an elaborate, three-part, quasi-encyclopaedic epitome of the history of German opera from the early eighteenth century to the present. One of its major points was its stress on the importance of the *French* school for the development of music drama: '... we are now only reluctantly waking up to the fact that to the Grand Opéra of Paris ... all Europe has been greatly indebted for the formation of dramatic as distinguished from musical opera' (573). The article concluded that German opera, despite its distinguished history, reached a dead end:

> The nightmares imposed on a helpless and astray public by Herr Wagner, may be "left alone in their glory" — for the moment at least. What manner of influence they have had, was to be heard last autumn in the horrible music of the Carlsruhe Festival, described in these columns. We imagine it to be already decaying. (22 July 1865: 611)[47]

The second of the operatic articles, 'Depths and Heights of Modern Opera' (9 October 1869: 450-54) criticized two specific performances of operas whose styles were worlds apart, and whose common trait was that both were worthless: Offenbach's *La Grande Duchesse de Gérolstein* in Paris, and Wagner's *Rheingold* in Munich. Offenbach's opera, analysed and denounced in the first section of the article, represented the 'depths' of modern opera — opera 'in the mire', as the subtitle had it — because the music was 'trite and colourless' (451). 'Lower in the setting of burlesque and in offence to delicacy, stage music can hardly sink' (451).

The concluding section of the article, 'In the Mist', took up the Wagner question in detail.[48] Printing such a detailed analysis represented a commitment on Dickens's part to fight the music of the future, an endorsement of his comment on the earlier article of Chorley's: 'them's my sentiments, too'. Europe needed Gounod to give it another *Faust* or *Mireille* in order to stop the growing public interest in Wagner's music (450).

When 'Depths and Heights of Modern Opera' was published in 1869, London opera-goers had still not seen a production of any of Wagner's operas — the first, 'L'Ollandese Dannato' (*Der Fliegende Holländer*) was presented at Drury Lane under the joint management of Mapleson and Gye on 23 July 1870, twenty-seven years after its first performance in Dresden.[49] A year before that, Chorley made a journey to Munich in order to see *Rheingold* and report to his English readers that Wagner's acceptance by a 'band of enthusiasts' was a wonder for 'the Annals of Charlatanry' ('Depths and Heights', 451). Wagner has come a long way since the 'not altogether irrational Rienzi' (451), an opera in which Wagner showed some talent. Today the 'case' of Wagner 'is one not of principles in art carried out, but of the same utterly annulled: not of progress, but of destruction' (452).

The vitriolic diatribe continued: Wagner's vocal phrases 'can only strike the ear as so much cacophonous jargon' (452), and '[e]ven the most credulous of Herr Wagner's partisans become tepid, vague, apologetic, and scarcely intelligible, if they are called on to defend or explain Herr Wagner's text' (452). The inept handling of stage effects produced 'dull absurdities':

> There is a final effect of a rainbow, not greatly larger than a canal bridge, which keeps close to the earth for the convenience of the dramatis personae, who are intended to mount upwards on it. ... Add to these wonders mists that come and go on the open landscape without any apparent rhyme or reason, clouds, darkness, sunbursts, all so many hackneyed effects dear to our children and "groundlings" at Christmas time; and some idea may be formed of the shows to exhibit which the music has been bent and broken. The congregation declare that the utter want of success which attended the rehearsal was owing to the stupidity of the Munich machinists and painters. Yet these till now have borne a deservedly high character throughout Germany; and the stage of the Bavarian capital is one notoriously convenient for any purposes of change or effects of space. (453)

The relation between the staging of *Das Rheingold* and that of an English Christmas pantomime was stressed as preparation for an analogously reasoned denunciation of the music as being interesting only in so far as it is derivative:

> The absence of melody is, of course, in accordance with Herr Wagner's avowed contempt for everything that shall please the ear. This being the condition of matters, it is not wonderful that a common four-bar phrase of upward progression, repeated some thirty times or more in the prelude, should please, and (to be just) its effect at representing the ceaseless flow of water, is picturesque and happy. The river nymphs are next announced by a phrase borrowed from Mendelssohn's overture to Melusine. There is a pompous entry for the principal bass voice, there is an effect of nine-eight rhythm, borrowed from Meyerbeer's scene in the cloisters of Saint Rosalie

> (Robert [*Robert le Diable*]); and these are all the phrases
> that can be retained by those who do not believe in what
> has been described by the transcendentalists, as
> "concealed melody." (453)

The failure of the performance thus could be attributed directly to the work itself, not to an unsatisfactory production:

> It will not avail to plead that it is ungenerous or unjust to
> judge from a rehearsal; when, as in the case of Das
> Rheingold, such rehearsal was tantamount in correctness
> and spirit to any first performance ever attended by Euro-
> pean critic. (453)

Though further rehearsals were called off, guests were not so much disappointed as relieved to be 'spared another dismal evening, to be spent in wonder — at the mouse brought forth by the mountain, at the pigmy production of the self-styled Musician of the Future' (454).

5 Gounod Ascendant and Sullivan Ascending

At the same time as these depressing musical developments were underway, there were also developments which Chorley celebrated, most particularly the careers of Gounod and Sullivan: in Gounod's case Chorley saw in the spectacular success of Faust in London the vindication of his 'discovery' of 1850, and in Sullivan's case Chorley proclaimed another discovery: the long-awaited arrival of a English composer whose significance was expected to be universal rather than local.

Faust came to England by the back door, as it were, being performed in Canterbury Hall in 1860: Chorley commended this, but it was hardly the same as a 'real' production at one of the two Italian houses:

> There is no keeping a real reputation at home: if it cannot
> get out by the door, it will by the window — if not by the
> window, by the chimney. Of this truth a curious proof is
> now exhibiting in the production here of some of the
> music of M. Gounod's 'Faust.' Guess where: — at that
> wonderful place, Canterbury Hall, the enterprise and far-
> sightedness of whose proprietor put to shame those of our
> managements. (5 May 1860: 625)

From that time on, Chorley kept the *Athenæum* readers of 'Musical and Dramatic Gossip' informed of each step in the progress of *Faust* around Europe as soon as he heard about it. In 1861, for example, he noted that Darmstadt produced it 'with entire success' (2 March 1861: 300), as did

Mayence [Mainz] in May (4 May 1861: 455). In Brussels it was performed 'with the most complete success. After the opera has established itself every-where else, we may possibly be treated to it in London' (9 March 1861: 333). In 1862 he reported that Vienna had performed it more frequently than any other opera, as had Stuttgart (16 August: 218). Hamburg's fiftieth performance was announced (4 October 1862: 442). The next year he again suggested sarcastically that Londoners were deprived of it because it was successful:

> Mdlle. Artot, whose success is deservedly great wherever she is heard, is about to sing the part of *Margaret* at Ber-lin, in M. Gounod's 'Faust,' The opera is "running" for a second time in Paris. The curiosity to hear it in England is wide and increasing — accordingly it is not played (21 February 1863: 269)

Still, it was not only English managers who found *Faust*'s beauties hard to comprehend at first. Its first English conductor, Arditi, and one of its early Marguerites, Clara Louise Kellogg, help us understand some of its early difficulties. Arditi remembered that '[t]he members of the orchestra ... were not at first attracted by the music, the style and orchestration being so new to them, and during the first rehearsals they were scarcely favourably impressed' (Arditi, 105-6). Kellogg (whose Marguerite in London was later warmly commended by Chorley) remembered the diffi-culty of learning the opera for Maretzek's company in Philadelphia, November 1863: 'It was just as startling, just as strange, just as antagonistic to our established musical habit as Strauss and Debussy and Dukas are to some persons to-day. [The music] puzzled me vastly. Also, I found it very difficult to sing' (Kellogg, 79). In short, Kellogg wrote, 'everything was new, startling, overthrowing all traditions' (87).[50] Mapleson, too, recalled after the initial London performances that many opera-goers said 'it was wanting in melody' (Mapleson, 1888, 1: 71).

Finally the opera was given three London productions: the first at Her Majesty's Theatre, 11 June 1863, quickly followed at Covent Garden by a rival production 2 July 1863 (with Miolan-Carvalho), and finally once again at Her Majesty's a few months later, this time in Chorley's English translation. Mapleson related that Chappel, the English publisher of *Faust*, was willing to pay him £200 to perform the opera, another £200 after four performances, and another, undisclosed sum after ten performances. Advance ticket sales were miserable. In a ruse like one of P.T. Barnum's, Mapleson gave away most of the seats to the first three performances in order to advertise 'everything sold' and thereby stir up interest (Mapleson, 1888, 1: 67-9 and Northcott, *Gounod's Operas*, 16-19).

Wilhelm Kuhe recollected the audience reception at the first performance

as 'by no means favourable'. It became enthusiastic at the third performance (*Recollections*, 170). His account verified the statement of Arditi, the
conductor of these performances; 'frankly', he asserted, *Faust*

> did not immediately force its way into the hearts of the
> people. The work had many enemies, and encountered a
> great deal of opposition and unmerited abuse; and,
> although the opera was constantly repeated [twenty per-
> formances], it was not a financial success during the first
> year. (Arditi, 109)

This account, however, did not clarify why Gye mounted a competing
production so quickly, nor did it entirely square with Mapleson's recollection:

> [A]fter the third performance the paying public, burning
> with desire to see a work from which they had hitherto
> been debarred, filled the theatre night after night. No fur-
> ther device was necessary for stimulating its curiosity; and
> the work was now to please and delight successive
> audiences by its own incontestable merit. It was given for
> ten nights in succession, and was constantly repeated until
> the termination of the season.

Chorley's account of the success of the first performance differed from
Arditi's and Mapleson's. In it, he analysed changes made to the opera and
reported its 'triumph':

> ... without doubt [*Faust* is] the opera which has most
> thoroughly *satisfied* the stage of Europe since 'Les
> Huguenots' appeared. ... The opera, as it now stands in
> London, is not as it then stood in Paris. The original
> spoken dialogue has been replaced by sung recitative —
> perhaps too much after the elaborate fashions of the time,
> which tend towards converting opera into a sung
> symphony. — The "Walpurgis" music has vanished — the
> spinning song, too; and in the prison-scene the duett and
> the trio have been retouched. The scenes of the church
> and of the combat ending in Valentine's death have
> changed places — every alteration being for the better. ...
> There is nothing in the whole range of opera more effec-
> tive, more impressive ... [than the death of Valentine]. ...
> [*Faust* is] by many degrees the best among modern
> operas. The crowd assembled at Her Majesty's Theatre on
> Thursday week obviously was aware of the fact. Rarely
> has a stronger sensation been produced — rarely has a

more complete triumph been achieved. (20 June 1863: 816-17)

Tietjens, as Marguerite, was, though variable, especially strong in the final trio because her voice was so powerful. Gassier's Mephistopheles was only 'mediocre', but Santley's Valentine was extraordinary:

> [W]e were not prepared for so admirable a piece of acting and singing as this is ..., [W]e must stop after having again expressed our pleasure in a success which has outdone all expectation, and which has silenced for ever those who have sneered at M. Gounod as a man whose productions in no respect justified the pretensions and professions of his admirers, — among whom we were the earliest. (817)

In an undated letter to D---- [Dilke? Dickens?] Chorley emphasized that the success was the culmination of twelve years of supporting Gounod, during which his support was viewed in England as eccentric. He insisted that his support had been disinterested, since he personally despised Gounod:

> I don't wonder at every one being charmed with "Faust," & after my having run the gauntlet of twelve years' abuse in the press, I can't help feeling something besides wonder. — & I don't wonder at your liking the man: who is most cultivated & agreeable. It has been one of my greatest literary griefs, in a life which has had many, that I was obliged many years ago abruptly to terminate an acquaintance very near a friendship, owing to an outrageous & deliberate manifestation of baseness on his part (*not to myself*)[51] which rendered it impossible for me any longer to keep anything but the most formal terms of intercourse with a man whom I despise as heartily, as I admire his music cordially. I can have no objection that any one should know this, because it relieves me from all possible suspicion of having, during a long & lonely advocacy of his music, been influenced by personal likings & dislikings. ...[52]

Dickens understood how important the success of *Faust* was to Chorley as a vindication of his long-suffering foresight. This reference to a 'gauntlet of twelve years' abuse in the press' may explain an otherwise obscure point which Dickens made in a letter about Chorley which he sent from the offices of *All the Year Round* to his sister-in-law, Georgina Hogarth, at Gad's Hill, on 18 June 1863, just after the first performance of *Faust* at

Her Majesty's Theatre:

> Chorley is made so happy by the success of Faust ... that
> it is quite impossible to understand what he means. When
> he told me what his feelings were, he drew a dial in the
> air, and punched with his forefinger all the twelve hours
> in it. Then he said "*You* understand?" and I said (with
> deep feeling) "I do."[53]

In July, Gye mounted a rival production at the Royal Italian Opera,
Covent Garden. Chorley's review of it was important because in it he
makes clear that *Faust* was of central importance to the modern repertory
because it provided a legitimate continuation of lyric drama from the central
position occupied up to now by *Les Huguenots*. In effect, it was a genuine
example of the direction to be taken by the 'music of the future', not the
false direction taken by Verdi and Wagner:

> Let us first record that the scenic luxuries are on a scale
> and of a finish never before reached in an English theatre;
> rivalling the best days of M. Véron's management of the
> Grand Opéra of Paris. ... No common credit is due to
> Messrs. Beverley and Harris, who, by aid of the new
> effects of light discovered, have wrought these
> unparagoned shows. [It may become more popular than
> "Huguenots"] for one simple reason. There is as much
> effect in the opera of M. Gounod as in M. Meyerbeer's,
> — there is much more reality, and far more tenderness.
> ... Against any other operas than M. Meyerbeer's, it
> would be a folly to measure 'Faust.' The school to which
> the two men belong is the same; ... [It is] the most
> remarkable opera of modern times, standing midway (not
> meanly, therefore) betwixt the flimsy violences of Signor
> Verdi and the shallow obscurities of Herr Wagner. ...
> Madame Miolan-Carvalho, [is] the *Margaret* of whom
> every one has dreamed. ... Her acting throughout is per-
> fect, and her appearance that of a figure which has
> stepped forth from the frame of one of Ary Scheffer's
> 'Faust' pictures. (11 July 1863: 56)

Tamberlik as Faust was the 'weak point' (56); Faure as *Mephistopheles* was
excellent, and Graziani presented 'a fair *Valentine*, though less good than
Mr. Santley' (56).[54]

The next month, as the Italian operas closed for the season, Chorley
reiterated for his readers the significance of the season:[55]

> A season more laborious is not in our recollection, nor

one so interesting, since that of the 'Huguenots,' which
broke the ice for M. Meyerbeer in this country. 1863 will
be remembered as the 'Faust' year. A like excitement has
not possessed itself of London since Madame Grisi, Signor Tamburini, and Rubini and Lablache enraptured it by
their marvellous "consent" in 'I Puritani.' As a musical
success, M. Gounod's is far higher than Bellini's was; and
if what competent witnesses report of his 'Mirielle' [*sic*]
be true, there is small fear of its not being followed up. (1
August 1863: 154)

The Italian translations of *Faust* were followed by a winter season at Her
Majesty's during which the repertory consisted solely of performances of
Faust in English. The translator was Chorley. This translation, which he
had prepared as far back as 1859,[56] was influential. Arditi said it brought
the opera 'nearer to the hearts of the public than it had as yet been'
(*Reminiscences*, 112), and tickets were in great demand. Fixed to Arthur
Sullivan's edition of the opera's vocal score, originally published by Boosey
& Company and widely distributed in the twentieth century by Schirmer, it
helped the opera become widely known among English-speaking audiences
in both hemispheres.[57]

Santley asked Gounod for an aria, suggesting that its melody could be
taken from the overture (*Student and Singer*, 197). Gounod obliged, and
Chorley put English words to it: 'Even bravest heart may swell / at the
impulse of farewell' (retranslated variously as 'Dio possente' or 'Avant de
quitteur ces lieux').[58]

Chorley repeatedly mentioned that the English version was about to be
presented, and discussed it in relation to the two other versions of *Faust*
then current:

> The opera will shortly be presented at Her Majesty's
> Theatre, with the cast already announced, and the English
> version prepared four years ago by Mr. Henry F. Chorley
> (Chappel & Co.) — Each of the three versions, the
> French, the Italian, and the one in question, has variations
> and modifications of its own sanctioned by the composer.
> We understand that at the coming performance the Wal-
> purgis scene, suppressed because of its length in the
> Italian versions, will be presented. (9 January 1864: 45)

Chorley reviewed the first performance of the English version, avoiding
direct comment on the quality of his own translation (except in the new aria
for Valentin/Santley), and focusing instead on the singers (Lemmens-
Sherrington being new to the cast at Her Majesty's):

> Her Majesty's Theatre. — *'Faust' in English.* — So much

has been written on the sudden and unparagoned success of 'Faust' in this country that there is no need to expatiate on the subject when recording that the performance, in the form above described, took place duly on Saturday last, to the entire satisfaction of the audience. Three of the four principal artists were the same as sang the opera in Italian, on the same boards, in October; Signor Arditi conducted, as then. The chorus is stronger and fresher than it was. Madame Lemmens-Sherrington, as *Margaret* proved herself competent to her task; she stands midway betwixt Mdlle. Tietjens and Madame Miolan-Carvalho, inclining not to the forcible, but to the delicate reading of the character — that of an innocent girl, pure and heart, yielding to a two-fold fascination, earthly and supernatural. But for her tendency to drag the time, as in the "Thule" ballad, and the final trio, her singing would have left little to desire. Her acting is sufficient. Madame Florence Lancia, as *Siebel*, pleased, in spite of a costume tasteless to absurdity. The best performance, in every point of view, was Mr. Santley's. The new song, taken from the second theme of the Introduction, with an episodical second part, is about as happy as are usually such *quasi-impromptu* movements, and owes its effect to the exquisite finish and feeling of the singer. Signor Marchesi has improved his *Mephistopheles*, though it is still a touch too *buffo*. His English is better than we had expected; and the words of the part are, from first to last, difficult, the author, with dramatic intentions, having overweighted them with sarcasm, always difficult to render in music. Mr. Sims Reeves, who was in thorough voice, sang the music well, — with great care. (*Athenæum*, 30 January 1864: 163)

The popular success of the translation would undoubtedly have gratified Chorley more had there not been some controversy over liberties taken with his words by the principals. Sims Reeves seems to have led a movement by the singers to change Chorley's words on the grounds that they were, as Reeves's biographer explained, 'unsingable':

> The production of the opera at Her Majesty's was not unattended by difficulties, as it was discovered that many of Mr. Chorley's lines were quite unsingable. Even before the first rehearsal complaints were made to Messrs. Chappell, by Mr. Sims Reeves, Mademoiselle Florence Lancia, and Mr. Santley, about the impossibility of singing Mr.

Chorley's words. So strenuous and persistent were the complaints that Messrs. Chappell — much against their inclination, it was said — were compelled to have the greater part of the words of Faust, and one scene of Valentine, rewritten. Mademoiselle Lancia had all the verses of Siebel directly translated from the French, while Reeves had his own version written for him by Charles Lamb Kenney. All this was done unknown to Mr. Chorley — perhaps no one had the courage to tackle the autocrat — and the first intimation of the hacking and altering was conveyed to him as he sat listening to the first performance on January 23rd [1864]. It must have been a terrible shock. ... (Pearce, 241)

It was indeed a shock. Chorley regretted the 'damage done' (*Athenæum*, 27 February 1864: 307). The newly-established journal, *The Orchestra*, mentioned the alterations in its review of the production:

[T]he new adaptation [is] from the experienced pen of Mr. H.F. Chorley. That this gentleman has done his work well we will at once admit with pleasure; and that the singers should in many instances have made changes in the text is neither here nor there; for do not singers delight in altering the words they have to sing to suit their voices? (*The Orchestra*, 30 January 1864: 278)

Elsewhere in the same issue a correspondent terming himself 'Mephistopheles' wondered whether Mr. Chorley would not have altered 'unvocal' passages had he been asked (283). 'The English Translator of "Faust"' responded in the next issue that he was 'invariably' ready to go over his translations with singers. Nobody consulted him. 'I conceived that my services were not required; and was proportionately surprised on the evening of the performance. It is surely needless to point out that had the other characters in the opera, with a similar want of self-respect, each indulged in like private independent measures, the result would hardly have been intelligible or satisfactory' (*Orchestra*, 6 February 1864: 299). Rubbing salt in Chorley's wounds, the *Musical World* pronounced the alterations to Chorley's words 'indispensable' (5 March 1864: 153) and, the following week, reprinted 'a Poet in a Pet' from *Punch* (173-4), which mocked 'Poet Chorley's divine verses' (173).

Because of the popular success of *Faust*, Chorley was eager to attend in Paris the first performance of Gounod's new opera, *Mireille*, produced at the Théâtre Lyrique in March, 1864, hoping to find his predictions validated. Instead, Chorley had some reservations, insisting that the opera needed careful revision:

> [There are] two acts of perfect enjoyment, then one of wondering disapprobation, and, afterwards, two of admiration, with large exceptions. Let us enter into details which will explain what has been said, and explain, too, what we distinctly state that this chequered pleasure in M. Gounod's new work does not, in the smallest possible degree, shake our opinion of him as a composer ... To praise [Miolan-Carvalho] too highly would be impossible. ... But even such consummate art and feeling as hers may fail to save 'Mireille,' unless a thorough reform and compression of three fifths of the opera be undertaken and carried out. (2 April 1864: 478-9)

The revisions were forthcoming, and when the opera was presented at Her Majesty's Theatre in July, Chorley termed them 'effective and necessary'. No one alive 'could write anything for the stage comparable to it' (9 July 1864: 57).

Gounod's popularity being now firmly established in England, Chorley found it gratifying from time to time to remind his readers of his early support, providing them with 'I told you so' commentary. In February 1866 Chorley reminded them how Gounod had first been treated by 'signal contumely' by all 'save by ourselves' (17 February 1866: 245). That same week, however, when *The Orchestra* suggested that credit for introducing Gounod to London belonged to the *Athenæum*, it erred in attributing that article not to Chorley but to M. Viardot:

> it is a curious fact that the first really important notice of [Gounod's] works was written by the musical critic of a London paper — the *Athenaeum* — in a *compte rendu* he gave of a concert at St. Martin's Hall, at which four of M. Gounod's works were produced. The article, which was most favourable ... was generally attributed to M. Viardot (who has never declined this 'soft impeachment'),[59] and being reproduced in French a few days later, created great interest. (17 February 1866: 330).

Responding the very next week (as 'The Writer in the "Athenaeum"'), Chorley zealously defended his reputation for perspicacity. His letter to the editor set the record straight as to where credit was due:

> I first heard of M. Gounod from that distinguished lady, Mdme. Pauline Viardot. ... I mentioned [Gounod's music] to Mr. John Hullah. ... The result was that performance at St. Martin's Hall in 1851, which called out a storm of doubt, derision, and abuse, the like whereof I hardly recollect. With what was published here, concern-

ing that concert, M. Viardot had nothing to do. He was not in England. ... (*Orchestra*, 24 February 1866: 348)

Chorley's determination to defend his own critical acumen remained acute, but his interest in fostering Gounod's career became less intense after the English success of *Faust*. He had been right; the canon had been enlarged; he could now happily remind people from time to time of his own role since 1850 in establishing Gounod, 'without question' as 'the first opera-composer now before Europe' (25 May 1867: 700).

Gounod's *Roméo et Juliet* was first performed in Paris at the Théâtre Lyrique on 27 April 1867. When it arrived soon afterwards at the Royal Italian Opera, Covent Garden, Patti was declared better than ever, but Mario, though 'picturesque', seemed perhaps too old for the role of a young lover. 'For the moment, the new opera is incontestably, brilliantly, successful. Whether it will have as wide and long a reign on the stage as "Faust" remains to be seen' (20 July 1867: 91).

A newer discovery had come along, whose talent needed nurturing: the young Arthur Sullivan. Unlike Gounod, Sullivan retained Chorley's personal friendship as well as his professional respect. Moreover, the new discovery provided a happy answer to that nagging question: is England a musical nation? As far back as his long review-essay summarizing the musical season of 1837 (in *The London and Westminster Review*, July 1837), Chorley had claimed that one reason England's composers were inferior to continental composers was that they sought the quickest route to the 'mob popularity' and riches, rather than the soundest route to mastery and excellence: but, he added hopefully, 'a change *may* be at hand' (58).[60] At last, after twenty-five years of finding no composer to meet his criteria, he discovered Sullivan, the first (and for many years, the only) 'Mendelssohn Scholar', trained at Leipzig in the conservatory Mendelssohn had started. For much of the 1860s, the columns of the *Athenæum* frequently proclaimed his accomplishments and his promise. Moreover, Chorley struck up a personal friendship with Sullivan, as did Chorley's friends Dickens and Frederick and Nina Lehmann.

Chorley's 'Musical and Dramatic Gossip' column announced the completion of Sullivan's studies in Germany:

> From information on which reliance is to be placed, we may announce that at a late pupils' concert given at the Conservatory at Leipsic, some music to Shakespeare's 'Tempest' (six numbers), by our young Mendelssohn Scholar, Mr. Arthur Sullivan, excited attention as of remarkable promise. The Conservatory, by the way, is just now rich in English scholars. Mr. Sullivan has returned to England to enter on his professional career.

(27 April 1861: 568)

And the next week: 'We are able, from perusal, to confirm the favourable account of Mr. Arthur Sullivan's "Tempest" music alluded to a week since'. (4 May 1861: 454). Moreover, he informed his readers on 15 February 1862, this work was about to be performed in London (233).

The following excerpts from his columns in 1862 revealed his excitement at Sullivan's promise, and the kind of encouragement and commendation Chorley felt was publicly appropriate. On 5 April 1862, Sullivan made his English debut with a performance of the 'Tempest' music conducted by Manns:

> Crystal Palace. — 'The Tempest' Music by Mr. A Sullivan. ... We now have the pleasant task of recording the very remarkable and legitimate success gained at the Crystal Palace this day week by the illustrations to the same drama written by Mr. Arthur Sullivan. — It was one of those events which mark an epoch in a man's life; and, what is of more universal consequence, it may mark an epoch in English music, or we shall be greatly disappointed. Years on years have elapsed since we have heard a work by so young an artist so full of promise, so full of fancy, showing so much conscientiousness, so much skill, and so few references to any model elect. ... The dance of nymphs and reapers, which closes the [fourth] act (*encored*), is the number in the work calculated to remind the hearer the most that Mr. Sullivan is the Mendelssohn scholar, in the quick *staccato* figure harmonized, which every one has been used to consider as Mendelssohn's own particular property; yet not so, since it is in Cherubini's Quartetts. ...
>
> ... In brief, it is a real gratification to think that there is already such good justification of the hope on which he was sent to study abroad. We can imagine no doubt for his future — life and leisure permitting.
>
> But — it must be added that, for a beginner, Mr. Sullivan had a great chance. The performance of his work was excellent. Too much praise cannot be given to Herr Manns for the admirable nerve, spirit and delicacy and the capital measurement of *tempo* which he threw into all the freaks and fantasies and brilliant passages of the music. ...[61] The day was a pleasant day altogether for those who wish well to English music. (504-5)

In the next issue he wrote:

> Mr. Arthur Sullivan's 'Tempest' music was repeated on
> Saturday last at the Crystal Palace, with an increased
> effect and success, rare in *second* performances, which
> have the reputation of going off flatly. ... There has been
> no such first appearance in England in our time.

On 7 June he wrote again of Sullivan's success and promise:

> It is pleasant, and should encourage all who do and
> deserve well, to record that the favourite English song of
> the season, in request everywhere, is Mr. A. Sullivan's
> setting of "Where the bee sucks." His 'Tempest' music
> has permanently established itself. Is it too new, too
> elegant or too difficult, and is the composer too promising
> or too English, for his work to be thought worthy of
> notice by the Philharmonic Directors? (752)

On 21 June 1862, Chorley discussed the prospectus of the English
Opera, to be conducted by Henry Leslie. Unwilling since the 1830s to join
enthusiastically in searches for a foreign scapegoats on which, or whom, to
place blame for the precarious existence of English opera, Chorley insisted
that the prospectus would do well to drop its charge that the English
encouraged foreign music more than English music:

> There has never been fit and fair response wanting to
> British music or musicians meriting response. Take such
> widely differing illustrations as Bishop's and Mr. Balfe's
> operas, — Dr. Bennett's 'May Queen,' — the well-
> merited and not ill-recompensed success of such ex-
> ecutants as Mesdames Novello and Sainton-Dolby,
> Messrs. Sims Reeves and Santley, — the popularity of the
> elect musical director's Part Choir, — the instant accept-
> ance of Mr. Sullivan the other day. ... Insomuch as the
> English musicians have been either true to their art, or
> individuals have shown either style or proficiency, they
> have never lacked encouragement. ... [w]e are at a loss to
> see in what point the scheme on which we have com-
> mented differs from many schemes past and gone. ...
> (830)

That summer Chorley announced in 'Musical and Dramatic Gossip' that
Arthur Sullivan was 'engaged in the composition of an opera' (5 July
1862: 26),[62] and Cramer published *Thoughts*, piano pieces by Sullivan.
Chorley noted that

> Mr. Sullivan's *Thoughts*, Nos. 1 and 2 (Cramer & Co.),
> are real thoughts — real devices and desires, — justifying

> to every one the remarkable reputation won by his 'Tempest' music. (30 August 1862: 283)

And in October he deemed 'clever' the four-hand piano arrangement of the 'Tempest' prepared by Franklin Taylor and published by Cramer (18 October 505). He reminded his readers again on 10 January 1863, that '[t]here have been few cases of more complete and legitimate success than this in our time' (59). Sullivan's 'March' is commended — 'very good; and, what is more, new' (14 March 1863: 368).

Chorley glowed, gratified by the public success of Gounod's *Faust* and Sullivan's *Tempest*. Privately, however, he found much to worry him. His family situation was difficult.[63] He was shaken by the final stages of his sister's decline. In increasingly bad health since the death of Mrs Chorley in 1851, in 1863 she died. In writing of his sister's death in a private journal, Chorley reflected keenly its effect not only on himself but also on his brother, John Rutter Chorley, who had cared for their sister for years. This train of thought led him to eulogize his brother and to praise his life as 'a series of sacrifices, met by him with a sense of duty which was too severe, too unselfish'. John Rutter Chorley had been

> ... compelled, by circumstances needless to recount, by his own accuracy and justice as a man of business, to undertake the administration of family affairs, some of which were of no common perplexity. He watched over the declining health of my mother till the last; and hardly had she departed, when it became evident that another charge of the kind, far more serious, was thrown on him — the ministry to a hopeless invalid, suffering and decaying more and more during many years; one endowed with every gracious gift and capacity for enjoyment, who was doomed in the prime to life to expect and to endure the slow extinction of every hope that cheers, of every talent that alleviates acute and wearing bodily pain. The patience with which this grievous trial was braved is not to be exaggerated; but the inevitable result was to increase my brother's seclusion among his own pursuits. (Hewlett, 2: 282-3)

Sullivan wrote Chorley a letter of sympathy, to which Chorley responded warmly on 19 September 1863:

> My dear boy.
>
> Thank you for your affectionate note. — My dear sister's release is no cause for sorrow: so terribly painful had her life been for the last ten years. — Had she lived it must have become still worse: & perhaps with none to

care for her! — But it seems to deprive my life of its main object — & leaves me virtually alone in the world. Thus, I repeat, I am more sensible of kind thoughts than those who are richer in family affection: — & I appreciate yours with all my heart — I am *very* fond of you & when I have scolded you it has been because I have a right to expect great things from you.

I *was* at Norwich — & heard your "Tempest" music rehearsed. It seemed to please extremely. You have only to go on: & to think that you must not disappoint those who are attached to you — I hope you will come very often to me this winter: since I shall keep very quiet. After Monday I shall be visible again —

Aff[ectionate]ly yours.
Henry F. Chorley[64]

Sullivan's next major work, *Kenilworth*, a cantata with words by Chorley, was presented at the Birmingham Festival in 1864. Chorley managed to praise Sullivan and himself without quite violating the code of ethics which prevented him for reviewing or puffing his own works:

> Mr. Sullivan's music contains four numbers, out of the nine, with which the rhymester has nothing to do. Of these the critic may speak. They are an instrumental prelude, a slow and a brisk dance, the former with a choral burthen, and a setting of the lovely dialogue between *Lorenzo* and *Jessica* from 'The Merchant of Venice,' introduced (under peril of its being blamed as an anachronism) as the play set before the Queen, among other of the pleasures of Kenilworth. All these, it may be said without hesitation, will do more than bear out every favourable impression excited and retained by the writer's 'Tempest' music, the first hearing of which set him in a foremost place among English composers ... [Sullivan's melody and treatment of orchestra] mark another step upward in a career which it rests with himself to render remarkable in the annals of Art. [The singers were Lemmens-Sherrington, Miss Palmer, Mr. Cummings replacing Mario at the last minute, and Santley.] (17 September 1864: 378)

He concluded by terming the Birmingham Festival 'the most remarkable musical meeting at which we have ever been present' (379).

In March, 1866, the Crystal Palace presented an important Sullivan premiere, his Symphony in E major ('Irish').

> *Crystal Palace Concerts* — A new and a long Symphony, by an English composer to boot, which can retain the attention and awaken the applause of a crowd of thousands, must, it is clear, possess no ordinary merit, — since no favouritism could leaven so vast and miscellaneous an audience. Mr. A.S. Sullivan, then, may count on having gained a real success this day week, in one of the most difficult forms of composition; ... [Analysis of each movement follows.] Let Mr. Sullivan choose his first thoughts well, write with fluency and decision, and write frequently, and he has a great and universal celebrity within his reach, if ever man had. The 'Kenilworth' duett, the 'Orpheus' Shakspeare [*sic*] song, and this Symphony, all subsequent to his charming 'Tempest' music, are all entirely his own: all three of a high and refined order of beauty, skilfully expressed. (31 March 1866: 371-2)

Davison in *The Times* corroborated Chorley's judgment of the symphony. This unanimity of opinion prompted Chorley to send Sullivan a congratulatory note, dated 12 March 1866. With its 'paternal' advice and a touch of self pity, the tone of Chorley's letter is similar to that of letters to Charles Santley written towards the end of the 1850s:

> My dear Sullivan,
>
> I really must write to you ... to express the very great pleasure which the *Times* gives me this morning. As you know, I *don't* care for criticism: but your good people naturally do: — & though I have the most profound contempt for the writer's insincerity, I have never, as you know, denied his possession of knowledge. & if the impression was made on him — it is clear that this time. it must have been a genuine one: — & as such creditable to yourself. — If you will only be true to yourself, & try for decision as a necessary element in *mastery*, I am satisfied that there is nothing to stand between you, & a great Europian [*sic*] success.[65]
>
> You observed, I hope, the *slap* at me: in re Schumann — I was "a jaded connoisseur" about ten days ago, — What *does* it matter? — If it amuses any one to abuse me, let *he she or it* be amused. — [66]

1866 was a prolific year for Sullivan, and Chorley kept his readers apprised of every detail in the composer's progress. In June, 1866, he reported a private entertainment in his 'Musical and Dramatic Gossip' section, not something he normally did. This was 'Cox and Box', Sullivan's comic collaboration with F.C. Burnand, preceding his first full collaboration with W.S. Gilbert (*Trial by Jury*, 1875) by about nine years:

> Only some circumstance of exceptional curiosity and interest can justify any journalist, not belonging to the *Jenkins* family,[67] from alluding to private festivals, be they ever so brilliant. Such a one presents itself in the fact of a new work having been produced in what may be advisedly named as the most artistic, original and hospitable musical house in London. (2 June 1866: 745)

That same month, thoughts of the Mendelssohn/Sullivan connection stirred Chorley to comment graciously on Lind-Goldschmidt, who was to sing at a concert 'given by Mr. A.S. Sullivan' soon:

> This act of grace must not pass without the reader being reminded that it was mainly by the lady's singing, on her first appearance in English oratorio, and the splendid receipt of that concert, that the solitary Mendelssohn Scholarship, which is such a monument of lasting dishonour to the inhabitants of North Germany, was founded. The excellence of the first Mendelssohn scholar need not be dwelt on. (30 June 1866: 873)

The concert brought back memories of the 1840s — Moscheles was visiting London from Leipzig and attended it. Lind-Goldschmidt was praised: 'The main vocal attraction of the evening was, of course, Madame Lind-Goldschmidt. ... So magnificent a display of executive power has never been heard in the St. James's Hall' (14 July 1866: 57-8). Sullivan's new overture to 'his MS. opera' was singled out for praise. This was, I assume, the overture to *The Sapphire Necklace*, an unfinished opera, to Chorley's libretto:[68] 'As a stage overture compelling attention and increasing in interest from the first note to the last, we could name very few specimens, since Weber's in any respect so good, — none better' (57). All in all, the performance formed '*the* concert of the season' (14 July 1866: 57).

On 24 November 1866, Sullivan's violoncello concerto in D major had its premiere at the Crystal Palace, played by Piatti:

> This marks another step forward in a true and earnest career. The music is elegant, full of contrast and effect, — the *solo* instrument excellently set off by the orchestra, which, in the case of this peculiar instrument, is not an easy task. ... [T]here is an inherent dullness in the tone of the instrument which cannot be gainsaid, neither wholly conquered. It is the business of a *solo* instrument to dominate, not to be lifted up. So much the more credit,

> then, is in our judgment, the due of Mr. Sullivan for the
> brightness and character thrown into his latest work; but
> then he owes no common debt to his interpreters. Herr
> Manns is always admirable when conducting instrumental
> (not vocal) music; and the playing of Signor Piatti was
> marvellous — the playing of one who obviously enjoyed
> his occupation. (1 December 1866: 722)

The year 1866 did not seem a particularly magnificent one musically, but when Chorley summed up the season, he showed how he responded favourably to the music which connected with his long established predilections: He had been pleased with Gluck's *Iphigenia in Tauris* at Her Majesty's with Tietjens and Santley (somewhat less pleased with the quality of the performances in Paris of *Alceste*, prepared by Berlioz), supportive of the initial successes of one of Viardot's pupils, Aglaja Orgeni, and still more supportive of the continuing success of Sullivan.

Next, Sullivan's overture 'In Memoriam', composed to commemorate the death of his father, was performed in January 1867 at the Crystal Palace. Chorley reported:

> Mr. A. S. Sullivan's overture, 'In Memoriam,' produced
> an impression even greater than it did at Norwich. Being
> familiar with most of the overtures which have made the
> tour of orchestral concerts, we have no hesitation in plac-
> ing this among the best. ... (2 February 1867: 162).

He urged Sullivan not to follow the example set in the Beethoven's late works, written 'when his powers of self-judgment (not his fancy) decayed', since those works have had 'a fatal influence on young would-be poets' (162).

In April 1867 Chorley reported that two songs from the still uncompleted Chorley-Sullivan opera, *The Sapphire Necklace* were 'cordially received', and that the 'elegant overture' seems to be already 'established in favour' (20 April 1867: 526). Then in November there is a passing reference in 'Musical and Dramatic Gossip' to another collaboration between Sullivan and Burnand for a light work (*The Contrabandista*):

> Mr. German Reed has secured the Bijou Theatre in St.
> George's Hall, with a view of giving light operettas there.
> He will open, we are told, with a new work by Messrs.
> Burnand and A. S. Sullivan. (30 November 1867: 731)

This too was soon praised:

> [Music and the Drama. St George's Opera House under
> German Reed's management] Mr. Sullivan's new comic
> opera. Enough for the moment to state our conviction that

the music is thoroughly charming, and marks another step
upward in the career of our young composer (21 December 1867: 856).

Chorley's support for the music of Gounod and Sullivan continued up to
and beyond his retirement from the *Athenæum*. In Gounod, there was a
connection with the spirit of French Grand Opera which had so stirred him
in the 1830s; in Sullivan, there was a connection with the beloved music of
Mendelssohn. As alternatives to the corrupt 'music of the future' offered by
Wagner and Schumann, they were Chorley's best, and last, hopes.

In 1866 there was a new director, William Cusins, for the much-scorned
Philharmonic:

> A more amiable gentleman, a more honestly intentioned
> member of the English musical profession than he, could
> not be named; but it remains to be proved how far he
> commands experience, authority and independence of
> coterie influence, to reinstate the dilapidated fortunes of
> an establishment which, after having been one of the lead-
> ing musical institutions of Europe, has now, in what-
> soever aspect it be viewed, sunk to a position below
> mediocrity. (8 December 1866: 759)

Chorley soon complained about the election, writing that there were many
excellent conductors now in London: Herr Manns, Mr Hallé, Mr Mellon,
and Mr Benedict. Therefore why did the Philharmonic elect Mr Cusins? (16
March 1867: 345). Still, he was not entirely implacable:

> Enough to say that the orchestra was correct, but rough,
> and its new director, apparently, not nervous; certainly
> more animated than his predecessor (Sterndale Bennett),
> who too often let matters take their own way, and, like
> Mr. Merdle's chief butler in [Dickens's] 'Little Dorrit,'
> looked on. (16 March 1867: 345)

But the Philharmonic seemed to continue in the wrong direction. 'There is
no evidence that Cusins became more competent with experience', according to Cyril Ehrlich, 'nor that his presence was ever regarded as an attraction to ticket-buyers; yet there was no attempt to replace him for a single
concert, throughout seventeen seasons' (*First Philharmonic*, 116).

These developments at the Philharmonic were overshadowed, however,
by the fire which, once again, destroyed Her Majesty's Theatre. This time
it was not reopened until 1877, when Chorley was no longer alive. Its burning prompted Chorley to elegiac musings on the history of the theatre. For

thirty-five years Her Majesty's Theatre had been intertwined with his own life in opera. He recalled the days when it had been the only Italian opera house:

> As a theatre for the display of the voice, it was unequalled. When it was reared, the demands for scenic display in Italian Opera were trifling in comparison with those we have lived to see enforced during the last five-and-thirty years. The stage of late must have been felt as comfortlessly small and inconvenient. But the aspect of the theatre, especially when court plumes and full dress figured in the boxes and in "Fops' Alley," was brilliant and pompous in no common degree. ...
>
> From the first, our Haymarket Opera-house has commanded for its service all that was richest and choicest in Europe, before St. Petersburg and New York were thought of as markets, and before the great art of singing had followed the law of all arts, and, from a splendid noon, waned into a dull twilight. What a procession of queens of song rises as we recall the names of Billington, Banti, Grassini, Catalani (with her "five supplementary dolls"), Pasta, Sontag, Malibran, and the three last, but not three least, of the great vocalists, happily all living, Mesdames Grisi, Viardot and Lind! Only such consummate "singing-men" as David, Donzelli, Rubini, Lablache, and Signor Tamburini. Then, in the history of Opera at Her Majesty's Theatre, it must never be forgotten how, during many a long year, the performances were wrought up by Mr. Costa to a point of perfection utterly unknown till then in this country. (14 December 1867: 807)

6 Final Creative Works

The year 1861 saw performances of Henry Leslie's setting of Chorley's cantata, *Holyrood*. The score was published by Addison, Hollier & Lucas, with the following dedication page: 'The Words and Music Dedicated to Mrs Benson Rathbone,[69] by Henry F. Chorley, and Henry Leslie'. The book for *Holyrood* was pastoral, and somewhat whimsical. On a beautiful June day, Queen Mary and courtiers are rejoicing. Suddenly stern Puritan voices disturb them; John Knox predicts future sorrow for Queen Mary, predicting 'Murder of a bridegroom sleeping', then 'battle', 'prison', and finally 'scaffold'. The chorus's angry reaction to such predictions is stilled by Queen Mary who calmly rejects them, adding that even if the predictions are true, she 'would *die* — as fits a Queen!' — with dignity. Knox then leaves and Mary sings: 'Let him go, and hear our laughter! / Mirth to-day, whate'er come after!' These two lines form the transition to a final chorus of praise to Queen Mary:

> Music to her honour,
>> Sing in hall and bower,
> Peace and joy upon her,
>> Scotland's lily flower!

Since it was not appropriate for Chorley to review his own works, the *Athenæum* made only passing favourable comment in its 'Concerts of the Week' section for 2 February 1861.

The opera libretto, *The Amber Witch*, was an much more ambitious undertaking than *Holyrood*. The libretto was adapted by Chorley from Meinhold's novel *Bernsteinhexe* (Lady Duff Gordon's translation, published by John Murray, appeared in 1844).[70] It was produced at Her Majesty's Theatre on 28 February 1861. Chorley mentioned it briefly in his columns, pleased by its success:

> The reasons which precluded any review of Mr. H. Leslie's 'Holyrood' from appearing in the *Athenaeum* apply to 'The Amber Witch' of Mr. Wallace. ... The incidents of the tale present combinations and situations analogous to those of 'La Gazza Ladra'. ... The new scenery is by Mr. Beverley, which announcement renders epithet needless. ... The artists and the composer could not have been better received, nor more enthusiastically applauded. Both, we conceive, have reason to rate 'The Amber Witch' as a real success, so far as their share in the opera is concerned. (2 March 1861: 299-300)

Mapleson recalled with some pride that the opera owed its existence to his managerial support.[71]

Chorley was pleased that Wallace's music was in the French operatic tradition; he emphasized that tradition, and its relevance to *The Amber Witch*, the following year in a review of *Love's Triumph* by Wallace and Planché:

> There is a consistent style in 'Love's Triumph' — such a style as befits a French Court-story — showing an advance on that of his 'Maritana,' or 'Matilda,' or 'Lurline,' or 'Amber Witch.' The style is French. Has it ever (by the way) been sufficiently admitted that a leaven of this very marked style may be traced throughout the

> whole modern world of European Opera? — that French
> effect is half the secret of even Signor Verdi's *cabalettas*,
> with their skips and their syncopations and their sur-
> prises? — that the one single tune in Herr Wagner's
> Mediæval 'Lohengrin,' where *Elsa's* maidens disrobe her
> on her bridal night, might have been signed "Adolphe
> Adam"? — that the chorus opening the second part of
> Schumann's 'Paradise and Peri' resembles a rather dry
> theme by Halévy or M. Ambroise Thomas (treated, we
> admit, canonically)? — How long will it be ere the sug-
> gestive power of France in dramatic musical art is fairly
> recognized? Mr. Wallace, at all events (no doubt partly
> with meritorious regard for local colour), is successfully
> French throughout a large part of 'Love's Triumph.' (8
> November 1862: 599)

Chorley was engaged with oratorio as well as opera. In 1866 he reported the success at the Norwich Festival of Julius Benedict's setting of his text for 'St Cecilia':

> We are spared the necessity of dwelling at length on Mr.
> Benedict's Cantata, 'St. Cecilia,' not merely by circum-
> stances which there is no need to specify [Chorley wrote
> the book], but because our contemporaries have given suf-
> ficient publicity to the intentions of the writer of the
> words, as set forth in his introductory advertisement. ...
> [Sims Reeves sang. Tietjens was St. Cecilia; also Sant-
> ley and Drasdil] The reception of 'St. Cecilia,' we repeat,
> was a genuine triumph. We have rarely seen an audience
> more rapt — more completely and unanimously kindled to
> admiration. (10 November 1866: 614)

From his office at *All the Year Round*, Dickens wrote to congratulate Chorley. He 'heartily rejoiced' in the success of the cantata, and recalled the
'fine dramatic force' of Chorley's words.[72] The following month, Chorley
cited his collaboration with Benedict as an example of the major musical
events of 1866:

> The European musical events of the year may be
> described as under: — At home, the revivals of 'Iphigenia
> in Tauris' and 'Le Nozze,' the success of Mr. Benedict's
> 'Legend of St. Cecilia,' of Mr. Sullivan's Symphony and
> serious Overture, and the real impression made by Herr
> Wilhelmj.[73] The Crystal Palace has kept up its reputation
> as giving the most interesting and best-executed orchestral
> concerts within reach, to the great credit of our London

societies. The attempt to popularize Schumann's music has been earnestly continued. We can but attribute such success as has attended this to the wretched dearth of modern music in Germany. No new singer who deserves to bear the name of an artist has appeared, save Mdlle. Orgeni. ... On the whole, the year just over, though busy enough, cannot be called a rich one. (29 December 1866: 885)

Unfortunately, a later collaboration begun with Benedict ended with hard feelings between poet and composer. Benedict was not satisfied with the words provided by Chorley for *St Peter*, an oratorio to be performed at the Birmingham Festival, 1870. He turned to Joseph Bennett, saying that the libretto was his to do what he pleased — he had paid Chorley £80 for it — and what he pleased was to have it revised. Bennett agreed that the libretto needed extensive rewriting — everything except the opening scene — and, after consulting with his mentor (and Chorley's rival critic) Davison, agreed to do the job. 'Chorley was, of course, informed of all this, and great was his indignation, great also was the display of it' (Bennett, *Forty Years of Music*, 58).

After the performance of *St Peter* in Birmingham, Chorley 'opened fire', in signed letters to the *Athenæum* deploring the changes made to his libretto. To discuss what their response should be, Bennett and Davison arranged to dine with Benedict in Manchester Square. Bennett and Davison drafted a letter to the *Athenæum*, then pressured Benedict to sign it. The intensity of the paper war then increased, with Gruneisen (Bennett habitually writes 'Grüneison') taking Chorley's side in objecting to the changes, and Davison and Bennett vehemently defending them. The tempest subsided finally when Benedict appealed to Bennett in October 1870, asking that Bennett and Davison 'grant my request to leave old Chorley, with all his misstatements and even falsehoods, alone' (quoted in *Forty Years*, 61). Compassion for 'old Chorley' was not Benedict's sole motivation in seeking to end the press war: he was alarmed that the quarrel could lead to a misunderstanding with Costa, whose goodwill he needed. 'I am most anxious if possible not to increase my enemies', he pleaded (*Forty Years*, 61).

Not all of Chorley's creativity was directed at writing texts for music.[74] In 1866 Chorley's final novel, *The Prodigy*, appeared. Dickens had considered it for *All the Year Round*; deciding against publishing it, he wrote to the publishers Chapman and Hall on 28 January 1865 enthusiastically recommending it to them:

> I have at the office, the MS of a novel by Mr. Chorley.
> I have been for some time considering it, with a view to

> its publication in *All the Year Round*. At length I have
> come to the conclusion that the story so turns itself as that
> it could hardly be held in hand by some readers, if it were
> published in small serial portions. But it is so far beyond
> my expectations in respect to merit and variety, and it has
> such remarkable and new pictures of student and profes-
> sional life in Germany — as well as here — that I can
> very strongly recommend it to you as well worth your
> consideration. It has an excellent name (The Prodigy, or
> the Adventures of a Prodigy), and is full of character and
> incident. My doubt of it as a serial does *not* apply to it as
> a book. If on my warranty, you would like to see it, I will
> tell Mr. Chorley that I have taken it upon myself to sub-
> mit it to your firm.[75]

The novel was, appropriately, dedicated 'to Charles Dickens, Esq., As a
Poor Expression of Admiration, Gratitude, and Affection, on the Part of
the Author'.

The three volumes relate the fortunes of a genius — a musician (pianist
and composer) — and his difficult relations with other people, who variously injure, betray, disappoint or, occasionally, try to help him. The narrative centres consistently on Charles Einstern himself — he is 'our hero'
(3: 87) the musical prodigy — and how the Prodigy is affected — usually
hurt — by the insensitivity, selfishness, malice, or thoughtlessness of
others: his mother (Sarah Jane, at first termed Baroness Einstern — her
German husband, the Baron, has died before the novel begins — then
termed Lady Caldermere after her second marriage to a rich English indus-
trialist and newly created Lord). She is seen as betraying him by contract-
ing a second marriage with a rich man who is hostile to him. His childhood
sweetheart, Susanna Openshaw, is a Quaker who comes to see and
'emancipate' herself from the narrowness of the Friends' mentality. His
friend Becker, a fellow student with him in Germany, poor but honest and
loving, accidentally drowned himself in the first volume. His wife, Marie,
is the sister of this same Becker and a dancer, who he discovers after their
impetuous marriage is too shallow for him to love. His half-brother Adalbert is the illegitimate son of his German father and, like his father, is supposed to be dead before the novel begins but is in fact masquerading first as
'Zuccaglio' and later as 'Dr. Mondor' in order to harm the Prodigy and
avenge himself on the Prodigy's mother, Sarah Jane/Baroness Ein-
stern/Lady Caldermere, because when Adalbert was a child she favoured
her own children, especially her Prodigy.

A few worthy minor characters wish the Prodigy well. His brother Justin
is a faithful friend, although for a time Charles mistakenly thinks his
brother shares the hostile attitude of their stepfather, Lord Caldermere.

There is also Dr Orelius, the German Rector in whose house the Prodigy lived before he was expelled from the music school for 'profligacy of conduct' (1: 186), and Colonel Vandaleur, revealed as the true owner of the Caldermere mansion and estate. A host of additional minor characters function frequently as commenting characters, observing the foibles of both high society and Quakers.

The Prodigy is narrated straightforwardly by a single 'omniscient' narrator and thus is unburdened by the story-within-a-story rambling style which Chorley adopted — awkwardly — during his fascination with 'Paul Bell' as a narrator and pseudo-author for *Roccabella*. The plotting and the style are melodramatic (there are several fatal or nearly fatal knife attacks; one character's features reveal the 'terror of one convulsed by the sudden sight of some supernatural vision' (2: 179).

Chorley's career-long interest in the '*Kunst-roman*', which he mentioned in his preface to *Conti the Discarded* (1835), led nowhere intellectually, beyond certain broadly conceived stereotypes. Artists are sensitive, easily irritated by others, moody, and good-looking. They are not appreciated by the rich who pay them to perform at private parties but don't listen carefully. Thus *The Prodigy* is not 'a novel of music', *pace* its subtitle, but, more conventionally, a novel of adventures experienced by a musician. Chorley created plot opportunities to engage musical issues, then ignored or bypassed them. At a party, for example, it is annouced that Grisi will sing. A few pages later it is announced that she has sung — so much for Grisi's appearance (2: 273; 3: 11). Her cameo appearance serves only to show that the party is an expensive one for the hostess, like Pasta's appearance in chapter 51 of Thackeray's *Vanity Fair*.

Elsewhere the narrator suggests that music is undervalued in England by stating that a character agrees with the 'old-fashioned English idea which prevailed so universally at the commencement of this century, that so lovely an art [music] was unworthy the attention of a man'. (1: 216) When the Prodigy astounds his audiences with his playing of Weber's 'Concert Stück', the narration uses stock phrases of generalized response:

> Every musician knows what can be made of this glorious
> work by one having poetry at his heart and fire in his fin-
> gers; — every listener can recollect some lucky evening
> when composer, player, and audience, have had each a
> share in the complete rapture — every human creature,
> save the envious and sour, has some time or other yielded
> to the generous enchantments of youth and promise ... (1:
> 159)

The use of stock phrases and stereotypes extends from music to failed marriages: 'The outside world does not reckon what it is for women and men to live on, and to approach age, without the attachment of friends and kindred' (1: 122). A Colonel from Kentucky (later 'Major Kentucky Browne') is a little like the hypocritically self-righteous Americans in Dickens's *Martin Chuzzlewit*, and also like the American society-obsessed reporter in *Vanity Fair*, obsequiously fawning on rank and fashion. His vulgar 'twang' and misplaced self-confidence are alike mocked, and when his obtuse social-climbing is checked (temporarily), he complacently remarks on 'the insolent manners of the British aristocracy' (1: 127). Stereotypes of womanly behaviour are evoked perfunctorily. When the Prodigy learns that his flighty wife is pregnant, he muses that her pregnancy may be a 'redeeming, rescuing, ripening influence, so fearfully wanted by that wayward, worldly creature!' (2: 245). A woman spiritually empty, hurting her husband, in need of a redeeming event is used as if anticipating (simplistically) Eliot's treatment of Rosamund in *Middlemarch* (1872), just as the character Rosamond in his previous novel, *Roccabella* (1859) had been given a yearning to be socially useful like Dorothea Brooke.

Several characters in the novel express anti-semitic stereotypes. When Meshek, 'an Israelite broker — a man of questionable repute', (1: 142) first appears, the Prodigy calls him a 'miserable creature' before 'spitting in the Jew's face' (the Prodigy has been pawning items to raise money to give to his friend Becker; Meshek, wondering if the items were stolen, reports him to Dr Orelius [1: 143]). Various characters identify Meshak's Jewishness with his baseness ('Sunk to keep company with a Jew!' [2: 72]; 'a Hebrew man ... kept his eyes fixed on the boy, ... Red wicked eyes they were' [1: 262]; 'a cunning Jew fellow' [3: 214]). When a character asks if the Prodigy is perhaps interested in investing his money, the Prodigy's self-congratulatory reply is: 'I have done with investing, since I promised dear old Orelius to have nothing more to do with the tribe of Meshek' (2: 17).[76] Another Jewish character is stereotyped as vulgar in Chapter 3, Part the Third ('Ears and Eyes at Baden-Baden'). It opens with an interesting balance of voices (anticipating in some respects the opening of Eliot's *Daniel Deronda*) and evokes the excitement and potential moral danger of a fashionable gambling resort. The newly-introduced, unnamed character is identified as 'the Hebrew female' (1: 248), 'the Hebrew maiden' (1: 253), and the 'Hebrew damsel' (1: 262); she is 'shrill and voluble at dinner' (1: 262). She returns later in the novel, finally (after converting to Christianity) given a name. As Countess Baltakis, rich beyond description, she gives parties attended by the well born and well connected. Like Melnotte's party in the opening section of Trollope's *The Way We Live Now* (1873),[77] her party 'shows' that enough money buys fashionable friends.

> Everybody agreed that Countess Baltakis was the most
> insufferable and vulgar woman in London. Every one,
> nevertheless, went to her parties; every one, on being

seen there, declared that she or he was there "only just for once, out of curiosity."

> Since the daughter of Israel had displayed herself at Baden, many changes had come over her. She had cast off the faith of her fathers with amazing intrepidity: and with her own face staring at herself in the glass, would talk of "those Jews" with as brave and distant a disdain as the most acrimonious of bleak Christians could have shown. ... Their house was a show ... [and was] of its size, the most perfect mansion in Babylon. (2: 264-6)

People tell themselves they go just 'out of curiosity' (2: 265), although a character remarks that 'we know of old that the Hebrews have a preference for what is tawdry' (2: 273). As a throwaway character Countess Baltakis is needed for gambling and party scenes. After a riot at the opera house,[78] the Prodigy's wife is in a life-threatening fit, and Countess Baltakis sends flowers and fruit — showing 'feeling in her own way' (3: 244), and earning a final dismissal from a minor character as 'a good creature, though coarse — and patronizes the Arts: when only one understands how to manage her' (3: 272).

In the *Athenæum*, John Doran, who had reviewed *Thirty Years' Musical Recollections* so enthusiastically, was gentle, but unimpressed:

> A generation has passed away, one-and-thirty years have been added to the account of Time, since we noticed Mr. Chorley's 'Sketches of a Seaport Town,' and later in the same year, 1835, his 'Conti the Discarded,' and other tales.
>
> Ten years subsequently, in 1845, Mr. Chorley published his 'Pomfret,' which exhibited progress in style, in imaginative power, and in conception as well as execution. In the following year, if we remember rightly, he produced his 'Roccabella,' anonymously [actually 1859, not 1846]. ... [T]here is genuine honest aim to achieve a certain perfection; and if he falls short of this, a good word is due to him for the earnestness of his attempt. ... Thus, trusting to our impressions, we should not be disposed to rank 'A Prodigy' so high as 'Pomfret'; but there are many traces of the quality which distinguished 'Pomfret' in every chapter of 'A Prodigy.' ... [As in his other works:] Whenever the writer leaves his maxims, or even his story, to deal with music, with the science, or with its professors, and to sketch some enthusiast in song or instrumental harmony, he at once arrests attention,

> secures the interest of his readers, and wins applause.
> With music we may include the drama. (529)

Hewlett thought that as 'a novel with a purpose' it 'may be thought to have failed' (2: 179). Doran's complaint that the hero seems a 'fool' was understandable.

Sour and disillusioned, throughout the 1860s he continued to live a bachelor life in the tiny house at 13 Eaton Place, in Belgravia, cared for by his servants. Though he continued to give his dinner parties, his emotional isolation and its accompanying self-pity increased, as various moaning letters attested.

To many he seemed absurd. Certainly he was an easy target for ridicule. He continued to wear the bright yellow and blue clothes of his youth well into a period when everyone else had stopped doing so. Many of Chorley's contemporaries remarked on his red hair and his red, or brick-coloured, complexion. Charles Lamb Kenney, a fellow critic and translator, was the source of the widely-reported cruel witticism about Chorley: 'everything was red about him but his books' (Bennett, *Forty Years of Music*, 307). His voice caused some to ridicule him as 'falsetto Chorley'. Turgenev, who knew him reasonably well, wrote to Viardot's daughter in 1869 that he looked terrible:

> He is fantastically ugly, more so than ever ... His face is
> completely covered now with little red or purplish-blue
> pimples, each with white icing on the top; they radiate out
> in all directions from his nose, which looks as if it were
> alight like a fire. (quoted in Waddington, *Turgenev in
> England*, 140)

R.C. Lehmann, son of Frederick and Nina Lehmann, vividly remembered how ludicrous Chorley appeared to him when he was a child:

> His eyes blinked and twinkled as he spoke; and his quaint
> pecking gestures and high staccato voice made an impres-
> sion which caused one of his friends to describe him as
> the missing link between the chimpanzee and the cock-
> atoo. (*Memories*, 228)

If it was indeed a witty 'friend' who described him as 'the missing link between the chimpanzee and the cockatoo', one may be sure that Chorley's enemies had no difficulty inventing still less flattering descriptions.

Twenty years earlier, Elizabeth Barrett had fretted over him; now it was Nina Lehmann's turn. In February, 1867, Chorley's bitterness was discussed by the Lehmanns — Frederick had less patience with him than Nina.

Writing from St. Jean de Luz, Nina Lehmann analysed Chorley's lonely situation to her husband, and counselled compassion:

> I had a letter to-day from Chorley. I enclose it for your strictly private inspection, then burn it. Poor fellow! you must only smile at his morbid vanity, and not be angry at it. I have answered it, and will quote bits to you that are answers to some of his statements. Of Madame Schumann, and of her admirers dropping him, I say I don't believe for a minute people that like Madame S. would give him up or like him less — why should they? ... I am sorry poor Chorley demeans himself to so much unmanly spite sometimes; but such is my pity for him and my old-standing feeling of affection and tolerance, that I never for a moment bear him a grudge; and for my sake be good, be lenient, to the lonely, much-forsaken, affection-seeking (and so seldom-finding) old man. Think, he is going on for sixty now, and only by his dinners can he gain or hold for an instant the least regard. To me all his vanity is most pathetic. So, for my sake, I say it again, be good to him, and pay him some little attention which will make him think you care a bit for him. Will you? (February 1867; Lehmann, *Memories*, 192-3).

In the summer of 1867, Chorley's brother, John Rutter Chorley, died. With his remaining brother, William Brownsword Chorley, he seems to have had relatively little contact. The money he inherited, added to the money he already had, meant Chorley no longer needed to work for a living. It was at last possible to retire.

In August, 1868, Chorley gave a retirement dinner at Wembley Hill. In a few words Chorley paid tribute to the workers in the publishing office. 'Not a single angry word or doubtful transaction had passed on either side' during the past thirty-five years, he said, and he thanked his colleagues 'with all his heart for their prompt and courteous punctuality, which had made not the easiest of tasks a comparatively light one' (Hewlett, 2: 213). His 'few kindly words of parting' were delivered not by Chorley himself but by the publisher of the *Athenæum*, John Francis, on his behalf.

The delicate state of Chorley's health kept him away from the party in his honour.

Notes

1.   Chorley commended Galitzin because in 1861-62 his 'entertainments' introduced Glinka's music to London: 'But for Glinka's incurably

debauched habits, which brought him prematurely to the grave, he might have established a school of Russian opera as individual as the schools of Italy, France and Germany' (*Athenæum*, 5 September 1863: 314).

2. Virginia Gabriel was a composer of popular ballads, "most simple and melodious" (Simpson, 145).

3. MS Liverpool Record Office, 920 SAN 1/8.

4. Irvine and Honan, 372, quoting *Dearest Isa*, 19 April 1860: 61.

5. Chorley also reviewed *Last Poems* by Mrs Browning, 29 March 1862: 421-2.

6. He was more sensitive to arbitrary concluding *rondos* when his own *Amber Witch* was required to have one, writing in the *Athenæum* that 'We are requested to state that the sprightly final *rondo*, which immediately succeeds to incidents so serious, was placed there in disregard of the protest of the arranger of the *libretto* [Chorley himself] ...' (2 March 1861: 299).

7. George Linley's hostile satire of Chorley in 1862 cited this review as an example of Chorley's bad character. He stated that Bunn had befriended Chorley by producing his *Brides of Venice* in 1844 (music by Benedict) and this obituary was Chorley's ungrateful return for Bunn's kindness:

> Praised, flattered, toadied by this Janus, Bunn
> Consented that his Opera should be done,
> And lent his skilful aid to make ship-shape
> The anti-English gibberish of an ape;
> But scarce could Bunn or Benedictus save
> Those Brides of Venice from a watery grave;
> For never, since Minerva oped her portal,
> Was verse so clogged with earth — so *un*-immortal;
> Time has elapsed — the waves still lash the shore —
> The managerial Lion is no more!
> The scribbling Ingrate, to the service blind
> That Bunn had wrought him, like one of his kind,
> Turns round, and, with a loud, defiant bray,
> Exults o'er his good Angel turned to clay,
> Maligns him in his journal of the day.
> O! worse than Judas! when thy sands run low,
> May other mercy then on thee bestow,
> The mercy that thy venom ne'er did show! (Linley, 13-14)

George Biddlecombe attributed the libretto of *The Brides of Venice* not to Chorley but to Bunn and Benedict (Biddlecombe, 334).

8. One stereotype of the conflict between the two houses had it that the old-fashioned aristocratic audience stayed at Her Majesty's Theatre,

while the forward looking, up-to-date music lovers moved to Covent Garden. Shirley Brooks's essay, 'The Opera', an example of pro-Lumley writing, stressed the high social position of Lumley's audiences. Brooks described two visits: at the first visit, during Laporte's management, he naively thought the house and the audience 'brilliant', but a barrister acquaintance pointed out all the low people (12). Years later, he attended *La Sonnambula* 'on a Jenny Lind night' (13) with 'a young lady who had never visited' Her Majesty's Theatre before. They witnessed an audience 'jewelled by that unrivalled beauty' which English aristocrats have, the 'gorgeous scenic displays of Grieve or Marshall' and 'a perfect chorus and orchestra' (16) (in Smith, *Sketches of London Life*, 1859, previously printed in Smith's *Gavarni in London* (1849: 1-6).

9.   Chorley's comrade-in-arms in the war of the late 1840s, Charles Gruneisen, again weighed in with a pamphlet, *The Opera and the Press* (1869), criticizing the artistic management of Covent Garden and comparing it to Lumley's mismanagement of Her Majesty's Theatre. Gruneisen became the music reviewer for the *Athenæum* in 1870, succeeding Cowden Clarke, who had followed Chorley in 1868. As the review of Gruneisen's pamphlet put it in *The Orchestra*: again there is 'operatic monopoly [,] ... heedlessness as to *ensemble*, carelessness as to art, and ingratitude towards Sir Michael Costa', and again the promises of the season's prospectus are not fulfilled (*Orchestra*, 30 July 1869: 295). In 1875, Covent Garden's manager, Frederick Gye, printed a pamphlet, *The Royal Italian Opera and the 'Athenæum' Newspaper*, in which he protested the incessantly negative coverage in the *Athenæum* of performances at Covent Garden:

> Mr. Gye feels that he ought, in justice to the many art-
> istes of his establishment, as well as towards himself,
> to make known to the readers of the "Athenæum" how
> untruthful are the criticisms and how incorrect is the
> information of that paper. (10)

10.   Herman Klein maintained that Patti's career in the second half of the nineteenth century fit this description, despite Chorley's prophecy (Klein, 85 *et passim*).

11.   London's Orfeo in 1860 (not identified by name in *Thirty Years' Musical Recollections*) was Czillag. In the *Athenæum*, of course, Chorley named her, complaining after the season was over 'that such an artist [as Viardot] ... should have been overlooked for one so unequal to the task as Madame Czillag must be signalized as a self-injurious piece of managerial perversity' (1 September 1860: 296).

12.   Wagner's operas were not produced in London during this period covered by *Thirty Years'*, but there were, nevertheless, a few direct

references to them, e.g. '[In this period] singer's-music has been stamped into bits as so much trash, by the Wagners of New Germany ... [and also injured by] the Verdis of infuriate Italy' (2: 320).

13. Chorley's remarks on the often played *Tannhäuser* overture reveal his fondness for pointing out similarities and influences: 'The overture [to Benedict's "Undine"] is delicious as a prelude to a faëry tale of lakes and streams. The opening of the *allegro* may be expressly commended to those who are disposed to be rapturists (Miss Burney's Johnsonian word) over the overture to "Tannhäuser." The effect which Herr Wagner has there tried for is got here. The second subject is elegantly flowing; the third, marked *scherzando* (page 7 of the Piano-forte score) happily fancied as an enhancement — not an intrusion. We know no modern overture better than this' (29 September 1860: 425).

    Several years later, after a performance Mozart's *Entführung* at Her Majesty's Theatre, he compared Mozart's overture to Wagner's:

    Parenthetically, let the passage at the sixty-fourth bar
    [of the overture] be noted as the first example of that
    peculiar effect, which has been made such account of
    in the 'Tannhäuser' Overture, as though it were
    invented by Herr Wagner (7 July 1866: 24)

14. Harold Rosenthal explained that the solo, written for the tenor Tamberlik (singing with the Royal Italian Opera at Covent Garden, whose management would not release him to sing it), was rearranged for the soprano Tietjens. She was a member of Mapleson's company and therefore available for the assignment (Rosenthal, ed. *Mapleson Memoirs*, footnote to 37).

15. Tongue in cheek, Henry Lunn maintained that young singers would soon refuse to sing bass roles since composers always made them villains. ('A Plea for Operatic Basses' in Lunn, 176-9).

16. One of three letters from Santley's father to Chorley which exist as drafts in the collection of the Liverpool Public Library, showing various corrections and additions. The final fair copies as sent to Chorley have not survived.

17. The letter was not dated, but the draft of the letter from Santley's father dated 20 November 1857 presumably refers to the same 'trial'.

18. MS, Liverpool Record Office, 920 SAN 1/5.

19. MS, Liverpool Record Office, 920 SAN 1/3/4.

20. He sang 'All' invito generoso' from Rossini's *Maometto Secondo*, and 'If Thou should'st mark iniquities' from Costa's oratorio *Eli* (Santley, 147).

21. 'Miss K' was presumably Santley's future wife, Gertrude Kemble.

22. In Balfe's *Armourer of Nantes* (Pyne-Harrison 'Royal English Opera')

Santley was 'hazardly using the upper notes of his voice. No strength will hold out after a time against such mistaken practice' (21 February 1863: 268).

23. Interestingly, *From Mendelssohn to Wagner* (1912), the account of the career of J.W. Davison written by his son, was 'Dedicated With Grateful and Affectionate Regard to Sir Charles Santley, K.S.G. By Henry Davison'.

24. 'The world was all before them, where to choose', Milton, *Paradise Lost*, 12: 646.

25. 'The *New York Herald* gives a great account of the success, at the Italian Opera there, of Signora Adelina Patti, the fourth daughter of Madame Barilli, a singer who had some renown in her time. On every account we hope the tale may prove true' (*Athenæum*, 'Musical and Dramatic Gossip', 24 December 1859: 858).

26. In 1920, Herman Klein made a similar point about early reports of Patti's success in US newspapers: 'Sixty years ago there existed a much wider disparity between American and English standards of operatic criticism [than today]. ... English critics of that day were wont to judge singers from a far loftier and more exacting standpoint' (Klein, 67).

27. Grisi joined Mario in a tour of the provinces under Mapleson's management beginning in January, 1866. The state of Grisi's voice emboldened Mapleson and her to decide on a reappearance at Her Majesty's Theatre, almost twenty years after she had last sung there. Her appearance in *Lucrezia Borgia* (5 May 1866), however, did not go well: Mapleson recalled that in Act 2 'she made an unsuccessful attempt to reach the A natural; and the failure caused her much confusion. ... The notices next morning were sufficiently favourable; but it was evident that the career of the great vocalist was now, indeed, at an end' (Rosenthal, *Mapleson Memoirs*, 1966, 63). Chorley's report of Grisi's one-night return was more severe:

> The appearance of Madame Grisi this day week must have been felt by the lady herself, as it was by all her zealous friends — grateful for the many years of great enjoyment afforded them by her — to be a complete mistake. Her engagement, it is understood, has been cancelled. (12 May 1866: 642)

Mario sang on. His final performances at Covent Garden were in July, 1871, when he was 62 years old. Gruneisen, now writing music criticism for the *Athenæum*, reported that in *Les Huguenots* 'Amidst a hurricane of cheering, after repeated realls before the curtain, the most popular artists of his age finally withdrew from his public career on the 19th of July, 1871' (22 July 1871: 121). Praising him for his acting, no longer for his voice, Gruneisen wrote, 'Let the sad scenes of 1871 be forgotten' (121). One week later, reviewing the season, he added, Chorley-like, that 'It is not agreeable to dwell on the final representations of Signor Mario' (*Athenæum*, 29 July 1871: 152). In the same performance, Patti's Valentine was a 'failure' because 'her physical powers were not equal to the calls upon the upper notes which Valentina has to sustain, and not to touch merely' (22 July 1871: 121).

28. He continued:

> For instance, throughout her first sleep-walking scene she soliloquized in full voice till the moment when the weary girl lies down to repose. — This was, to our thinking, the best part of her performance. In the rest of it there was nothing to displease, but we failed to discern traces of that sensibility which marks the distance betwixt talent and genius, no matter what the physical means be. In short, we cannot feel so sure, as the world on every side for the moment is, that another first-class artist, or one who may become such, has appeared. "Time tries all." If Mdlle. Patti do prove the *rara avis* so long desired — if the sensation of Tuesday be justified in her coming performances — so much the better for all who hear and for all who write on music. (670)

29. Statira and Roxalana, characters in Nathaniel Lee's *The Rival Queens* (1677).

30. The importance of these *Don Giovanni* performances was noted at the time, but understandably seemed even more impressive as years went on. From the vantage point of 1920, Herman Klein summarized the awe-inspiring position they occupied in the minds of some:

> For years did musical writers, members of the *vieille garde*, descant upon the glories of this great cast. In the days of the writer's youth it was still recalled with tender regret, as a treasured memory, as in a sense the operatic *clou* of the mid-Victorian era. And, indeed, it was never equalled as a galaxy of famous singers of that period. Even the fast-diminishing vocal strength of Grisi did not detract from the dramatic grandeur of her *Donna Anna*. Csillag, too, was a fine singer; she was considered the best *Donna Elivira* of her day. Faure, the renowned French baritone ... was just arriving at the summit of his powers [Don Giovanni]. (Klein, 85)

Patti was Zerlina, Tamberlik was Ottavio, Ronconi was Masetto,

Formes was Leporello, and Tagliafico was the Commendatore. Costa conducted.

31.   Originally published anonymously; attribution from the *All the Year Round* office book (Oppenlander, 252). Klein, who maintained that Chorley attacked Patti unfairly, reprinted these paragraphs, with a few omissions (Appendix I: 414-15), dating them 'December, 1861'. He inadvertently misused them as evidence that Dickens, like everyone except Chorley, admired Patti extravagantly. The paragraphs belie Klein's claim, however, since they were presumably written by Chorley, not by Dickens.

32.   Klein noted that these same critics (Desmond Ryan, Henry Lincoln, Sutherland Edwards, Davison)

> witness[ed] the gradual disappearance of every blemish that had at first evoked their adverse criticism. As a matter of fact, in the course of two or three seasons they ceased to entirely "pick holes"; and it is not only reasonable but fair to assume that they did so because by degrees they perceived no more holes to pick. In other words, by dint of assiduous study the youthful artist contrived to rid herself of her imperfections, one by one, until at last perfection alone remained. (Klein, 69)

He singled out Chorley as a foe, one who 'appeared to have regretted the utterance of a single kind word' about Patti after her debut (82). In fact, Chorley was, on the whole, an admirer of Patti's singing. For further comments on press reactions to Patti's debut and initial seasons see Klein, Chapters 6 and 7 (esp. 52-90), and Cone, 47-54.

33.   See, for example, *Athenæum*, 21 April 1866: 536.

34.   The 'new "school" of Wagner and Schumann', as Hueffer noted (68) was discussed favourably (for perhaps the first time) in 'Lyric Feuds', *Westminster Review*, July 1867. Chorley tended to criticize Liszt less vehemently, although he was part of the new school, perhaps because of his fond personal memories of Liszt's charm and their friendly intercourse in the 1840s.

35.   In general, he commended Covent Garden's production:

> Gluck, it is true, will possibly never be such a "bright particular star" in the world of fashionable *dilettantism* as the "Verdi of the minute," but the lovers of the great classical masters, those who frequent the shrines of Handel, Mozart, and Beethoven (a large and increasing public), will rejoice in the new pleasure now set before them. — The Covent Garden version of 'Orfeo' is virtually the one digested and arranged for

> the *Théâtre Lyrique*. ... Madame Penco is better as *Eurydice* than she has been in any former part. ... It is true that Madame Czillag, the *Orfeo*, must be credited with good intentions: having taken, we cannot but think, Madame Viardot's wonderful impersonation of the character for her model; but fascination is wanting to her voice. ... [and] she is not equal to the requirements of 'Orfeo.' (*Athenæum*, 7 July 1860: 33)

("'Twere all one / That I should love a bright particular star / And think to wed it, he is so above me.' *All's Well that Ends Well*, Act 1, Scene 1).

36. The published libretto (printed by J. Mitchell) to *Iphigenia in Tauris* states that the opera, with English words by Chorley, was 'performed at Dudley House, London, Wednesday, July 11, 1860'.

37. For specific musical examples of Viardot's performance of the role, see Fauquet (189-253).

38. It was less promising for those involved: the artistic relations between Berlioz and Viardot were deteriorating at this time (Fitzlyon, 345-62).

39. Both have been treated by later writers with disdain: Norman Demuth, for example, stated that Chorley and Davison were the first professional music critics, then added: 'There is no doubt about their loves, hates, and utter ineptitude for the task' (Demuth, xx).

40. According to Bourne:

> At the close of 1854 the circulation of 'The Morning Chronicle' averaged only about 2,500, while that of 'The Morning Post' was about 3,000, that of 'The Morning Herald' about 3,500, that of 'The Daily News' about 5,300, that of 'The Morning Advertiser' about 6,600, and that of 'The Times' about 55,000. The circulation of 'The Times' was thus nearly thrice that of the five other papers put together. ... (2: 159)

41. For Manns's programming of Schubert's works, see Musgrave, 96-8 *et passim*. Chorley's reaction to newly heard music by Schubert was generally very favourable.

42. Graves, 170, footnote 1. His story is implausible. There is nothing unusual about the two chords in the eighth measure (they are first inversion c minor and f minor triads). Moreover, Chorley discussed Schumann's Quintet on several occasions in ways inconsistent with a claim that he walked out when it was played. On 6 December 1862, for example, Chorley mentioned the performance of the quintet at Monday's Popular Concert:

> This work is still among the list of things, the value of which is debated in this country, and therefore should

have been tried while the attention of the audience was fresh [instead of being played at the end]. For this reason, having spoken of it before, we will not return to it till it is given again, which we understand may be the case. (741)

Less than two months later, he heard the Quintet again:

Our own impressions are, that whatever be the amount of aspiration conceded to Schumann, in his best works, he was deficient in fancy, and audacious, not only in taking, but also in making, those liberties, which can but be pardoned in consideration of consummate genius. ... Further, Schumann's taste in harmony is, throughout, impure — showing a perverse leaning to the use of those extreme chords and suspenses which are useful to give piquancy and heighten effect, but are no more admissible when employed as the universal medium of carrying on a movement from point to point than would be Cayenne pepper showered over a bill of fare from the soup to the dessert. So that, to sum up, our impressions stated last week have undergone no change in consequence of Monday's experience. ... (24 January 1863: 123-4)

And five years later he commented courteously on Madame Schumann's devotion to her husband's memory after still another performance of the Quintet at the Popular Concert on Monday:

At Monday's *Popular Concert* was given Schumann's Pianoforte Quintett, rather in propitiation of Madame Schumann (we suspect) than because the composition has really taken root here. Dislike for this music must be separated from the thorough sympathy every generous person feels for the devotion of a widow to the memory of the husband in whom she believed. (*Athenæum*, 8 February 1868: 221)

43.   Davison noted the earlier performance on 4 April 1853:

On that date, at the second concert of the Philharmonic Society, [Schumann's] Overture, Scherzo and Finale in E were played under Costa's bâton with but little success. (Davison, 182)

44.   Part one appeared 22 October 1864: 245-64; part two appeared 5 November 1864: 294-300. For discussion see Bledsoe, 'Dickens and Chorley', 159-61.

45. Oppenlander attributed the article to Chorley on the basis of this comment (253). Edgar Johnson stated that 'there is no indication that [Dickens] ever heard of Wagner' (2: 1130), a statement not supported by the publication of these articles in *All The Year Round*.

46. In another article about music, not specifically about opera, 'Music About Music' in two parts (*All the Year Round*, 9 March 1867: 256-9; 16 March 1852: 280-82), the author refers to 'the reign of Decay, began by Schumann, and continued by the usurpation of Delirium, under Herr Wagner's sceptre' (281). That this article too may by Chorley's is suggested by its praise for Viardot's Orphée (9 March 1867: 257), its praise for the setting of 'the "Orpheus" song' (16 March 1867: 282) [i.e. Shakespeare's lyric from *Henry VIII*, 'Orpheus with his lute'] by Arthur Sullivan, a friend of Chorley's, and its praise for Henrietta Sontag's performance in Auber's setting of Scribe's libretto 'L'Ambassadrice' (281), also praised by Chorley in his *Athenaeum* columns.

47. This reference to the article on the Carlsruhe Festival (i.e. to 'Old, New, and No Music') is one reason to believe that Chorley was its author. Three others are:
    1. the congruence of the comments about the importance of French opera with Chorley's opinions as consistently expressed in the weekly columns of the *Athenaeum* since the 1830s.
    2. the reference to the Orphée of 'that matchless artist among modern singers: — Madame Viardot' (part two, 15 July 1852: 583).
    3. the following reference to Mendelssohn: 'It was among his many unfulfilled plans, cut short by early death, to write an opera based on Shakespeare's Winter's Tale; and, in a letter on the subject which exists, besides due regard to the interest of Hermione and Perdita, an anxious wish is expressed that Autolycus shall be well seen after'. (part one, 8 July 1852: 575)
    The librettist of Mendelssohn's projected opera based on Shakespeare's *Winter's Tale* was to have been Chorley himself, who, as its recipient, would be in a position to refer to an unpublished letter 'which exists'. The letter may no longer exist, but several letters from Chorley to Mendelssohn about the possibility of collaborating on *A Winter's Tale* are in the 'Green Books' in the Bodleian Library, Oxford.

48. I assume this article was written by Chorley for the following reason: Chorley reported in a signed article (having retired from the journal's staff the year before, he no longer wrote anonymously) in the

Athenaeum (11 September 1869: 347-8) on the 'full dress stage rehearsal' of *Das Rheingold* at Munich (347). His sentiments were exactly the same as those expressed in *All the Year Round*, down to spotting the resemblances to Mendelssohn's *Melusine* overture and to Meyerbeer's *Robert le Diable* ('coolly appropriated by the unblushing insulter of Judaism in music!', 348). The report prompted a response from Walter Bache defending Wagner (*Athenaeum*, 18 September 1869: 378), the substance of which was in turn attacked by Chorley in the issue of 25 September 1869 (410-11).

49. Chorley's successor as the music reviewer for the *Athenaeum* was C.L. Gruneisen, whose review of that performance was largely favourable: 'The Music of the Future is still an open question in this country. If Wagner will produce another "Fliegende Holländer" there would be unanimity in musical Europe, and his return to the legitimate school of the lyric drama would be heartily welcomed' (30 July 1870: 154). The Dutchman of the production, Charles Santley, recalled in his memoirs that 'Wagner ... failed to attract the public. We only played it two or three nights, and to very poor houses' (285). But Davison remembered the occasions as 'a distinct success' (291).

50. Kellogg also stated her views on the Musical England question: 'But I believe from the bottom of my heart that, inherently and permanently, the English are an unmusical people. They do not like fire, nor passion, nor great moments in either life nor art' (Kellogg, 136).

51. Chorley may have been thinking of the falling out between Gounod and Viardot in 1852: Turgenev wrote to Viardot on 31 March 1864: 'I dislike the man more than ever. ... He is surrounded by a shell as resistant to the truth as that which surrounds kings. And then there is also the ooze of the erotic priest that bubbles to the surface ... I cannot stomach it!' (quoted in Huebner, 29, from Turgenev, *Nouvelle correspondance inédite*, ed. Alexandre Zviguilsky, 2 vols, Paris, 1971-72, i: 120-22).

52. MS, Harry Ransom Humanities Research Center, University of Texas at Austin.

53. MS HM 17584, Huntington Library, San Marino, California.

54. Morley characterized the performance of Tietjens at Her Majesty's Theatre as presenting a 'real' conception of the opera, that of Miolan-Carvahlo at Covent Garden as an 'ideal conception' — representing 'not so much the girl as the girl's soul' (Morley, 256).

55. By coincidence, in the same month when Chorley was proudly recalling his discovery of Gounod, he learned of, and related with indignant sarcasm, the plans by Wagner, 'the *Dalai-Lama* of opera', to conduct a 'colossal musical and dramatic festival about once in three years'. For this festival, 'colossal temporary theatres are to be

built ... and all the greatest artists ... are to be convened to display ... the splendour and genius of Herr Wagner's four *Nibelungen* operas!' (29 August 1863: 281).

56. Chorley announced in 'Musical and Dramatic Gossip' that Her Majesty's Theatre would use 'the English version prepared four years ago by Mr. Henry F. Chorley (Chappel & Co.)' (9 January 1864: 45).

57. Herman Kline wrote in 1920 that Chorley is 'best known to the present generation' by this translation; he termed it 'inept and commonplace' (Klein, 81).

58. As Budden noted, Verdi took a theme from the overture to *Stiffelio* to use for the tenor aria, 'Sotto il sole di Siria', when Verdi remade the earlier opera into *Aroldo*.

> The practice of keeping a neutral melody in hand in your overture to serve as basis for an additional aria, if one were required, seems to have been fairly common. Instances include Mercadante's *Il Reggente*, where for the Trieste revival a new scene for soprano was quarried from the overture's main theme, and Gounod's *Faust*, where a melody in the prelude was turned into the aria 'Even bravest heart' written for the baritone Charles Santley. (Budden, 2: 342)

59. 'I own the soft impeachment', Sheridan, *The Rivals*, Act V.

60. When Sullivan later wrote operetta music in the 1870s and 1880s, some former supporters were disappointed. Arthur Coleridge, for example, wrote of Sullivan's career bitterly:

> There was a time when Sullivan might have done great service by self-denial and devotion to his profession; in my judgment he forfeits all claim to gratitude of those who were eager to welcome him 20 years ago as the hope of English musicians. (Coleridge, 145)

61. I assume it was this performance to which Frederick Lehmann's brief note, quoted by his son, refers: 'With Dickens at Crystal Palace performance of Sullivan's "Tempest". Walked with Dickens from Crystal Place to Chorley's, 13, Eaton Place'. (Lehmann, *Memories*, 4)

62. Perhaps 'The Emerald Necklace', with libretto by Chorley; not completed (Wyndham, *Sullivan*, 80).

63. On 3 February he wrote to Mrs Story, in Rome, that the winter had been the hardest one he could recollect: 'I have been out of sorts and out of spirits, finding the day's work a very heavy burthen & finishing up with a sprightly fit of rheumatism which appears to have a particular affection for my right hand' (letter dated 27 January/3 February 1864, MS, Univ. of Texas, Austin).

64. MS, Gilbert and Sullivan Collection, Pierpont Morgan Library, New York City.
65. Chorley's spelling, 'Europian' with the 'i' underlined, is presumably a private allusion or joke.
66. MS, Gilbert and Sullivan Collection, Pierpont Morgan Library, New York City.
67. Jenkins: allusion to Rumsey Forster, termed a 'toady', by Thackeray and other *Punch* writers; applied in 1844 by Davison to Gruneisen, a *Morning Post* critic.
68. 'At about this time (1852) he [Sullivan] and Chorley were collaborating in a opera to be entitled *The Sapphire Necklace*, which, however, was eventually found unsuitable for the stage and was abandoned, the music being used by Sullivan in other works' (Wyndham, *Sullivan*, 80).
69. Wife of the nephew of Chorley's childhood friend.
70. The novel had been reviewed favourably in the *Athenæum*, 10 August 1844: 731-2 (no attribution in the marked file).
71. 'As regards English Opera, Macfarren's *Robin Hood* and Wallace's *Amber Witch* owe their very existence to me. It was I who, at Her Majesty's Theatre in 1860-61, brought out both those works which had been specially composed for the theatre' (Mapleson, *Memoirs*, 1888, 1: 283).
72. 7 November 1866, MS, Dickens House, London.
73. August Wilhelmj, German violinist (1845-1908).
74. One of his most popular texts was for a choral song, 'The Long Day Closes', music by Sullivan ('extremely melodious' and 'the conclusion ... is perfectly beautiful', *Musical Times*, 1 November 1868: 574).
75. Quoted from MS in Whitaker Collection, University of North Carolina, in Grubb, 106.
76. In *Genesis*, Meshek was a son of Jacob and Leah (30: 18).
77. Trollope's Madame Melmotte 'was fat and fair, — unlike in colour to our traditional Jewesses; but she had the Jewish nose and the Jewish contraction of the eyes. ... Miss Melmotte [was] very unlike her father or mother, having no traces of the Jewess in her countenance.' Although people said Melmotte was a 'gigantic swindler', nevertheless, because he was rich, 'a Royal Prince, a Cabinet Minister, and the very cream of duchesses were going to his wife's ball' (*The Way We Live Now*, chapter 4: Madame Melmotte's Ball).
78. Most of the ethnic slurs in the novel are anti-Semitic, but Kentucky Browne describes this riot as 'All those Italians screaming and making a noise like so many niggers at a frolic!' (3: 162). Chorley had him say this, I believe, to indicate that not only the English characters were bigoted.

CHAPTER EIGHT

A Gentleman of Independent Means:
Sick, Drunk, and Lonely

In 1868, Chorley carefully prepared his will. His first bequest was to Dickens: £50 'for a ring, in memory of one greatly helped by him'. A second bequest for a ring was to Costa. He left an annuity of £300 to his brother William Brownsword Chorley, another of £200 to 'Mary Dickens, the eldest daughter of said Charles Dickens', and another of £100 to Stephen and Mary Brake 'in memory of faithful service faithfully rendered'. The Life Boat Institution was given £600 to build a boat to be named the 'John Rutter Chorley', after the brother whose good opinion meant much to him.

As he settled into retirement, Chorley appeared pitiful to some observers. His drinking was not always sociable and charming. Continuing his frequent visits to the Lehmann family at Woodlands, he sometimes became disoriented, thinking he was at his own home. To their servant he repeatedly gave orders one evening at dinner, and was annoyed when Mrs Lehmann gave an order herself. He behaved even more grotesquely at another dinner which the Lehmanns gave in his honour. Again thinking himself the host, he paid special attention to a Mr Bockett, whom he did not know: 'Take the champagne to Mr. Bockett, please'. After dinner he confided to Mrs Lehmann, 'I shall certainly ask Mr. Bockett again, he's ver-r-y nice'. Later he 'recovered himself, and told us how confused he had been', but then became confused again. (Lehmann, *Memories*, 234).[1]

Dickens, too, saw this side of Chorley. He was moved by the pathetic appearance of his friend when he called on 2 February 1869, as he wrote to Mrs Lehmann:

> I saw Chorley yesterday in his own room. A sad and solitary sight. The widowed Drake,[2] with a certain gin-coherence of manner, presented a blooming countenance and buxom form in the passage; so buxom indeed that she was obliged to retire before me like a modest stopper before I could get into the dining decanter where poor Chorley reposed, like the dregs of last season's last wine. (Lehmann, *Memories*, 104)

During the 1860s it may have been only Nina Lehmann and Charles Dickens who did *not* at some time record their exasperation or irritation with him. He returned their indulgence warmly. Of course, Benson Rathbone's nephew, now a grown man with his own family in Liverpool was a consolation. On 8 December, 1869, Chorley thanked Benson for birthday greetings, and reminded him gently that his birthday was the 15th of December, not the 8th. Anyway, he concluded glumly, 'I doubt much whether I shall see another; but I think I have so arranged my affairs as to give very little trouble to those who are kind enough to administer them' (2: 312). That year Chorley did not plan to go to Gad's Hill for Christmas because his health was too bad. 'Meanwhile', he told Benson, 'keep a warm corner in your heart for me, remembering that you need not be anxious, because if I *really* want help I shall telegraph to you' (2: 313).

Chorley continued to contribute from time to time to periodicals and he wrote, or intended to write, more books. In January, 1870, the *Quarterly Review* published his review-essay on Jane Austen and Mary Russell Mitford, occasioned by the appearance of Austen-Leigh's memoir of Austen and A.G. L'Estrange's selection of Mitford's letters (196-218). He specifically excluded criticism of Austen's novels from the scope of his essay ('it has been well said that it may be taken as a new test of ability whether a person can or cannot appreciate her novels' 196), and recorded anecdotes of her life.[3] Much of the material in this article on Mitford was re-used in 1872, in the last book he published. In the article he contrasted Austen's 'happy' life (204) with Mitford's, who bore nobly the burden of caring for her reckless, worthless father. Like Chorley himself, Mitford had been drawn to the 'loadstone rock' ('to borrow one of Mr. Dickens's happy figures')[4] of play writing (214). He concluded by noting her 'abstinence from self-glorification', which was 'not common' among writers, especially women writers (218).

On 7 June 1870, Dickens wrote one of his cordial notes to 'my dear Chorley'. Chorley wanted to send Dickens a gift, a painting, but did not know the best route to send it. 'London Chatham and Dover will suit perfectly for the picture. I receive many packages by that route', Dickens told him. As editor of *All the Year Round*, he assured Chorley that 'Don Juan is gone to the Printer, who will send a proof to you'. Dickens expressed pleasure in the 'glimpse of hope' Chorley had given about a possible production of one of his plays, signing himself 'ever affectionately, CD'.[5]

For years, Chorley had received many similar notes, casual and kind, from his beloved friend. This was the last one. Two days later Dickens was dead, having collapsed at Gad's Hill at dinner. Chorley's happy days visiting Gad's Hill were over.

Chorley was devastated. He considered himself the invalid whose hold on life was precarious, not Dickens. Although he collected his wits to write an obituary for the *Athenæum,* he was emotionally devastated. Turgenev commented in a letter to Viardot 'What a shock for Chorley! I don't think he will survive it' (Waddington, *Turgenev and England,* 140).

Chorley's obituary outlined Dickens's literary career as 'possibly the most original English writer of English domestic fiction who has ever been seen' (*Athenæum*, 18 June 1870: 804). He took pains to refute the notion that Dickens could not create 'gentlemen and ladies'.[6] He objected, too, to considering Dickens a political radical:

> [T]hough he was by nature and experience a shrewd redresser of abuses — tracing them back to their primal causes — he was in no respect the destroyer it was for awhile the whim of fools of quality to consider him. One who redresses grievances is not, therefore, an overthrower of thrones. The life and works of Dickens expressed a living protest against Disorder — no matter what the Order. (804)

Because Chorley had so often experienced Dickens's generosity and hospitality, his emotional description of Dickens as friend is poignant. He was overcome at his remembrance of the great-hearted host at Gad's Hill, putting guests at their ease:

> Those who were admitted to know Charles Dickens in the intimacy of his own home cannot — without such emotion as almost incapacitates the heart and hand — recall the charm of his bounteous and genial hospitality. Nothing can be conceived more perfect in tact, more freely equal, whatever the rank of his guests, than was his warm welcome. The frank grasp of his hand — the bright smile on his manly face — the cheery greeting — are things not to be forgotten while life and reason last by those who were privileged to share them. ... There was no possibility of anything passing where he was which the most experienced woman or the simplest child might not have heard. There was for every guest, the smallest as the greatest, perfect ease and security in the shelter of his house. (804)

Chorley, like almost every commentator on Dickens, marvelled at the man's focus — 'Whatever he did, he did with all his heart and soul and strength' — and his energy:

> When the story of his life shall come to be told on some distant day, then, and not till then, this amazing vitality, which set him apart from every human being I have approached, will present itself as one of the most remarkable features in the life and works of one of the greatest and most beneficent men of genius England has produced since the days of Shakspeare [*sic*]. (804)

He ended by lamenting the 'miserable incompleteness' of his tribute, suggesting that someday he might publish more about Dickens, but he never did (805).

Chorley asked Dickens's daughter, Mamie, to cut two cedar branches from the trees at Gad's Hill for him as a remembrance of his happy days there. She did so, unaware that he had asked because he intended to have those cedar branches placed in his own coffin.

He survived Dickens's death barely two years. During that time, he corresponded with the publisher Richard Bentley about several literary projects: a book on Mary Russell Mitford, a book on Holbein (based on, or drawing on, Woltmann's German study),[7] and his own memoirs, which were intended to occupy six volumes in two series. The two men were resuming a business relationship that had been active during the 1840s when Chorley wrote numerous articles on miscellaneous subjects for *Bentley's Miscellany*. Bentley had been the publisher of Chorley's first book: *Sketches of a Sea Port Town* (1834).

Letters between the two men discussing these three projects began in the summer of 1870. Chorley wrote to Bentley from the Grand Hotel, Scarborough. Bentley had approached Chorley with an idea involving writing about Dickens. In June, Chorley expressed some interest:

> Your obliging letter of the 24th is one I cannot answer definitively for a few days, though I feel it best to acknowledge it at once. First as to its principal subject, I could not write a word more on it without the sanction of the family of my dear friend Dickens — after the express directions of his will — I cannot tell how far they will wish them wrought out. — Meanwhile, I am glad that the few paragraphs I forced myself to write, appear to have been kindly taken. — I think his wishes & *theirs* should be religiously respected, & I hope that whatever be the temptation of immediate profit, all unauthorized publication will be discouraged as much as possible, by all respectable persons. So soon as I can ascertain their wishes, I will write to you again.

He then turned to Bentley's other proposals:

> The Mitford matter does not press, so far as I am concerned. I have more to complete than I may have strength to do. This place, however, has always revived me & I shall try it as long as possible, I think for at least, a couple of months.
>
> Will you give me a little time to consider the Holbein proposal. I should like to do it very much, as my only

> refuge from very sad thoughts, will for some time to
> come, be in steady work, involving no great strain on the
> faculties. (26 June 1870)[8]

By 1 July, Chorley had taken a fancy to the Holbein proposal, though he was a little nervous about doing anything under pressure. He volunteered to Bentley that he was well qualified to write the book because 'I have rested myself largely from my musical labours by studying pictures at home & abroad, so am not altogether perhaps unprepared' (Wigan Archives Service). Four days later, Chorley, still in Scarborough, wrote to Bentley that he intended to travel to view an exhibition of Holbein works to be held in Dresden in September 'as nothing is so valuable as a complete knowledge of the subject one treats, though as in the present case, it be merely treated second hand' (5 July 1870).[9] In the same letter, Chorley expressed some annoyance with A.G. L'Estrange's life of Mary Russell Mitford, which Bentley had published earlier that year: 'As to the Mitford business — are you aware that the right, or otherwise, of printing letters is vested not in the possessors — but in the representatives or executors of the deceased. This was long ago decided in the case of Byron & Dallas. ...'[10]

Apparently Chorley thought about the Holbein book more than he actually worked on it. During the next several months references to it were coupled with references to his inability, or unwillingness, to proceed quickly. He asked Bentley for a modification of the contract so he would be paid on completion of the manuscript, rather than on publication:

> it will not suit me after giving some months' labour,
> which assuredly, it will cost me — to wait for the reward
> of said labour. The work will be one of great difficulty if
> it be to have any apparent freshness or novelty — & when
> I fairly enter on it, I shall lay every thing else aside — so
> that virtually I shall lose by it in any case. (Grand Hotel,
> Scarborough, Monday, 12 September 1870)

He then requested that all the illustrations be sent him. When he returned to Eaton Place West, he returned also to the question of payment, requesting that the contract be modified so that 'the £100 agreed on should be paid on my completion of the manuscript — & such payment be not dependant on the time of printing or publication — I am too old now to give prospective labour' (28 October 1870).[11] Chorley concluded this note more genially, expressing regret that Bentley has not been well and suggesting that, if he suffered from rheumatism, charcoal biscuits might be helpful. On 5 November 1870 he told Bentley that the book would take longer than originally thought. 'I cannot *force* myself in producing or arranging (as may be) what I should wish to last'. Therefore, Bentley was to consider himself free to commission the book from someone else; this he did not yet do, and next week Chorley wrote to him that all the material (presumably the illustrations) was complete and 'I shall begin next week to do a little every day, which is the only manner of dealing with tasks of the kind' (10 November 1870).[12]

An important figure in English nineteenth-century opera, Michael Balfe, died on 20 October 1870. Chorley contributed a signed obituary to the *Athenæum*. Its tone is cold, accusatory, even sarcastic: Balfe had wasted his talents for the sake of quick popularity. And yet his success 'gradually palled and paled, and the satiety and the waning were, of course, ascribed to national ignorance' (5 November 1870: 600). Balfe threw away his later opportunities, too:

> Then, for our London Italian Opera, Balfe had another amazing chance, in his 'Falstaff,' written on commission for *only* Grisi and Madame Albertazzi, *Falstaff* Lablache, Rubini and Tamburini, in the year 1838, when that company of artists was in its prime. "What would you," as Mrs. Quickly said (according to Goldsmith), even with such a brilliant opportunity as this, even when supported by the press, and petted by the nobility, he allowed the ground to slip from beneath his feet. A single *terzetto*, "Voglio parlar dell'ira," with its whimsical effect of female unisons at the close, is the only piece to be remembered.
>
> To speak of Balfe as an artist is either to mis-use the word, or to permit its meaning to depend on temporary success, no matter how acquired. He was indifferent to the quality of the stories he treated, to the words he set, to the situations he outraged; content if the clap-trap honours of the gallery and the shop-counter were secured. (600)

Meanwhile, his book on Holbein was not progressing well. Finally, in February 1871 Chorley wrote to Bentley, withdrawing from the project:

> When I undertook to arrange the Holbein book, I could not foresee the very long period of ill health through which I have passed during the autumn & early winter. — I have been so incapacitated as hardly to have had *two* working hours a day in place of my usual *ten*, & this, as you may believe, has made it impossible for me to sit down to a task of such solid importance, which cannot be properly executed by fits & starts. — I fear now, that it will be some time, under the best of circumstances, before I could betake myself to my work — & it is better to say so, at once, I think. I had best return the materials before

me, if you wish the work to be executed without much delay. I do not apologize for making this proposition, because, I repeat, I have not been to blame, though I feel seriously and sincerely vexed. ...

The same reasons do not apply to the Mitford letters — since I could look through & arrange those bit by bit.

I am sure you will acquit me of any discourtesy, or unhandsome treatment, in my laying before you a case, which no one can regret more sincerely than Yours. etc. etc. Henry F. Chorley. (16 February 1871)[13]

2

There remained two publishing projects which Chorley fully intended to complete: his book of Mitford's letters and his own reminiscences. In March Chorley wrote to Bentley that he was ready to begin:

So soon as I have materials in hand, I shall be glad to begin the Mitford book — *I* have had several offers of letters, but have desired my correspondents to send every thing to *you*, feeling this the simplest mode of proceeding. I conceive that the death of Mr Blackett releases me from my contract with him, — in regard to *my own* memoirs. I am making daily progress with them, having materials so ample as to have made me determine thus, with respect to them — There will be two series — the first to close some twenty years ago.

The second I shall complete while I can: — but it had better be deferred — I think the book will be as full of character & anecdote as most that have appeared & I will take care that there shall not be a word that can give private pain, to any of those who have known & trust me. — It will make two groups of three volumes each. What are you disposed to offer? — I do not wish to divide the work & should like to be paid on handing over the M.S. — I could not have believed I had so much to tell, as proves to be the case. ... (22 March 1871)[14]

Bentley must have written asking Chorley what terms he had agreed on with Blackett, because on 31 March 1871 Chorley responded:

As to the matter of business, — Mr Blackett promised verbally to give me whatever I asked for the first portion of my memoirs. — I think he had confidence in the work

& more, in my not being exorbitant. I have thought much about the matter — The book, as it will be full of anecdote, is worth to me £250. I mean the first three volumes. I could at once send in the M.S. to be printed, as I am now occupied with nothing else. — I can undertake for its being finished by late Autumn.

I wish I could have helped in the Holbein matter. — I think an intelligent English writer, who knew German well, — could possibly alter the translation you have so as to make it good — There would be, then, only the references for the insertion of the wood cuts. — And could you not get some known artist — try Millais — to write a preface? Ever yours truly, Henry F. Chorley. So soon as I get the Mitford matter I will take that in hand, — but I hope you recollect that I conditioned for her letters being copied. — If that be not done, there will be no amount of trouble in press mistakes to be paid for.

On 4 April 1871, Chorley gave Bentley an update, and distanced himself still further from any involvement, even peripherally, with the Holbein project.[15] Although it was he who had suggested asking Millais, he now seemed somewhat impatient with Bentley for taking up the suggestion.

Dear Sir,

I duly received the Mitford parcel & the moment I am able shall begin to work, — but I am beset on every side — & anything but equal to exertion. I have however made memoranda towards the preface. —

As to the Holbein affair. — I hardly know Millais well enough to ask him — & I do not think it would be advisable. First, I doubt whether he is in the habit of writing — Secondly whether he is up in his subject — Thirdly, because I do know — if I am to judge from his dealings as an artist, that his demand would probably be more than you could like to meet.

I should think R. Westmacott might do it, & do it *well*. He has written & lectured on art, & is a man of great general intelligence & culture, I would offer to propose it to him — but I *must* limit my self [two words, *sic*] to my own work — to which my present powers are miserably insufficient. — Perhaps you may care to mention it as my suggestion. — He has retired from the practice of sculpture, & I think would find the commission one to his taste.[16]

In August Chorley was eager to get back to Scarborough. It was to be his last summer visit there. By October 1871, in Chorley's last surviving letter to Bentley, the projects had moved closer to completion. Mitford was almost ready. But Chorley expressed poignantly his recognition that the works were not as good as they could have been:

> Let me do my very best, the book *must* be a patchy one — how different from what such a collection *might* have been made, I need not point out. — I have as little doubt that I shall be handsomely attacked for any failure which may present itself. — However, for this I don't care. What I want is a little breathing time, ere I turn to my own memoirs, if possible, to get away for a complete holiday in quite a new place. ...[17]

On Rossini's death in November 1868, Chorley, just retired from regularly journalism, contributed to the *Athenæum* a long tribute. It seemed like only yesterday when young Chorley and Mrs Hemans were discussing Chorley's attraction towards Europe's newest sensation. Enthusiasm for Rossini's operas was now left to those aging *laudatores temporis acti* who, like Chorley, were cranky and ill at ease in the present. Chorley placed Rossini in the Pantheon of geniuses that the nineteenth century had, until recently, so generously turned out:

> The last man of genius but one who belonged to the greatest musical period that Europe has yet seen, — the contemporary of Beethoven, Weber, Spohr, Mendelssohn, Meyerbeer, Paer, Mayer, Zingarelli, Donizetti, Pacini, Bellini, M. Auer, Paganini, De Bériot, Ernst, M. Moscheles, Hummel, Chopin, MM. Liszt, Thalberg, and a score of other artists, whose place there is small present chance of being filled, — almost, it may be added, the greatest man of genius in the glorious list — Rossini ... died on the 13th of this month, in Paris. (*Athenæum*, 21 November 1868: 685-6)

A review of the composer's works led to the fourth act of *Otello*, that touchstone of taste:

> If this marvellous piece of dramatic conception, where the wildest passion is combined with a beauty as symmetrical as that of the Greek statues, is now thought slow and cold by those who will swallow any amount of Verdi bombast or of Wagner trash, it may be that the great art of operatic singing and acting has died out.

Finally, he recalled those old days in England when Rossini visited —

1824, now almost beyond the reach of human memory:

> [Colbran] accompanied him to England; when Prince Leopold's Concerts, at Marlborough House, were "the rage" in our world of fashion; when Almack's was in full glory. What a by-gone time does this simple statement recall! There is probably one only of that brilliant society still in the world, — Lady Palmerston, then Lady Cowper. (21 November 1868: 686)

Chorley considered writing a book about Rossini's career. Although he never wrote it, he did publish in 1871 another tribute, which appeared in the *Edinburgh Review*, edited by Chorley's old friend and former housemate, Henry Reeve, as part of a twenty-five page essay-review on the significance of Rossini and Berlioz. The occasion was the publication of Sutherland Edwards's *Life of Rossini* in 1869 and Berlioz's *Mémoires* in 1870. The difference between Rossini and Berlioz, wrote Chorley, was that between a real genius and a 'self-imagined' one (*Edinburgh Review*, January 1871: 34). He quickly dismissed Sutherland Edwards's work as demonstrating neither good research nor 'delicacy of musical perception' (34-5). Rossini's operas were able 'to delight, to intoxicate, and revolutionise the public of Europe' (36). The Rossini revolution was the only European revolution that Chorley ever supported. Unlike Meyerbeer, Rossini sincerely encouraged younger musical talents, Chorley wrote. His creative methods were impossible to describe — theories of 'ripening and development' would be destroyed if a 'correct and chronological catalogue of Rossini's Italian operas' were written (41). Like many great composers, he was not averse to stealing and borrowing, either from himself or others; only the 'narrow minded', the 'bilious', and the 'pedantic' will misconstrue this characteristic (42). From the time of his appointment at the Opéra, 'he began to finish his compositions with scrupulous self respect' (42). He paid no attention to the quality of his libretti, unlike Bellini and Verdi. He was Italy's greatest composer for the stage (43), though his operas were no longer the popular favourites they once had been — 'their vogue, for the moment, has largely gone by' (43).

Chorley's mixed reaction to Berlioz had always been influenced by the fact that he saw Berlioz as a professional peer, a journalist, as much as a composer. In 1848, reviewing a concert of Berlioz's music in London, he termed him 'the cleverest of our confraternity' (*Athenæum*, 12 February 1848: 170). In his diaries Chorley commented on Berlioz's bitterness, and his 'vitriolic spirit', contrasting it unfavourably with Mendelssohn's nature (Hewlett, 2: 96, 97). Chorley may also have disliked Berlioz, at least in part, for being not only a journalist but also a composer, as he felt *he* should have been.

From Berlioz it was 'impossible to withhold pity, akin though that be to contempt' (*Edinburgh Review*, 44). The key to Berlioz's 'unlovely peculiarities' was seen in the portrait facing the title page: it revealed his 'mental distemperature', like Cowper's in the 'well-known likeness' (44). Despite Berlioz's ungrateful whining, '[n]ever was man more munificently assisted by others, never did artist do less in repayment, by holding out the hand of assistance and sympathy to those of a younger generation' (47). The episodes of his life were not so much romantic as lunatic. The adventure of Berlioz's love-sick rush from Italy to France, for example, armed with 'a pair of pistols, poison and ... a suit of woman's clothes for some undisclosed purpose', ended appropriately in his calmly going back to Rome, 'it is to be hoped, having left on the way his drugs and his feminine gear' (49).[18]

Chorley's insistence on Berlioz's lack of integrity as a critic was central to his basically unsympathetic reaction to the man. Chorley's own journalistic integrity is presented, by implication, as a model:

> With a view of eking out his resources, Berlioz became a newspaper critic. Such a position must always be perilous to anyone who, besides criticising, desires to create. Nothing in this book is more characteristic than the cynicism of the revelations of Berlioz on the subject. He consented to fulfil an avowedly loathsome task in order to earn money; — as if the calling were not one only to be carried through by severe reference to the standards of truth and duty. That, when thus exercised, it proves one of the least gainful occupations in which literary skill and fancy, borne out by special knowledge, can engage themselves is sadly true — nor less so that, therefore, there clings to it a perpetual temptation to favouritism and venality, hard to be resisted by any save those whose mental tone and moral standard are high. Berlioz turned its privileges and temptations to account with considerable adroitness. ... He managed to make himself followed and feared, and had no scruples to prevent his misusing the privileges of one in authority. What he suffered in forcing himself to write mystifying reports of musical works which he despised and could not recollect is not, he tells us, to be described. The suffering, it may be suspected, was not fatally keen; at best, degrading to the manhood of him who consented to endure it for lucre. (50-51)

He then related an anecdote discreditable to Berlioz's integrity: Recio, until she married Berlioz, was put on the payroll of the Opéra Comique fraudulently: the understanding was that she would *not* sing and that Berlioz would puff the establishment as much as possible. If this story were untrue, Chorley stated, it surely would have been refuted in Berlioz's book. Chorley's conscience in relaying the scandal is clear: 'Everyone who could be hurt by the exposure is dead; otherwise it would have been withheld' (52). It is also personally known to Chorley that Berlioz left a performance of Mendelssohn's 'Elijah', 'the greatest work of modern times', after the first part, but wrote his review as if he had heard it all (54). His lack of proper respect for Bach, Handel, and Rossini was as unbalanced as his 'immoderate deification' of 'the great Gluck' and 'the less great Spontini' (52).

Berlioz's success after 1841 on his tours in Germany was cited by some as evidence of his artistic worth. In fact, however, Germany's position as a land of superior musical understanding was already undermined: 'That the respect for law and order, without which Society becomes a chaos, and Literature and Art drivel and rave, fancying themselves simple or sublime, has been weakened throughout Germany, is a sad and serious truth. It was no wonder, then, that Berlioz should by the destructive party there be regarded as an inspired prophet' (53). Indeed, Berlioz's criticism of Wagner's music was 'suspicious', perhaps insincere, given his own music. *Benvenuto Cellini* and the Roman Carnival Overture were his best compositions (48); *Les Troyens*, too, had 'some indication of grandeur and beauty'. The second part only had been performed: 'That the opera was carefully and liberally set forth we can bear witness', and it enjoyed a modest 'success of curiosity'. But it was typical of Berlioz that he turned on Carvalho, who had 'risked so much in his behalf' to stage the second part (54).

Chorley wrote the words to the second part of *L'Enfance du Christ*. His views on Berlioz's work were therefore of special interest, but they are not especially enlightening:

> With regard to the 'Childhood of Christ' a curious anecdote may be told: its author wrote the second part of the work as it stands (the only one of the three which has any value), professedly in ridicule of the melodists, and palmed it off on the public as the work of a forgotten composer. The parody pleased more than any of the earnest efforts of its writer had done. Berlioz then conceived the idea of extending it, and added what is now the third portion, namely, the arrival in Egypt, a luckless example of his worst manner — grim, confused, pretending, and unmelodious — and conceived his work finished. On mentioning it to an acquaintance, the latter suggested that, to complete the subject, the terror from which the fugitives had escaped should be expressed or narrated. Berlioz caught at the suggestion eagerly; and added that

> which is now the first part, picturing the madness of Herod and the Massacre of the Innocents. The music to this is simply hideous, and, conjointly with the peroration, smothers the beautiful and delicate simplicity of the central portion of the Trilogy. It is characteristic that a fact like this should have been omitted; but a like disingenuousness runs through the entire record. (56-7).

For young composers, Berlioz's career was thus an example to be avoided.

In October, 1871, Chorley wrote a signed letter to the *Athenæum* protesting an announcement that his 'May Queen' would be performed as an opera. In the letter he rehearsed arguments he had used twenty-nine years earlier in objecting to Macready's spectacular Drury Lane stage presentation in 1842 of Handel's *Acis and Galatea* with Clarkson Stanfield's scenery.[19] Action, Chorley insisted, was crucial to staged dramatic presentations but antithetical to the nature of cantatas, which were unsuitable to stage presentation. In writing the *May Queen*, Chorley stated, he made use of only one dramatic action, the blow 'borrowed' from Scott's *Fortunes of Nigel*. Instead of imagining action, he imagined 'Leslie's charming picture' while writing the words (14 October 1871: 504). Thus, to alter the appropriate presentation and produce it as part of an English Opera season was to misunderstand the generic nature of the cantata, and to insult Chorley personally, although '[t]he discourtesy with which my expressed wishes have been set aside has nothing to do with the force of the argument, or the state of the case, as questions of Art' (504).

Discourtesy rankled; Chorley dwelt on it in his last published book. In 1870 Bentley had published a series of Mary Russell Mitford's letters in three volumes, edited by A.G. L'Estrange, who took over the editorial work when William Harness was unable to complete it. Early in 1872, Bentley published Chorley's work, the second series of the *Letters of Mary Russell Mitford* in two volumes. To these letters Chorley contributed a twenty-five pages prefatory essay, concluding remarks, and some explanatory footnotes. He wrote of major wrongs which Mary Russell Mitford had endured, of minor wrongs which he himself had endured in connection with his friendship with Mitford, and of L'Estrange's discourtesy to him.

The great wrong Mitford suffered was the burden of caring for a father who abused her. The charming Dr Mitford 'had a hold on the women of his family as oppressive and as noxious as the load laid by the Old Man of the Sea on the shoulders of Sindbad' (1: 3). He was, in short, 'the sorrow — the disadvantage — the mistake' of her life (1: 2) — a 'wasteful profligate' and a gambler. Chorley re-told the story, as it had first been told in 'an article which appeared in a leading review, at the time when the first series of

Miss Mitford's letters appeared' (1: 2), that is, his own essay in the *Quarterly Review* for January 1870, mentioned above. 'I believe that there is no living person who can be hurt by the whole story being set forth as explicitly as words can tell it. — This was not thoroughly done in the preface to the first series of letters' (1: 2). Her father, Dr Mitford, ruined his family through his recklessness. He was given a second chance by a stroke of luck straight from a fairy tale:

> By one of those chances which, if met with in one of Balzac's novels, would be pronounced forced and theatrical, his daughter became the possessor of an enormous lottery prize — twenty thousand pounds. That sum of money, too, sufficient to have reinstated himself and his family in their old position, Dr. Mitford gambled and muddled away in an inconceivably short period. And from that time forth, to the end of his days, Miss Mitford was the "breadwinner". ... (1: 3).

She became a household angel, one of those who 'will sacrifice herself to the most tawdry and inconstant being on whom she is ready, even unto death, to waste her heart's treasure of love' (1: 5).

Despite Chorley's claim to the contrary, this account did not differ drastically from Estrange's. L'Estrange too noted that on Dr Mitford's marriage to Mary Russell in 1785 he came into possession not only of property but also of £28 000, and went through it completely within eight or nine years. When his daughter Mary chose the winning lottery number, he wasted his second chance by being, as L'Estrange put it, 'utterly selfish at heart, and incapable of sacrificing the slightest inclination of his own for the welfare of his wife, or even of his daughter' and he remained 'recklessly extravagant' all his life (L'Estrange, Harper edition, 2: 17). Chorley discussed Dr Mitford's selfishness in greater detail than L'Estrange.

In one respect Chorley suggested that Mitford, though an angel, was a very sharp-tongued one. In a footnote to Mrs Acton Tindal's character sketch, he compared Mitford to Jenny Wren in Dickens's last novel *Our Mutual Friend*, who verbally abused her drunken father in a bizarre reversal of Dickens's earlier long-suffering and nurturing children (Little Nell in *The Old Curiosity Shop*, for example, and the eponymous heroine of *Little Dorrit*):

> While on the subject, I cannot but note the singular resemblance, in position, — nay, too, and in expression — between those of Miss Mitford and her father, and those of the doll's dressmaker and her drunken parent, in Dickens's "Our Mutual Friend" (1: 22-3)

Chorley's comparison of Mitford's behaviour to Jenny Wren's is revealing, since Jenny Wren's verbal abuse of her abuser is startling, not conventionally angelic. The allusion suggests that Mitford's relation to her father was less self-sacrificingly angelic than he was prepared to state directly.[20] Mitford endured another somewhat mysterious wrong, less drastic but still painful — this one at the hands of a young actor whom she befriended and who 'repaid this kindness by giving those, who chose to listen to him, reason to believe that she wished to marry him. The incident is too curious a one to be omitted; but it is an old tale of Woman's kindness, required by a vain and selfish man's indelicate ingratitude' (2: 223). At this point, Chorley inserted a ten-page character sketch of Mitford written by Mrs Acton Tindal, commenting that it reinforces his view of her character and her exploitation — 'the case ought to be stated from the mouth of more than one witness' (1: 15) — while reminding readers that Tindal's account of the paternal abuse is softened somewhat by her own womanly lack of understanding of 'what really make up the habits, and temptations, and indulgences of Man's life' (1: 14).

In addition to chronicling Mitford's wrongs, Chorley had his own set of grievances to ventilate. As a conscientious editor, he was disappointed by many of Mitford's correspondents who refused him permission to print her letters, reserving them for separate publication by themselves (2: 265). And he was sorry to read in L'Estrange's book that Mitford had told the Revd William Harness that he was too self-involved to perceive her final, fatal suffering: 'Mr. Chorley is gone away under the impression that I have nothing the matter with me — because he and his sister grumble and fret and whine — which you know is not my way ...' (16 December 1854, L'Estrange, 3: 304). According to L'Estrange, Mitford suggested that she wrote for Chorley's magazine, *Lady's* [*sic*] *Companion* only under pressure: '... he is such a very old friend, that I really could not persist in saying No to him' (to Miss Goldsmid, 1 December 1852, L'Estrange, 3: 220).[21]

Prompted by such written comments, as well as by comments others had passed on to him, he responded eloquently, proclaiming to his readers his trust in Mitford's affection for him and reiterating his for her. He recalled that Mitford had dedicated *Recollections of a Literary Life* to him. In it she called him her 'dear friend', adding: 'But for you this book would never have existed'.

> I have been assured that my dear old friend changed her
> opinion of me, and that her regard for me cooled, during
> the later years of her life. This was not the case. Like all
> quick-witted women, and some quick-witted men, she
> may have said or written sharp things in a moment of
> petulance. I now hear of them for the first time. But a few
> hasty or sarcastic words, if such things were, or exist,

count for nothing when set against long years of pleasant intercourse and good understanding. The dedication of Miss Mitford's "Records of Literary Life," and the fact that we were in perpetual communication till within the last three weeks of her life, — when after seeing her, I did not certainly (as has been told in one of her last letters), think the end so near at hand — are sufficient evidences to myself of her unbroken regard and confidence. Only those who are paltry in their friendships and not sure of themselves, can be soured or shaken by any such poor and passing expressions of temper. (1: 25)[22]

Chorley's volumes of Mitford's letters were noticed in the lead review in the *Athenæum* on 9 March 1872 (297-8). In it John Doran, who had reviewed Chorley's *Thirty Years' Musical Recollections* ten years earlier, remarked that this was 'Mr. Chorley's last service to literature' (297). Like many nineteenth-century reviews, Doran's deals less with the qualities of the book ostensibly under review than with the reviewer's own knowledge of the book's subject. Doran, like Chorley, emphasized Mitford's 'extravagant adoration of her impure idol', her father (297). Without explicitly intending to do so, Doran also summarized in his conclusion why Chorley was attracted to Mitford, placing her among those who have endured nobly life's disappointments. The passage unintentionally but effectively complemented the *Athenæum's* obituary of Chorley himself:

[W]e find Miss Mitford, from first to last, a truly good Englishwoman, hopeful in youth, resignedly content in age; a noble worker ever; and with that brave philosophy which enables a few when young to bear well the sharp anguish which comes with disappointment, and when years gather round them, to meet it with a faint smile — the homage paid to another illusion departed. (9 March 1872: 298)

This seems to be how Chorley, too, wanted to be regarded.

He wrote to Henry Hewlett on 2 October 1871 that he intended to turn his full attention to his own memoirs after he completed work on Mitford's letters:

There are things that I feel I ought to put on record, especially as I have destroyed a large correspondence. The book will be a curious one, and I have been writing at it, as I think you know, for the last ten years.

... I am behind hand with all periodicals, not even having read up the 'Athenæum.' My time for them seems to be over, as you would not wonder, did you know what

> my inner life, during my thirty-five years' apprenticeship, comprehended. (Hewlett, 2: 326)

In January 1872, Chorley's obituary of Turgenev appeared in *The Orchestra*.[23] Turgenev, however, was not dead. Instead, he was greatly offended by the obituary's estimate of his work, which, though generally laudatory, termed it occasionally 'fatiguing'. A correction was duly printed in the *Athenæum*. In February, Chorley submitted an essay to Henry Reeve with his final thoughts on Hawthorne. Although Reeve, editor of the *Edinburgh Review*, was his old housemate and friend, the *Edinburgh Review* did not print it. Chorley's final letter, the last of his long stream of complaints about his failing health, referred to that essay:

> My Dear Reeve, — I send you what I have done *in re* Hawthorne. I offer a character rather than a review, proved by extracts; since had I gone on *in extenso* I don't know where I should have stopped. Nothing but my strong wish to get my subject before the public could have made me carry out my article, poor as it is, seeing that I have written it half a leaf at a time, and with a weak, weary hand, the end of which will not impossibly be palsy. But I think as character, when duly corrected, my work may not come out amiss. Ever yours faithfully, Henry F. Chorley. (8 February 1872, in Laughton, 2: 205-6.

Chorley was beyond caring much about Hawthorne or Turgenev. His own death was only days away. He had planned another exclusive dinner party for that evening: Michael Costa was expected, as were Lady Downshire, Henry Hewlett, Dickens's daughter Kate, and others. In the morning, however, he was suddenly seized with what Hewlett termed 'syncope'. He lay unconscious for several hours, giving no signs of suffering. And then the much-predicted and occasionally longed-for end of his life finally came (Hewlett, 2: 334).

His passing was the occasion for appropriate expressions of professional respect and personal fondness. He had understood, rightly, that his death would not be a deep personal blow to anyone. Georgina Hogarth, keeper of flame for her brother-in-law, Dickens, wrote to her Boston friend Annie Fields:

> — Poor Mr. Chorley! his death was a shock, from its extreme suddenness — and it was very sad to me also, from the associations connected with him — and to Mamie it was really a *grief*, for she liked the kind[?] man very much — and he was really fond of her — I never cared much about him — I mean as a personal friend — I

had a respect for him, knowing him to be an upright-
honourable man — and a regard for him knowing his
great regard for Charles and gratitude to him — He felt
his death *terribly* — he lost his very best friend. I am
happy to say that during the latter months of his life he
had been better as to his drinking habits — Mamie and
Harry met['?] him *at a Ball* — two nights before his death
— and Mamie told me the next day she had never seen
him look and *seem* so well — and Katy was to have dined
at his house — at a party — on the very day of his death!
So it *was* shockingly sudden. (3 May 1872)[24]

Chorley's obituary in the *Orchestra*, the journal he had often contributed
to in his last years, appeared on 23 February 1872. The author maintained
that music critics really have little influence on public taste, a possibility
that would have distressed Chorley:

Musical criticism and musical 'recollections', have little
influence in making a name even in musical society so-
called. As far as such a reputation can be earned, it has
been done by Mr. Chorley; and deservedly so: for in
addition to his natural and acquired qualifications, and to
his constant rectitude, he threw all his energy into the
work of the hour: whatever he did he did with all his
might. (331)

At his funeral at Brompton Cemetery, noted the *Orchestra*, important
figures in England's musical life were among the mourners (23 February
1972: 328): Sir Michael Costa, Arthur Sullivan, Henry Leslie, Charles
Hallé, C.L. Gruneisen, John Thomas, Mr Payton (Secretary of the
Birmingham Festival), and Edward Dannreuther. Also present were the
actor Mr Bancroft, Henry Hewlett, and the publisher of the *Athenæum*,
John Francis. Around the grave were Joseph Joachim, Tom Taylor, George
Grove, Mamie Dickens, Mrs Lehmann, and the nephew of his childhood
friend from Liverpool, Benson Rathbone. He was buried next to John Chorley, his beloved brother.

In a later issue, the *Orchestra* summarized for a new generation of
readers some aspects of a career which was already beginning to seem
faded and obscure. It recalled that before Chorley, from 1830 to 1834, Ella
had written criticism for the *Athenæum*, and that Chorley's books about
music had once made some impression.

Chorley's pleasant volumes of "Modern Music and Manners in Germany" have been recently translated and
printed in the Paris *Musical Gazette*. It was reviewed in
the *Times* in a severe and very unjustifiable manner. It is

> to be hoped that the materials prepared for a life of Ros-
> sini will fall in to the hands of a competent person, for
> publication (*Orchestra*, 1 March 1872: 344).

And the journal reported that the Welsh remembered gratefully Chorley's appreciation of their music and musicians: 'The claim of the late Mr. Chorley to the grateful remembrance of Welshmen is asserted by the *Carnarvon and Denbigh Herald*' (345).

The writer for the *Musical Times* stated that he 'wrote with an honest conviction of the truth of the principles he advocated, and endeavoured to uphold the dignity and independence of an office which, for thirty-give years, he worthily filled'. It predicted that 'his name will not be easily forgotten, even by those who differed from him in his earnestly expressed strictures upon art and artists' (1 March 1872: 413).

Chorley's colleague and successor, Charles Gruneisen, wrote his obituary for the *Athenæum*. Gruneisen retold the story of the young Chorley, a misfit in the world of the Friends, a misfit in the world of Liverpool merchants. On coming to London he became and remained the *Athenæum's* music critic, 'down to 1868, when the state of his health necessitated his retirement; and the acquisition of a fortune from a brother enabled him to gratify his taste as an amateur for the remainder of his days' (24 February 1872: 249). Chorley had reached a position of critical power, and he exercised

> a powerful influence on musical art in this country. He
> effected this by his thorough independence, by his dis-
> cernment, by his instinct, which enabled him to distin-
> guish the true from the false, to detect with unerring
> sagacity the signs and tokens of a future in aspiring
> novices. His own training, after his early studies, was
> confined to lessons from Herr Hermann [sic]. Yet he was
> not only a practical player, but a theorist as regards
> music. He became a linguist, and he read the works of the
> classic masters of antiquity as well as those of the modern
> writers. (24 February 1872: 249)

Gruneisen reminded readers that Chorley's main legacy was to his fellow critics: 'Critics ought to reverence his memory, for he fought a stout and determined battle in vindication of their independence' (249-50). Gruneisen concluded by alluding gently to Chorley's difficult personality:

> The versatility of Mr. Chorley's attainments was only
> equalled by his uprightness and by his truthfulness, and if
> he sometimes concealed from the outer world his
> innermost qualities by peculiarities and eccentricities,
> those who knew him best, or those who had occasion to

seek beyond the mere surface, had reason to be proud of
coming in contact with such rare intelligence and
unflinching integrity. (250)

Mamie Dickens came with Nina Lehmann to view Chorley's body. She
wrote to Hewlett of her surprise at seeing again the two cedar branches
from Gad's Hill which he had requested when Dickens died:

> My friend, and *his* dear friend, Mrs. Lehmann, saw him
> lying calm and peaceful in his coffin, with a large green
> branch on each side of him. She did not understand what
> this meant, but I did, and was much touched, as, of
> course, he had given orders that these branches should be
> laid with him in his coffin. So a piece of the place he
> loved so much, for its dear master's sake, went down to
> the grave with him. (Hewlett, 2: 240)

Chorley's life's work, accomplished industriously though sometimes
despairingly, was over. In his depressed moods, he had considered himself
a failure as an artist and as a human being. It is true that his novels, plays,
and poems, were unsuccessful, and for the most part understandably so. His
books on music and musicians were not always appreciated by his contemporaries, but they are of permanent value. The enormous body of his
journalism and critical writing about composers and performers in the nineteenth century has contributed greatly to our knowledge of the reception
and significance of nineteenth-century art. It was written by a man
determined to surround himself with prominent writers, composers, and
performers who could create art and make it live, a man burning with love
for words and for music. His best critical skills were used to analyse
writers, composers, and performers; his worst were used to analyse himself.

Though many people disliked him, many others wished him well and a
few, like Dickens, were devoted to him. To the end, he honoured the
domestic ideals of the mentor of his young days in Liverpool, Felicia
Hemans. His belief in the centrality of self-sacrifice and suffering in life
both created and nurtured dissatisfaction. The pains resulting from his
inability to find emotional wholeness in a life spent alone were doubled
because he had no resources to assure him that he was successful other than
those which equated success with happiness. Unable to locate and exist in a
permanent state of happiness any more readily than the rest of the human
race, he too often assumed that he was a failure. As an earnest and insight-
ful participant in humanity's ongoing efforts to understand how to create
and to criticize art, he was a significant figure for his contemporaries and
for the generations that succeeded them.

Notes

1. In 1871, Harriet Martineau wrote to Henry Reeve asking about Chorley's drinking:

   > One private word with you. I lately saw in a letter that Mr Chorley is *lost in drink*. I have not mentioned this, & shall not, — except here, to ask whether you can tell me that this *is not true*. (15 March 1871, *Selected Letters*, ed. Sanders, 227)

2. Presumably Chorley's servant Mary Brake.

3. Although his focus was on Austen, he paid passing tribute to Gaskell:

   > Only one candidate to her peculiar honours, who has approached her finish and excellence, during the half century which has elapsed since her decease occurs to us. This is the late Mrs. Gaskell — whose 'Cranford' and 'Wives and Daughters' will long keep a place by the side of 'Mansfield Park' and 'Persuasion.' (204)

4. Book 1, Chapter 24, *A Tale of Two Cities*.

5. MS, Liverpool Record Office. Chorley hoped for a revival of *Duchess Eleanor*.

6. He noted:

   > It has been said that he could not draw gentlemen and ladies (as footmen understand the designation). This is false. The characters of Sir Leicester Dedlock, in 'Bleak House,' that of Mrs. Steerforth, in 'David Copperfield,' and fifty indications more may be cited in disproof. That he found greater pleasure in selecting and marking out figures where the traits were less smoothed or effaced by the varnish of polite society than in picturing those of a world where the expression of individual characters becomes less marked, is true. To each man his own field. (*Athenæum*, 18 June 1870: 804)

7. Chorley mentioned to Bentley on 10 November 1870 that he had received his copy of Woltmann; on 16 February 1870 he used the phrase 'I undertook to arrange the Holbein book'.

8. MS, Wigan Archives Service.

9. MS, Wigan Archives Service.

10. Chorley's knowledge of legal issues involving publication of letters had impressed Mrs Gaskell when she published her *Life of Charlotte Bronte* in 1857: he warned her that the legal rights to Charlotte

Brontë's papers lay with her husband, Mr Nicholls (Barker, 794-5).

11. MS, Wigan Archives Service.

12. MS, Wigan Archives Service.

13. MS, Wigan Archives Service.

14. MS, Wigan Archives Service.

15. In 1872 Bentley published F.E. Bunnett's translation of Woltmann's *Holbein and His Time*.

16. MS, Wigan Archives Service.

17. 18 October 1871, MS, British Library, Add. MS H6.654.

18. Chorley saw Berlioz's marriage to Harriet Smithson when her acting career was over and she was in debt as 'the one generous transaction of his life', although the marriage was 'a most unhappy one' (*Edinburgh Review*, 50).

19. In 1860 Chorley had stressed one criterion of a good cantata — 'The less action that it contains the better' — when discussing his *Undine*, set by Benedict:

> In spite of the capital groupings and gesticulations of
> the crowd on the stage, and Mr. Stanfield's pictorial
> scenery, the chorus, 'Wretched lovers,' in Gay's 'Acis
> and Galatea,' is more effective as concert-music than it
> was when forced into dramatic form by Mr. Macready.
> (29 September 1860: 425)

The *Athenæum* printed Chorley's objections to the Macready/Stanfield version of Handel's *Acis and Galatea* on 12 February 1842: 149, and 19 February 1842: 172.

20. Harriet Martineau, commenting privately in a letter to Henry Reeve (15 March 1871) on L'Estrange's edition of Mitford's letters, portrayed Mitford as a parasite in collusion with her father:

> — In course of years I became aware of her essential
> falseness, & of the undercurrent of ill nature w^h in this
> book comes to the surface so fearfully towards the end
> of her life. — Mr Harness & I were good friends; & he
> used to come & pour out his griefs & vexations about
> his most troublesome charge; — about the way in w^h
> she *encouraged* her father's unprincipled doings, —
> enjoying her share of the good things she begged in his
> name. (Sanders, 224)

21. Chorley knew that Mitford's view of the writers on the *Athenæum* staff was cynical:

> ... they proclaim loudly and proudly that they treat
> their friends worse than strangers, and their enemies
> best of all; so one does harm in mentioning a book to

> them. (Chorley, *Mitford*, 1: 225)

Chorley's footnote contradicted this passage: 'A misstatement. I believe that no journal was ever less talked about by its proprietors and contributors than the one in question: — hence an amount of error in imputation, which not seldom amounted to the ridiculous' (1: 225). He may not have known that, writing to Barrett in a passing fit of exasperation, Mitford once termed him a 'presumptuous coxcomb' (Kelley and Hudson, 8: 326).

22. In self-defence, Chorley indignantly repudiated L'Estrange's allegation that he refused to cooperate with the earlier series of letters 'on the score of insufficient remuneration' (2: 266). He asserted that he was never approached for assistance in the first place; this charge was therefore baseless and the most 'flagrant' of all L'Estrange's errors.
23. Attribution from Waddington, *Turgenev in England* 220.
24. MS FI 2706, Huntington Library, San Marino, California.

Works Consulted: Selected List

Among the nineteenth century periodicals consulted, in addition to the *Athenæum*, are *Bentley's Miscellany, Blackwood's, Daily News, Douglas Jerrold's Shilling Magazine, Dublin Review, Edinburgh Review, Fraser's, Harmonicon, Illustrated London News, Macmillans', Morning Post, Musical Times, Musical World, New Monthly Magazine, Orchestra, Quarterly Review, Tait's, The Times*, and *Westminster Review*

Ackroyd, Peter, *Dickens*, New York: Harper Collins, 1990.
Allen, Reginald, in collaboration with Gale R. D'Luhy, *Sir Arthur Sullivan: Composer and Personage*, New York: Pierpont Morgan Library, 1975.
Allsobrook, David Ian, *Liszt: My Travelling Circus Life*, Carbondale: Southern Illinois University Press, 1991.
[Anon], 'The English Orchestra: The Philharmonic Society', *The New Monthly Magazine*, 44 (July 1835): 289-95.
[Anon], 'Notes of a Musical Student. Progress of English Music in the Past Year', *The New Monthly Magazine*, 43 (February 1835): 145-55.
[Anon], Review of [Chorley's] *Sketches of a Sea Port Town* (1834), *The London Literary Gazette; and Journal of Belles Lettres; Arts, Sciences, &c, Athenæum* (7 March 1835): 150-51.
[Anon], 'Musical Criticism in 1844', *Musical Times*, (1 June 1894): 383-4.
[Anon], 'A Few Conversationalists', *The Cornhill Magazine*, New Series 12 (1902): 526-41.
Arditi, Luigi, *My Reminiscences*, ed. and compiled by the Baroness von Zedlitz, New York: Dodd, Mead and Company, 1896.
Armstrong, Isobel, *Victorian Poetry: Poetry, Poetics, and Politics*, London: Routledge, 1993.
Ashbrook, William, *Donizetti and his Operas*, Cambridge: Cambridge University Press, 1982 (reprinted 1984).
Audubon, John James, *The 1826 Journal of John James Audubon*, transcribed with introduction and notes by Alice Ford, Norman: University of Oklahoma Press, 1967.
Audubon, Maria R., *Audubon and his Journals*, 2 vols, London: John C. Nimmo, 1898.
Auerbach, Emily, 'John Bull and his "Land Ohne Musik"', *Victorian Literature and Culture* (vol. 21), ed. John Maynard and Adrienne Auslander-Munich, New York: AMS Press, 1993: 67-88.
Auerbach, Jeffrey A., 'What They Read: Mid-Nineteenth Century English Women's Magazines and the Emergence of a Consumer Culture ', *Victorian Periodicals Review*, 30 (1997): 121-40.
[Ayrton, William], 'The *Revue Musicale* and the Harmonicon', *Harmonicon*, (1829): 154-6.
Bache, Constance, *Brother Musicians: Reminiscences of Edward and Walter Bache*, London: Methuen & Co., 1901.
Barbier, Patrick, *Opera in Paris, 1800-1850: A Lively History*, trans. Robert Luoma, Portland, Oregon: Amadeus Press, 1995.
Barker, Juliet, *The Brontës*, London: Weidenfeld and Nicolson, 1994.
Barnett, John Francis, *Musical Reminiscences and Impressions*, New York: B.W. Dodge & Co., n.d.

Barrett, Wm. Alexander, *Balfe: His Life and Work*, London: William Reeves, [1882].

B[ayley], T[homas] H[aynes], 'My Opera Box', *New Monthly Magazine*, 42 (December 1834): 431.

[Bayley, Thomas Haynes], 'Oh, Take Me a Box at the Opera', *The New Monthly Magazine*, 43 (April 1835): 498.

Beale, Willert, *The Light of Other Days: Seen Through the Wrong End of an Opera Glass*, 2 vols, London: Richard Bentley, 1890.

Becker, Heinz and Gudrun, *Giocomo Meyerbeer: A Life in Letters*, trans. Mark Violette, Portland, Oregon: Amadeus Press, 1989.

Bennett, J[ames] R[obert] Sterndale, *The Life of William Sterndale Bennett*, Cambridge: University Press, 1907.

Bennett, Joseph, *Forty Years of Music: 1865-1905*, London: Methuen, 1908.

Berlioz, Hector, *Correspondance Générale*, ed. Pierre Citron et al., vols 1-6, Paris: Flammarion, 1972-95.

Biddlecombe, George, *English Opera from 1834 to 1864 with Particular Reference to the Works of Michael Balfe*, New York: Garland, 1994.

Blaze de Bury, Henri, *Meyerbeer et son temps*, Paris: Michel Lévy, 1865.

Bledsoe, Robert, 'Dickens and Chorley', *The Dickensian*, 75 (1979): 157-66.

Bledsoe, Robert, 'Henry Fothergill Chorley and the Reception of Verdi's Early Operas in England', *Victorian Studies*, 28 (1985): 631-55. reprinted in Temperley, *The Lost Chord*: 119-42.

Bledsoe, Robert, 'Dickens and Opera', *Dickens Studies Annual: Essays on Victorian Fiction*, 18 (1989): 93-118.

Bledsoe, Robert, 'Critics and Operatic Performance Practice in London During the 1830s', *Victorian Review: Victorian Studies Association of Western Canada*, 16 (Summer 1990): 59-70.

Bloom, Peter, ed., *Music in Paris in the Eighteen-Thirties*, Stuyvesant, NY: Pendragon Press, 1987.

Bourne, H.R. Fox, *English Newspapers: Chapters in the History of Journalism*, 2 vols, London: Chatto & Windus, 1887.

Bowen, José A., 'Mendelssohn, Berlioz, and Wagner as Conductors: The Origins of the Ideal of "Fidelity to the Composer"', *Performance Practice Review*, 6 (Spring 1993): 77-88.

Budden, Julian, *The Operas of Verdi*, 3 vols, New York: Oxford University Press, 1973.

Bunn, Alfred, *The Stage: Both Before and Behind the Curtain From 'Observations Taken on the Spot'*, 3 vols, London: Richard Bentley, 1840.

Carse, Adam, *The Orchestra From Beethoven to Berlioz: A history of the Orchestra in the first half of the 19th century, and of the development of orchestral baton-conducting*, New York: Broude Brothers, 1949.

Casale, Stephen, 'A Newly-Discovered Letter from Verdi to Léon Escudier', *Verdi Newsletter*, 11 (March 1983): 6-10.

Cesari, Gaetano e Alessandro Luzio, *I copialettere di Giuseppe Verdi*, Milano: S. Ceretti, 1913.

Chorley, Henry F., *Sketches of a Sea Port Town*, 3 vols, London: Richard Bentley, 1834.

Chorley, Henry F., *Conti the Discarded; With Other Tales and Fancies*, 3 vols, London: Saunders and Otley, 1835.

Chorley, Henry F., *Memorials of Mrs. Hemans with Illustrations of Her Literary Character from her Correspondence*, 2 vols, London: Saunders and Otley, 1836 (also Philadelphia: Carey, Lea & Blanchard, 1836).

Chorley, Henry Fothergill, 'The Crucifixion; an Oratorio. By Louis Spohr ... *Malek Adel*; A Tragic Opera ... by M Costa. *Catherine Grey*; ... The Music by M. W. Balfe' [review article], *The London and Westminster Review*, 37 (July 1837): 52-77.

Chorley, Henry F., *The Authors of England: A Series of Medallion Portraits of Modern Literary Characters, Engraved from the Works of British Artists by Achille Collas*, London: Charles Tilt, 1838.

[Chorley, Henry F.], *The Lion: A Tale of the Coteries*, 3 vols, London: Henry Colburn, 1839.

Chorley, Henry F., *Music and Manners in France and Germany: A Series of Travelling Sketches of Art and Society*, 3 vols, London: Longman, Orme, Brown, Green, and Longmans, 1841.

Chorley, Henry F., *Pomfret; or, Public Opinion and Private Judgment*, 3 vols, London: Henry Colburn, 1845.

[Chorley, Henry F.], 'Madame Viardot Garcia: A Glance at the Italian Opera', *Bentley's Miscellany*, June 1848: 35-40.

[Chorley, Henry F.], 'Musical Notes for April by Tartini's Familiar', *Bentley's Miscellany*, 25 (May 1849): 519-26. [attribution from *Wellesley Index*, 5: 151].

[Chorley, Henry F.], 'Musical Notes for March by Tartini's Familiar', *Bentley's Miscellany*, 25 (April 1849): 404-11 [attribution from *Wellesley Index*, 5: 151].

[Chorley, Henry F.], 'Musical Notes for May by Tartini's Familiar', *Bentley's Miscellany*, 25 (June 1849): 645. [attibution from *Wellesley Index*, 5: 151].

[Chorley, Henry F.], 'Musical Traits and Memorials. By Tartini's Familiar. Frederic Chopin', *Bentley's Miscellany*, 27 (February 1850): 185-91 [attribution from *Wellesley Index* 5: 151].

[Chorley, Henry F.], *Duchess Eleanour. A Tragedy in Five Acts by the Author of 'Old Love and New Fortune', 'White Magic', &c*, London: Thomas Hailes Lacy [Lacy's Acting Edition of Plays], [1854].

Chorley, Henry F., *Modern German Music*, 2 vols, London: Smith, Elder & Co., [1854].

Chorley, Henry F., ed., *Fairy Gold for Young & Old In Eighteen Tales From the French of Savinien Lapointe*, London: G. Routledge, 1857.

[Chorley, Henry F.], *Roccabella: A Tale of a Woman's Life* [by 'Paul Bell'], 2 vols, London: James Blackwood, [1859].

Chorley, Henry F., trans., *Iphigenia in Tauris*, London: J. Mitchell, 1860.

[Chorley, Henry F.], 'Amina and the Mill-Wheel', *All The Year Round*, 29 June 1861: 320-23.

Chorley, Henry F., 'On English Poetry in reference to Music' [*Notices of the Proceedings at the Meetings of the Members of the Royal Institution of Great Britain*, vol. III: 1852-1862], London: William Clowes, 1862: 317-20.

Chorley, Henry F., *Thirty Years' Musical Recollections*, London: Hurst and Blackett, 1862; reprinted with new index, New York: Da Capo, 1984.

[Chorley, Henry F.], *A Prodigy: A Tale of Music*, 3 vols, London: Chapman and Hall, 1866.

[Chorley, Henry F.], [review of Austen-Leigh's *Austen* and L'Estrange's *Mitford*], *Quarterly Review*, January 1870: 196-218.
[Chorley, Henry F.], [review of Lives of Rossini by Sutherland Edwards and Berlioz's *Memoirs*], *Edinburgh Review*, January 1871: 33-57.
Chorley, Henry F., *Letters of Mary Russell Mitford. Second Series*, 2 vols, London: Richard Bentley and Son, 1872.
Chorley, Henry F., *Thirty Years' Musical Recollections* (abridged), ed. with an introduction by Ernest Newman, New York: Alfred A. Knopf, 1926.
Chusid, Martin, Luke Jensen, and David Dauy, 'The Verdi Archive at New York University: Part II.', *Verdi Newsletter*, 9/10 (November 1981-82): 1-52.
Citron, Marcia J., *Gender and the Musical Canon*, Cambridge: Cambridge University Press, 1993.
Clarke, Norma, *Ambitious Heights: Writing, Friendship, Love — The Jewsbury Sisters, Felicia Hemans, and Jane Welsh Carlyle*, London: Routledge, 1990.
Coleridge, Arthur, *Reminiscences*, ed. J.A. Fuller-Maitland, London: Constable and Company Ltd, 1921.
Cone, John Frederick, *Adelina Patti: Queen of Hearts*, Portland, Oregon: Amadeus Press, 1993.
Cox, H. Bertram and C.L.E. Cox, eds, *Leaves From the Journals of Sir George Smart*, London: Longmans, Green, and Co., 1907.
[Cox, John Edmund], *Musical Recollections of the Last Half-Century*, 2 vols, London: Tinsley Brothers, 1872.
Crosten, William L., *French Grand Opera: An Art and a Business*, New York: King's Crown Press, 1948.
Crum, Margaret (compiler), *Catalogue of The Mendelssohn Papers in the Bodleian Library, Oxford, Vol. I: Correspondence of Felix Mendelssohn and Others*, Tutzing: Verlegt bei Hans Schneider, 1980.
Davison, Henry, *From Mendelssohn to Wagner: Being the Memoirs of J.W. Davison, Forty Years Music Critic of 'The Times'*, London: Wm. Reeves, 1912.
Dean, Winton. 'Some Echoes of Donizetti in Verdi's Operas', *Atti del III° Congresso Internazionale di Studi Verdiani* [Milan, Piccola Scala, 12-17 June 1972], Parma: Istituto di Studi Verdiani, 1974: 122-47.
Demuth, Norman, *Anthology of Musical Criticism*, London: Eyre and Spottiswoode, 1947.
Devrient, Eduard, *My Recollections of Felix Mendelssohn-Bartholdy, And His Letters to Me*, trans. Natalia Macfarren, London: Bentley, 1869; reprinted New York: Vienna House, 1972.
Dickens, Charles, *The Letters of Charles Dickens* [Nonesuch edition], ed. Walter Dexter, 3 vols, Bloomsbury: Nonesuch Press, 1938.
Dickens, Charles, *The Letters of Charles Dickens* [Pilgrim Edition], ed. Madeline House et al., 10 vols, Oxford: Clarendon, 1965-98.
Dilke, Sir Charles Wentworth, *The Papers of a Critic: Selected from the Writings of the Late Charles Wentworth Dilke With a Biographical Sketch by his Grandson*, 2 vols, London: John Murray, 1875. 'Memoir': [1]-91.
Duckles, Vincent, 'A French View on the State of Music in London [1829]', in *Modern Musical Scholarship*, ed. Edward Olleson, Stocksfield [Northumberland]: Oriel Press: 233-7.

Ebers, John, *Seven Years of the King's Theatre*, 1828: reprinted New York: Benjamin Blom, 1969.

Edwards, F.G., *The History of Mendelssohn's Oratorio 'Elijah'*, 1896; reprinted New York: AMS Press, 1976.

Ehrlich, Cyril, *The Music Profession in Britain since the Eighteenth Century: A Social History*, Oxford: Clarendon, 1985.

Ehrlich, Cyril, *First Philharmonic: A History of the Royal Philharmonic Society*, Oxford: Clarendon, 1995.

Ella, John, *Musical Sketches, Abroad and At Home*, London: Ridgway, 1869, vol. 1 (only vol. published).

Ellis, Katherine, *Music Criticism in Nineteenth-Century France: La Revue et Gazette Musicale de Paris, 1834-80*, Cambridge: Cambridge University Press, 1995.

Ellis, William Ashton, *Life of Richard Wagner*, 6 vols, London: Kegan Paul, 1900-08 (first four volumes are a translation of C.F. Glasenapps, *Das Leben Richard Wagners*).

Fauquet, Joël-Marie, 'Berlioz's version of Gluck's *Orphée*', in Peter Bloom, ed., *Berlioz Studies*, Cambridge: Cambridge University Press, 1992.

Fenner, Theodore, *Opera in London: Views of the Press 1785-1830*, Carbondale: Southern Illinois University Press, 1994.

Fétis, [François Joseph], *Curiosités Historiques de la Musique*, Paris: Janet et Cotelle, 1830: 169-271 (reprinted from *Revue Musicale*).

Finck, Henry T., *Wagner and His Works: The Story of His Life with Critical Comments*, 2 vols, London: H. Grevel and Co., 1893.

Fitzball, Edward Esq., *Thirty-Five Years of a Dramatic Author's Life*, 2 vols, London: T.C. Newby, 1859.

Fitzlyon, April, *The Price of Genius: A Life of Pauline Viardot*, London: John Calder, 1964.

Forbes, Elizabeth, *Mario and Grisi: A Biography*, London: Victor Gollancz, 1985.

Forster, John, *The Life of Charles Dickens*, 3 vols, London: Chapman and Hall, 1872-74.

Foster, Myles Birket, *History of the Philharmonic Society of London: 1813-1912*, London: John Lane, 1912.

Francis, John. D., compiler, *John Francis, Publisher of the Athenæum: A Literary Chronicle of Half a Century*, introductory note by H.R. Fox Bourne, 2 vols, London: Richard Bentley, 1888.

Fryckstedt, Monica Correa, *Geraldine Jewsbury's Athenaeum Reviews: A Mirror of Mid-Victorian Attitudes to Fiction*, Uppsala: Acta Universitatis Upsaliensis, 1986 [Studia Anglistica Upsaliensia].

Fulcher, Jane F., *The Nation's Image: French Grand Opera As Politics and Politicized Art*, Cambridge: Cambridge University Press, 1987.

Fuller Maitland, J.A., *English Music in the XIXth Century*, London: Grant Richards, 1902.

Gallenga, Antonio, *Episodes of My Second Life*, 2 vols, London: Chapman and Hall, 1884.

Ganz, A.W., *Berlioz in England*, 1950; reprinted New York: DaCapo Press, 1981.

Gardiner, William, *Music and Friends; or, Pleasant Recollections of a Dilettante*, 2 vols, London: Longman, Orme, Brown, and Longman, 1838.

Garibaldi, Luigi Agostino, ed., *Giuseppe Verdi nelle lettere di Emanuele Muzio ad Antonio Barezzi*, Milan: Fratelli Traves, 1931.

Garlington, Aubrey S., '*Mega*-Text, *Mega*-Music: A Crucial Dilemma for German Romantic Opera', *Musical Humanism and its Legacy: Essays in Honor of Claude V. Palisca*, ed. Nancy Kovaleff Baker and Barbara Russano Hanning, Stuyvesant, NY: Pendragon Press, 1992: 381-93.

Gerhard, Anselm, *Die Verstädterung der Oper: Paris und das Musiktheater des 19. Jahrhunderts*, Stuttgart: Verlag J.B. Metzler, 1992.

Gettmann, Royal A., *Turgenev in England and America*, Urbana: University of Illinois Press, 1941.

Gettmann, Royal A., *A Victorian Publisher: A Study of the Bentley Papers*, Cambridge: Cambridge University Press, 1960.

Gotch, Rosamund Brunel, ed., *Mendelssohn and His Friends in Kensington: Letters from Fanny and Sophy Horsley Written 1833-36*, London: Oxford University Press, 1934.

Godefroy, Vincent, *The Dramatic Genius of Verdi: Studies of Selected Operas*, 2 vols, London: Victor Gollancz, 1975-77.

Graves, Charles L., *The Life & Letters of Sir George Grove, C.B.*, London: Macmillan, 1903.

Grubb, Gerald G., 'Dickens and Chorley', *The Dickensian*, 52 (Summer 1956): 100-109.

Gruneisen, C.L., *The Opera and the Press*, London: Robert Hardwicke, 1869.

Gye, Frederick, *The Royal Italian Opera and the 'Athenaeum' Newspaper*, London: Privately Printed, 1875.

Harden, Edgar, ed., *The Letters and Private Papers of William Makepeace Thackeray*, 2 vols, New York: Garland, 1994 [supplement to Ray].

Hewlett, Henry G., compiler, *Henry Fothergill Chorley: Autobiography, Memoir, and Letters*, 2 vols, London: Richard Bentley and Son, 1873.

[Hogarth, George], 'Musical Literature', *Blackwood's Edinburgh Review*, 27 (March 1830): 471-80.

Hogarth, George, *Musical History, Biography, and Criticism: Being a General Survey of Music, from the Earliest Period to the Present time*, London: John W. Parker, 1835.

Hogarth, George, *Memoirs of the Music Drama*, 2 vols, London: Richard Bentley, 1838 [revised edition as *Memoirs of the Opera in Italy, France, Germany, and England*, 2 vols, London: Richard Bentley, 1851].

Hogarth, George, *The Philharmonic Society of London; From its Foundation, 1813, to its Fiftieth Year, 1862*, London: Bradbury & Evans, 1862.

Holland, Henry Scott and W.S. Rockstro, *Memoir of Madame Jenny Lind-Goldschmidt: Her Early Art-Life and Dramatic Career 1820-1851*, 2 vols, London: John Murray, 1891.

Houghton, Walter E. and J.H. Slingerland, eds, *The Wellesley Index to Victorian Periodicals*, 5 vols, Toronto: University of Toronto Press, 1966-89.

Howe, Susanne, *Geraldine Jewsbury: Her Life and Errors*, London: George Allen & Unwin, 1935.

Huebner, Steven, *The Operas of Charles Gounod*, Oxford: Clarendon, 1990.

Hueffer, Francis, *Half a Century of Music in England: 1837-1887, Essays Towards a History*, London: Chapman and Hall, 1889.

[Hullah, Frances], *Life of John Hullah, LL.D. By His Wife*, London: Longmans, Green, 1886.

Irvine, William and Park Honan, *The Book, the Ring, and the Poet: A Biography of Robert Browning*, New York: McGraw-Hill, 1974.

Jacob, Heinrich Eduard, *Felix Mendelssohn and His Times*, trans. Richard and Clara Winston. 1963; reprinted Westport, CT: Greenwood Press, 1973.

Jacobs, Arthur, *Arthur Sullivan: A Victorian Musician*, Oxford: Oxford University Press, 1984.

Jenkyns, Richard, *The Victorians and Ancient Greece*, Cambridge: Harvard University Press, 1980.

Jensen, Luke, 'The Emergence of the Modern Conductor in 19th-Century Italian Opera', *Performance Practice Review*, 4.1 (Spring 1991): 34-62.

Jerrold, Walter, *Douglas Jerrold: Dramatist and Wit*, 2 vols, London: Hodder and Stoughton, [1918].

Johnson, Edgar, *Charles Dickens: His Tragedy and Triumph*, 2 vols, New York: Simon and Schuster, 1952.

Johnson, James H., *Listening in Paris: A Cultural History*, Berkeley: University of California Press, 1995.

Kelley, Philip, Ronald Hudson, and Scott Lewis, eds, *The Brownings' Correspondence*, vols 1-14, Winfield, Kansas: Wedgestone Press, 1984-98.

Kellogg, Clara Louise [Mme. Strakosch], *Memoirs of an American Prima Donna*, New York and London: G.P. Putnam's Sons, 1913.

Kemble, Frances Anne, *Records of Later Life*, 3 vols, London: Richard Bentley and Son, 1882.

Kennedy, Michael, ed., *The Autobiography of Charles Hallé: With Correspondence and Diaries* [1896], New York: Harper & Row, 1973.

Kent, Christopher, 'Introduction' in Alvin Sullivan, *British Literary Magazines: The Victorian and Edwardian Age, 1837-1913*, Westport, CT: Greenwood Press, 1984, 2: xiii-xxvi.

Kenyon, Frederic G., ed., *The Letters of Elizabeth Barrett Browning*, 2 vols, New York: Macmillan, 1898.

Kimbell, David R. B., *Verdi in the Age of Italian Romanticism*, Cambridge: Cambridge University Press, 1981.

Kimbell, David, *Italian Opera*, Cambridge: Cambridge University Press, 1991.

King, R. W., *The Translator of Dante: The Life, Work and Friendships of Henry Francis Cary (1772-1844)*, London: Martin Secker, 1925.

Klein, Herman, *The Reign of Patti*, 1920; reprinted New York: Da Capo Press, 1978.

Klingemann, Karl, ed., *Felix Mendelssohn-Bartholdys Briefwechsel mit Legationsrat Karl Klingemann in London*, Essen: G.D. Baedeker, 1909 [the editor was Klingemann's son].

Kuhe, Wilhelm, *My Musical Recollections*, London: Richard Bentley and Son, 1896.

Langley, Leanne, 'The Musical Press in Nineteenth-Century England', *Notes: Quarterly Journal of the Music Library Association*, 46 (March 1990): 584-91.

Laughton, John Knox, *Memoirs of the Life and Correspondence of Henry Reeve, C.B., D.C.L.*, 2 vols, London: Longmans, Green & Co, 1898.

Lawrence, Vera Brodsky, *Strong on Music: The New York Music Scene in the Days of George Templeton Strong*, vol. 1, New York: Oxford

University Press, 1988; vol. 2, Chicago: Chicago University Press, 1995.

Leach, Joseph, *Bright Particular Star: The Life and Times of Charlotte Cushman*, New Haven: Yale University Press, 1970.

Lehmann, John, *Ancestors and Friends*, London: Eyre and Spottiswoode, 1962.

Lehmann, R.C., *Memories of Half a Century: A Record of Friendships*, London: Smith, Elder & Co., 1908.

Le Huray, Peter and James Day, *Music and Aesthetics in the Eighteenth and Early-Nineteenth Centuries*, Cambridge: Cambridge University Press, 1981.

Leighton, Angela, *Victorian Women Poets: Writing Against the Heart*, Charlottesville: University Press of Virginia, 1992.

L'Estrange, the Revd A.[lfred] G., ed., *The Life of Mary Russell Mitford ... Related in a Selection From Her Letters to Her Friends*, 3 vols, 2nd and revised edn, London: Richard Bentley, 1870 (also: 2 vols, New York: Harper, 1870).

Ley, J.W.T., *The Dickens Circle: A Narrative of the Novelist's Friendships*, London: Chapman and Hall, 1918.

Linley, George, *Musical Cynics of London, A Satire (Sketch the First)*, London: G. Bubb, 1862.

Lippman, Friedrich, 'Verdi und Donizetti', *Opernstudien: Anna Amalie Abert zum 65. Geburtstag*, Tutzing: Hans Schneider, 1975.

Lohrli, Anne, *Household Words ... List of Contributors*, Toronto: University of Toronto Press, 1973.

Lootens, Tricia, 'Hemans and Home: Victorianism, Feminine "Internal Enemies", and the Domestication of National Identity', *PMLA*, 109 (March 1994): 238-53.

Lumley, Benjamin, *Reminiscences of the Opera*, London: Hurst and Blackett, 1864.

Lunn, Henry C., *Musings of a Musician; A Series of Popular Sketches Illustrative of Musical Matters and Musical People* [1846], new edition, London: Robert Cocks and Co., 1854.

Luzio, Alessandro, ed., *Carteggi Verdiani*, 4 vols, Rome: Reale Accademia d'Italia, 1935-47.

Mackerness, E.D., 'Henry Fothergill Chorley (1808-1872) — I', *The Monthly Musical Record*, (July-August, 1957): 134-40.

Mackerness, E.D., 'Henry Fothergill Chorley (1808-1872) — II', *The Monthly Musical Record*, (September-October, 1957): 181-8).

Mackinlay, M. Sterling, *Garcia: The Centenarian and His Times*, 1908; reprinted New York: Da Capo, 1976.

[Mapleson, James Henry], *The Mapleson Memoirs 1848-1888*, 2 vols, 2nd edn, London: Remington & Co., 1888.

[Mapleson, James Henry], *The Mapleson Memoirs: The Career of an Operatic Impresario 1858-1888*, ed. Harold Rosenthal, New York: Appleton Century, 1966.

Marchand, Leslie, *The Athenaeum: A Mirror of Victorian Culture*, Chapel Hill: University of North Carolina Press, 1941.

Margalioth, Daniel, 'Dickens contra Wagner', *The Hebrew University Studies in Literature*, 10 (Spring 1982): 39-68.

Mellor, Anne K, *Romanticism and Gender*, New York: Routledge, 1993.

Mermin, Dorothy, *Elizabeth Barrett Browning: The Origins of a New Poetry*, Chicago: University of Chicago Press, 1989.

Meyerbeer, Giacomo, *Briefwechsel und Tagebücher*, ed. Heinz und Gudrun Becker, Berlin: Verlag Walter de Gruyter & Co., [1985], vol. 4: 1846-49.

Morley, Henry, *The Journal of a London Playgoer: From 1851 to 1866*, London: George Routledge and Sons, 1891.

[Moscheles, Charlotte, ed.], *Aus Moscheles' Leben: Nach Briefen und Tagebüchern*, 2 vols, Leipzig: Verlag von Duncker & Humbolt, 1872, 1873.

[Moscheles, Charlotte, ed.], *Life of Moscheles, With Selections from His Diaries and Correspondence, by His Wife*, Adapted from the original German by A.D. Coleridge, 2 vols, London: Hurst and Blackett, 1873 [omits some references to Chorley found in the German edition].

Moscheles, Felix (ed. and translator), *Letters of Felix Mendelssohn to Ignaz and Charlotte Moscheles*, 1888; reprinted, Freeport, NY: Books for Libraries Press, 1970.

Mount-Edgcumbe, Richard Edgcumbe [2nd Earl of], *Musical Reminiscenses of the Earl of Mount Edgcumbe: Containing an Account of the Italian Opera in England from 1773 to 1834*, 4th edn, 1834; reprinted. New York: Da Capo, 1973.

Murphy, Kerry, *Hector Berlioz and the Development of French Music Criticism*, Ann Arbor: UMI [University Microfilms Incorporated] Research Press, 1988.

Musgrave, Michael, *The Musical Life of the Crystal Palace*, Cambridge: Cambridge University Press, 1995.

Nalbach, Daniel, *The King's Theatre 1704-1867: London's First Italian Opera House*, London: The Society for Theatre Research, 1972.

Nettel, Reginald, *The Orchestra in England: A Social History*, London: Jonathan Cape, 1946.

Newman, Ernest, *The Life of Richard Wagner*, 4 vols, New York: Alfred A. Knopf, 1946.

Northcott, Richard, *Beethoven's "Fidelio" in London*, London: The Press Printers, 1918.

Northcott, Richard, *Gounod's Operas in London*, London: The Press Printers Ltd, 1918.

Northcott, Richard, *Opera Chatter*, London: Novello, 1921. ['English Opera at Covent Garden', 5-14; 'The Composer of "Faust"', 44-56.]

Oppenlander, Ella Ann, *Dickens' All the Year Round: Descriptive Index and Contributor List*, Troy, NY: Whitston Publishing Co., 1984.

[Owenson, Sydney], *Lady Morgan's Memoirs: Autobiography, Diaries and Correspondence*, 2 vols, London: W.H. Allen, 1862.

Parke, W.T., *Musical Memoirs; Comprising an Account of the General State of Music in England, from the first commemoration of Handel, in 1784, to the year 1830. Interspersed with numerous anecdotes, musical, histrionic, &c*, 2 vols, London: Henry Colburn and Richard Bentley, 1830.

Pearce, Charles E., *Sims Reeves: Fifty Years of Music in England*, London: Stanley Paul, 1924.

Pendle, Karin, *Eugène Scribe and French Opera of the Nineteenth Century*, Ann Arbor, Michigan: UMI Research Press, 1979.

Phillips, Henry, *Musical and Personal Recollections During Half a Century*, 2 vols, London: Charles J. Skeet, 1864.

Phillips-Matz, Mary Jane, *Verdi: A Biography*, New York: Oxford University Press, 1993.

Planché, J.R., *The Jewess, A Grand Operatic Drama, in three acts, founded on M. Scribe's Opera 'La Juive'*, London: Porter and Wright, 1835.

Planché, J.R., *Recollections and Reflections: A Professional Autobiography*, 2 vols, London: Tinsley Brothers, 1872.

Plantinga, Leon B., *Schumann as Critic*, New Haven: Yale University Press, 1967.

Pollard, Arthur, *The Letters of Mrs. Gaskell*, Manchester: Manchester University Press, 1966.

Pollock, Sir Frederick, ed., *Macready's Reminiscences, and Selections From His Diaries and Letters*, 2 vols, London: Macmillan and Co., 1875.

Praeger, Ferdinand, *Wagner As I Knew Him*, London: Longmans, Green, 1892.

Praz, Mario, *The Hero in Eclipse in Victorian Fiction*, London: Oxford University Press, 1956.

Procter, Bryan Waller [Barry Cornwall], *Autobiographical Fragment and Biographical Notes, With Personal Sketches of Contemporaries, Unpublished Lyrics, and Letters of Literary Friends*, London: George Bell and Sons, York Street, Covent Garden, 1877.

[Pückler-Muskau, Hermann Ludwig Heinrich], *Tour in Germany, Holland and England, In the Years 1826, 1827, & 1828*, 4 vols, London: Effingham Wilson, 1832.

Rainbow, Bernarr, *The Land Without Music: Musical Education in England 1800-1860 and its Continental Antecedents*, London: Novello, 1967.

Rathbone, Eleanore F., *William Rathbone: A Memoir*, London: Macmillan, 1905.

Rathbone, Emily A., ed., *Records of the Rathbone Family for Private Circulation Only*, Edinburgh: R. &. R. Clark, 1913.

Raumer, Frederick von, *England in 1835: Being a Series of Letters Written to Friends in Germany During a Residence in London and Excursions Into the Provinces*, trans. Sarah Austin, 3 vols, London: John Murray, 1836.

Raumer, Frederick von, *England in 1841: Being a Series of Letters Written to Friends in Germany During a Residence in London and Excursions into the Provinces*, trans H. Evans Lloyd, 2 vols, London: John Lee, 1842.

Ray, Gordon G., *The Letters and Private Papers of William Makepeace Thackeray*, 4 vols, Cambridge: Harvard University Press, 1946.

Raymond, Meredith B. and Mary Rose Sullivan, *The Letters of Elizabeth Barrett Browning to Mary Russell Mitford 1836-1854*, 3 vols, [Waco, Texas]: Armstrong Browning Library [Baylor University], 1983.

Reid, Charles, *The Music Monster: A Biography of James William Davison, Music Critic of* The Times *of London, 1846-78, With Excerpts from His Critical Writings*, London: Quartet Books, 1984.

Répertoire International de la Presse Musicale (Ann Arbor, Michigan: UMI): *The Musical Examiner 1842-1844*, ('Calendar' prepared by Diana Snigurowicz) 1992; *The Musical Times 1844-1900*, 9 vols ('Calendar', vols 1-5, prepared by Edward Clinkscale), 1995; *The Musical World 1836-1865*, 11 vols ('Calendar', vols 1-5, prepared by Richard Kitson), 1997.

Roger, Clara Kathleen [Clara Doria], *Memories of a Musical Career*, Boston: Little, Brown, 1919.

Rosenberg, Edgar, *From Shylock to Svengali: Jewish Stereotypes in English Fiction*, Stanford CA: Stanford University Press, 1960.

Rosenthal, Harold, *Two Centuries of Opera at Covent Garden*, London: Putnam, 1958.

Ruprecht, Werner K., 'Felicia Hemans und die englischen Beziehungen zur deutschen Literatur im ersten Drittel des neunzehnten Jahrhunderts', *Anglia*, 48 [neue folge, band 36] (1924): 1-357.

Ruskin, John, *Sesame and Lilies* (1864), London: George Allen, 1899.

Sala, George Augustus Henry, 'The Musical World', *Household Words* (29 July 1854): 561-7.

Sanders, Valerie, ed., *Harriet Martineau: Selected Letters*, Oxford: Clarendon Press, 1990.

[Santley, Charles], *Student and Singer: The Reminiscences of Charles Santley*, London: Edward Arnold, 1892.

Séchan, Charles, *Souvenirs d'un Homme de Théâtre 1831-1835*, Paris: C. Levy, 1883.

[Schindler, Anton], *The Life of Beethoven Including his Correspondence with his Friends, Numerous Characteristic Traits, and Remarks on his Musical Works*, ed. Ignace Moscheles, 2 vols, London: Henry Colburn, Publisher, 1841. (A translation of Schindler's biography of Beethoven. Moscheles contributed the notes bearing his signature and the appendices to vols 1 & 2. [iv-v], as well as the signed Preface.)

Scholes, Percy A., *The Mirror of Music 1844-1944: A Century of Musical Life in Britain as reflected in the pages of the* Musical Times, 2 vols, London: Novello and Oxford, 1947.

Schumann, Robert, *Tagebücher: vol. III: Haushaltbücher* (Part I, 1837-47) Gerd Nauhaus, ed. Leipzig: VEB Deutscher Verlag für Musik, 1982.

Shaw, George Bernard, *London Music in 1888-89 as heard by Corno di Bassetto*, New York: Dodd, Mead, 1937.

Simpson, Harold, *A Century of Ballads, 1810-1910: With Some Introductory Chapters on "Old Ballads and Ballad-Makers*, London: Mills & Boon, 1910.

Smith, Albert Richard, 'Theatrical Ashes', *Household Words*, 13 (22 March 1856): 217-20.

Smith, Albert Richard, *Sketches of London Life and Character*, London: Dean and Son, 1859.

Smith, Albert, *Wild Oats and Dead Leaves*, London: Chapman and Hall, 1860.

Soubies, Albert, *Documents inedits sur le Faust de Gounod*, Paris: Fishbacher, 1912.

Stebbins, Emma, *Charlotte Cushman: Her Letters and Memories of Her Life*, Boston: Houghton, Osgood and Company, 1879.

Steinberg, Michael P., 'The Incidental Politics to Mendelssohn's *Antigone*', in R. Larry Todd, *Mendelssohn and His World*, Princeton: Princeton University Press, 1991: 137-57.

Stendhal, *Life of Rossini* (1824), trans. and annotated Richard N. Coe, New York: The Orion Press, 1970.

Stephenson, Glennis, 'Poet Construction: Mrs Hemans, L.E.L., and the Image of the Nineteenth-Century Woman Poet', in *Reimagining Women: Representations of Women in Culture*, ed. Shirley Newman and Glennis Stephenson, Toronto: University of Toronto Press, 1993: 61-73.

Stolzenberg, Ingeborg, 'Paul Mendelssohn-Bartholdy nach dem Tode seines Bruders Felix: Ein Brief vom 10. Dezember 1847 an Karl Klingemann nebst drei Briefen von Eduard Magnus', (*Mendelssohn Studien*, vol. 8, Festschrift for Cécile Lowenthal-Hensel), ed. Rudolf Elvers and Hans-Günter Klein, Berlin: Dunker & Humblot, 1993: 179-95.

Strachey, Lytton and Roger Fulford, eds, *The Greville Memoirs 1814-1860*, 8 vols, London: Macmillan & Co, 1938.

Stradlin, Robert and Meirion Hughes, *The English Musical Renaissance 1860-1940: Construction and Deconstruction*, London: Routledge, 1993.

Straus, Ralph, *Sala: The Portrait of an Eminent Victorian*, London: Constable and Company, 1942.

Temperley, Nicholas, ed., *Music in Britain: The Romantic Age 1800-1914*, London: Athlone Press, 1981.

Temperley, Nicholas, ed., *The Lost Chord: Essays on Victorian Music*, Bloomington: Indiana University Press, 1989.

Temperley, Nicholas, 'Schumann and Sterndale Bennett', *Nineteenth Century Music*, 12 (Spring 1989): 207-20.

Thackeray, William Makepeace, *Works: With Biographical Introductions by His Daughter Lady Ritchie* (Centenary Biographical Edition), 26 vols, London: Smith, Elder, & Co., 1911, vol. 24: 'Cox's Diary', 289-346; vol. 25: 'A Word on the Annuals', 74-86.

Thackeray, William Makepeace, *Vanity Fair: A Novel Without A Hero*, ed. Geoffrey and Kathleen Tillotson, Boston: Houghton Mifflin, 1963.

Tinsley, William, *Random Recollections of an Old Publisher*, 2 vols, London: Simpkin, Marshall, Hamilton, Kent & Co., 1900.

Todd, R. Larry, ed., *Mendelssohn and His World*, Princeton: Princeton University Press, 1991.

Todd, R. Larry. ed., *Mendelssohn Studies*, Cambridge: Cambridge University Press, 1992.

Tomlin, E.W.F., 'Charles Dickens and Henry Fothergill Chorley', *Études Anglaises*, 32 (1979): 434-48.

Tucker, Herbert, 'House Arrest: The Domestication of English Poetry in the 1820s', *New Literary History*, 25 (Summer 1994): 521-48.

Vann, J. Don and Rosemary T. VanArsdel, *Victorian Periodicals and Victorian Society*, Toronto: University of Toronto Press, 1994.

Waddington, Patrick, 'Dickens, Pauline Viardot, Turgenev: A Study in Mutual Admiration', *New Zealand Slavonic Journal*, no. 1 (1974): 55-73.

Waddington, Patrick, 'Turgenev and Gounod: Rival Strangers in the Viardots' country nest (Part I)', *New Zealand Slavonic Journal*, no. 2 (1976): 11-32.

Waddington, Patrick, 'Turgenev's relations with Henry Fothergill Chorley (with an unpublished letter)', *New Zealand Slavonic Journal*, no. 2 (1978): 27-39.

Waddington, Patrick, 'Henry Chorley, Pauline Viardot, and Turgenev: A Musical and Literary Friendship', *Musical Quarterly*, 67 (April, 1981): 165-92.

Waddington, Patrick, *Turgenev and England*, New York: New York University Press, 1981.
Walker, Alan, *Franz Liszt*, 3 vols, New York: Knopf, 1983, 1988, 1996.
Walker, Frank, *The Man Verdi*, Chicago: University of Chicago Press, 1982.
Wallace, Robin, *Beethoven's Critics*, Cambridge: Cambridge University Press, 1986.
Weaver, William, *Verdi: A Documentary Study*, London: Thames and Hudson, 1977.
Weaver, William and Martin Chusid, eds, *The Verdi Companion*, New York: Norton, 1979.
Werner, Eric, *Mendelssohn: a New Image of the Composer and His Age*, trans. Dika Newlin, New York: The Free Press of Glencoe [Macmillan], 1963.
Werner, Eric, *Mendelssohn: Leben und Werk in Neuer Sicht*, Zürich: Atlantis, 1980.
White, Eric Walter, *A History of English Opera*, London: Faber and Faber, 1983.
Williams, A. Susan, *The Rich Man and the Diseased Poor in Early Victorian Literature*, Atlantic Highlands, New Jersey: Humanites Press International, Inc., 1987.
Williamson, Rosemary, *William Sterndale Bennett: A Descriptive Thematic Catalogue*, Oxford: Clarendon Press, 1996.
Wyndham, Henry Saxe, *The Annals of Covent Garden Theatre From 1732 to 1897*, 2 vols, London: Chatto & Windus, 1906.
Wyndham, H[enry] Saxe, *August Manns and the Saturday Concerts: A Memoir and a Retrospect*, London: Walter Scott, 1909.
Wyndham, Henry Saxe, *Arthur Seymour Sullivan: 1842-1900*, London: Kegan Paul, 1926.
Yates, Edmund, *His Recollections and Experiences*, 2 vols, London: Richard Bentley, 1884.
Young, Percy M., *Beethoven, A Victorian Tribute: Based on the Papers of Sir George Smart*, London: Dennis Dobson, 1976.
Zimmermann, Reiner, *Giacomo Meyerbeer: Eine Biographie nach Dokumenten*, Berlin: Henschel Verlag, 1991.

Index